Y0-BNE-123

NEW MODEL 44 ARMY PISTOL.—SMITH & WESSON, SPRINGFIELD, MASS.

AMERICAN INVENTIONS

AND

IMPROVEMENTS

IN

Breech-Loading Small Arms,

HEAVY ORDNANCE,

MACHINE GUNS, MAGAZINE ARMS, FIXED AMMUNITION,
PISTOLS, PROJECTILES, EXPLOSIVES,

AND OTHER

MUNITIONS OF WAR,

INCLUDING A CHAPTER ON

SPORTING ARMS.

COMPILED BY

CHARLES B. NORTON,

Brevet Brig Gen. U S V, United States Commissioner to Paris Exposition,

Author of "History of American Breech-Loading Small Arms," "Reports on Munitions of War," "Fortifications of the City of New York," and "Treasures of Art and Industry."

SPRINGFIELD, MASS.:
CHAPIN & GOULD.
LONDON: N. TRÜBNER & CO.
1880.

Springfield Printing Company,
Printers, Electrotypers and Binders,
Springfield, Mass.

TO

NATHAN APPLETON,

Brevet Captain Fifth Battery, Massachusetts Artillery.

THIS VOLUME IS DEDICATED,

in remembrance of many never to be forgotten acts of kindness.

CHARLES B. NORTON

PREFACE.

The favorable reception given to the work on "AMERICAN BREECH-LOADING SMALL ARMS," published by the compiler in 1872, has led to the preparation of the present work. While it contains much that appeared in the former volume, relating to Small Arms, there will be found large additions bringing the description of each Arm down to the present time, and also a sketch of the rise and progress in the manufacture of Heavy Ordnance and Projectiles. Reference has also been made to the new systems of Magazine Guns, the manufacture of Gunpowder and Fixed Ammunition. The compiler again avails himself of this opportunity to express his thanks to the United States War Department and the several inventors and arms companies, for their readiness to furnish him with every information.

CONTENTS.

AMERICAN BREECH-LOADING SMALL ARMS.

CHAPTER I.

EARLY INVENTIONS.—OFFICIAL REPORTS.

THE invention of breech-loading fire-arms dates back to a very remote period of antiquity; but, to quote the Emperor Napoleon III in his admirable treatise on the "Past and Future of Artillery": "Inventions that are before their age, remain useless until the stock of general knowledge comes up to their level." And again: "Whatever is complicated fails in producing good results in warfare; the promoters of systems forget always that the object of progress ought to be to obtain the greatest possible effect with the least possible effort and expense."

He blames, however, the opposition of *routine*, "which, being enamored with old ways, has presented for ages practices that are most stupid. And, not only does *routine* scrupulously preserve, like some sacred deposit the errors of antiquity, but it actually opposes might and main, the most legitimate and the most evident improvements."

Gunpowder is supposed to have first become generally known in the latter part of the thirteenth, or early in the fourteenth century. Artillery was used as early as 1327 in European warfare, and small-arms a few years later; meanwhile, there is good reason to believe that the Chinese were acquainted with the use of gunpowder and employed it in warfare full two thousand years ago, — though the art, like many others, was lost until its revival in the middle ages.

The chief improvements in the practical use of fire-arms were at first confined to modes of firing; the old *match* being superseded by the wheel, or German lock, invented in 1577 in Auremberg: by this lock, friction was occasioned by rapid rotary motion, sparks following, which ignited the powder. This improvement was followed, about 1630, by the flint-lock. After this and until 1840, when the percussion-lock — invented in 1800 — was first adapted to military muskets, improvements were confined chiefly to lessening the weight of small-arms, and modifying complications in their mechanism.

Rifling, as a method of insuring accuracy in firing, like breech-loading, dates back to ancient days; though the principle cannot be authentically traced to an earlier period than the fifteenth century. It, however, fell into disuse for nearly a century, and it was not until 1830 that it came into vogue again, and grew to rapid popularity among military men.

Thus it was with breech-loading arms. In the *Musee d'Artillerie* in Paris, is a breech-loading gun of the time of Henry II, prior to 1550, and a match-lock revolver of the same period. In the United Service Museum, London, there is likewise a revolver which is described as follows: No. 1168 — A snap haunce self-loading petronel, probably of the time of Charles the First. The contrivance consists of a revolving cylinder, containing seven chambers, with touch-holes. The action of lifting the cock causes the cylinder to revolve, and a fresh chamber is brought into connection with the barrel. Six of the seven chambers are exposed to view, and the charges are put in without the need of a ramrod. All of this goes to illustrate the old saying that there is "nothing new under the sun," and shows further, that inventions which are novel to us, may, on investigation, prove to be old discoveries, impracticable when first brought to light, but which the growing necessities of man have unearthed when required, and when the march of knowledge has made men's minds ready to apply them judiciously and usefully.

Improvements in fire-arms date back specially to the time of Henry VIII, who was one of the first to observe the power and to foresee the influence of these weapons. Two weapons, manufactured in England during his reign, were exhibited in London in 1867, and with some difference in minor details, were found to be veritable Snider rifles. As has been before mentioned, all the early cannon and primitive hand-guns were loaded at the breech. The method did not continue in favor, however, and was superseded, because of the inability of the gun-makers of those days to meet all the requirements of the design. Still the attempt continued to be made from time to time, and in the collection of specifications of British Patents, we find mention of new inventions of this character among the very earliest recorded. In 1664 is noted one by Abraham Hall of a "gun or pistoll, which hath a hole at the upper end of the breech to receive the charge, which hole is opened or stopped by a piece of iron or steel that lies along the side of the piece, and moveable by a ready and easy motion."

The adaptation of the principle of breech-loading to small arms did not find favorable consideration until long after this date; and during the whole of the eighteenth century there were but five patents recorded in England having this object in view. The first recorded patent in the United States was dated May 21st, 1811, and the evidence, sustained by the records of the Ordnance Bureau in the War Department, prove that John H. Hall, of North Yarmouth, the patentee, was the inventor of the first breech-loading arm receiving attention from the Government of the United States. In a letter addressed to Col. Bomford of the Bureau of Ordnance, dated Jan. 24th, 1815, Mr. Hall writes as follows: "I invented the improvement in 1811, being at that time but little acquainted with rifles, and being perfectly ignorant of any method whatever of loading guns at the breech."

He at a later date suggested the manufacture of one thousand of his patent rifle for use in the campaigns of 1812. The official records indicate that in 1816 one hundred of these arms were made and issued to a company of riflemen, and that the reports thereon were favorable. In 1825 two companies of United States troops stationed at Fortress Monroe were armed with Hall's rifles, and had the same in use in 1827, during which year two thousand stand were completed. The Committee of the Staff of the School at Fortress Monroe reported "its perfect conviction of the superiority of this arm over every other kind of small arm now in use." Hall, in his letters to the War Department, writes as follows:

"Only one point now remains to bring the rifles to the utmost perfection, which I shall attempt, if the Government contracts with me for the guns to any considerable amount, viz.: to make every similar part of every gun so much alike that it will suit every gun, so that if a thousand guns were taken apart and the limbs thrown promiscuously together in one heap, they may be taken promiscuously from the heap and will all come right. This important point I conceive practicable, and although in the first instance it will probably prove expensive, yet ultimately it will prove most economical, and be attended with great advantages."

"A favorite and important part of the American small-arms would then be at the heighth of perfection, and would vastly excel those of any other nation. They would be strong, durable and simple, easily kept in order, easily repaired when out of order, perfectly accurate and capable of being fired with the greatest quickness which a gun can admit of, and we have more marksmen capable of using them to advantage than can be found in the army of any other nation."

There is evidence that Hall's breech-loading carbine and rifle were used with great success in the Black Hawk and Seminole wars, and possibly also in the war with Mexico.

In 1836 public attention was so largely directed to the special value of this arm, that a resolution was passed by Congress to pay Hall $10,000, and also that he should be employed at Harper's Ferry in superintending the manufacture of the arm. As the sum paid was at the rate of one dollar per arm, it is positive proof of the manufacture of 10,000 breech-loading arms up to that date. As there are arms in the museum of the Ordnance Bureau bearing the date 1839, it is also evidence of a subsequent issue. Mr. Hall describes his arm as follows:

"The gun consists of a receiver, which contains the charge, and to which the lock is attached, it (the receiver) has two shoulders near its muzzle or fore-end, by which it is kept to the barrel and is prevented from recoiling when it is discharged. The receiver is prevented from recoiling wholly by these shoulders, which bear against the core-hardened chocks placed behind the shoulders. But no direct support is given by the butt-piece behind the receiver, nor by the axis-pin on which the receiver turns; on the contrary, the receiver does not even touch the butt-piece; a vacancy is left between that and the end of the receiver to freely permit all the expansion which takes place in the receiver as it grows warm with repeated discharges, viz.: all the expansion from the back part of the shoulders to the back end of the receiver. That expansion which takes place forward of the shoulders is provided for in the joint where the receiver meets the barrel. The holes in the receiver through which the axis-pin passes are made long for the same purpose, viz.: to freely admit of expansion in the after part of the receiver. The bore of the barrel increases gradually in size toward the breech, beginning about one foot from the muzzle and enlarging very rapidly in the last half-inch next the receiver somewhat in the form of a trumpet, so as to be rather larger at the butt than the bore of the receiver, even if its bore were not exactly to correspond with the bore of the barrel."

One special advantage claimed by Hall, was the fact that upon his plan all parts could be made interchangeable, thus rendering it very easy to supply missing parts when desired. The price put upon this arm as manufactured by himself was $20, and the result of its adoption by the War Department, was the appointment of a Congressional Investigating Committee to examine into the expense, whose report, however, was favorable. As there is no evidence of the adoption of a breech-loading small-arm by any European nation till many years after the above dates, the United States War Department should have the credit of being the *first in the field* to recognize the great value of this improvement, and also by a continued series of experiments to the present day to secure the most practical tests of the relative merits of the various arms.

From the introduction of Hall's breech-loading rifles and carbines to the commencement of the War of the Rebellion, there were but few systems of breech-loaders presented to the War Department; the principal ones being Sharps, Burnside's, Maynard's and Spencer's, of each of which, issues were made to troops between the years 1845 and 1860. An Army Board convened at West Point in 1857, examined a large number of systems of breech-loading small-arms, and gave their opinion as unfavorable to the introduction of breech-loaders until more perfected, but at the same time giving preference to the Burnside arm.

The attention of the War Department was specially directed towards the adoption of a breech-loading arm which should meet the wants of all branches of the service, and the results obtained up to 1859 are here referred to.

Report of the Secretary of War, 1859.

"Under the appropriations heretofore made by Congress to encourage experiments in breech-loading arms, very important results have been arrived at. The ingenuity and invention displayed upon the subject are truly surprising, and it is risking little to say that the arm has been nearly, if not entirely, perfected by several of these plans. These arms commend themselves very strongly for their great range and accuracy of fire at long distances; for the rapidity with which they can be fired; and their exemption from injury by exposure to long-continued rains. With the best breech-loading arm, one skillful man would be equal to two, probably three, armed with the ordinary muzzle-loading gun. True policy requires that steps should be taken to introduce these arms gradually into our service, and to this end preparations ought to be made for their manufacture in the public arsenals."

As is well-known, at the commencement of our war in 1861, the Ordnance Bureau was strained to its utmost by demands for arms, and as a natural result, every opportunity was seized to secure whatever could be made of service, without special regard to any practical test or examination; the only point being to obtain the arms and proper ammunition. The following list will give some idea of the variety of American systems of breech-loaders manufactured or purchased from January 1st, 1861, to June 30th, 1866.

1,509	Ballard,	20,002	Maynard,
1,002	Ball,	1,001	Palmer,
55,567	Burnside,	20,000	Remington,
9,342	Cosmopolitan,	80,512	Sharps,
22,728	Gallagher,	30,062	Smith,
1,052	Gibbs,	94,156	Spencer,
3,520	Halls,	25,603	Starr,
11,261	Joslyn,	4,001	Warner,
892	Lindner,	151	Wesson.
14,495	Merrill,		

It is believed that the above arms were issued almost entirely to mounted troops, and the general result of their use was so satisfactory as to lead to the following from the

Report of General Dyer, Chief of Ordnance, 1864.

"The use of breech-loading arms in our service has, with few exceptions, been confined to mounted troops. So far as our limited experience goes, it indicates the advisability of extending this armament to our infantry also, and this experience is corroborated by that of several foreign nations, into the military service of which the breech-loader has been or is about to be introduced as the exclusive fire-arm for both cavalry and infantry. It is therefore intended to make this change of manufacture at our national armories so soon as the best model for a breech-loader can be established by full and thorough tests and trials, and the requisite modifications of the present machinery for the fabrication of that model can be made. The alteration of our present model of muzzle loading arms is also a very desirable measure, both on account of economy and improvement in the character of these arms. It is thought that they can be altered at a moderate cost and in a short time to very efficient breech-loading arms. The details for effecting both these measures will receive the early attention of this Bureau."

Report of the Chief of Ordnance, 1865.

"In my last report I stated that it was in contemplation to change the manufacture at the national armory as soon as the best model for a breech-loading musket could be established, and that details for effecting this measure would receive the early attention of this Bureau. Extensive experiments have been made by a board of officers, and also under my direction and supervision to effect that object, but as yet no arm has been presented which I have been willing to recommend for adoption. The selection of a proper model is considered so important a measure, that I have preferred to act slowly and with great care in its selection rather than take a false step and have to retrace it.

"I hope to be able very soon to recommend a model for your approval. A plan for altering the muzzle-loading musket into efficient breech-loaders has been devised by the master armorer at the Springfield Armory, which appears to be superior to any other that I have seen. I have taken measures to have five thousand muskets altered to it, and will have some of them issued to troops for trial as soon as the alterations can be made."

Report of the Chief of Ordnance for 1866.

"No arms have been manufactured at the Springfield Armory during the past year, the operations at that post having been confined to cleaning and repairing arms which were turned in after the war, and to making the necessary preparations for converting the Springfield muskets into breech-loaders. About 5,000 muskets have been converted into efficient breech-loaders, and the conversion will be continued as fast as practicable. It is believed that two hundred of these muskets will be turned out daily in February."

Report of the Chief of Ordnance, 1868.

"Reports from the army in regard to the small arms which have been converted from muzzle-loaders into breech-loaders, and to the special ammunition therefor, continue to be highly favorable to the efficiency and superiority of these converted arms and their ammunition. The work of conversion, which had been limited to a small number of muskets, all of which have been issued for service, has been resumed, with such improvements as experience has dictated, which will be applied to a further supply which has been authorized and is now in preparation."

Report of the Secretary of War, 1869.

"The cavalry have been supplied with Spencer carbines and with Sharp's carbines, altered to use the musket metallic ammunition. The infantry, heavy artillery and engineers have been armed with the Springfield breech-loading rifled musket. All these arms have given great satisfaction."

Report of General Sherman, 1869.

"All our troops are now supplied with breech-loading small-arms of the best kind, fully equal to any in use in foreign armies."

Report of the Chief of Ordnance, 1869.

"The operations at the Springfield Armory have been chiefly confined to fabricating the necessary machines, tools and fixtures required for converting the Springfield rifled muskets into breech-loaders. The Springfield Armory is now adequate to the conversion of two hundred muskets per day of eight hours. The Spencer carbine continues to be regarded as a superior arm by the cavalry. The altered Sharps carbine gives great satisfaction, in some respects, particularly in the ammunition, which is the same as the breech-loading musket ammunition; it is decidedly superior to the Spencer carbine. All the infantry, heavy artillery and engineer troops have been provided with the Springfield breech-loading rifled musket. Many of them have had these arms for more than two years. The reports from the different branches of the service in all parts of the country have been highly favorable to this arm and its ammunition."

"Arms now being made at Springfield Armory, it is thought, will be free from any and all the defects heretofore found. In comparison with other breech-loading arms it is confidently believed that this new pattern musket will stand unsurpassed."

Report of the Chief of Ordnance, 1870.

"The operations at the Springfield Armory have been confined chiefly to the conversion of Springfield rifle muskets into breech-loaders of the model of 1868, under the order of the Secretary of War to alter 50,000. Of this number, 45,500 had been altered at the end of the last fiscal year, and the order has now been completed. The armory is now occupied in manufacturing 10,000 Remington muskets for the navy; a few thousand cadet muskets to issue to colleges in pursuance of the joint resolution of Congress, approved May 4th, 1870, and about the same number of arms for competitive trial in the field, in pursuance of the recommendations of the board of officers which convened at St. Louis, in obedience to General Order No. 72 of 1869, as modified by me and approved by you on the 16th of July, 1870."

"The Springfield breech-loading muskets with which the troops have been armed for more than three years, continue to give satisfaction. There are about 35,000 on hand of the model of 1868. It is believed that the arm is one of the very best that has been devised, and it is worthy of consideration whether the alteration of the Springfield muzzle loading muskets upon this system, should not be resumed at once at the national armory."

Report of the Secretary of War, 1871.

"Several kinds of experimental rifles and carbines, as recommended by the St. Louis board, have been manufactured at the Springfield Armory for comparative trial in the field Sufficient information will doubtless be derived from the use of the experimental arms in the field, to enable a board to recommend a breech-loading system for adoption. The armament of State troops should be like that of the national forces, who now use breech-loading small arms."

Report of the Chief of Ordnance, 1871.

"The operations at the Springfield Armory have been confined chiefly to the conversion of a small number of Springfield rifle muskets into breech-loaders for issue to troops and to the States and colleges; to the manufacture of 22,000 Remington rifles for the Navy Department, and three or four kinds of experimental muskets and carbines, for comparative trial by troops in the field. Three of these systems have been put into the hands of the troops, and monthly reports are made to this Bureau upon them, as was directed by you on my indorsement of July 8th, 1870, submitting the report of the board of officers of June 10th, 1870, of which Major-General Schofield was president.

"It is expected that sufficient information in regard to these experimental arms will be derived from troops using them to warrant the appointment,—some time next summer,—of the board which is to select and recommend to the War Department a breech-loading system for adoption for the military service. It is highly important that this board shall act as soon as possible upon the subject, and that a breech-loading system shall be adopted as soon as possible, and adhered to until a large number of breech-loaders can be made for the Government Now there are less than 10 000 breech-loading muskets in the arsenals for issue. This number of muskets is not half sufficient to supply the States with the muskets they are now entitled to receive under their apportionment of the permanent appropriation for arming and equipping the militia. It is important that the arms of the States should be like those used by the Government, and I believe the States are anxious to get the same kinds of arms For these reasons I have been anxious to furnish them, to the extent of the ability of the Department and of their credits, with arms like those our troops are armed with, and I have not been willing to encourage any State in getting any other arms. This Department should, as soon as possible, be placed in a condition to fill all proper requisitions by the States upon it, and should also have on hand in store a large number of breech-loading muskets and carbines to meet any emergency that may arise. Ten years ago the country felt that not less than a million of muskets should be kept in store in the arsenals. We are making very few arms at present, and for the reason that no breech-loading arm has yet been adopted for our military service."

During the fiscal year 1871, the following breech-loading arms were issued to States by the Ordnance Bureau:

6,874 Springfield breech-loading rifle muskets, calibre .50.
291 Springfield cadet breech-loading rifle muskets.

The official evidence that has been given, is a gratifying proof of the steady and consistent attention paid to the introduction of a satisfactory model of a breech-loading arm, on the part of the Ordnance Bureau. The three systems above referred to, viz.: the Springfield model of 1868, the Remington and the Sharp, have been sometime in the hands of troops, and the monthly reports are being regularly forwarded to the Ordnance Department, upon the results of which will be based a permanent decision. A fourth system, the Ward-Burton, is now being manufactured at Springfield, and will be issued in the same manner for competition. The decision of the War Department in reference to these various systems, will probably be made during the present year.

A special interest has been awakened in the various State military organizations in reference to the introduction of breech-loading arms for service as the arm of the State militia and the National Guard. Rifle clubs are being formed, and at a meeting of the New York State Military Association, a special lecture on this subject was delivered by Col. W. C. Church, the able editor of the *Army and Navy Journal.* The following extracts from State Reports will indicate the feeling on this subject:

Message of Gov. Claflin of Mass., Jan. 7th, 1871.

"Only one regiment is armed with breech-loaders. A large proportion, if not the whole, of the infantry should be armed in like manner, if we desire to keep them prepared for effective service. The war in Europe has created such a demand for fire-arms, that their cost has materially increased; but still, careful inquiry should be instituted to ascertain whether early preparation ought not to be made for arming all of our infantry with these new guns."

Report of Adjt.-Gen. Cunningham, State of Mass., 1871.

"The militia should be armed and equipped in the most approved manner, and in every respect equal to the troops of the United States. The infantry of the army has been supplied with breech-loading muskets for the past two years. I recommend that an appropriation be made for the purchase of a sufficient number of these muskets to arm the infantry."

Message of Gov. Washburn, of Mass., 1872.

"I am informed that $50,000 was appropriated last year for the purchase of breech-loading arms. As no expenditure has been made, and as the general government has now under advisement a plan for furnishing the militia of all the States with a uniform arm of this description, I suggest the propriety of awaiting the action of the authorities at Washington."

Report of Adjt.-Gen. Townsend, State of New York, 1871.

"Now that the superiority of breech-loaders has been so fully demonstrated in actual warfare, it seems to me that there should be no further delay in exchanging the muzzle-loading rifled muskets, with which the infantry of the National Guard is armed, for the most approved arm of the kind loading at the breech.

"Referring to what is contained in my last annual report relating to this matter, I would now remark that, although I still hope that there may be recovered from the United States on account of the war claims, a sufficient sum, in excess of the special tax due from this State, to pay the expense of the proposed exchange of arms. There is so much unavoidable delay in getting those accounts settled, that I would recommend that an appropriation be asked for to accomplish the object at once."

Report of Gen. Shaler, 1st Division, N. G. S. N. Y.

"I believe it to be the policy of the State to arm the National Guard with the most approved weapons; and I would, therefore, strongly recommend that this command be supplied with the most approved pattern of breech-loading muskets. The superiority of this weapon has been so well proven, and the efficiency of the Corps would be so much promoted thereby, that I hope the suggestion may meet with the consideration which in my opinion it deserves."

Report of Adjt.-Gen. Stryker, State of New Jersey.

"I would recommend at an early day the exchange of the muskets now in the hands of the military force of the State, for breech-loading rifles. As, however, the War Department, on inquiry, has not yet adopted a new arm for the regular army, it would manifestly be inexpedient for us hastily to adopt one at present. I think there is no one thing would encourage the men more than an accurate, effective breech-loading weapon. At the earliest moment possible, I would urge your serious attention to this matter."

Report of Adjt.-Gen. Burrell, State of Pennsylvania, 1870.

"By direction of your Excellency, in the month of August last, I called the attention of the Chief of Ordnance of the War Department to the quota of arms due Pennsylvania, and after the necessary preliminary correspondence, drew, on your requisition on the Ordnance Department, 4,500 Springfield breech-loading rifle muskets, model of 1868. These guns have been distributed as indicated by law, 'in such manner as in the judgment of the Commander-in-Chief would most effectually subserve the military interests and necessities of the Commonwealth.'"

Annual Report of Adjt.-Gen. Allen, State of California.

"The application of the breech-loading principle to small-arms has marked a new era in the science of war. This great improvement, which threatens to revolutionize tactics and modify the principles of strategy, has been accepted with a promptitude and unanimity remarkable in view of military conservatism, and indicative of the unqualified appreciation of its merits. Since the various exhibitions of the superiority of this improved arm, it has been adopted by a number of the States, and already the several European governments have either adopted the new system, or are making preparations for the conversion of old arms, or the substitution of new ones. The regular army of the United States is being rapidly armed with guns converted into breech-loaders.

"It is to be hoped that your Excellency, seeing the importance of these facts, and through you the Legislature, will cause to be constituted a board of officers by Legislative action, to determine the most efficient arm for the use of the National Guard. In view of the importance of a speedy adoption of a new armament for the National Guard, it is earnestly recommended that a special appropriation be made for the conversion of at least five thousand during the next year."

American invention and genius has been largely directed towards the production of a simple form of a breech-loading small arm. Prior to 1860 there had been less than two hundred patents taken out for this purpose; from 1860 to 1871 this had increased to the large number of over seven hundred, more than quadruple the inventions of all the rest of the world in the same direction. It may be as well to remark here that with the single exception of the needle-gun, every arm on a breech-loading system used in Europe is of American origin, both in its principle and application; a large portion being of American manufacture.

1880.

In this continuation of the history of inventions and improvements in the manufacture of fire-arms, it is desirable to show the energy shown, and advance made, by the Ordnance Department of the United States, and by the various states in the adoption of recent inventions, and the general adaptation of all breech-loading arms to one calibre, and for that reason the following extracts are made from the reports of the Chief of Ordnance and the State Adjutant Generals:

Report of Chief of Ordnance, 1872.

"Arms upon the system adopted ought to be manufactured without delay, in quantities sufficient to supply the entire army with them, and fill requisitions for the militia; and it is earnestly recommended that liberal appropriations may be made to enable this department to manufacture, from year to year, a sufficient number to accumulate a reserve for the exigencies of war. In the adoption of an arm for the military service, it should be the policy of the Government to determine and fix upon the best arm that can be had for present manufacture, and to be provided in quantities for future emergencies, and retained as the standard arm only so long as none more perfect and efficient as a military weapon has been invented. The object of this department is, and has been, to secure for the army and militia the very best military arm that the inventive genius of the age can devise."

Report of Chief of Ordnance, 1873.

"The Springfield Armory is now engaged in the manufacture of rifles and carbines on the new model for the military service. * * * * It is not presumable that the new system of breech-loader selected after such exhaustive tests of all inventions brought before the world, will soon be superseded by any more valuable and efficient system; and it is a grave question of public policy, deserving serious consideration, whether the new arm that has been adopted, after such intelligent and careful trial by a competent board, ought not to be manufactured in such quantities for a reserve supply in case of war, as will place us in this part of our national armament on a footing with other first-class powers."

Report of Secretary of War, 1874.

"Every nation that aspires to the dignity of a first-class power, has cast aside its obsolete muzzle-loading arms, and at immense cost has been, and is, providing newest and most approved models by hundreds of thousands. The sudden occurrences that end in war, and the startling rapidity with which wars are waged and terminated, demand complete preparation in time of peace. With us the want of a large standing army can only be compensated by keeping on hand, ready for any emergency, a complete supply of every description of war material."

Report of Chief of Ordnance, 1874.

"The production of rifles and carbines upon the adopted plan, has been pushed forward at the National Armory with energy and success, and the new arms issued to the troops will, no doubt, give great satisfaction."

Report of Chief of Ordnance, 1876.

"That a better arm than the Springfield may some day be invented is not at all improbable, and a magazine-gun will no doubt be the arm of the future, but until such an one suitable for our military service has been perfected and approved, a reserve stock of Springfield is a necessity."

Report of Chief of Ordnance, 1877.

"The rifle issued to the army and the militia, compares favorably with the best breech-loader either here or abroad. This was conclusively shown recently in the 'inter-state military match' at Creedmoor. In the hands of the California team from General McComb's brigade, the score made is said never to have been equaled in a military team match. It is an arm that may not be superseded for many years to come, and if it be obliged to yield to one of superior merit, the effect will not be to render it obsolete, but to make it secondary to one using the same cartridge, but having greater rapidity of fire, so that the present single breech-loader will always be a powerful weapon, even when compared with the possible magazine-gun of the future. We cannot be wrong then in laying up a reasonable supply of these, therefore, especially as the magazine-gun that may some day be adopted for army service, may require years of invention and improvements to reach that degree of simplicity in its mechanical arrangements necessary to render it suitable for the soldier."

Report of Chief of Ordnance, 1878.

"The present approved arm cannot be rendered worthless by the introduction of an improved weapon, because as long as small-arms are fired from the shoulder, and the propelling force is gunpowder, the calibre of gun and dimensions of cartridge, new regulation, will not be changed, and the improvements will only consist in more rapid manipulation and increased rapidity of fire."

Report of Chief of Ordnance, 1879.

"During the last fiscal year, there were manufactured at the National Armory 20,085 Springfield rifles, and under the law authorizing it, 1,000 of the experimental Hotchkiss magazine rifles. The former have been produced at a much less cost than heretofore, owing to the increased number manufactured and the improvement of the plans employed, and as there is now available a larger appropriation than usual for the present year, it is confidently expected that the cost will yet be further reduced in the future."

Report of Adjutant-General of Conn.

"The perfection to which the breech-loading musket with metallic cased cartridge has been brought, and its enormous efficiency compared with the muzzle-loader, have caused a revolution in modern tactics." * * * * * * "A good deal of interest has been manifested by the members of the National Guard, in perfecting themselves in the use of the breech-loading rifles, by frequent target practice."

Report of Adjutant-General of Georgia.

"The breech-loading rifle has been in use by most of the Georgia Volunteers for a number of years, and has afforded general satisfaction."

Report of Adjutant-General of Michigan.

"During the American civil war and since, the demand for superior arms, both for this and other nations, has increased, and their manufacture in this country has been proportionately enlarged, and with such improvements that the American arms need only to be brought into contrast with those of European make, to fully establish their superiority."

Report of Adjutant-General of California.

"The application of the breech-loading principles to small arms has marked a new era in the science of war. This great improvement, which threatens to revolutionize tactics and modify the principles of strategy, has been accepted with a promptitude and unanimity remarkable in view of military conservatism, and indicative of the unqualified appreciation of its merits." * * * * * * * * * * * "I have made frequent trials of all patterns of breech-loading arms to test their accuracy, force, range, and their rapidity of fire, as also the comparative usefulness of these arms with the old style, and have demonstrated that the improved breech-loader can be loaded and discharged with facility twenty times in a minute, while the old muzzle-loading arm can only be fired three times in a minute and that with considerable labor, as compared with the new."

Fig. 1.

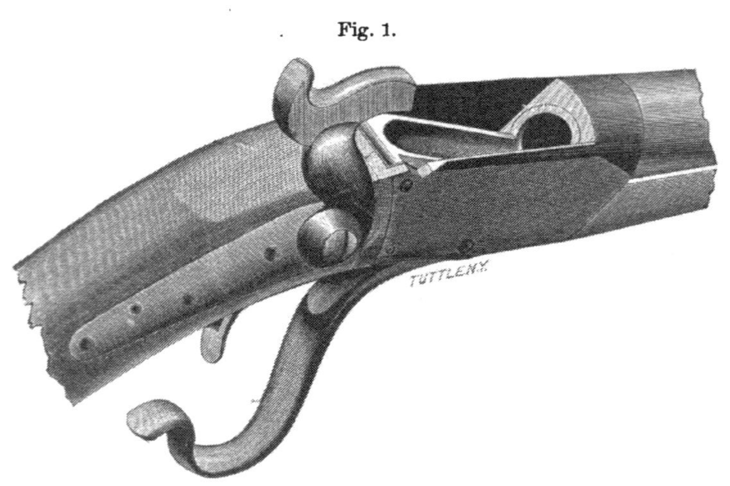

THE PEABODY SYSTEM.

CHAPTER II.

THE PEABODY SYSTEM.

The record of this arm entitles it to a front rank among the productions of American industry. The inventor, Henry O. Peabody, of Boston, an active and thoughtful mechanic, had his attention first directed to the subject of breech-loading arms at the commencement of the war. After careful labor and study he worked out the original idea of the mechanism of the Peabody gun, which is to-day, as he made it, unimproved and unchanged, the first and only patent in the United States, having been taken out July 22d, 1862.

Since its origin, this arm has been manufactured and controlled by the Providence Tool Company, of Rhode Island, who have spared no expense in machinery and workmen to produce an arm complete and satisfactory in all its parts, and with a capacity sufficient to turn out 10,000 guns per month. The interests of this system have been represented in this country and Europe by Marshall F. Benton, Esq., of New York City, through whose kindness and attention the following facts have been obtained. The arm was presented to the United States Army Board, assembled at Springfield in January, 1865, to examine it, together with sixty-four other systems of breech-loading fire-arms.

The severe practical tests instituted by the Board soon reduced this large number to eight, and then to four. The character of these experiments was such as the exigencies of actual service might require, and comprised trials for strength, accuracy and penetration. The mechanism was also allowed to rust, and afterwards covered with sand. The eight arms selected from the sixty-five systems, were exposed to variable weather for ten days and daily drenched with water. The weather during this period was so cold as to cover the guns with snow and ice, and again so warm as to remove both by a sudden thaw.

They were also dried suddenly by exposure to a very high temperature. After this test the four best arms, comprising the Peabody, were selected and fired with heavy charges, sixty grains of powder and three balls, each ball weighing four hundred and fifty grains. The charges were gradually increased to eighty grains of powder and five balls without injury to the Peabody rifle, the only arm which successfully passed the ordeal. A charge of one hundred and twenty grains of powder and five balls was subsequently used in the Peabody arm with the same result. The Board who had witnessed these experiments recommended the Peabody gun for military service.

The report concludes as follows: "Having examined and tested all of the breech-loading arms submitted for their consideration, the Board recommend the breech-loading arm known as Peabody's."

Signed by Major T. T. S. Laidley, Ordnance Department,
"Major J. G. Benton, " "
"Major H. E. Maynadier, 12th U. S. Infantry,
"Capt. J. D. O'Connell, 14th " "
"Capt. J. H. Kellogg, 1st U. S. Cavalry,
"Capt. T. F. Rodenbough, 2d U. S. "
"First Lieut. J. R. Edie, Ordnance Department.

The war having closed during the session of this Board, the Government did not find it necessary to act at once upon the report, and the Chief of Ordnance, General A. B. Dyer, under date of July 12th, 1866, states "the necessity for the immediate selection of a model having ceased to exist with the termination of hostilities, further action was suspended with the view of ascertaining whether additional improvements in some of the arms which had been tried might not be made. It is contemplated to have a further trial of the arms which were deemed the best."

On the 10th of March, 1868, another Board, convened by order of the Secretary of War, met at Washington, its duties being the selection of the best breech-loading system for new arms, and also the best system for the conversion of the Springfield muzzle-loaders to breech-loaders. Over sixty arms were presented for examination and trial, many of these being special systems for conversion. The tests made by this Board were similar in character and identical in result with those carried out by the Springfield Board. The details of the report of this Board were not officially announced, but it is stated that their deliberations were terminated by an order from the Secretary of War, requiring the report to be submitted on the 4th of June.

A recommendation was made for a system of conversion of the Springfield rifle, that being the immediate object of the trial. The credit for superiority was awarded to the Peabody arm by this Board, which was composed of the following officers :

Major-General Winfield Scott Hancock, U. S. A.
Brevet Major-General R. C. Buchanan, Col. 1st Infantry,
" Brigadier-General P. V. Hagner, Col. Ordnance,
" " " Charles Griffin, Capt. 5th Artillery,
" Colonel J. G. Benton, Major Ordnance,
" " Horace Porter, Capt. "
Lieut.-Col. Wesley Owens, 5th Cavalry,
" C. C. Parsons, First Lieut. 4th Artillery.

With reference to calibre the Chief of Ordnance stated, "The Board did not recommend any particular calibre." The report was partially acted upon, and a number of muzzle-loaders were converted according to the system recommended. The more important subject of the adoption of a new breech-loading arm was resumed on the appointment of a third Board to meet at St. Louis, Mo. This Board made a report under date of June 10th, 1870, giving a decision in favor of six different systems of breech-loading arms, among which the Peabody arm was not included.

The decision of this Board was disapproved by the Chief of Ordnance in the following language : "The opinion expressed by the Board in regard to the relative merits of the several breech-loading systems for small arms is not wholly concurred in by this Bureau ; and is not, it is thought, sustained by the record of the proceedings which accompanies this report, which shows that serious defects existed in the Remington arms not observable in the Springfield or the Sharps, such as frequent failures to explode the cartridges, occasional sticking of the empty shell in the chamber, and the difficulty of moving the hammer and breech-block after firing with heavy charges.

The first two of these defects, and also the objection arising from the arm being loaded only at a full-cock, have been brought to the notice of this Bureau by the commanding officers of all companies using this arm. These defects show that the Remington arm should not be adopted before being thoroughly tested in service."

To this is subjoined the endorsement of the War Department as follows: "The recommendations of the Chief of Ordnance are approved by the Secretary of War. Signed Ed. Schriver, Inspector-General," under date of July 16th, 1870. In consequence of these contradictory results, a fourth Board, it is officially stated, will be convened during the present year to take into further consideration the question of the adoption of breech-loading arms for the United States army. Against the decision of the St. Louis Board the proprietors of the Peabody issued a protest, which, as belonging to the history of this arm, is quoted nearly in full. After recapitulating the decisions of the two Boards preceding, the protest continues:

These deliberate and formal opinions of *two* boards in favor of the Peabody gun, might appear conclusive of the merits of that arm. But at this juncture persons who had anxiously urged the adoption of another system, succeeded in securing the appointment of a board of naval officers, for the purpose of reporting upon the merits of small arms. This board consisted of the following persons:

Captain William Reynolds, President of the Board,
Commander S. Nicholson,
Commander K. R. Breese,
Captain McLane Tilton, U. S. Marines,
Second Lieutenant George C. Reid, U. S. Marines, Recorder

No considerable publicity was given to the fact of the appointment of this board, and *the manufacturers of the Peabody gun knew nothing of its existence until their deliberations were nearly concluded.* No opportunity was afforded the makers to present the Peabody system to this board, and *their report was made with no sample of the arm having been before them.* The board naturally recommended the adoption of the Remington system for the naval service.

A third army board was ordered on the 23d of October, 1869, and the members of it were

Major-General J. M. Schofield,
Brevet Brigadier-General J. H. Potter, Lieutenant-Colonel Fourth Infantry,
Brevet Major-General Wesley Merritt, Lieutenant-Colonel Ninth Cavalry,
Major James Van Voast, Eighteenth Infantry,
Brevet Colonel John Hamilton, Major First Artillery.

In the General Order convening this board, it was ordered as follows:

This board will act in conjunction with a board of naval officers, and endeavor, if possible, to adopt small arms of a pattern and calibre suitable to both branches of the service, with common ammunition and parts interchangeable.

The Navy Department, however, appears to have ignored the action of the War-Office, having already adopted the Remington system and ordered 10,000 guns to be made. Admiral Porter says: "The naval officers were invited to attend as a matter of courtesy, and the results of the board will affect only the army." *Under the orders of the War Department, therefore, the St. Louis board was called upon to endeavor if possible to adopt the same arm already adopted by the Navy Department.* The deliberations of the board seem to have been hurried, and their conclusion was quickly and easily made. In their report they altogether ignore five different models of the Peabody system submitted for trial. In fine, they not only did not recommend the Peabody for adoption, but agreed so little with the opinion of their predecessors, as to place it behind several other arms known to committees, but only known to be discarded; for not one of the guns so recommended, except the Remington, has been actually introduced in any army whatever as the standard service rifle. This decision against the Peabody proves too much · for not only have *two* United States boards decided in its favor as the best arm for military service, but *all* of the committees of Europe have, after long trial, placed it in the very first rank of breech-loaders; *several* have recommended it to their governments for adoption (the English committee accepting it with only the modification made in it by M. Martini), and it has been *actually adopted* in the armies of Switzerland, Roumania, Canada, Spain and Cuba, and now forms a large proportion of the armament of the two countries first named. In addition to these the manufacturers of the Peabody gun have had the *first refusal* of the orders of several other countries, which offers were declined for business reasons.

It will not, therefore, seem strange that the manufacturers of the Peabody arm believe themselves to have been unjustly treated by the board in question, especially as Major-General Dyer, Chief of Ordnance, not only strongly disapproves of the conclusion of the Board, but declares that such conclusion was not only unwarranted by the facts elicited by the trial, but, on the *showing of the report of the board, was directly opposed to them.*

That his severe censure was amply deserved, may be seen from the following extracts from the committee's report;

Remington arm tested for endurance:

First hundred rounds—One cartridge failed to ignite; cases extracted with difficulty.

Second series—One cartridge failed to ignite; distance between extreme shots, 34 inches.

Third series—Six cartridges failed to explode; distance between extreme shots, 68 inches.

Fourth series—Six cartridges failed to ignite; balls ranged wild.

Fifth series—Five cartridges failed to explode; shots all over the target.

The arm worked well. *Many of the cases were drawn with difficulty; the main spring worked with much friction on the hammer; and small particles of iron were found in the breech-mechanism; barrel much fouled and leaded.*

While thus specifying the points which prove conclusively that the gun did not work well, the board states that it did work well.

In the face of these facts, the manufacturers of the Peabody rifle ask why *three* boards were necessary before a verdict against the Peabody could be obtained? What were the excellences of the arm now preferred, and the defects of the Peabody, which two boards failed to discover, and which at this late day have caused a reversal of their decision by a third? Why was a naval board invited to assist informally at the deliberations of the army board, the former composed only of known supporters of the Remington system?

Let these questions be answered. But whether they are answered or not, the manufacturers of the Peabody arm—in view,

1. Of the favorable decision of the two United States army boards, after a long and exhaustive series of trials, in which the Remington was an unsuccessful competitor;
2. Of the testimony of the committees of Europe to the superiority of the Peabody arm;
3. Of the actual adoption of this arm in the countries before named; and
4. Of the evidence of the good opinion entertained of it by other countries, in giving to the Peabody manufacturers the first refusal of orders—maintain that they are fully justified in protesting against the decision of the St. Louis committee, and in continuing to claim for the Peabody rifle one of the first places, if not the very first place, among modern breech-loading arms.

PROVIDENCE TOOL COMPANY,
JOHN B. ANTHONY, *Treasurer.*

PROVIDENCE, R. I., U. S. A., September 20th, 1870.

Above published in the *U. S. Army and Navy Journal*, September 24th, 1870.

In justice to the Peabody arm, a statement is here given of the character of the defects alleged to have been developed by this Committee, as will be perceived from the following extracts from their report:

I.

"The Peabody rifle (Spanish model), calibre .43, sent by Providence Tool Company, was dismounted, examined and found to consist of sixty parts.

II.

"The arm was fired with the Berdan cartridge for accuracy. Target Record, No. 1. The sixth and seventh cases were not ejected by the extractor, and were forced out by the ramrod.

III.

"The arm was fired for rapidity. *Time for twenty-three shots, four minutes.* The cases generally being extracted with difficulty.

IV.

"Arm tested for endurance. Cases did not extract easily. The greater portion of them were removed with a screw-driver. Twelve cases were forced out with a rammer. *The cases were scored near the base and cartridges did not fit the chamber. The test was therefore discontinued.*"

This explanation as to the difficulty in loading and extracting the shells is certainly conclusive, but it is to be regretted that on this account this model should have been put aside, as such action appears to be irreconcilable with a purpose to arrive at the true merits of the arm under consideration, and with the duty of the committee.

By comparison with reports of the performances of the Peabody gun before other committees, the number of shots obtained before this board was remarkably small, being only 5.3 shots per minute as against 27 shots per minute before the Connecticut Board, and 25 shots in the same time when tested before the official Boards of New York and Massachusetts. The number given by the St. Louis Board, has been largely exceeded by every other committee of which there is a record. In other respects, the results arrived at by this Board are at variance with those obtained elsewhere and with the experience of seven years in the practical operation of the arm.

In Europe the Peabody has been extensively introduced, and has received the highest encomiums. After exhaustive trials of all available breech-loading arms extending over a year, the Swiss Committee selected the Peabody as superior to all of its competitors, and despatched Captain Michel of the Swiss Ordnance Corps to the manufacturers in this country, with an order for the immediate completion of 15,000 of these arms of .41 calibre, with rim-fire ammmunition.

This order was filled promptly, and obtained for the arm a wide reputation, principally on account of the high standing of the Swiss in every detail connected with small arms. The action of Switzerland was soon followed by Denmark, which government despatched officers to the United States for the purpose of contracting for the Peabody arm, but the terms not being acceptable to the manufacturers, negotiations were abandoned.

The Government of Roumania also sent Captain Dabija of the artillery to this country, who brought an order for 15,000 Peabody rifles, which gave such entire satisfaction that the order was supplemented soon after by an additional one for 10,000, of .45 calibre, brought over by Captain Demetresco, who was under orders to superintend the construction of the arms, which were adapted to use the centre-fire cartridge. Orders amounting to about 24,000 have also been received from Cuba, Canada and Mexico, where the arms have been for several years in actual service in the field.

The French Government has also endorsed the Peabody arm by orders to the extent of 39,000, mostly of calibre .43, using a centre-fire cartridge. The reports which have been received fully testify to the efficiency of the arm in the hands of troops in the field, thus corroborating the favorable reports of the several Boards and Committees upon whose recommendation it was adopted and issued for service. In several of the European nations considerations of price and a desire to foster home industry, has prevented the adoption of the Peabody arm, but even there they have cheerfully acknowledged its merits, as the following reports fully indicate:

REPORT on a trial made at the 'Manufacture Royale d' Armes' (at Liege, Belgium,) with a Peabody musket of calibre 11 *millim.* (0.43 1-4 *inch,*) *disposed for Boxer cartridges:*

The arm is presented by Mr. H. Renard, representative of the inventor. The cartridge (central fire,) is manufactured at the Government Pyrotechnic establishment at Antwerp, the lead weighs 24 1-2 grams (378 1-2 grains), and the charge is 5 grams (77 1-4 grains) of infantry powder.

THE TRIAL COMPRISES:

1. A shooting at 100 metres (328 feet) to appreciate the precision.
2. A shooting at 100 metres, to estimate the penetration.
3. A quick shooting.

PRECISION.

The marksman of the Manufacture Royal fired twenty rounds from a rest; the result is shown in the copy of the target:

PENETRATION.

Eleven planks of white wood (poplar), had been placed at a distance of 100 metres (328 feet), each plank having a thickness of 25 millimetres (0.98 inch), with a similar distance of 25 millim. between each of them.

Seven rounds were fired:

The 7 balls went through the first 6 planks.
6 " " " " 7 "
5 " " " " 8 "
3 " " " " 9 "

Consequently the penetration gave an average of 200 milimetres (7 7-8 inches).

"QUICK SHOOTING AT 50 METRES (164 ft).

The cartridges were passed to the marksman by a soldier placed at his right side. Notwithstanding some difficulty to introduce the cartridges, owing to the circumstance that the chamber of the barrel had not the exact dimensions required, the sergeant of the manufactory obtained seventeen rounds in the minute; fifteen balls struck the target.

The working of the mechanism was examined after the trials. It acted regularly. The automatic extraction of the discharged cartridge shell was perfect; not a single cartridge missed fire, and no signs of dirt were found in the breech-piece.

(Signed) COUSTURIER,
Captain Commandant, and President of the Commission.
(Signed) TERSSEN, *Inspector of Arms.*
(Signed) De GHESELLE, *Captain, Reporter.*

ROYAL DANISH LEGATION AND CONSULATE GENERAL,
NEW YORK, 15th October, 1866.

To the President of the Providence Tool Company, Providence, R. I.

SIR: His Danish Majesty's Government has instructed me to communicate to you the report on the Peabody Gun, made by the Royal Commission for examining and trying experiments with breech-loading arms.

"REPORT:

The breech-loading system of the Peabody gun is simple and convenient, and under the whole firing its mechanism has acted very satisfactory.

It was subjected to the following trials:

1. 100 shots from rest, distance 600 feet.
2. 75 quick shots, with and without rests, distance 400 feet.
3. Three days later; 25 shots from rest, distance 600 feet.
4. 210 shots at target, distance 200 to 2,400 feet.

During these trials the gun was not cleaned. Incessant quick firing did not influence the hitting quality, and the mechanism continued to act perfectly to the last shot.

12 shots were fired in one minute.

No change was perceptible in the different trials; good hitting shots were obtained at a distance of 2,400 feet. The Commission, composed of the officers of the Royal Artillery, close their report thus:

The Peabody gun, has, on the whole, given a very satisfactory result, and must be considered the best single shot breech-loading weapon, with which copper cartridges are used.

I have the honor to be,
Your obedient servant,
(Signed) H. DOLLUER,
Charge de Affairs, ad inter. and Acting Consul General.

REPORT on a trial made with three Peabody rifles at the Hague, Holland, on 11th of March, 1867, *in presence of the Commission for selecting breech-loaders.*

The arms presented by Mr. H. Renard, of Liege, representative of the Providence Tool Company, R. I., are of the calibre of 11 m. 4 (45-100 inch), but their chambers are of different dimensions.

The chamber of Musket No. 1 (manufactured at Liege) is disposed for centre-fire Boxer cartridges, charged with 5 grammes (17 1-4 grains of powder); that of Muskets No. 2 and

3 for metallic cartridges with rim-fire, and charges of respectively 3 gr. 88 (60 grains) and 4 gr. 58 (70 grains).

The trials, made in one single sitting, comprised,

1. A shooting to appreciate accuracy. 2. Another to test rapidity. 3. One with filed cartridges and heavy charges. 4. One with dirt in the block.

Precision, at 300 metres (984 feet). A sergeant fired 20 shots from rest, with 60 grains cartridges. (Diagram A, accompanying original report.) And other 20 shot, equally from rest, with 70 grains cartridges. (Diagram B, also accompanying original report.)

2. Quick shooting at 300 metres, (984 feet.) The sergeant fired 20 shots with gun No. 2 in 2 minutes and 15 seconds, from the shoulder, the cartridges being placed in an outside pocket of the man's coat. It must be remarked that the shooter did not know the arm, and that one shot missed fire.

3. Filed cartridges and heavy charges. With gun No. 1, one Boxer cartridge filed and cut at the rim, so as to cause its bursting, was fired. The escape of gas was considerable, but the mechanism remained closed, and the shooter was not molested.

One shot was then fired with 6 grammes (92 1-2 grains) powder and two balls (loaded from the muzzle), and another with 8 grammes (123 1-2 grains) and 3 balls. At these shots the bottom of the cartridge shell was completely torn, and there was a great escape of gas and smoke; the mechanism remained intact, and the shooter was in no way molested.

4. Shooting with obstructed breech lock. The mechanism was filled with sand, and the sergeant, after having more or less cleaned it with his fingers, shot three rounds. The mechanism operated quite conveniently.

The Hague, 11th March, 1867.

The Lieutenant-General, President of the Commission,
(Signed,) HAPPE.

The Captain, Secretary of the Commission.
(Signed,) SMISSAERT.

SPANDAU, PRUSSIA, 5th September, 1867.

To Messrs. James R. McDonald & Co., Hamburg, Representatives Providence Tool Company, in Europe:

GENTLEMEN:—By order of the War-Office, dated August 27th, we take the liberty to communicate you the results of the experiments made with the two Peabody Guns, Musket and Carbine, which you sent to the Department of War, by transmitting you herewith an extract of our report to the Royal Artillery Department.

Said report speaks, at first, of the construction of the gun. The manipulation of loading is simple, and equally easy to the soldier, in standing upright or in laying down. The mechanism, leaving the percussion-lock out of consideration, is solid, and independent of the effects of moisture in the atmosphere.

After fourteen days trial, in changing weather, during which time only the barrel was cleaned, the inside of the breech-block showed only some rust, which prevented, however, in no way, the regular movement of the same. The explosion failed hardly ever in the Peabody gun. Amongst 700 to 800 shots, there was only a single failure, but when this cartridge was turned it exploded likewise.

The connection between the barrel and stock and mechanism is sufficiently secured, and no fears are to be entertained that the gun, if used for fighting instead of shooting, will be broken easier than a gun, the stock of which is made of one piece.

As to the ammunition for the Peabody gun, which has proved itself very satisfactory, it may be mentioned that eight cartridges deposited, for twenty-three days of the most changeable weather of the spring, into the free air, showed no increase of weight, and lost only little of their explosive power, while eight cartridges, deposited for nearly four days, into water, weighed three "cent" a piece more than before. These latter cartridges had kept their capacity of igniting, but lost their explosive power almost entirely.

If it is required, by means of the copper cartridge, to establish a safe closure, which is always renewed, it appears that the Peabody cartridge has been perfectly successful in this point. Even after a great number of shots, neither a bursting of the shells, nor an obstruction of the mechanism by dirt, came to our notice.

As to the shooting capacity of the gun, we found the following results:

(The results, for Accuracy, Penetration and Trajectory, are not copied here, because the figures are not given in English measure, nor are they clearly understood.)

Rapidity.--Repeated experiments showed thirteen shots by average, and fifteen shots as a maximum, per minute, with twelve hits, on the common small target, at 400 paces distance, cartridges given to the marksman, who is a master of his art.

Regarding the carbine; it agrees in the principle with the musket, and therefore most of what is said of the musket might be applied to the carbine also.

We resume our report, in the words that the Peabody gun, musket as well as carbine, are weapons perfectly adapted for military service.

The Directors of the Military Shooting School,

(Signed,) VON KALINOVSKY, *Major and Director.*
VON ANNEZTSKY, *Captain and Member.*
PEKRSEN, *Captain and Member.*
MEINHARD, *First Lieutenant.*
HENTSDEN, *First Lieutenant.*

IMPERIAL ROYAL BREECH-LOADING ARMS COMMISSION, OF AUSTRIA.

Results of the trials with the breech-loading arm, system "Peabody."

The trials with the Peabody arm were conducted in two series, according to the quantity of ammunition on hand; 1882 rounds in all being fired.

The first of these two series consisted in:

a. Firing for accuracy;

b. Firing for rapidity;

c. A series of rounds solely for testing the durability of the breech;

d. Firing with cartridges purposely damaged.

The second of the two series consisted in a further testing of the breech, as to its efficiency, under a variety of circumstances, 1371 rounds in all being fired.

e. A series of rounds during which the recoil was measured, and rapidity of fire repeated, noted, and finally,

f. Firing for accuracy, at targets respectively at a distance of 300 and 600 yards, in order to compare the accuracy of the firing during a large number of rounds, with the results obtained in the beginning of the trial.

With reference to *a.* The firing for accuracy in the first series was commenced on the 18th of September, 1866, and consisted in,

32 shots at a target, distance 300 yards.
30 " " " " 600 "

The results obtained are shown in accompanying diagrams of targets 1 and 2.

With reference to *b.* Firing for rapidity was conducted both with aiming from a rest, and from the shoulder without a rest.

In the first manner fourteen shots in one minute were fired, the cartridges having been placed on a table near the marksman. Of these shots nine bullets struck the target, the same being 8' square.

In firing from the shoulder thirty-two shots were fired in two minutes. The cartridges, in this case, were also placed on a table.

With reference to *c.* Besides the 108 shots above referred to, the following were fired from the Peabody gun, solely for the purpose of testing the breech:

401 { 24 shots in 1 series, on the 18th September;
160 " " 5 " of 32 rounds ea., } on the 21st September;
57 " " 1 " —————— }
160 " " 5 " of 32 rounds each, on the 22d of September, 1866.

The firing in the single series was continued without intermission, and the pause between the series was only long enough to enable the gun to cool. During these 401 rounds as well as during the 108 before mentioned, or together 500 rounds, the breech operated perfectly well, and had completely retained its easy movement, although the gun had not been cleaned during the whole course of the trial. In short, no difficulty or objection had presented itself during the various series. The breech-apparatus performed its functions with perfect efficiency, only when loading, it was necessary to insert the cartridge completely into its chamber, as otherwise the closing of the breech would be impossible, and the cartridge would be liable to be deformed in case the breech-piece should be brought up with a violent motion. Of the 500 shots mentioned, there was one misfire, but this cartridge also exploded after having been slightly turned in its chamber. The cartridge cases were not injured by firing, and no escape of gas took place. After the fourth day of the trial, the gun was taken apart and examined; some rust was found on the barrel, and a deposit from the powder-smoke in some parts of the breech, but the easy movement of the breech-apparatus was not in any manner affected. The gun was now cleaned, and firing continued.

With reference to *d*. Firing with cartridges purposely injured was commenced, in order to learn the effect upon the breech consequent upon the bursting of a cartridge case, respecting the damage to be apprehended from escape of gas to the marksman. To this end, the gun was screwed on a rest, and two shots were fired with cartridges which had been filed and slightly split. The effect of these shots was, that the base of the cartridge was almost entirely torn off, the gas escaped upwards and downwards, tore and scorched a paper which had been adjusted over the breech, and about four to five inches from it. The breech, however, remained without any injury, and was covered only with a slight deposit of powder smoke.

In the second series, the following trials are made with the Peabody gun:

With reference to *a*. On the 18th of October, 1866:

481 { 320 shots, in 10 series of 32 shots,
62 " " 2 " " 31 "
30 " " 1 "
64 " " 1 "
5 " " 1 " the latter for the purpose of measuring the recoil in the measuring apparatus, which showed a mean of 41.6 pounds. There were seven misfires but all the seven cartridges exploded upon being slightly turned.

After each series of rounds, the barrel was cooled by pouring water upon it. The last 164 shots were fired with greased bullets, by which the somewhat irregular effect, which had been observed with ungreased bullets, was obviated. At the termination of the firing the breech was opened, and water poured into it, and without being cleaned, was put aside until the next trial, which took place on the 19th of October, 1866.

The gun was examined before being fired, and was found to be somewhat clogged with rust, powder dirt, and hard grease, but the breech worked with its usual facility. The gun was then again put together and firing recommenced, as follows:

411 { 59 shots in 1 series;
256 " 8 " of 32 shots;
64 " 1 " aiming from a rest in 6' 8";
32 " rapid firing without aiming, in 1' 5".

The gun from which, in two days, 892 shots had been fired without cleaning, was now examined, and the middle of the barrel was found somewhat covered with powder dirt. In the breech was also powder dirt, but the grease which had been dissolved from the firing, had lubricated the breech parts, and dissolved the rust. The breech worked with perfect facility. Before continuing firing, the gun was cleaned.

On the 20th of October, 1866, the trials with the Peabody were continued with greased cartridges. 128 shots were fired in 4 series of 32 shots, without any difficulty. During the last trial, the marksman was provided with an American cartridge-box or pouch, containing 32 cartridges. 32 shots were fired from the pouch in 2' 45", without a rest, but aiming at the target, being 13 shots per minute.

Further, then were fired, 159 shots, in four series;
64 " " one " At the beginning, and during these

rounds, a quantity of dirt was thrown into the breech. After each time the breech opened with somewhat more difficulty than usual, but at the second or third round it recovered its regular easy movement. During the first series on this day, tests were made to prove whether, if the cartridge be inserted while the hammer is down, the cartridge will not explode upon closing the breech. This did not take place. It was also found admissible, and without damage, to fire the gun at exactly the same moment that it was closed. The gun out of which 1,754 shots had now been fired was again covered with dirt, and was exposed to the damp night air, until the following day, for continuing trial, namely:

On the 23d of October, 1866. Upon examining the Peabody gun, which had been left in the condition above described, it was found, that although the breech was partially covered with rust, and completely clogged with dirt, it was still capable of performing its functions with perfect efficiency, though a somewhat greater force was necessary to operate it. Hereupon, the following shots were fired:

64 shots, in one series, in order to compare the results with those obtained in the early stage of the trial for accuracy.

With reference to *f.* 32 shots, at a target 300 yards distant;
32 " " " 600 " "

The very satisfactory results, as to accuracy, obtained, are shown in the accompanying diagrams of target No. 3 and 4. After the first few shots, the breech apparatus had recovered its smooth movement, and continued to operate thus throughout. Upon taking the gun apart, and examining it, after 1,882 shots had been fired, no alteration or injury of any part of the breech could be discovered.

With this trial, the tests with the Peabody gun were concluded, which, with good cartridges, has been found to answer every requirement for a military arm.

(Signed) ARCH DUKE WILHELM,
VIENNA, January 6, 1867. *Lieutenant-General.*

I herewith confirm with pleasure that the 15,000 Peabody guns of 10 1-2 millimetres calibre, purchased by the War Department of Switzerland from the Providence Tool Company's Armory in the United States, have given full satisfaction in the hands of the troops, regarding the accuracy of shooting, as well as regarding their solidity and the working of the mechanism.

(Signed) WURSTEMBERGER,
BERNE, SWITZERLAND, 26th August, 1870. *Colonel.*

The State of Connecticut having decided upon the adoption of breech-loaders, the Peabody arm was submitted in competition with other well-known arms. After elaborate tests, similar in character to those instituted by the State of New York, the Peabody arm was recommended for adoption by unanimous vote of the Board as the arm of the State of Connecticut. This recommendation was approved and acted upon by the Governor, and the arms were promptly furnished. The report of the Committee is as follows:

To His Excellency Marshall Jewell, Governor and Commander-in-Chief:

SIR: The Board appointed by your Excellency to examine and recommend for adoption by this State some suitable breech-loading rifle for the use of the Connecticut National Guard respectfully report: That they have had under consideration several breech-loading rifles, all of which have been subjected to such trials and tests as to their comparative merits as the time at the disposal of the Board would permit of, and that, while each system that has been tested has peculiar merits of its own is not to be denied, and without going into an extended, detailed report of the several trials and tests to which the arms have been subjected, or reproducing the arguments in favor of, or unfavorable to, the several systems examined, the Board are unanimously of the opinion that the Peabody rifle is a safe, efficient, and easily managed weapon and best adapted to the use of our State Militia, and they therefore recommend that the Peabody rifle, calibre .433, be adopted as the arm of the State of Connecticut. Signed by the whole Board.

After the reception of these arms and their distribution to the various companies of the National Guard, a special committee was appointed by the Adjutant-General, whose duty it was to develop, if possible, any defect of the arm by which harm might result to those inexpert in its use, if any such defect existed, and to form a manual for the handling of the arm in accordance with such experience. The results of the trials instituted by this auxiliary Board are stated in the following certificate from the Quartermaster-General of the State:

STATE OF CONNECTICUT, Q. M. GEN.'S DEPT.,
HARTFORD, December 28th, 1871.

M. F. Benton, Esq., Agent Peabody Rifle Co.:

DEAR SIR: In accordance with your request of this date, I beg leave to say that the Peabody breech-loading rifles purchased by this State of the Providence Tool Company have all been received in good order, and a large proportion of them have been issued to our troops, and I am pleased to say are giving very general satisfaction, much more so than I anticipated, the change in this State from a muzzle-loader to breech-loader being a radical one. Since the issue of the arms to our troops they have been subjected to severe trials, to test the liability of danger to the soldier using them, and the result has been such as to confirm Adjutant-General Merwin and myself in our opinion as to the safety and efficiency of the Peabody arm. As to the calibre adopted by this State, .433, I have seen nothing to change my mind that for efficiency and accuracy it is superior to that of 50.

Very respectfully, your obedient servant,

S. A. DICKINSON, *Q. M. General.*

The New York State Board for the examination of breech-loaders having issued notices to inventors and others to present their systems for examination, twenty-two different models were submitted. After due investigation, five of these arms, the Peabody being one of the number, were selected for elaborate trials. These trials were commenced at Springfield, Mass., on the 23d of September, 1871, and were continued for four days.

The report of the Board states: "After careful examination and full explanation by the exhibitors of the various arms submitted, the Board selected from among them those which, in their opinion, were best adapted to the use of the National Guard, and caused circulars to be sent to the owners of such arms, asking for proposals to furnish the State with 15,000 new arms of their respective models, and to receive an equal number of the Springfield rifle musket, cal. .58, now in the hands of the National Guard, at such price as might be deemed favorable, in part payment thereof." To this condition the owners of the Peabody would not conform, and the report therefore states: "The proposals of the agent of the Peabody arm was defective, in failing to fix a price for the Springfield muskets owned by the State." The arm offered at "the lowest net price" was selected, although the report admits that it was in some respects surpassed by several of the arms tested.

In explaining the reasons for the selection made, the Report continues: "The experiments resulted satisfactorily, and demonstrated that all the arms possess great merit in point of accuracy, durability, and facility of manipulation. In fact, were the choice of an arm to be determined by the actual results of the experiments upon the arms themselves, the Board would have great difficulty in arriving at a decision, all the arms having undergone the various tests without injury and unexceptionably to the satisfaction of the Board." The result of the trials with the Peabody arm are condensed as follows:

Rapidity of Fire.—Calibre .43.

First trial: 18 shots in one minute.
Second " 25 " " "

Accuracy of Fire.

For 100 yards, see Target No. 10.
" 300 " " " " 11.
" 700 " " " " 12.

Effects of sand and dust.—No perceptible difference in the working of the gun, excepting, perhaps, a very little stiffness.

Effects of defective ammunition.—After No. 8, the extractor did not withdraw cartridge (this is explainable by the fact that the heads of the shells were purposely damaged, being filed in four places). No escape of gas was perceptible on the paper.

Simplicity of construction.—The piece was dismounted and found uninjured by the several tests. It was dismounted in twenty-five seconds. The liability of several arms to premature explosion by closing the breech violently having been elsewhere proven, and serious accidents having occurred with an arm by the projection of the firing-pin, a trial was made with the Peabody to demonstrate its "safety in the hands of troops comparatively inexpert in the use of arms." The result of which is as follows: "In the Peabody gun a piece of wood was inserted in the rear of firing-pin so as to render it immovable; in this condition the gun could not be fired."

The adoption of a breech-loading arm by the State of Massachusetts was recommended by the proper authority as early as 1868. But the great variety of arms to be tested postponed the final decision from year to year, and we have but barely opportunity to obtain and record the ultimate choice of the committee appointed. The tests which led to the result were instituted both at Boston and at Lowell, and extended over a considerable period. These trials were in accordance with the usual formula observed, and were so ordered as to bring out the best and worst features of the arms submitted. Between the Remington and Peabody the contest was a close one, but the superiority of the latter was finally vindicated, and expressed in the following report:

[*Copy.*]

BOSTON, March 18th, 1872.

To His Excellency William B. Washburne, Governor and Commander-in-Chief:

The Board of Officers appointed and convened under Special Order No. 14, May 26th, 1871, respectfully

REPORT,

That the Peabody breech-loading rifle should be adopted for the use of the militia of the Commonwealth of Massachusetts; that the appropriation of $50,000 made by the Legislature of 1871 for the purchase of breech-loading arms for the infantry of the volunteer militia should be forthwith expended for the purpose.

(Signed) { JAMES A. CUNNINGHAM, HOBART MOORE, EBEN SUTTON.

CONSTRUCTION OF THE ARM.

The theory upon which the Peabody arm is constructed is:

First.—The reception of the recoil upon a horizontal block situated in a line with the axis of the bore.

Second.—The pivoting of this block at its rear end, dropping its forward end and grooving the top as a guide for the cartridge, so that when lowered it coincides with the barrel and admits of the easy passage of a cartridge down this groove into the chamber.

Third.—The operation or movement of the block at almost right angles to the barrel, thus avoiding a horizontal movement of the block towards the cartridge when in its chamber.

The result of these principles is:

First.—The greatest resistance against the force of recoil.

Second.—A guide or bridge for the passage of the cartridge into its chamber.

Third.—Security against premature explosion of the cartridge in closing the breech-block.

Fig. A.

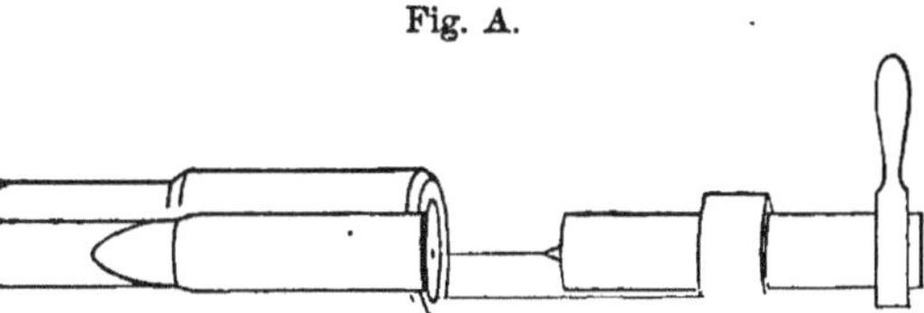

In order to present more clearly the peculiarity of this system and the advantages claimed for it in comparison with other systems, the following illustrations are given. They may be classified under four heads, viz.:

First.—Bolt gun, in which the bolt containing the firing-pin moves in a direct horizontal line, as in Fig. A.

Second. — Block guns, in which the block is pivoted at the forward end above the barrel, moving downward and toward it, and

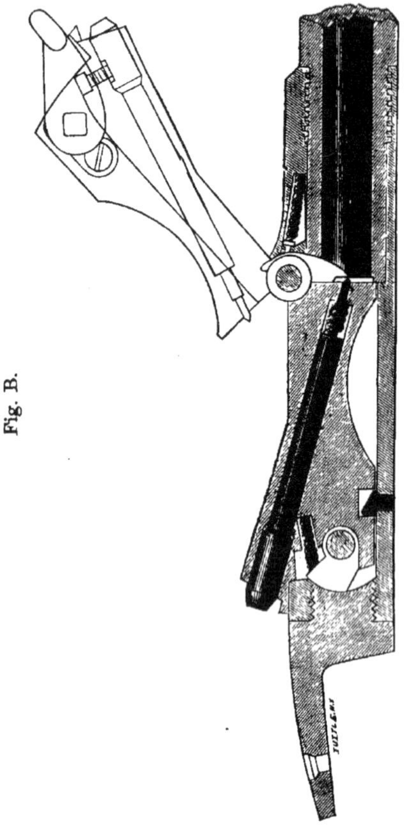

Fig. B.

which, when performing its curved passage, approaches the cartridge at the last moment almost horizontally, and with an effect upon the cartridge equivalent to that which might be produced by the sudden impact of the bolt of a bolt gun, as in Fig. B.

Third.—Guns in which the block is pivoted below the barrel, moving upward and towards it, communicating a similarly sudden impact upon the head of the cartridge.

Fig. C.

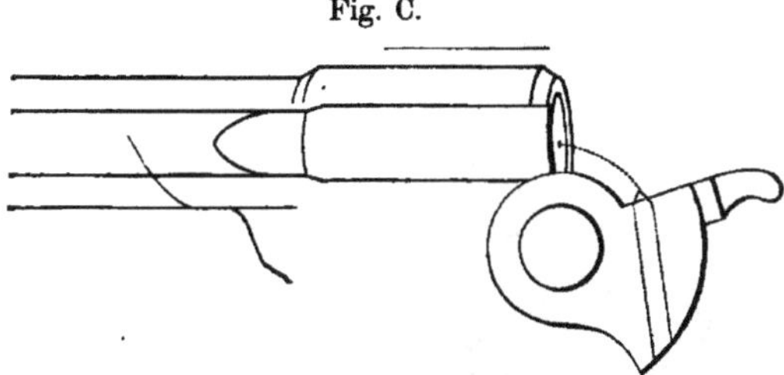

It is claimed by the manufacturers of the Peabody arm that the above three systems are liable to premature explosion, either in consequence of the projection of the firing-pin or of the impact of the block or bolt upon the head of the cartridge, should the same be more than ordinarily sensitive, inasmuch as in each of the systems already referred to, the block containing the firing-pin, in the act of closing, moves horizontally or nearly so towards the primer in the head of the cartridge, and threatens to cause an explosion of the same. Experience having shown that premature explosions have occurred from such causes, many devices have been adopted to secure a positive withdrawal of the firing-pin and thus reduce the probability of such accidents. *On the other hand, it is maintained that where the breech-block moves at a right angle, similar accidents may be regarded as practically impossible, from the fact that the action of the block against the head of the cartridge is a pressing and sliding action by which the sudden impact necessary to explode the cap or primer cannot be produced.* To arms of this fourth class belong the Peabody, in which the block, with reference to the cartridge, moves on a curve slightly varying from a right angle; also the Martini-Henry, in which the movement is identical with the original Peabody; the Sharps, which moves at right angles verti-

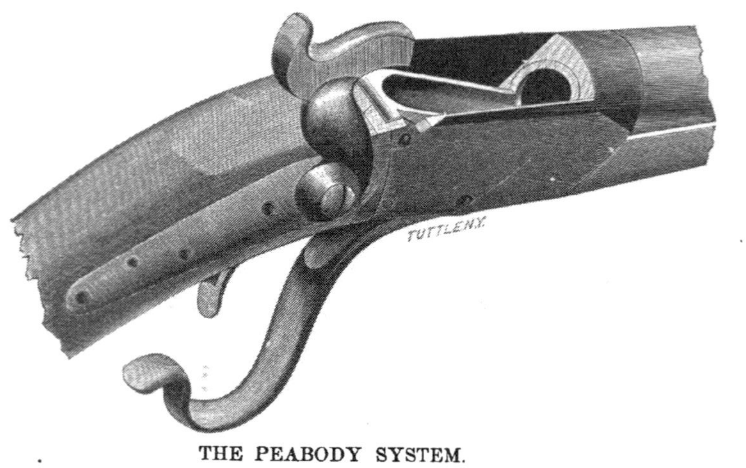

THE PEABODY SYSTEM.

cally; the Werndl (Austrian), at right angles laterally; the Snider the same, and the Werder (Bavarian), similar to the Peabody.

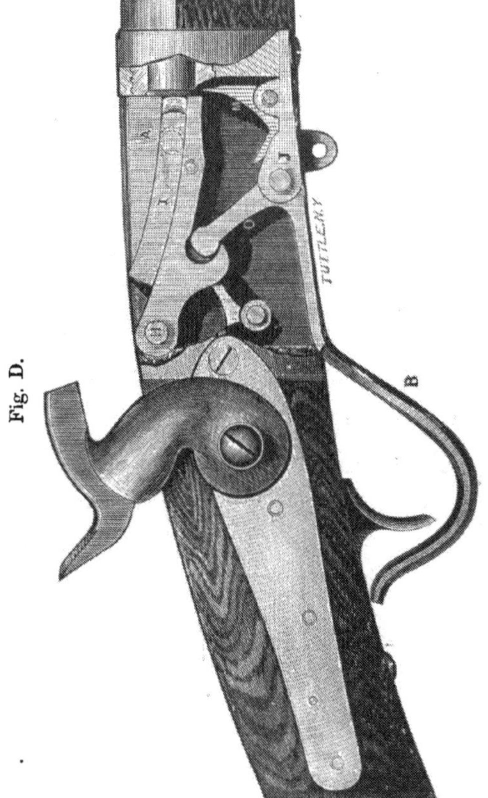

Fig. D.

In the Peabody system the whole movement of the block is performed within the stock, and there are no parts rising above the arm itself, which may be liable to injury or interfere with convenience in carrying or handling. The end of the trigger-guard falls but little more than an inch, so that there is no difficulty in manipulating the lever while lying down, as the angle between the end of barrel and of stock is such as to leave ample room therefor. This arm cannot be discharged until the breech-block is in its proper position, as will be evident from a glance at the drawing. The rapidity with which it can be fired is believed to be equal, if not superior, to any other single loader. It has been fired off-hand thirty-five (35) times in one minute, and the average rate in the hands of an inexperienced person loading from the cartridge-box may be fixed at ten to fifteen shots per minute. The weight of the Peabody arm for the use of infantry is nine and three-quarter pounds, and that of the carbine six and three-quarter pounds. The rapidity with which the breech-mechanism of this arm is manipulated may be seen from the following manual. The movements for loading and firing being but four, as follows:

MANUAL FOR PEABODY RIFLE OR CARBINE.

Fig. 7. Fig. 8.

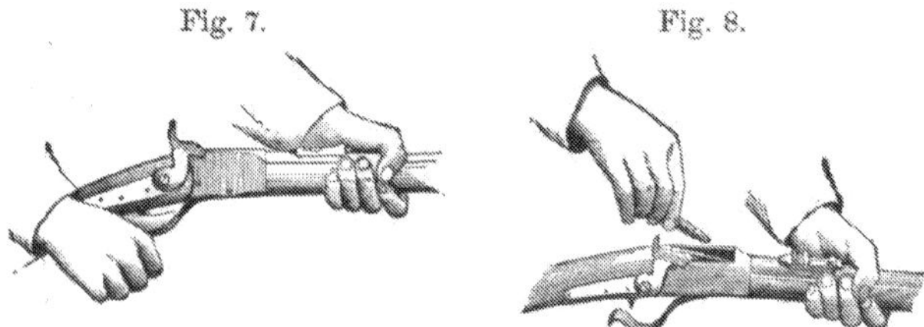

1. Place the ball of the thumb of the right hand on the guard-lever, and throw the lever down *smartly*.

2. Insert cartridge with thumb and forefinger, pushing cartridge home with thumb.

Fig. 9.

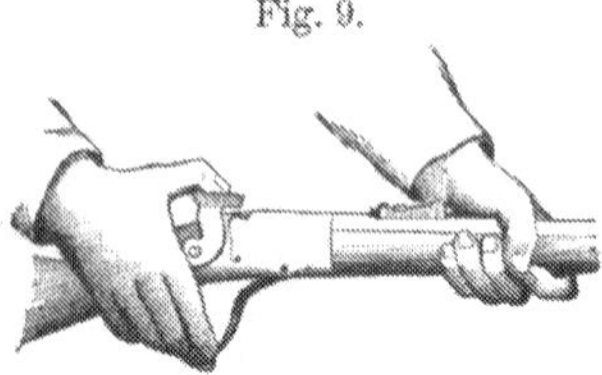

3. Cock hammer with thumb, and *simultaneously* close guard-lever with fingers of right hand. 4. Fire.

TO TAKE OUT BREECH-BLOCK.—Remove pivot-screw only.

TO REPLACE BREECH-BLOCK.—Bring the guard-lever up, drop the block in the receiver, forward part first, then press on the rear end of the block until the hole in receiver and in block coincide, and insert pivot-screw.

PEABODY SYSTEM FOR TRANSFORMING MUZZLE-LOADERS TO BREECH-LOADERS.

The essential principles of the original arm have also been successfully applied to the transformation of muzzle-loading arms to breech-'oaders. In order to preserve the trigger-guard, lock, etc., of the nuzzle-loader, the lever in the transformation is situated at the top of the stock instead of beneath the same, and forms one piece with the block, as shown in cut.

Figure 1 represents a longitudinal section of the breech part of the arm, showing the metal breech-frame with one side and a portion of the stock removed to give a clear view of the interior mechanism.

To effect the conversion, a portion of the rear end of the barrel of the muzzle-loader is cut off, and the frame or section *A* is substituted in its place, being screwed on to the barrel and bedded in the stock prepared to receive it, a tang connected with the receiver fitting in the same place from which the breech-pin has been removed.

B is a hinged falling breech-block, pivoted at *a* by a pin passing through the same and the sides of the receiver *A*, and operated by placing the finger in the loop of the tail piece and pulling upward. *C* is an elbow lever pivoted at *b*, its upper end catching behind the rim of the cartridge. The block in its downward movement strikes the lower short arm of this lever, and extracts the cartridge, removing it entirely from the gun. On the under side of the breech-block is a brace spring, secured by a screw to its front lower side, and with its rear end so made that it rests upon notches *c*, *c*. This spring is provided with a roller which enables it to move smoothly over the notches. The shape of the notches with the aid of the brace spring causes the block to be held either in the position for loading or firing. On the rear end of the firing-pin is a projection, forming a shoulder which has a bearing on a portion of the breech-frame raised at that point to correspond with the angle of the shoulder, and forming a stop for the hammer, which cannot touch the firing-pin until the gun is in exact position for firing. *Figure* 2 shows the block and firing-pin. LOADING AND FIRING CAN BE EFFECTED IN FOUR MOVEMENTS.

The entire breech-mechanism consists of but 8 parts and can be cleaned by the removal of the pivot-screw only. These parts are: 1, breech-receiver; 2, breech-block; 3, firing-pin; 4, pivot-pin; 5, brace spring; 6, brace roller; 7, notch piece; 8, extractor. SPRING-

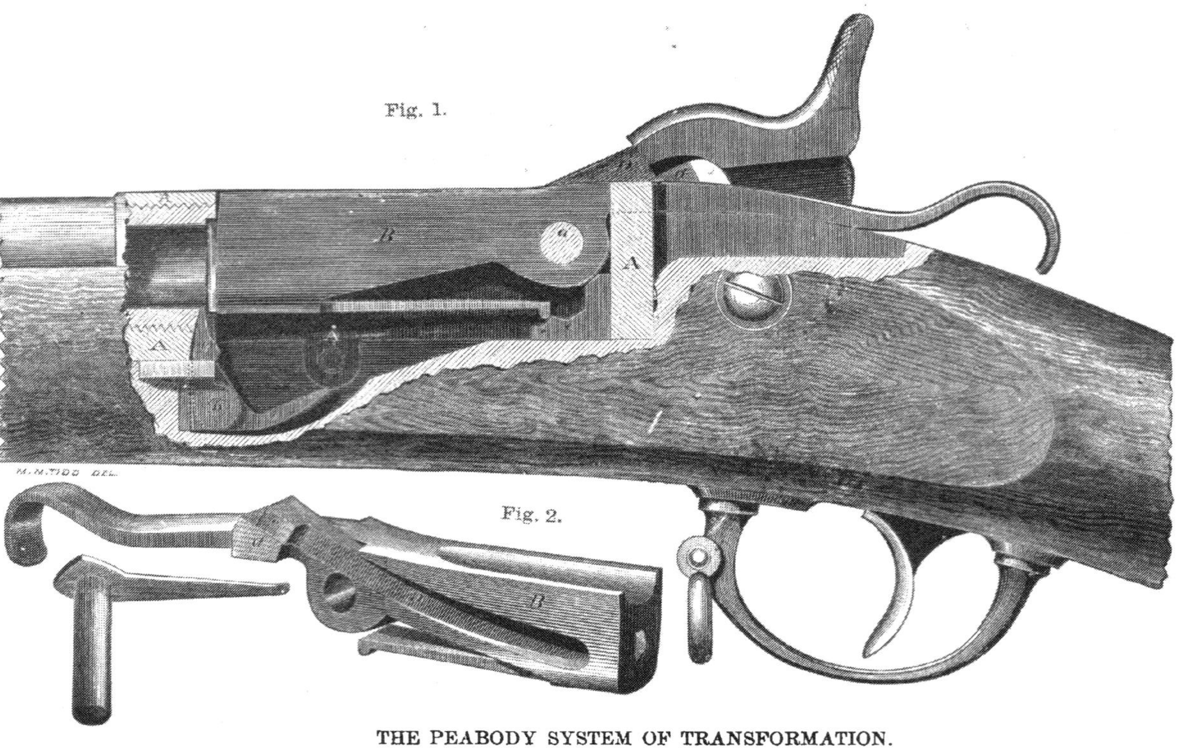

THE PEABODY SYSTEM OF TRANSFORMATION.

FIELDS OR ENFIELDS, WHEN THUS CONVERTED TO THE PEABODY SYSTEM, MAY BE FIRED 15-20 TIMES PER MINUTE.

Some of the distinguishing points of merit of this arm are the small amount of metal required for the breech-mechanism combined with strength, the small number of parts, the easy manner of taking out the breech-block ; using an entire stock, retaining the ordinary permanent guard and the regulation lock, the tail-piece rising only three-quarters of an inch above the gun. Locking the hammer and closing the breech is effected in one movement, as exemplified in the following manual. The alteration of muzzle-loaders to breech-loaders on this system adds but one-quarter pound of the weight.

DIRECTIONS FOR HANDLING.

Fig. 11. Fig. 12.

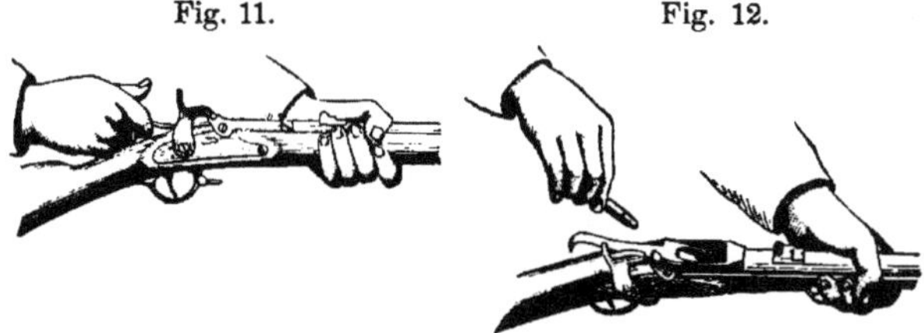

1. Raise the tail-piece or lever by inserting forefinger in the loop, and pulling upwards *smartly*. The shell will then be ejected clear of the gun.

2. Insert cartridge with thumb and forefinger, pushing cartridge home with thumb.

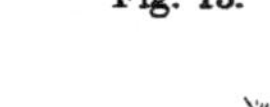

Fig. 13.

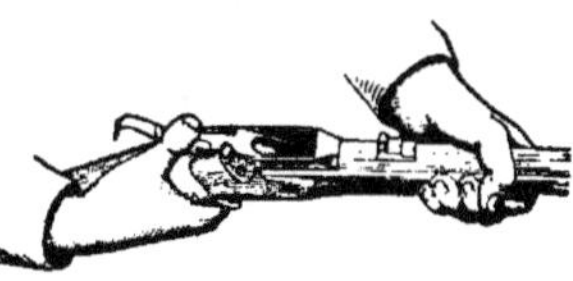

3. Cock hammer, and bring down lever *simultaneously* with the thumb. 4. Fire.

TO TAKE OUT BREECH-BLOCK.—Remove pivot-screw only.

TO REPLACE BREECH-BLOCK.—Drop the block in the receiver, forward part first, then press on the rear end of the block until the hole in receiver and in block coincide, and insert pivot-screw.

The Peabody arm has not been lacking in imitators. In 1866–7, soon after it became known in Europe, a device was added for the purpose of cocking the hammer simultaneously with the closing of the block, by a connection between hammer and lever. This modification received little attention. Subsequently the same inventor, Friedrich Martini of Frauenfeld, Switzerland, produced another modification of the Peabody arm, using a spiral spring as a means of operating the firing-pin in place of the ordinary side lock. In order to illustrate the identity of construction of the so-called Martini gun with the Peabody, we annex a drawing of the

Fig. 14.

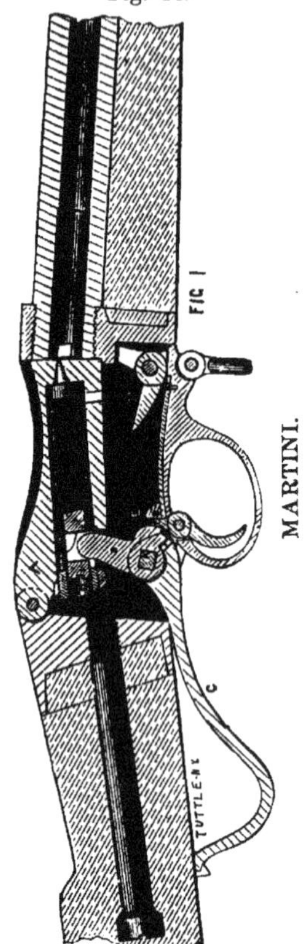

former and also one of the latter using a spiral spring, which was invented by Mr. Peabody in 1862. The prejudices then existing against the use of a spiral spring as a motor for the firing-pin, and the danger of accident, caused this arm to be temporarily put aside.

It will be seen by the preceding cut (Fig. 14) that: 1st, the block, 2d guard lever, and 3d, the extractor of the Peabody are used in the combination covered by Martini's patent, as before described, as is evident from a comparison of the same with the following cut of the Peabody arm:

Fig. 15.

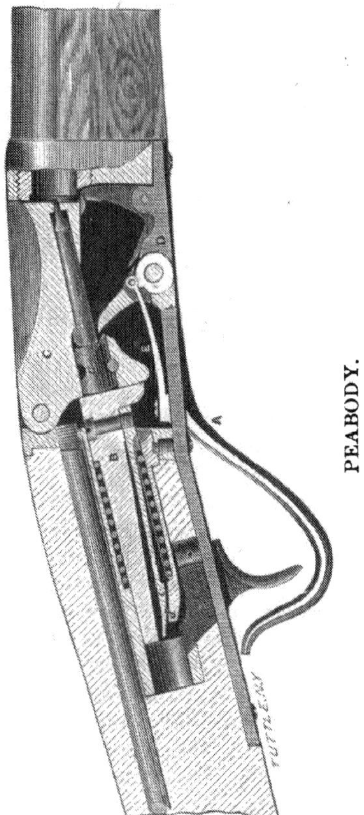

PEABODY.

In addition to these features the employment of a spiral spring in the Peabody as a motor for the firing-pin renders the identity between it and its imitator still more complete. Within a short time after the production of this Peabody modification it was offered and described by Martini himself as "my invention, consisting in an improvement of the Peabody breech-loading system." The English patent of the Peabody system dates from 1865, and the adoption of the Martini-Henry by the English Government, which is now regarded as definitely settled upon, appears to violate the rights of the American owners of the Peabody arm.

The arm adopted by Bavaria, the Werder gun, is also very similar in its general construction to the Peabody, especially in its combination of the breech-block and extractor. It was not until the Bavarian Government had experimented during the period of a year with the Peabody gun, that Mr. Werder, who had full access to the trials and frequent consultations with the committee, produced the arm to which his name has been given.

The combination of parts constituting the Peabody arm and covered by patent is:

First.—Constructing the breech-block with a groove corresponding with the bore of the chamber, for the purpose of facilitating the introduction of the cartridge.

Second.—Controlling the motion of the breech-block by combining the guard-lever with the breech.

Third.—Combining an elbow lever with the breech-block for the purpose of ejecting the cartridge case by dropping the said breech-block on one of the arms of the lever.

This arm can be made of any calibre required, and admits of the application of either the ordinary side lock, or a simple main or spiral spring in connection with the firing-pin.

The following cut (Fig. 5) shows the construction of the arm, the breech being represented as open and the shell partially withdrawn. B is the breech-block pivoted at *a* and grooved at the top to form a guide for the cartridge; E is the guard lever, its short arm D, engaging in the recess of the block and controlling its movement; G is the elbow lever extractor, which catches forward of the rim of the cartridge and throws out the same clear of the arm, more or less violently, according to the force with which the lower elbow of the lever is struck by the block. This elbow-lever or extractor is a strong single piece operating without the need of a spring upon its pivot screw, F. C is the firing-pin operating in a groove in the side of

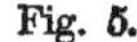

Fig. 5.

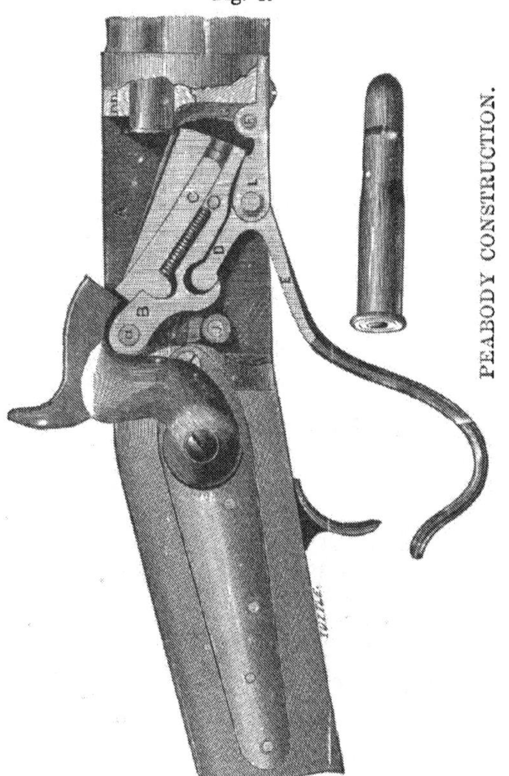

the block and withdrawn by the aid of the small spiral spring shown. This spring can be dispensed with if desired. J is the roller, held by a pin passing through the sides of the receiver A, and upon which the notches of the guard lever brace K so operate as to retain the breech block in its position both when closed and when open. A is the receiver in which the mechanism is enclosed and into which the barrel is screwed. The receiver is connected with the butt stock by a bolt passing through the stock and screwed into the rear of the receiver, and is further held by the lock plate and side straps. *The amount of metal employed in effecting this jointure gives a greater longitudinal strength than exists with an unbroken stock from end to end.* The ordinary side lock is retained in the present model, although the system of this arm permits the application of a simple main or spiral spring. The cartridge used is the centre-fire Berdan brass system, the charge of powder being 77 grains and the weight of ball 370 grains. The following cut (Fig. D) represents the breech mechanism closed and in position for firing:

Fig. D.

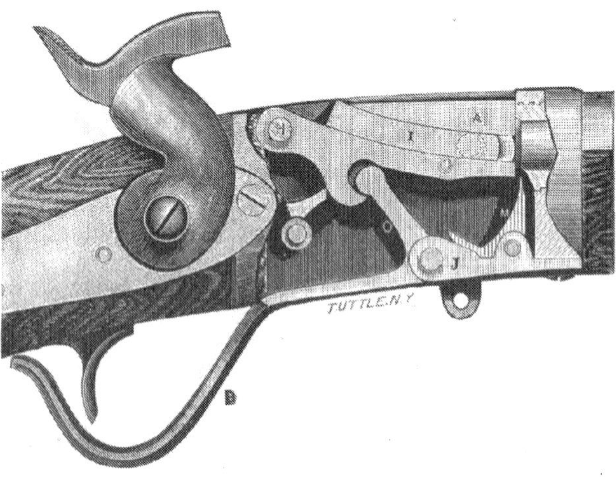

The targets annexed indicate firing with the Peabody rifle at 100, 300, and 700 yards off-hand, selected at random.

TARGET RECORD, "PEABODY." CAL. .43.

No. of shots.	Distances from center of target in inches.				Distances from center of impact in inches.				Remarks.
	Vertical.		Horizontal.		Vertical.		Horizontal.		
	Above.	Below.	Right.	Left.	Above.	Below.	Right.	Left.	
1	2.0	.....	.....	10.0	1.3	.....	.....	11.55	Fired by Mr. Wentworth.
2	.0	0.	4.5	.....	.....	.7	2.95	.....	
3	.....	3.5	14.0	.....	.....	4.2	12.45	.....	
4	.....	15.5	7.5	.....	.....	16.2	5.95	.....	
5	3.0	.....	4.5	.....	2.3	.....	2.95	.....	
6	2.5	.....	2.0	.....	1.8	.....	.45	.....	
7	7.0	.....	.....	0.5	6.3	.....	.....	2.05	
8	.....	1.5	.....	1.5	....	2.2	.....	3.05	
9	.0	.0	7.0	.....	.....	.7	5.55	.....	
10	4.0	.....	4.5	.....	3.3	.....	2.95	.....	
11	3.0	.....	2.0	.....	2.3	.....	.45	.....	
12	5.5	.....	0.5	.....	4.8	.....	.....	1.05	
13	.....	4.5	.0	.0	.....	5.2	.....	1.55	
14	....	2.0	.....	2.0	.....	2.7	.....	3.55	
15	2.5	.....	0.5	.....	1.8	.....	.....	1.05	
16	.....	1.5	.....	1.0	.....	2.2	.....	2.55	
17	.....	1.0	1.0	.....	.....	1.7	.....	.55	
18	1.5	.....	2.5	.....	.8	.....	.95	.....	
19	4.5	.....	.0	.0	3.8	.....	.....	1.55	
20	8.0	.....	.....	4.5	7.3	.....	.....	6.05	
	43.5	29.5	50.5	19.5	35.8	35.8	34.65	34.55	
	.7 above.		1.55 right.		3.58		3.46		

C. of I., 1.12. Absolute deviation, 4.89. Range, 100 yards.
Ammunition: Weight of ball, 370 grains. Weight of powder, 77 grains.

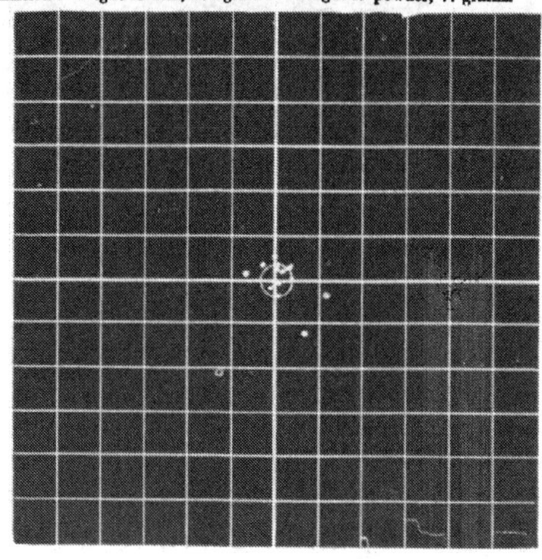

TARGET RECORD, "PEABODY." CAL. .43.

No. of shots.	DISTANCES FROM CENTRE OF TARGET IN INCHES.				DISTANCES FROM CENTRE OF IMPACT IN INCHES.				Remarks.
	VERTICAL.		HORIZONTAL.		VERTICAL.		HORIZONTAL.		
	Above.	Below.	Right.	Left.	Above.	Below.	Right.	Left.	
1	4	......	16	......	6.95	......	......	4.85	Fired by Mr. Wentworth.
2	18	......	29	......	20.95	......	8.15	......	
3	1	......	27	......	3.95	......	6.15	......	
4	13	......	17	......	15.95	......	......	3.85	
5	......	6	13	......	......	3.05	......	7.85	
6	......	10	20	......	......	7.05	......	.85	
7	......	1	12	......	1.95	......	......	8.85	
8	7	......	19	......	9.95	......	......	1.85	
9	2	......	28	......	4.95	......	7.15	......	
10	......	27	25	......	......	24.05	4.15	......	
11	......	10	36	......	......	7.05	15.15	......	
12	......	27	31	......	......	24.05	10.15	......	
13	8	......	24	......	10.95	......	3.15	......	
14	......	1	17	......	1.95	......	......	3.85	
15	......	10	31	......	......	7.05	10.15	......	
16	......	12	17	......	......	9.05	......	3.85	
17	......	6	12	......	......	3.05	......	8.85	
18	......	1	13	......	1.95	......	......	7.85	
19	13	......	7	......	15.95	......	......	13.85	
20	......	14	23	......	......	11.05	2.15	......	
	66	125	417	......	95.95	95.45	66.35	66.35	
	2.95		20.85		95.45		6.635		

C. of I., 21.04. Absolute deviation, 11.62. Range, 300 yards.
Ammunition: Weight of ball, 370 grains. Weight of powder, 77 grains.

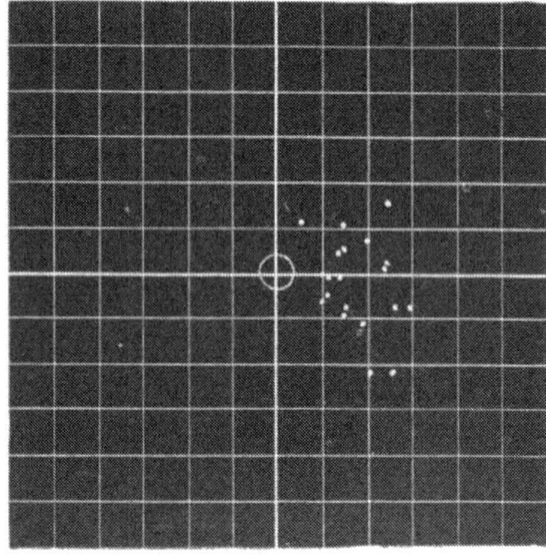

TARGET RECORD, "PEABODY." CAL. .43.

No. of shots.	DISTANCES FROM CENTRE OF TARGET IN INCHES.				DISTANCES FROM CENTRE OF IMPACT IN INCHES.				Remarks.
	VERTICAL.		HORIZONTAL.		VERTICAL.		HORIZONTAL.		
	Above.	Below.	Right.	Left.	Above.	Below.	Right.	Left.	
1	2	......	50	.....	13.3	......	10.9	.. ..	Fired by Mr. Wentworth.
2	......	29	47	.....	......	17.7	7.9	.....	
3	......	48	49	.....	......	36.7	9.9	....	
4	....	13	27	.....	......	1.7	......	12.1	
5	.....	61	46	.....	......	49.7	6.9	.....	
6	2	......	36	.....	13.3	......	......	3.1	
7	32	......	40	.....	43.3	......	.0	.....	
8	......	2	35	.....	9.3	......	.. ...	4.1	
9	12	......	6	.....	23.3	......	......	33.1	
10	......	8	55	.....	3.3	......	15.9	.....	
	48	161	391	......	105.8	105.8	52.4	52.4	
	11.3		39.1		21.16		10.48		

C. of I., 40.79. Absolute deviation, 23.60. Range, 700 yards.

Ammunition: Weight of ball, 370 grains. Weight of powder, 77 grains.

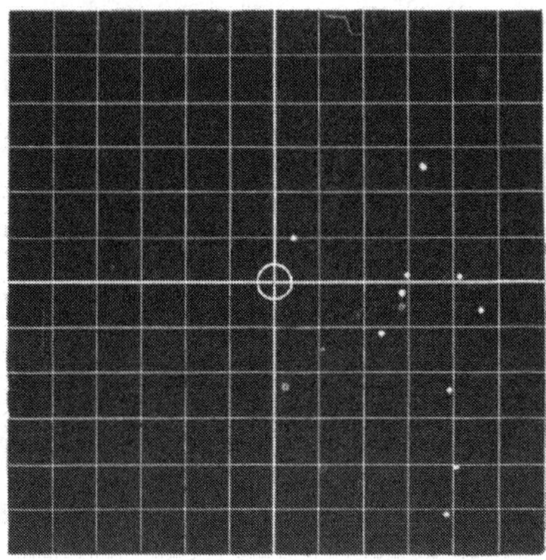

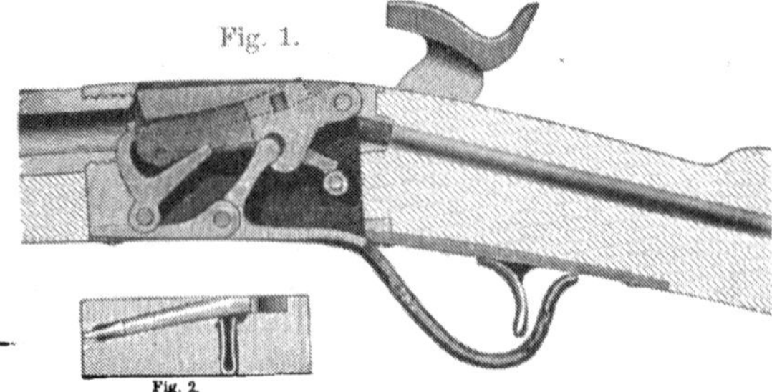

THE IMPROVED PEABODY.

The improvements in this model consist, firstly, in so shaping the breech-block and receiver, as to make a snug closure, and also to effect a positive stop to the movement of the block upwards. Secondly, in the application of a direct firing-pin, acted upon by a simple flat spring running through the block as seen in Figs. 1 and 2, instead of the usual spiral spring. But *two* springs of any description are now to be found in the entire breech-mechanism. Thirdly, in the application of two single and disconnected accelerating extractors, so made as to grip the sides of the cartridge case, though without breaking the continuity of the bore of chamber, and so adjusted to the breech-block, that the latter in falling immediately presses upon the extreme ends of the lower arms of the extractor, where the leverage is greatest, and in its further descent constantly changes its point of bearing to a point nearer the fulcrum pin of the extractor, and thus imparts to the latter a gaining or accelerating motion. The length of movement of the extractor is thus very great, and renders the extraction of any shell a positive certainty. By these changes the arm is improved both as to simplicity, strength, and certainty of extraction, though in these respects there was little to be desired in the original model.

IMPORTANT LETTER FROM GOV. JEWELL OF CONNECTICUT.

[*Copy.*]

EXECUTIVE DEPARTMENT, STATE OF CONNECTICUT,
HARTFORD, March 21, 1872.

Providence Tool Co., Providence, R. I.:

Mr. Benton having requested me to give the reasons influencing the selection of a breech loader by the State of Connecticut at the present time, I take this opportunity to do so.

In view of the fact that the General Government has from time to time appointed examining boards for the testing of new improvements, and are ever ready to try any recent invention, and as it may be some years before any decision will be reached, and no certainty that it will finally be in favor of any of the present styles of breech loaders, it seemed best that the State of Connecticut should not await the action of the General Government, but should at once furnish her militia with an arm equally effective as that used by any of her sister States.

That the calibre of our arm should differ from that finally selected by the General Government seems to me no objection, as in the event of war the number in the hands of our militia would be small compared with the number required to arm the soldiers we should send out, and naturally would be kept at home, while our men would be furnished with the same gun as the United States troops.

The only way to ensure a high state of efficiency in the militia is to furnish them with the best and latest improvements in arms and equipments; and the interests of the State would not permit us to go on with the old muzzle loaders of ten years ago.

I have the honor to be your obedient servant,

(Signed) MARSHALL JEWELL.

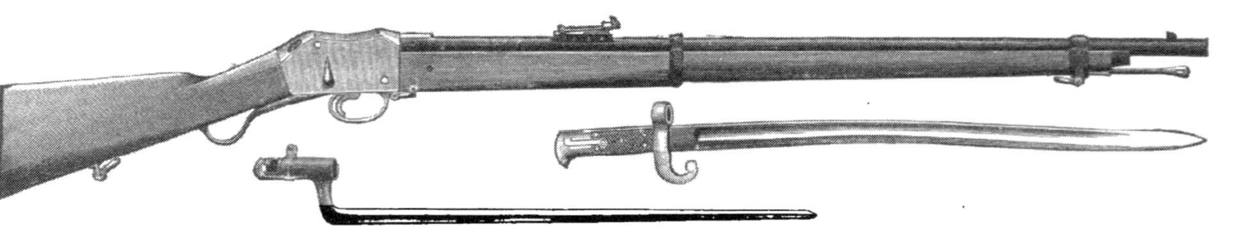

PEABOBY-MARTINI MILITARY RIFLE. (Turkish Model.)

With Quadrangular and Sabre Bayonets.

Entire Length of Peabody-Martini Military Rifle,	49 inches.	Weight of Quadrangular Bayonet, ...	15 ounces.
Length of Barrel, ...	$32\frac{1}{2}$ "	Entire Length of Sabre Bayonet, ...	$28\frac{7}{16}$ inches.
Weight, without Bayonet, ...	$8\frac{1}{2}$ pounds.	Length of Blade of Sabre Bayonet, ...	$22\frac{1}{8}$ "
Length of Quadrangular Bayonet, ...	$23\frac{1}{4}$ inches.	Weight of Sabre Bayonet, ...	2 pounds.
Length of Blade of Quadranglar Bayonet, ...	$20\frac{1}{4}$ "	Calibre, ...	.45 inch.

CARTRIDGE FOR PEABODY-MARTINI MILITARY RIFLE. (Turkish Model.)

Calibre, .45 inch. Powder, 85 grains. Bullet, smooth-patched; weight, 480 grains. Lubricating disc in shell.

1880.

THE PEABODY-MARTINI RIFLE.

Since 1872, the year of the publication of the first edition of this book, no rifles of the distinctive "Peabody" model have been manufactured. The system is, however, at the present time more prominently before the world than ever before, as the basis of the Peabody-Martini rifle, the weapon which has made such an excellent record in the hands of Turkish troops during the late Russo-Turkish war, and which is universally pronounced to be the foremost military rifle of the world. The modification of the Peabody system by Mr. Friedrich Martini was referred to in our first edition, but at that time it had attracted but little attention. It consists in combining a special device for igniting the cartridge with the breech-closing mechanism, thus doing away with the side-lock as it existed in the Peabody system. The Peabody mechanism for closing the breech and for extracting the empty cartridge shell, after firing, remains as the essential feature of the Peabody-Martini.

A very complete and perfect article on the Peabody-Martini rifle and its relation to the original Peabody is given in a recent number of that valuable and well-known authority, "The Army and Navy Journal," from which we make, by permission, the following extracts.

In all of the English and, with rare exception if any, all of the Continental publications that have treated of the Russo-Turkish campaign, the breech-loading rifle which was found so terribly effective on the Turkish side is misnamed. The Russian Guard and a considerable number of the best corps of the Czar were armed with an American breech-loader, the invention of Col. Berdan. This arm has never borne any other designation than the name of its inventor, though designed and manufactured, both in this country and Europe, under the supervision of a Russian officer, selected for his mechanical proficiency, General Gorloff. It would be quite as just to call the Russian arm the Gorloff-Berdan, as it is to term the Turkish arm the Martini-Henry. The proper name of the latter is the Peabody-Martini.

The original of this arm known to Europeans, simply through English assumption, as the Martini-Henry, is the breech-loader invented by Henry O. Peabody, a skillful, and more than usually intelligent, mechanic of Boston, Mass.

In 1864 he disposed of his patent rights to the Providence Tool Company, which has since with such remarkable business results developed their value. About this time the War Department was considering the question of a new service arm, and a Board of Officers had been appointed to inspect and thoroughly test the large number of guns of the new style offered from all parts of the Northern States. The first Peabody rifle turned out by the Tool Company was a model designed to be submitted to this Board, which was to convene in January, 1865, at Springfield. Sixty-five different inventions entered into the competition for official preference. Of this number, though several others possessed recognized merits, the Peabody secured the award for superior excellence in all respects, and was recommended to the Secretary of War for adoption. By the time the report was rendered, however, the Rebellion had been subdued, and any immediate necessity for a general re-equipment of the army was over. In view of this fact, and of the probability that inventive skill would develop still greater improvements in the new theory of both guns and ammunition, the Chief of Ordnance, Gen. Dyer, whose opinion was deferred to, deemed it inadvisable to select any particular design for re-armament at so early a day.

In September, 1865, the first contract for the Peabody was received, 3,000 stand being purchased by the Canadian Government—a small affair for an establishment which has since executed an order for 600,000 rifles, but worthy of remark from the circumstance that the arm secured its first practical recognition from a British dependency.

Undeterred by the adverse action of the U. S. Ordnance Bureau, which indeed could not seriously depreciate the favorable finding of the Government commission, in the autumn of 1865 Mr. Anthony went to Europe with the Peabody, during which visit he submitted the American breech-loader in England and on the Continent to the Ordnance authorities. Though no immediate result attended upon the trip, its effects were manifest in the large interest which soon thereafter developed in the military inventions of the United States, from which not only the Tool Company, but other establishments gathered profitable harvest. In 1867, the Swiss Republic, which had determined to arm its troops with breech-loaders, after a thorough test of a large number of models, adopted the Peabody. A contract was awarded for 15,000 stand, which was executed at Providence under the supervision of an ordnance officer detailed for that purpose. During the trial before the Swiss Board, which extended over a twelvemonth, Friedrich Martini, a native artisan of pronounced mechanical and inventive ability, devoted himself to a study of the several systems submitted, with a view to an original construction of his own. The principles and practical excellences of the Peabody, however, impressed him so strongly, that instead of evolving a new design, his inventive faculty could simply compass a fancied improvement upon one already made.

To appreciate how immaterial a change in the American system was effected by the Swiss improvement, it should be stated that Mr. Peabody in securing his patents originally produced two systems. That which had been the generally accepted Peabody, and which was submitted to our own Small Arms Board of 1865, 1868, and 1872, had its side lock and hammer outside of the receiver, or frame. The other combined these features with other parts of the action, so that no external part was apparent, and, of course, produced a more symmetrical general effect, and possibly a more naturally manipulated system. The latter, however, was not regarded with favor by experts because its firing-pin was controlled by a spiral spring, the reliability and safety of which was seriously questioned. It is needless to say that a most ample experience has since unquestionably demonstrated the fallacy of this prejudice; but its existence for some years influenced the Tool Company to produce only that model which was operated by an external lock and hammer.

Though no essential difference of principle distinguishes the two, it is easy enough to fancy Martini's change of one system an actual improvement, while it is quite as difficult to detect an essential feature of his design which is not practically developed in the second system. So slightly appreciated, indeed, was the Swiss alteration, that, among the ordnance experts of Continental Europe, it soon became the fashion to term it "*Peabody-fils.*" To do M. Martini justice, he has never, in fact, claimed for his mechanical changes any greater merit than that of an improvement; in his own specifications for a patent, terming them

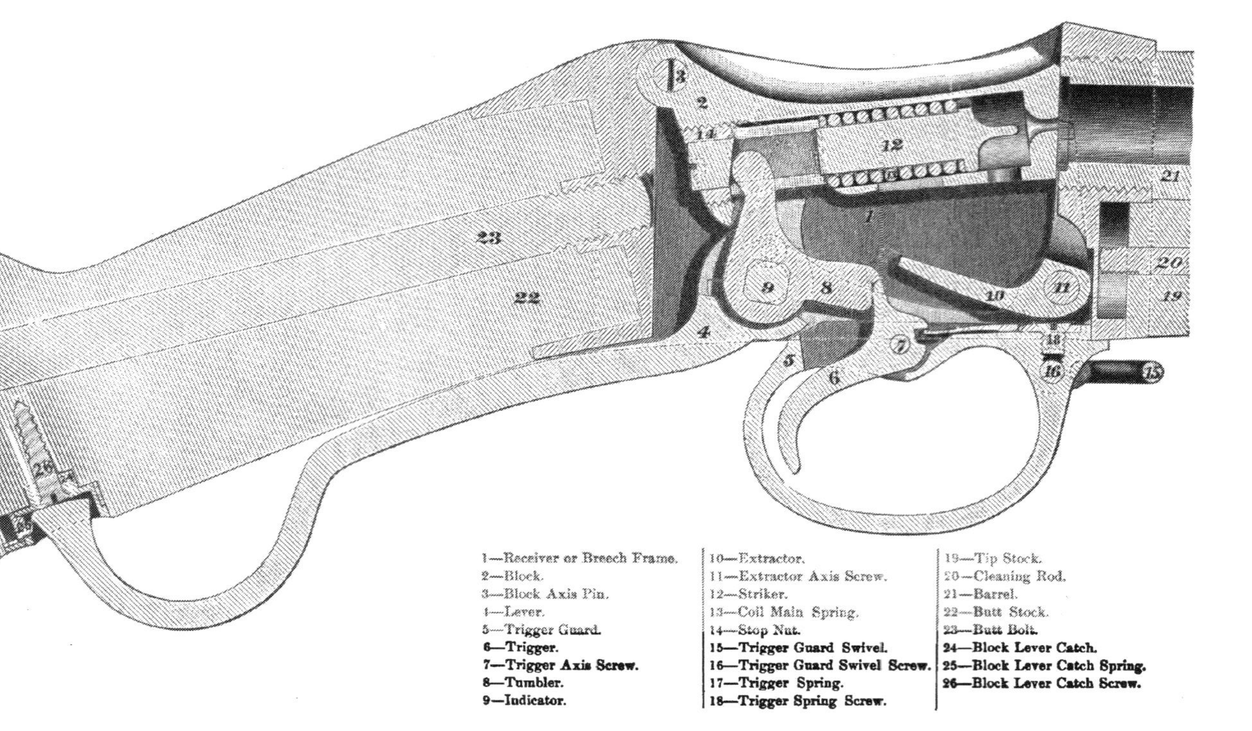

1—Receiver or Breech Frame.
2—Block.
3—Block Axis Pin.
4—Lever.
5—Trigger Guard.
6—Trigger.
7—Trigger Axis Screw.
8—Tumbler.
9—Indicator.
10—Extractor.
11—Extractor Axis Screw.
12—Striker.
13—Coil Main Spring.
14—Stop Nut.
15—Trigger Guard Swivel.
16—Trigger Guard Swivel Screw.
17—Trigger Spring.
18—Trigger Spring Screw.
19—Tip Stock.
20—Cleaning Rod.
21—Barrel.
22—Butt Stock.
23—Butt Bolt.
24—Block Lever Catch.
25—Block Lever Catch Spring.
26—Block Lever Catch Screw.

"an improvement on the Peabody breech-loading system." Whether the alleged "improvement" has a practical existence is a question for experts, who must decide if it has sufficient merit to compensate for a greater number of parts required, and the consequent elaboration of the system. Certainly there is no antagonism of interest or feeling between M. Martini and the American manufacturers.

We come now to the appearance of the Peabody in England, in which country patents had been granted for it in 1865.

In April, 1867, an English Commission convened to test the various breech-loaders then invented, for the purpose of deciding upon a new system for the British army in the place of the Snider. Among the most improved American arms the Peabody was conspicuous. Up to this time the Martini type of the gun had met with no favor from any European power, while several were using the original in their armament. Out of the thirty-eight different models finally admitted to the competition (seventy-four out of the one hundred and twelve first entered having been ruled out because they had not barrels long enough—as if length of barrel was decisive merit or demerit of a breech-loading system—or would not take the abominable Boxer cartridge), both the Peabody and the Martini stood the tests with about equal success. The Board, headed by Lord Spencer, continued its labors off and on, for more than a year. In the meantime the Martini system was assimilated to the Boxer cartridge and fitted to a barrel rifled upon the theory of Alexander Henry, a Scotch gunsmith.

It would be traveling away from the subject to discuss the merits of the Henry rifling; but it is necessary to speak of its claims to originality. Mr. Henry had patents in England and the United States for his alleged invention; but there is no maxim better substantiated by experience than that which declares a patent to be good for nothing till it has stood the test of litigation. We believe it was in 1874 that Mr. Henry came to the United States and instituted suits for damages for violation of his patent-rights against our arms manufacturers. The judgment of our courts was adverse to his claims, it being shown that whatever was alleged to be his invention had been the common property of American armorers for many years, each and all of its features having been experimented upon over and over again in our sporting and target rifles.

It is well known that the issue of the British trial was the adoption of the Swiss improvement upon the Peabody; and that the new service arm of England was by experts, officials and publicists at once termed the Martini-Henry. A more palpable injustice than this utter ignoring the original invention could hardly be conceived, but injustice is aggravated in the present instance by appending to the name of one man whose simple claim is that of an improvement, the name of another who has been proven, at his own instance, to have no claim at all to anything.

In 1872, however, occurred an event which has in all material respects compensated the representatives of the Peabody Patent for the indignity received from the English officials. This was the conclusion of the Turkish contract, by which was secured to the Providence Tool Company the most important order for arms known in the history of the industry.

EXECUTION OF THE CONTRACT WITH TURKEY.

The Government of Turkey, having, after the long-continued session of a Board of Ordnance Officers, decided to adopt the breech-loading system which was being introduced into the English army, during the summer of 1872, called upon the considerable number of arms manufacturers then assembled in Constantinople for propositions to supply the quantity of arms needed for a re-equipment of the Turkish troops. On the 1st of January, 1873, the contract was awarded to the Providence Tool Company, whose only serious competitor had been a large English company having its shops at Birmingham. The first order for arms under the contract contemplated 200,000 stand, but subsequent contracts increased the total number demanded to 600,000. To execute an order so unprecedented in its magnitude necessitated a very large increase of shop room and machine plant. The works of the Tool Company, already very extensive, occupied two distinct structures in the city of Providence, almost the entire breadth of the city intervening between them. Soon after closing the contract Mr. Anthony set about securing new shops, and was fortunate enough to find two unoccupied buildings, which he leased for the Tool Company. These two buildings were at some distance from each other, so that the working upon the Turkish contract was prosecuted at four separate localities. Under such circumstances it would be a natural and logical inference that the details of production should be more numerous and difficult and its cost enhanced. The perfect organization of the labor system in the different departments, and the exceeding care with which the progress of operations was harmonized in all, assuring a constant and steady stream of parts toward the assembling room, however, triumphed over all inconveniences of locality, and it would be hard to persuade the shrewd, untiring manager and superintendent of the company that they could have conducted their enormous industry in a new armory, especially designed and erected for the exigency, with a whit more economy than was secured in their isolated workshops.

The machines available for the construction of the Peabody were far from adequate to supply the parts for the extraordinary demands of the new enterprise. Co-incident with the leasing of the two new shops, thorough estimates were made of the additional machine plant required, and orders were at once given to several of the best establishments in New England for its construction. The work of preparing the shops for their respective operations and setting up new machines commenced in April. In the succeeding March (1874) the first thousand rifles had been inspected and delivered, and the great contract was fairly under way. But before a single arm was completed, the investment account for new buildings, machinery, and other imperative details of preparation, had nearly reached a total of two millions of dollars.

During the ten months of 1874, the first year of the work, the total product numbered 54,600 rifles. Of course the results of this year were affected by the many difficulties inseparable from the commencement of any extraordinary undertaking, and the production correspondingly limited.

In 1875, the entire number of arms delivered was 172,600, being very nearly the maximum aimed at in the plan of operations, which contemplated a production of 600 stand per working day.

The contract was finally completed in the late summer of 1879, circumstances growing out of the Turkish situation after the war causing a delay which was in no other sense necessary. At certain periods during its fulfillment 800 stand per day were turned out, and somewhat larger results could have been reached had an imperative exigency demanded.

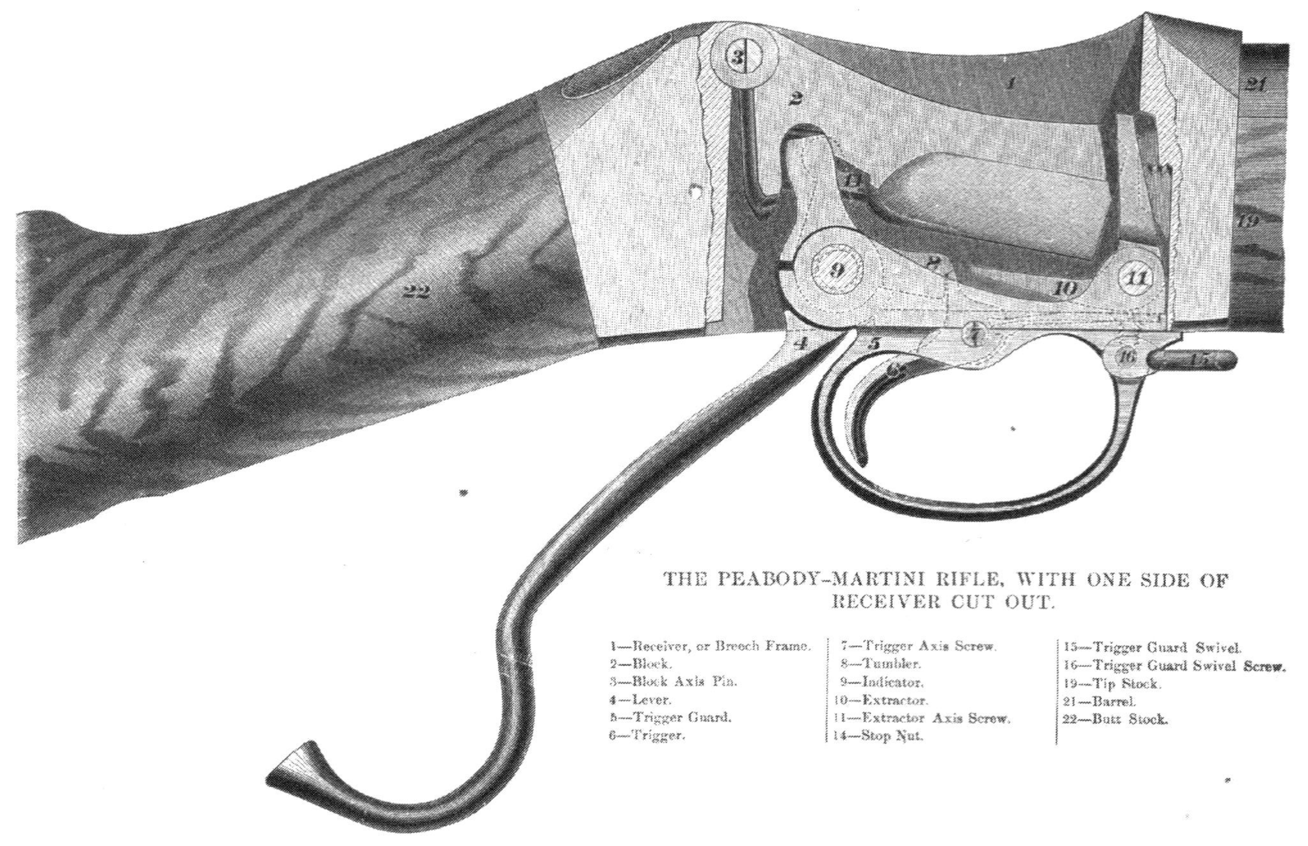

THE PEABODY-MARTINI RIFLE, WITH ONE SIDE OF RECEIVER CUT OUT.

1—Receiver, or Breech Frame.	7—Trigger Axis Screw.	15—Trigger Guard Swivel.
2—Block.	8—Tumbler.	16—Trigger Guard Swivel Screw.
3—Block Axis Pin.	9—Indicator.	19—Tip Stock.
4—Lever.	10—Extractor.	21—Barrel.
5—Trigger Guard.	11—Extractor Axis Screw.	22—Butt Stock.
6—Trigger.	14—Stop Nut.	

The American theory of manufacture upon the interchangeable plan may be fairly said to have attained its perfect development in the execution of the great Turkish contract. The Peabody-Martini has sixty-nine distinct parts, and out of the 600,000 rifles delivered, the first instance has yet to be made known of any one part being unfitted to take its particular place in any one whole. To assure this perfection and harmony of construction, not only the most thorough organization and administration of various branches of work had to combine with resources of machinery and tools never before collected in an armory, but an inspection of unprecedented severity was constantly enforced. This inspection followed each stream of parts from their first rude shaping out of the raw metal, through each process of development, to their full completion in the assembling room. Only an enterprise involving the largest returns would have justified the investment of time and money absolutely requisite to a mechanical achievement so extraordinary in every respect.

THE SYSTEM OF INSPECTION.

The system of inspection instituted at the beginning of the enterprise was, so to speak, a dual one. General Tevfik, with a detail of Turkish officers and subalterns, superintending the general progress of the work, while forty-five expert artisans, furnished, at the instance of the Ottoman Minister, from the Government armories, under the command of Lieutenant (now Captain) Henry Metcalfe, of the United States Ordnance, tested by gauge, not only each part as it was finished by the contractor, but again when it came to the assembling room. The Turks at the armory, numbering as high as twenty-seven at one time, as the contract advanced, acquired a growing acquaintance with its mechanical requirements, and though at first unpracticed and unappreciative, before its close, not a few of the detail were far from inexpert judges of fine machine work. In the second or third year of the contract, an officer of the detachment, having time on his hands, took a fancy to test the excellence of the interchangeable system by his own trial. He accordingly, with a squad of his men, ascended to the packing-room, and in a short time had fifty rifles reduced to their original condition of parts, each half hundred parts forming a pile by itself. Having thus effectually destroyed the identity of the guns, he proceeded with his purpose to attempt to re-assemble. Within a reasonable time for inexpert men, forty-eight rifles had been made out of the fifty piles. Two incomplete systems, however, remained, each having its recalcitrant part which could not be induced to take its position. Repeated efforts to solve the difficulty were unsuccessful, and it goes without saying that serious doubts of the invariable reliability of the interchangeable plan were being entertained.

At this juncture, the superintendent of the company made his appearance, having heard of the officer's sudden inspiration, and being curious to observe the degree of his mechanical expertness. He at once took the obstinate systems in hand, and discovered that the trouble in one instance was due to a fragment of dirt which had crept into the action, and in the other to the mistake of an unpracticed hand by which the proper position of a part had been reversed. This little episode, which at the time afforded no little amusement for both Turks and Americans, was of lasting importance, not merely as a demonstration of the correctness of the theory of construction, but as an incentive to the men who were to use the arms to acquire a practical knowledge of their mechanism.

THE SYSTEM OF GAUGES.

The system of gauges, which is the essence of the interchangeable theory, was of course a conspicuous preparatory feature at the commencement of work. Absolutely necessary to the details of inspection, they were equally indispensable in the stages of production. When the contract was undertaken, it was understood that the English standard arm should be the model, and the Turkish officers, sent over to superintend the execution of the contract, brought with them a number of original Martini-Henry rifles, designed as patterns. The design of the Martini-Henry was followed therefore in the execution of the contract, with very slight changes of machining, agreed upon by both parties as judicious, and but two important radical alterations—the introduction of a new extractor, and an essentially improved chambering—were made. The gauges used had to provide for these changes. As the work advanced under the supervision of the most intelligent and practical mechanics in the United States, the gauge system marched *pari passu* with it, new theories of detection and safeguards against imperfection being added, until the absolute precision of every process was assured.

Reference has been made to two radical changes in the Peabody-Martini from the English models. Though these changes were necessitated by the decision of the Turks to adopt the Berdan or folded-headed, drawn cartridge for their arm, instead of the Boxer used by the English army, they are still of original design and so important as to merit attention. The Boxer is a considerably more bulky cartridge than the same calibre of American metallic ammunition, its original type, a wrapped cone headed by a thick iron base, being both ugly and clumsy. The drawn Boxer cartridge is somewhat better, but retains the iron base, and is far from symmetrical. A series of experiments prosecuted at Bridgeport by the Ottoman officers, while the Tool Company was making its preparations for work, terminated in the approval of a bottle-shaped cartridge of considerably less diameter than the Boxer, though about the same length. The cartridges each weigh respectively as follows: The solid-head Boxer 822 grains, wrapped metal 791 grains, Berdan for Peabody-Martini 747 grains.

A very considerable difference in weight, notwithstanding the Berdan is a stronger shell than the English one; but the more important result is found in the chambering of the gun. The dimensions of the chamber of the Martini-Henry are, for instance: length 2.87 inches, diameter under head, .672 inch, varying to .507 inch over ball. The Peabody-Martini chamber for its cartridge has the following proportions: depth 2.86 of an inch, diameter .587 of an inch under head, varying to .481 over ball, and .465 of an inch at the commencement of the rifling.

As the weights of powder and ball are the same in the cartridges of the Martini-Henry and the Peabody-Martini, by its improved chambering the latter arm gains two obvious advantages—a greater strength at the breech and a concentration of the explosive effects by which their force is expended more directly upon the missile.

To assure the perfect proportions of the Peabody-Martini chamber, five different gauges were used, two sizes of each, the condition being that the chamber shall receive a cartridge .587 of an inch under the head, and reject one of .589 diameter, and similarly at four other points in its length. After these sectional gauges had performed their test, a single micrometer gauge was applied, measuring the chamber at each interval of an eighth of an inch, and detecting a default of 1-1000 of an inch.

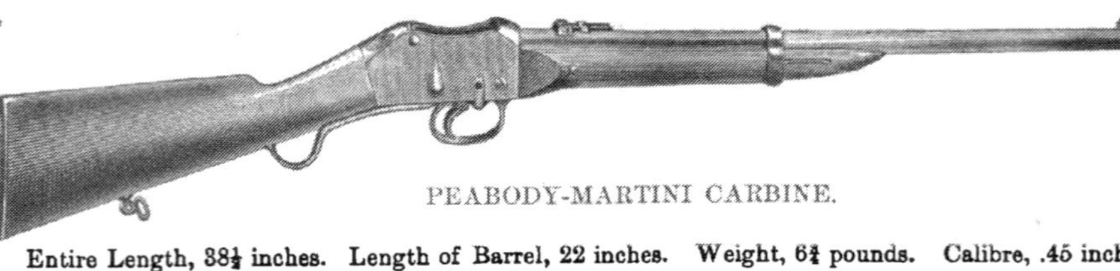

PEABODY-MARTINI CARBINE.

Entire Length, 38½ inches. Length of Barrel, 22 inches. Weight, 6¾ pounds. Calibre, .45 inch.

CARTRIDGE FOR PEABODY-MARTINI CARBINE.

Calibre, .45 inch. Powder, 60 grains. Bullet, smooth-patched; weight, 400 grains. Lubricating disc in shell.

In testing the metallic ammunition made at New Haven and Bridgeport for the Ottoman government, Peabody-Martini rifles were used. One of these—and it is not an exceptional instance—which had been subjected to 30,000 discharges with the service ammunition, 85 grains of powder and 480 of lead, is shown to the visitor at the Tool Company's Armory. After it had been withdrawn from its work, curiosity suggested the application of the chambering gauges. The tests discovered an enlargement of the mouth of the chamber, amounting to barely 1-1000 of an inch, and extending 3.16 of an inch back from the cartridge head. In all other respects no effect was manifest of this extraordinary trial, barrel and action being in perfect working order, and the arm altogether serviceable. Had a coincident trial been commenced with a Martini-Henry chamber and Boxer ammunition, it is hardly probable that the thirtieth thousand round would have been fired.

A recent article in an English journal, evidently from the pen of an expert, giving a comparative view of the arms of different European powers, with tables of ranges and calibre, closes with the deduction that less importance attaches to the particular breech-loading system than to the perfection of its construction. Probably this opinion will not be accepted by American gun-smiths or inventors, yet so far as it credits a large part of the efficiency and safety of the system to the controlling judgment and mechanical skill that have secured the light weight and thickness of metal in proper places, correct relations of receiver to barrel, exact chambering, and fine mechanism in the action, it need not be altogether rejected. In the execution of the Turkish contract, each one of the 600,000 rifles delivered was fired at least six rounds, with a service charge, at the armory. Out of this great number of rounds not only not a single accident occurred, but, with very rare exceptions of defective cartridges, miss-fires were absolutely unknown. Giving all the credit it manifestly deserves to the Peabody-Martini breech-loading system, had not the workmanship of the arm been as near perfection as is possible, this remarkable record of immunity from casualties, to which the best design of a fire-arm is liable, might not have been made.

As a still further proof of the perfect workmanship, the following fact is cited: In the specifications of the contract it was stipulated that a proportion of one-tenth of certain parts of the system should be made in addition to the arms delivered, and held as a reserve to draw upon in

Shop No. 1.

Shop No. 2.

PROVIDENCE TOOL COMPANY,

PROVIDENCE, R. I., U. S. A.

the event of breakage by use or accident. This provision was complied with; but no instance occurred of an extra part being used or called for.

From the great number of favorable reports about the Peabody-Martini rifle we give the following:

"General Todleben, in a letter to General Brialmont, states that the number of Turkish bullets which fell among the Russian ranks when they were still 2,000 yards away from the defenders' position was such, that divisions which at the outset numbered from 10,000 to 12,000 men were speedily reduced to a strength of from 4,000 to 5,000; that, in other words, they lost half their effectives. Captain Kouropatkine, speaking of the attack upon Loftcha, states that, at 2,000 yards from the Turkish position, Russian soldiers were struck down by the defenders' bullets, and that, at 1,500 yards, men were falling rapidly on all sides; and General Zeddeler, who was present with the Russian Guard when it received its 'baptism of fire' at Gorni Dubniak, states that, at 3,000 paces from the defenders' position, the Russians began to suffer loss; that, at 2,000 paces, men were falling rapidly, and, as the attack progressed, the reserves suffered nearly as much as the firing line.

"Here is the narrative of a non-commissioned officer of the Vladimir regiment, which, on the 11th of September, on the day of the last grand attack upon the Turkish lines round Plevna, formed a part of General Skobeleff's command. During the forenoon of the day, this regiment had been ordered to move up into a position in some vineyards and maize-fields, two versts, or about 2,200 yards, away from the central Turkish redoubts on the Green Hill. The most advanced of the Turkish trenches were some 200 to 300 yards in front of this redoubt, and were, therefore, presumably from 1,700 to 1,900 yards from the Russian position. After describing these preliminary movements, the narrator continues: 'We had not been long in the vineyard when the Turks began to fire at us. Many of our men were wounded before the order was given for us to advance, and among them the captain of my company, who was lying down among the vines. When at last we moved forward, the bullets fell upon us like hail. They pelted upon us on all sides. Men fell on all sides, in the front ranks and in the rear sections alike. We had not gone more than fifty paces when the officer of my sub-division was struck in the chest. He died two days afterwards. The other peleton officer led on the company, but 100 yards further on he was hit too. We could not fire. Our Krink rifles were only sighted up to 600 yards, and the Turks were a verst-and-a-half away.' Here is an instance, related by an eye-witness, of what long-range fire can do; a company loses all its officers, and becomes naturally seriously demoralized, before it can arrive within a mile of the position it has to assault. The particular battalion to which this company belonged did not, it is almost needless to say, carry the Turkish trenches. In the words of the narrator, 'Long before we got near the trenches there was no one left to advance.'"

A London *Times* correspondent at Russian head-quarters says: "The American rifles used by the Turks have a tremendous range; I have seen dug out of a hard clay bank, bullets which had penetrated sixteen inches after traversing a distance of over 2,000 yards."

"The rifle used in the Turkish army is a breech-loader made by the Providence Tool Company and called the Peabody-Martini; it can be fired by an expert hand at the rate of once in two seconds, and the soldier's capacity for killing is therefore only limited by his dexterity and supply of cartridges; it suffices to know, that in the crucial test of war on the large scale, this American weapon does its appointed work, and keeps the Russians at bay whenever the Turks can get behind a cover in strong force. The possession of 500,000 of these rifles—that number having already been supplied by the American contractors, with 100,000 more to be delivered—used by brave men behind defenses, may not decide the final issues of the war for the Turks, but it will undoubtedly protract the conflict, and make it frightfully costly to the Russians. American arms, and the American style of earthworks which the Turks have copied will give the Russians even more trouble than that fanaticism and valor which make the Turks foemen worthy of any nation's steel."—*New York Journal of Commerce*, 1877.

"This skirmish proved, as every recent engagement has shown, the incontestable superiority of the Turkish over the Russian soldier, and also the vastly superior shooting power of the Peabody-Martini rifle over that carried by the Russian troops. At 350 yards the Russian rifle ceases to be deadly, while the Peabody-Martini at that range inflicts tremendous loss. The Turks thoroughly appreciate the superiority of the American weapon which they carry, and being naturally excellent marksmen they pour a tremendous fire upon the enemy *before* he is within his own fighting distance."—*New York Herald*, 1877.

The London *Times* of January 29th, 1880, says: "The rifles carried by the Turkish infantry were the best in existence." Also, "The infantry rifles of the Turks were the best known."

General Whistler, of our own army, speaking of a comparative test he had personally witnessed, says: "This rifle I consider the best possible one which could be adopted for the soldier, on account of its accuracy, penetration, and wonderfully long range.

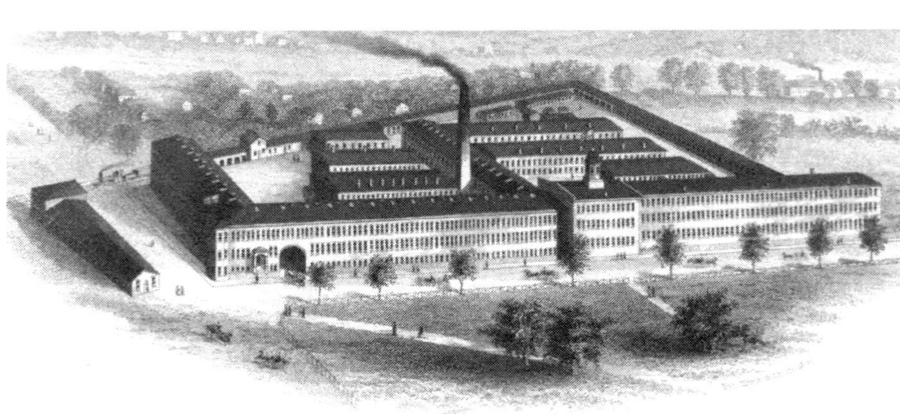

CHAPTER III.

THE WINCHESTER SYSTEM—THE HOTCHKISS SYSTEM.

THE Winchester Repeating Rifle is, as its name implies, a repeating or magazine gun, and differing from single breech-loaders in this, that, while it may be used as a single breech-loader with as great rapidity as any of the latter class, the magazine, filled with from ten to seventeen cartridges, forms a reserve to be used in emergencies, when greater rapidity of fire is desired. While retaining the same breech mechanism as the Henry, the entire structure of the magazine and method of filling it is so changed that it is filled from the rear or breech end, through a spring cover, which closes automatically after the insertion of each cartridge, and may be replenished as the cartridges are used, even without removing the gun from the shoulder. From this magazine, the cartridge is transferred to the barrel by a carrier block, actuated by a finger lever (occupying the place of the trigger guard in other guns), which, by a single motion, cocks the gun, ejects the shell of the last cartridge fired, brings a fresh cartridge from the magazine into the barrel and securely closes the breech, leaving but one motion, viz.: pulling the trigger, to complete the operation of loading and firing. These two motions, being simple and in direct line with the gun, can be performed with the gun at the shoulder and without removing the hand from it, securing to the Winchester a greater rapidity of firing than any other gun, as no other possesses all these advantages.

This gun is strong and durable, and not liable to get out of repair, as its mechanism is simple and constructed of the best material, in the best manner and thoroughly tested. Instances are known of these guns having fired 20,000 to 25,000 cartridges without a single repair being needed. The total amount of parts sold for repairs during the last twelve years is less than three cents for each gun sold during that time.

In *accuracy* and *efficiency*, it is equal to any other gun using the same charge of powder and lead. These qualities, which are undisputed by those who have used the gun, were publicly demonstrated at *Creedmoor* in the combined *rapidity and accuracy match*, as shown by the following score, the gun being used as a single loader only:

Competitions for the prize offered by Messrs. Schuyler, Hartley & Graham, No. 19 Maiden Lane, N. Y., for rapidity and accuracy. Open to all comers. Distance 200 yards. Position standing. Any rifle. *Magazine guns to be used as single loaders only.* Two sighting shots, to be fired consecutively. Competitors may fire as many shots as possible within half a minute (30 seconds), and to have two chances; the aggregate score made in both rounds to be counted; half the entrance money to be divided among the three highest scores as follows: The first taking the badge and half the money, the second two-sixths, and the third one-sixth. No restriction as to the manner of taking cartridges. Badge to be won three times (not necessarily consecutively), before becoming the personal property of the winner. Competitors will stand at firing-point with rifle loaded and cocked, butt below elbow, until the command "Fire." The scorer will command, "Are you ready? Fire!" and invert a half minute sand-glass; at the end of thirty seconds he will call "Time." A bull's-eye will be deducted from the score for every shot fired after "time" is called.

WINNERS.

DATE.	Number of Competitors.	NAME.	RIFLE.	SCORE.
1—July 22d............	19	William Robertson....	W B.	37
2—August 19th........	6	George Wood.........	Spg.	34
3—September 16th.....	10	J. E. Stetson..........	Win	52
4—October 21st........	5	J. E. Stetson	Win.	73
5—November 18th......	6	J. E. Stetson.	Win.	63

Finally won by Capt. J. E. Stetson, who entered only on the last three days, using a Winchester Rifle as a *single breech-loader only*, in competition with Ward-Burton, Remington, Springfield, Sharps, and Peabody Rifles.

From 1866 to 1873, the success of the Winchester Arm was such that over 150,000 of the model of that year were sold and are now in use. The demand for a more powerful arm resulted in the production of the model known as 1873, comprising many most important improvements.

The first and most important improvement consists in adapting it to the use of a longer and a center-fire cartridge, holding a charge of 40 grains of powder instead of 28, as in the model of 1866, retaining the same calibre, $\frac{44}{100}$, and the same weight of ball, viz.: 200 grains.

The effect of this change is to increase the initial velocity of the arm from about 1,125 to 1,325 feet per second, reducing or flattening the trajectory and increasing the power and accuracy of the arm, and giving it a penetration of about four inches, in pine board, at 1,000 yards.

A second improvement in the sporting arm is the addition of a set, or hair trigger. This differs from the ordinary hair trigger, in that it can be used precisely as if this trigger was not on the gun, if as in hunting, it is not wanted.

For fine shooting, as in target practice, it is made available thus: After setting the hammer at full cock, the trigger should be pressed forward slightly, and it is thus set. If it is found too delicate, or not delicate enough, it can be adjusted to suit the wishes, by turning a set screw in or out. This screw will be found by the side of the trigger.

A third improvement consists in a sliding lid, which covers the opening in which the carrier-block moves up and down. This lid, by the action of the finger lever, opens automatically when the gun is loaded, and should always remain open until closed by hand after firing. The object of this lid is to keep dirt and snow out of the lock.

A fourth improvement consists in the substitution of iron, in place of gun-metal or brass, in the manufacture of the lock-frame, butt-plate, and other parts, thus increasing the strength of the arm and reducing its weight. The-gun metal is, however, retained in the carrier-block and the lid in the butt-plate, opening into the receptacle for the cleaning-rod; the object being to avoid the liability to rust, so as to impede the movement of these parts, which would exist if made of iron.

A fifth improvement consists in a device which absolutely prevents accidental or premature explosions. In most breech-loading fire-arms, the firing-pin, after the explosion of a cartridge, depends upon a spiral spring to be thrown back even with the face of the breech-closing bolt. If this spring is very strong, so as to insure its operation, it tends to break the force of the blow of the hammer; but if not strong enough for the purpose, it soon gets so foul as not to work, and the firing-pin then projects, and if the breech is closed with a quick motion the car-

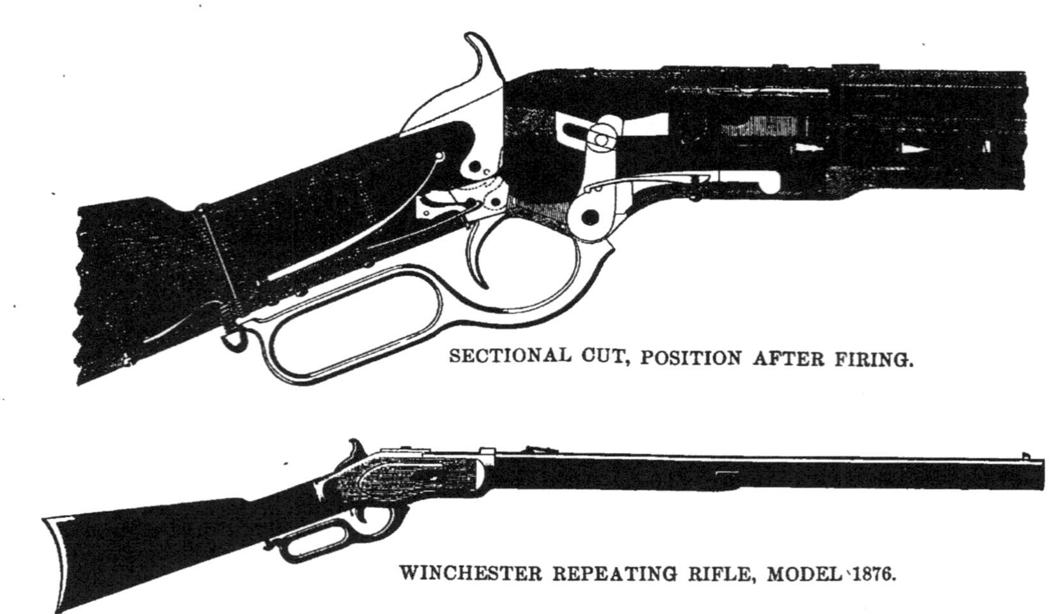

SECTIONAL CUT, POSITION AFTER FIRING.

WINCHESTER REPEATING RIFLE, MODEL 1876.

tridge is exploded prematurely. To obviate this, no spring is used, but the firing-pin is carried back by a positive motion retractor, and avoids all danger from the cause above mentioned.

In 1876 still farther improvements were made, securing an arm of greater power and efficiency, retaining all the essential mechanical elements of the former model, and adding such improvements as seemed possible, the result has been a gun carrying a central fire cartridge, capable of reloading, calibre $\frac{45}{100}$, with 75 grains of powder and 350 grains of lead, being nearly double the charge used in model 1873, about the same as that adopted by the U. S. Government, and giving an initial velocity of 1,450 feet.

The materials used in the construction of the gun are the same in kind and quality as in the Model 1873.

Both set and plain trigger rifles are made, and all guns with plain trigger are provided with an attachment which renders premature explosion of the cartridge, even from carelessness, absolutely impossible.

In both Infantry Musket and Carbine, the magazine is covered by the forearm its entire length.

Another gun of this model has been manufactured, chambered to carry a cartridge having a *straight* shell containing 60 grains of powder and a bullet weighing 300 grains, having greater power and range than Model 1873, but less power, range and recoil, than the regular Model 1876.

The factories, store houses and other buildings of the Winchester Repeating Arms Co., occupy about six acres, comprising all the appurtenances necessary for the purposes of their business. At present over nine hundred operatives are regularly employed, and when fully at work over seventeen hundred are kept busy. The Winchester Arms have been largely sold to the Governments of Turkey, France, Spain and the South American Republics, also to Australia, China and Japan. It has also been adopted by the Italian navy, and is in use for special service by British naval officers. Large sales of cartridge machinery have been made to the Turkish and Spanish Governments.

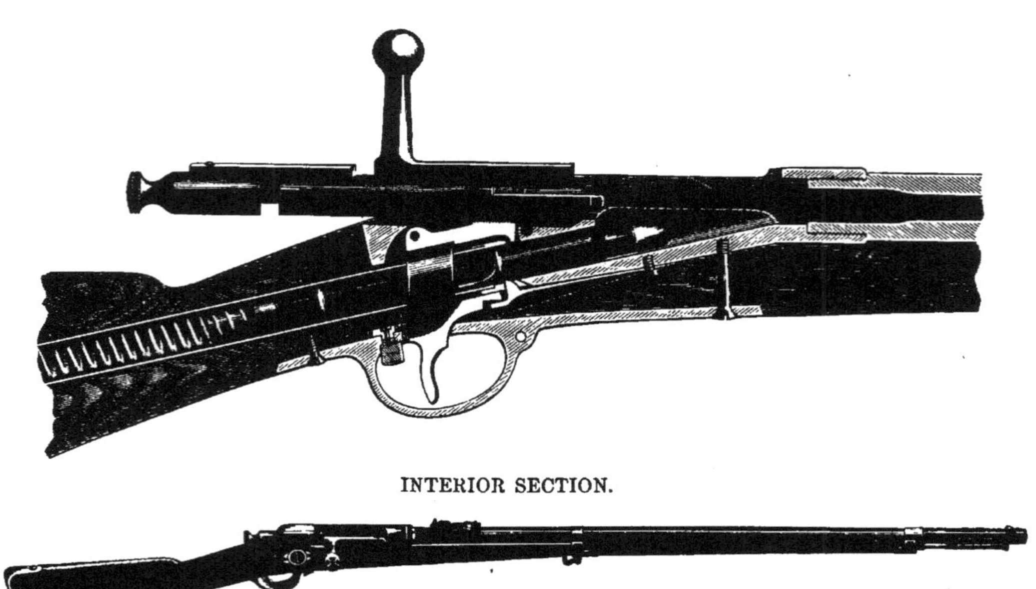

INTERIOR SECTION.

HOTCHKISS MAGAZINE GUN.

THE HOTCHKISS MAGAZINE GUN.

This arm is the invention of Mr. B. B. Hotchkiss, an American residing in Paris, who first brought it to this country in the spring of 1876, and exhibited it at the Centennial in Philadelphia where it attracted general attention from its simplicity. The patent was purchased by the Winchester Repeating Arms Co., who have since secured other patents for improvements in the arm, and now control the entire right to its manufacture.

The gun thus improved was presented for trial by the board of Ordnance officers appointed for the selection of a repeating arm for the use of United States troops, and as the result of this trial, the proceedings of which are published in the report of the Chief of Ordnance for 1878, that form of the Hotchkiss repeater now offered for sale was recommended for trial in the hands of the troops, in the following words:—"*From the satisfactory manner in which the Hotchkiss Gun, No.* 19, *has passed these tests, and from its combination of strength, simplicity, and great effectiveness as a single loader, the Board is of the opinion that the Hotchkiss Gun, No.* 19, *is suitable for the military service, and it does, therefore, recommend it as such.*"

The Chief of Ordnance farther states as follows:

"The report of the board is herewith submitted. It recommended the *Hotchkiss Magazine Gun*, and upon my recommendation the Secretary of War has approved the action of the board, and of the expenditure under the law of $20,000 in its manufacture. When we take into consideration the many months of patient labor devoted to this subject by so competent a board, and that its investigations were presided over by Lieutenant Colonel Benton, whose great expert knowledge and high scientific attainments are known and acknowledged throughout the profession, there can be no doubt that the conclusion arrived at will receive general approval."

The following rules for operating and dismounting the piece, will give to the reader a clear idea of the details of the Hotchkiss System:

TO OPERATE THE GUN.

1. To open the breech-bolt.—Hold the stock firmly with the left hand, a little in front of the receiver, and with the right hand grasp the handle, unlock and draw back the bolt, making but one motion.

2. Close the bolt by an inverse motion. This operation cocks the piece.

THE HOTCHKISS MAGAZINE GUN.

3. To cock the piece without withdrawing the bolt. — Grasp the handle as before, unlock the bolt and immediately re-lock it by turning the handle down.

4. To load the magazine.—Unlock and draw back the breech-bolt. Take a cartridge between the thumb and middle finger, placing the point of the forefinger on the bullet; insert the head of the cartridge in the receiver, just in front of the point at which it narrows down, and press it back in the magazine until a distinct click—the head passing the cartridge-stop—is heard. Repeat the operation until 5 cartridges have been inserted; another may then be placed in the chamber.

5. To unload the magazine.—Unlock and draw back the bolt; the cartridge in the chamber will be thrown out. Close the bolt and *pull the trigger;* a cartridge will then be released from the magazine. Open the bolt, and the cartridge will usually feed into the chamber; if not, it may be removed with the fingers; otherwise close the bolt and again open it, when the cartridge will be thrown out. Again close the bolt and pull the trigger; a second cartridge will be released, and so on.

THE MAGAZINE CUT-OFF.

This device serves a double purpose, viz.:—

1. To lock the magazine, enabling the piece to be used as a single loader.

2. To lock the bolt and trigger when the piece is carried loaded and at full-cock.

TO OPERATE THE CUT-OFF.

1. To use the piece as a magazine gun.—Rotate the cut-off in the direction of the hands of a watch until the pins spring in their corresponding holes in the escutcheon, the *notched end* being either *to the front or rear.*

2. To use the piece as a single loader.—Rotate as before, until the notched end is down.

3. To lock the bolt and trigger.—*Cock the piece* and rotate as before, until the notched end is up.

N. B.—The cut-off cannot be turned to the left, nor can it be turned through an entire circle *without cocking* the piece. The position which necessitates the cocking of the piece is that of the notched end to the rear. In all other positions it may be turned whether the piece be cocked or not.

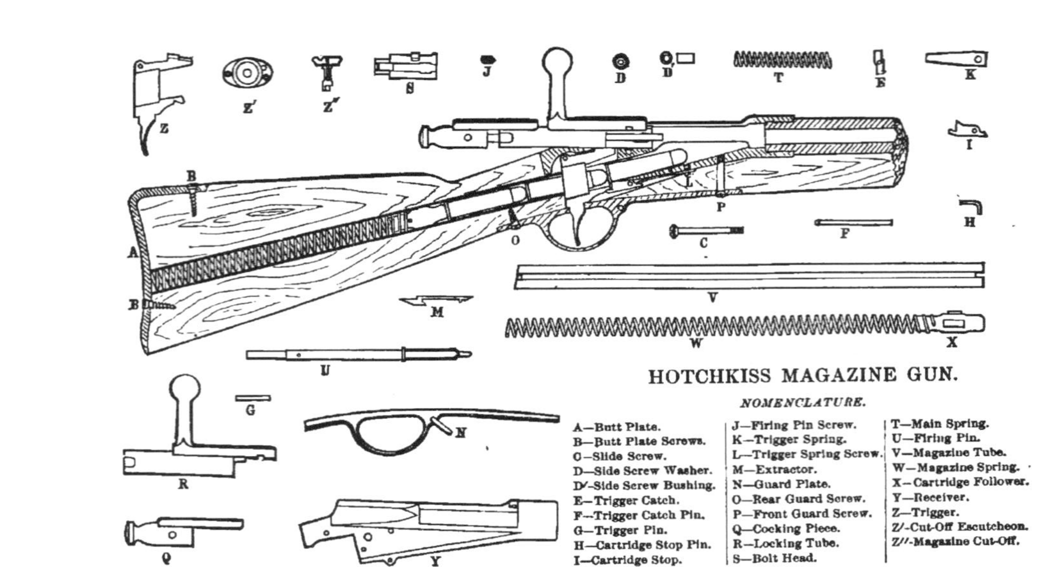

HOTCHKISS MAGAZINE GUN.

NOMENCLATURE.

A—Butt Plate.
B—Butt Plate Screws.
C—Slide Screw.
D—Side Screw Washer.
D′—Side Screw Bushing.
E—Trigger Catch.
F—Trigger Catch Pin.
G—Trigger Pin.
H—Cartridge Stop Pin.
I—Cartridge Stop.
J—Firing Pin Screw.
K—Trigger Spring.
L—Trigger Spring Screw.
M—Extractor.
N—Guard Plate.
O—Rear Guard Screw.
P—Front Guard Screw.
Q—Cocking Piece.
R—Locking Tube.
S—Bolt Head.
T—Main Spring.
U—Firing Pin.
V—Magazine Tube.
W—Magazine Spring.
X—Cartridge Follower.
Y—Receiver.
Z—Trigger.
Z′—Cut-Off Escutcheon.
Z″—Magazine Cut-Off.

TO DISMOUNT THE GUN.

1. Remove the magazine cut-off. To do this, turn the notched end to the front; place the point of a screw-driver under the rear end and bear down gently, slightly supporting the front end against pressure with the fingers of the left hand.

2. Remove the breech-bolt. To do this, press on the trigger, and at the same time unlock the bolt and withdraw it.

N. B.—The bolt can be removed in the following manner: Unlock and draw back the bolt until the cocking-piece just clears the receiver; then, letting go the handle, take hold of the cocking-piece and turn it down to the right until the projection of the bolt-head leaves the groove under the front end of the locking-tube. The latter may be drawn out at the rear, and the head at the front of the receiver. To return the bolt, the head must be inserted from the front and the other part from the rear, unless the cut-off be removed.

3. Remove the butt-plate screws and plate.

4. Remove the magazine-spring and cartridge-follower. Place the point of the firing-pin in the hole at the rear of the magazine-tube, and draw out the tube.

5. Remove the guard-screws and guard.

6. Remove the side-screw.

7. Remove the wiping-rod.

8. Remove the bands.

9. Remove the barrel from the stock. To do this, turn the barrel downward, holding it loosely in the hand just in front of the receiver, and tap the muzzle gently against the foot. This will start the barrel without danger of splitting the stock.

N. B.—The barrel cannot be removed until the magazine has been taken out. It will not ordinarily be necessary to remove the side screw washer, side-screw bushing, escutcheon, band-springs, tip, etc.

10. Remove the trigger-spring screw and spring.

11. Remove the cartridge-stop pin and stop.

12. Remove the trigger-pin and trigger. Use a punch to drive out the pin.

13. Remove the trigger-catch pin and catch. Use the point of a screw-driver in the notched end of the pin to draw it out.

The barrel should not be unscrewed from the receiver.

TO DISMOUNT THE BREECH-BOLT.

1. Remove the bolt-head. To do this, hold the cocking-piece firmly in the left hand, and with the right turn down the handles as in the act of locking the bolt. The head will then slip off.

2. Turn out the firing-pin screw.

3. Slip the bolt-head partly on the projecting end of the firing-pin, and use it as a wrench to unscrew the pin. The main-spring may then be removed.

4. Remove the extractor by tapping gently on its projecting end with a piece of wood.

To assemble, proceed in the inverse order.

THE WINCHESTER METALLIC CARTRIDGES.

This company is extensively engaged in the manufacture of every description of Metallic Cartridges, having the most extensive set of machinery for this purpose in the country, with a capacity of manufacturing over a million of Cartridges per day, for military and sporting use.

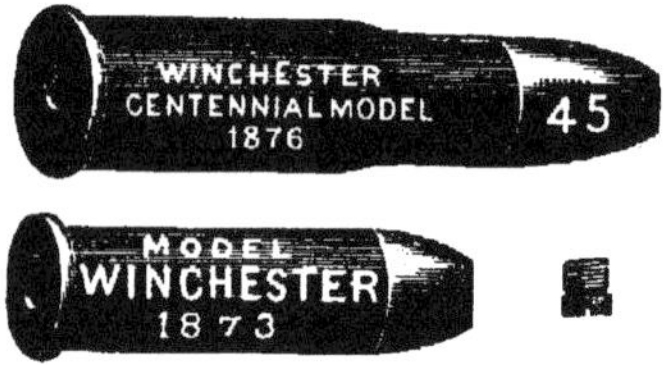

Appreciating the fact that like causes are required to produce like results, it is evident that, in order to obtain uniform shooting from a gun, the charge should be invariable; hence, the marksman with his muzzle-loading rifle, or the sportsman with his fowling-piece, uses the utmost care in weighing his charge of powder and lead, and equal care in placing them in the barrel. Neglecting these points, no matter how finely the gun may be sighted, the result must be wild shooting; for in any gun, the barrel, if kept clean, is an unalterable fact, and the variations in its work must be due either to the variation of the aim or charge. With breech-loading guns the same holds true, that to obtain good shooting cartridges must be used.

In view of these facts, the company have concentrated their efforts to the end of producing a cartridge combining all points of excellence.

This perfection has been attained by the adoption of a system of machinery which produces invariable results, by the exercise of constant and close inspection in all stages of the work, and in the use of none but the best material.

All bullets, from the smallest to the largest sizes, are swaged by patented machinery controlled by this company, which not only gives perfect uniformity in size, but also in weight and density of metal.

The ball is so inserted in the shell that its axis coincides with that of the shell, and consequently with that of the barrel of the gun.

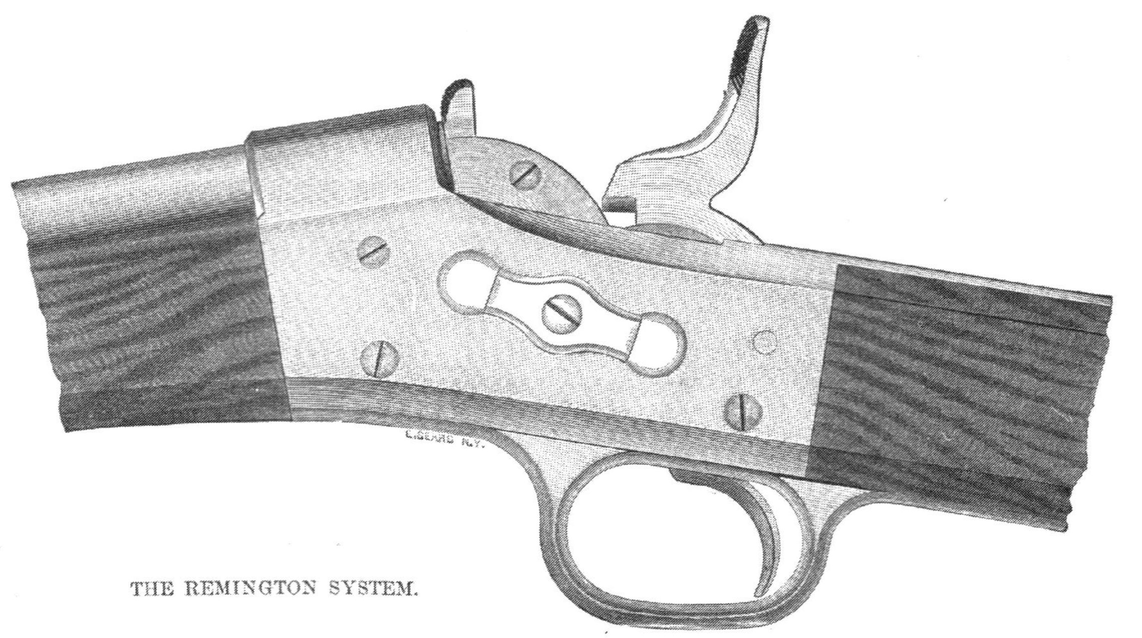

THE REMINGTON SYSTEM.

CHAPTER IV.

THE REMINGTON SYSTEM—MAGAZINE GUN, KEENE'S PATENT.

This American breech-loader, issued in greater numbers to troops than any other arm, with the single exception of the needle-gun, is one of the most recent inventions of its class. Its first public appearance, though in a shape hardly more than a suggestion of the principle developed fully in the present system, was before a Board of United States Army officers, convened at Springfield, Mass., in January, 1865. At this competition, sixty-five different guns were represented, among them the well-known Peabody, in its present perfection, though patented some three years previous; the Roberts of still earlier date; the Sharps and Burnside, the former with a record at least as old as 1850, and several other models of recognized merit. The system of Remington carbine tried at Springfield, while — as has been said — suggesting the principle of the present arm, was radically different in construction, the disposition of strength of parts being faulty, and other errors existing in the mechanism which have been discovered and remedied by experience. The Springfield Board having been, in a practical sense, resultless, since its finding was not endorsed by the Secretary of War, a second body of army officers, under the direction of Major-General Hancock, met at Washington in March of the succeeding year. In the meantime the Remington had been modified in certain details. In the original the hammer was made to work through a slot in the back of the breech-block, while in the second essay it was placed on the right exterior of the frame, as in the old muzzle-loader, with its horn projecting toward and striking into a recess cut in the block. It is questionable, however, if any material improvement was wrought by this change. In each one of these early shapes of the arm, the supporting shoulders were placed under and close to the pivot of the breech-block, so that the strain, due to recoil, upon that piece and its fastenings, was augmented: the hammer was also relatively light and inadequate in stability and strength of metal to execute the work indicated for it by the theory of the system. The new model, however, found greater favor with the Board of 1866, than with its antecedent body. Gen. Hancock's commission, setting aside the conclusion of the Springfield trial, which recommended the Peabody, reported: first, that the following modes of transformation be tested in the hands of troops, fifty muzzle-loaders being converted for that purpose according to each system, viz.: the Berdan, the Yates, the Remington, the Roberts, the Allin; second, that fifty original breech-loaders be made at Springfield Armory of each of the following systems, named in order of merit, viz.: the Remington, the Laidley, the Peabody, and the Sharps.

It will be remembered that the Hancock Commission, like its predecessor at Springfield, had no definite result, the Secretary of War and Lieutenant-General Grant declining to endorse a proposition tending to a general conversion of muzzle-loaders, or a permanent adoption of a new system at the time.

During the same year, and not long after the adjournment of the Commission, the Remington system, as now in use by so many nations of both hemispheres, was perfected. In the interval, a carbine had been produced which claims a qualified approval from the fact that it lessens the manual by one movement, though its mechanical complexity and the awkward feature of an outside hammer obviously outweigh this possible advantage. Other models were likewise constructed, each discovering a greater or less approach to the present arm, which has been termed, by the head of the American army, "the most perfect breech-loader in the world."

The first endorsement of the new Remington breech-system by the Government of the United States, was from the Marine Service, Capt. Henry A. Wise, the highly accomplished Chief of the Ordnance Bureau of the Navy, signing, on the 14th of November, 1866, a contract for 5,000 single-shot pistols of .50 calibre, similar to the terribly effective weapon afterward recommended by an army commission, and now in large numbers issued to the cavalry. This order was extended, till 6,500 pistols were made and delivered. On the 24th of October, 1867, actual trial having thus demonstrated the extraordinary fitness of the system for sea service, the same thorough officer concluded a contract for 5,000 carbines, which were delivered within a short period.

It was this partial introduction of a weapon, acting upon new principles, into the Navy, probably, which inspired an officer, distinguished as much for his progressive and improving policy, as for his *esprit du corps*, to initiate a general change in the small-armament of that branch of the service. On the 24th of March, 1869, Rear-Admiral Dahlgren, successor of Captain Wise in the Ordnance Bureau, ordered a Board of officers to convene at Washington, to "make an examination of the best systems of breech-loading, and test them fully in respect to endurance, convenience and general efficiency." This body, comprising Captain William Reynolds, *senior* member, with Commanders S. Nicholson and K. R. Breese, U. S. N., and Capt. McLane Tilton, United States Marine Corps, as associate members, held its first meeting on the 25th of March. Public notice having been previously given of the session, during the succeeding month several of the most approved American inventions were presented for trial, conspicuous in the number being the well-known Sharps rifle, the Roberts, the Burton — now called the Ward-Burton — and the Remington. The series of tests conducted by the Board were of the severest character, anticipating every possible incident of service. The report, dated August 2d, endorsed the Remington system, its recommendation being expressed as follows: "While each system of breech-loading examined or tested by this Board has its own peculiar merits, the Board is unanimous in preferring the Remington system for naval use in the service of the United States, and therefore recommend that it be adopted for the naval service."

In accordance with the above determination, ten thousand rifles were ordered constructed at the Springfield Armory, but this was not done before the finding of the Commission had been repeatedly confirmed, by a personal inspection of the several small arms factories of the country, and of a number of systems not entered during the session of the Board. The ultimate decision, after so thorough and patient a trial, regarding not only the qualities of inventions, but the facilities for production, is indicated by the subjoined official conclusions:

"OCTOBER 1, 1869.

"Having visited these different establishments for the manufacture of breech-loading arms and of their ammunition, and having carefully considered all the information we have thus obtained, we find ourselves confirmed in the recommendations made in our first report of August, and adhere to each and all of them.

Very respectfully, your obedient servants,

WM. REYNOLDS, *Captain and President*, S. NICHOLSON, *Commander U. S. Navy*,
K. R. BREESE, *Commander U. S. Navy*, McL. TILTON, *Capt. U. S. Marine Corps*.
CARLISLE P. PORTER, *Lieutenant U. S. Marine Corps and Recorder*.

"NOVEMBER 20th, 1869.

"Each of the breech-loading systems presented have their peculiar merits, and may be classed among the most serviceable; but the Board are still of the opinion that for naval purposes the Remington system is the best.

K. R. BREESE, *Commander U. S. Navy*,
McLANE TILTON, *Captain U. S. Marine Corps*."

The subsequent experience of the Navy with the arm has been altogether favorable. Its peculiar adaptation for boat service, due to the simplicity of manual by which it is loaded and discharged, without removal of the eye from its objective, or any change of the position of the hand, is universally remarked. The superlative excellence of the system, in its freedom from the clogging effects of humidity in every shape, has been proved by actual service. Since its adoption by the Navy, the arm has been subjected to probably the most severe trial that could be suggested, in the recent Corean expedition, throughout the reports of which, both official and private, it is without exception commended for efficiency and reliability. In this connection may be quoted the following letter from the accomplished officer now at the head of the Ordnance Bureau of the Navy, written in refutation of an anonymous charge that the Remington arms issued to that service had been returned to the United States Armory for repairs:

"BUREAU OF ORDNANCE, NAVY DEPARTMENT,
WASHINGTON CITY, November 25th, 1871.

"*Messrs. E. Remington & Sons*,

"SIRS: In answer to your letter of this date, calling its attention to the article in the *New York Times* of the 24th inst., in relation to the Remington gun, the Bureau has to inform you that there is not a particle of truth in the statement relating to the arms furnished by you for the navy. Not one single gun of the ten thousand (10,000) has been returned to the Springfield, or any other armory, 'to be overhauled.' On the contrary, six hundred (600) are now on board the ships of the Asiatic fleet, and the guns have been supplied to every ship which has been commissioned since the deliveries commenced. Nothing in relation to these arms has transpired to shake the confidence of the Bureau in them; a confidence based upon the unanimous report of a Board of Officers who had subjected the system, and that of *every* other gun submitted, to a most searching examination and trial. The above statement also applies in full to the paragraph in the *New York Tribune* of the 17th inst., under the head, 'Objections to the Remington Gun;' to which you have also called the Bureau's attention.

"I am, Sirs, your obedient servant,

A. LUDLOW CASE, *Chief of Ordnance*."

In the army of the United States the Remington system has been known for some years, a few hundred guns of reduced calibre having been transformed upon its plan in 1866–7. Its present relations to this branch of the service, properly claim an adequate statement at this stage of our article.

The exhaustive trial of breech-loaders conducted by the Navy, with the actual service tests to which the system had necessarily been subjected during the time following the original issue of carbines and pistols, would have probably justified a similar determination as to re-armament on the part of the army. Aside from the fact, however, that examples set by the marine are rarely copied by the land force in the war offices of nations, the Ordnance Bureau of the United States Army has always pursued a course as marked for its independent and thoughtful consideration, as for its progressive spirit. A professional staff corps which, in 1818, first of all bureaus throughout the world, entertained the new conception of an arm, would hardly risk its well-earned *prestige* by adopting, out of hand, the conclusion of a cognate body, however elaborate and thoroughly constructed its premises and arguments. The exact appreciation of the necessities of the service, which distinguishes the veteran chief of the Army Bureau of Ordnance, was in favor of independent action, and his opinion was endorsed by the General of the army. In the early part of August, 1869, General Sherman issued an order for a Board of officers to meet at Fort Leavenworth, Kansas, for the purpose of practically testing systems of tactics, etc. On the 23d of October, this body, empowered by the order organizing it to adjourn to another locality, and having assembled at St. Louis, was further instructed "to examine and report on the best small arms for the use of the Army of the United States," to conclude its labors by the 1st of May, 1870, if possible, and, in its final report, "*to designate the six best muskets for infantry, and carbines and pistols for cavalry and artillery, in the order of merit.*" The Commission was composed of the following officers:

Major-General J. M. Schofield, U. S. Army,
Brevet Brigadier-General J. H. Potter, Lt.-Col. 4th Infantry
Brevet Major-General Wesley Merritt, Lt.-Col. 9th Cavalry,

Major James Van Voast, 18th Infantry,
Brevet Colonel John Hamilton, Major 1st Artillery.

Lieutenant-Colonel Potter was, upon the meeting at St. Louis, charged with the direction of experiments and tests. With regard to the general conduct of the trial, the *Army and Navy Journal* remarks:

"The trials prosecuted at St. Louis were conducted by Lieutenant-Colonel Potter, of the Fourth Infantry, and in point of exactness of detail and thoroughness of experiments, are examples for all succeeding commissions. As authorities upon the working and enduring capacity of breech-actions, the character of the mechanism and the number of parts entering into different systems, the several reports rendered by this accomplished officer, are a final and decisive resort for all desirous of information."

The number of distinct systems represented at St. Louis, was but fourteen, a notable falling off from the crowd of competitors upon the two previous occasions. Among these fourteen, besides the Remington in its perfected shape, were the Allin, the Peabody, the Berdan, the Roberts, the Sharps, the Ward-Burton and the Martini-Henry. On the 10th of June the Board submitted its report, embodying the following conclusion:

"Our investigations have been limited to the determination of the relative merits of the various SYSTEMS of breech-loading small arms, without regard to questions of caliber, rifling, ammunition, etc. The main elements of excellence considered are: strength, durability, and simplicity of breech mechanism; ease, certainty, and rapidity of firing; and security against injury to arms, or accidents from use in the hands of troops.

"The following are the results of the deliberations of the Board, in view of our experiments with, and examinations of the several *systems* of small arms.

"We have selected the following six systems for infantry muskets, in the order of relative merit:

First. — The Remington,
Second. — The Springfield,
Third. — The Sharp,
Fourth. — The Morgenstern,
Fifth. — The Martini-Henry,
Sixth. — The Ward-Burton.

"For cavalry carbines the order of relative merit is, in the opinion of the Board, the same as for muskets; but it is regarded as essential for cavalry service that the Remington carbine be so modified as to load at the half-cock.

"Only the first three systems named possess such superior excellence as warrants their adoption by the government for infantry or cavalry without further trial in the hands of troops. Of these three, considering all the elements of excellence and cost of manufacture, the Board are unanimously and decidedly of the opinion that the REMINGTON is the best SYSTEM for the Army of the United States."

The report likewise recommends the adoption of the single-barreled Remington pistol, of a breech system similar to the rifle, for the United States Cavalry, suggesting that it be made to load at half-cock.

The Chief of Ordnance, to whom the papers and determination of the Board, were in due course referred by the Adjutant General, returned them with the following endorsement:

"I agree with the Board that the Remington, the Springfield, and the Sharps systems are decidedly superior to all other systems which have been brought to their notice, and I recommend that one thousand muskets and three hundred carbines be prepared according to each of the three systems and issued for comparative trial in service — companies of infantry and artillery to have an equal number of muskets of each system, and companies of cavalry an equal number of carbines of each system — monthly reports on the comparative merits of which to be made regularly to this Bureau, by company commanders, during a period of not less than twelve months after their first introduction into service, upon forms to be furnished by this Bureau; which reports, at the end of that time, to be laid before a board of officers to be appointed, to select a breech-loading arm for adoption by the War Department for the military service."

The exceptions taken to the proposition of the Board, by General Dyer, seem to have been mainly based upon reports received from commands to which the few hundred guns transformed upon this system had been issued, the defaults ascribed to the system being its failure to discharge cartridges, and the occasional sticking of the empty shell in the chamber. In justice to the arm, it should be stated that no such trouble, as is suggested, as to the efficient working of the system, has occurred with the cartridges made by the different private establishments of the country. The Government metallic ammunition, of less perfect finish and uniformity of gauge than that of individual production, has been shown not only by the trials at St. Louis, but by general experience, to be badly adapted for the greater number of systems. A reference to the tests with other arms indicates, moreover, the fact that the alleged failure with the United States cartridges, was not singular to, nor even especially marked in, the Remington, which worked invariably well, as did all its competitors, while using the Berdan and other ammunition of private manufacture.

It is, besides, a recognized premise in the theory of modern armament, that the cartridge is made for the gun, and not the gun for the cartridge; in support of which may be cited the introductory condition of Gen. Schofield's report: "Our investigations have been limited to the determination of the relative merits of the various systems, *without regard to questions of calibre, rifling, ammunition, etc.*"

The objection that the system does not load at half-cock, — if it be an objection at all, — concerns merely the particular lots of arms thus constructed. The Remington carbine produced in 1866 possessed this feature, as well as that of ejecting the shell. At the naval trial this particular form of the system having been submitted, with others, the Board reported, after careful deliberation, that "in rapid firing, which is the first object in the use of breech-loaders, there does not seem to be any disadvantage in full-cocking to load. The Board do not consider this requisite of this arm as a disadvantage." It is noticeable that in systems loading at half-cock, this operation is very rarely practicable when in action, the soldier naturally drawing back the hammer to its extreme pull.

It should be stated in this connection that, since the issue of the 1,300 trial arms to the army, the construction of a quantity possessing the half-cock loading and the shell ejecting features, has been ordered by the Chief of Ordnance. Gen. Dyer has, besides, within the last year, ordered the construction of 5,000 cavalry pistols of the original full-cock action, which will soon be issued to troops in the field. The reports from commands using the original issues, are understood to be generally corroborative of the recommendation of the Board.

The most recent triumph of this well-known arm, is its adoption by the State of New York, a tribute to its superiority awarded after the most thorough trial of all the approved systems, and certainly quite as creditable as the greatest of its foreign victories, since it is an exceptional merit to be honored in one's own country. The question of re-armament in this State was first considered in 1867. January 10th of this year, a special Board of officers was convened by the Adjutant-General of the State for the "examination and trial of the recent improvements and inventions in the breech-loading military small arms, and especially of such inventions and improvements as have been made for alterations of the muzzle-loading military arms now in use." This Board was composed of the following officers:

Brigadier-General George W. Palmer, Com.-Gen. of Ordnance.
Brigadier-General William G. Ward, Com.-Gen., 1st Brig., N. G.
Colonel George M. Baker, Commanding 74th Regiment, N. G.
Colonel Silas W. Burt, Assistant Inspector-General.

The following breech-loading arms were presented in competition:

The Joslyn swing-breech rifle,	Morganstern rifle,
Allin "	Roberts "
Aronson "	Ballard "

Berdan	rifle	Miller	rifle
Chabot	"	National	"
Cochran	"	Poultney	"
Empire	"	Peabody	"
Fitch & Powers	"	Remington	"
Gray's	"	Robertson	"
Hubbell's	"	Sharps	"
Joslyn's	"	Thunderbolt	"
Lamson	"	Ball's repeater,	
Milbank's side-gate	"	Spencer repeater,	
Meigs	"	Gray's repeater.	
Montstorm	"		

After a most complete and exhaustive series of experiments, extending over nearly a month's time, this Board reported in favor of the Remington gun as first in order of merit of new arms. Owing to the adjournment of the Legislature of the State, no action was taken upon the report of this Board. January 30th, 1868, by an order of the Adjutant-General, the same Board of Officers was reconvened for further tests, the following arms being submitted:

Morganstern rifle,		Needham rifle,	
Allin	"	Burton	"
Roberts	"	Berdan	"
Miller	"	Lamson	"
Conroy	"	Hinden & Schweikart's needle-gun,	
Empire	"	Montstorm rifle,	
Hubbell's	"	Yates	"
Cochran	"		

This Board convened on the 9th day of July, and continued its sessions at various dates for twenty-eight days. "The guns presented for competition embraced the best systems invented, and the Board is convinced that all practicable methods of breech-block movement have been already applied, and that future efforts in this direction must be confined to details or combinations." As before, the tests were exhaustive, and so far as the Remington arm was concerned, the Board reported as follows: "The favorable opinion of the Remington arm as expressed in the previous report is reaffirmed."

(Signed,) GEO. W. PALMER, Com.-Gen. Ordnance, S. N. Y.
W. G. WARD, Brigadier-General.
GEO. M. BAKER, Col. Com. 74th Regt., N. G. S. N. Y.
SILAS W. BURT, Col. and Asst. Inspector-General.

In addition, the following letter was written after the conclusion of the trials above referred to:

NEW YORK, March 26th, 1868.

E. Remington & Sons,

GENTLEMEN: Replying to your inquiry, and for your satisfaction, we would state that, the Board for examination of breech-loading small arms, which was convened by the Governor of the State of New York, after having examined a great variety of breech-loading systems, during a series of severe trials, lasting through many months, have affirmed, and in conclusion have reaffirmed their preference of the Remington system for new arms.

GEORGE W. PALMER, *Com. Gen. of Ordnance, President of Board.*
SILAS W. BURT, *Assistant Inspector Gen., Secretary of Board.*

The proposition for re-armament, so strongly recommended by these successive Boards, was, however, dropped until the beginning of 1871, when it at last assumed practical shape in a bill, which passed the State Legislature, appropriating $250,000 for the purchase of breech-loaders, of such model as a Commission, to be appointed by the Commander-in-Chief, should decide upon. In pursuance of this legislation, early in May, a Board, comprising the Adjutant-General, Inspector-General and the Chief of Ordnance, was ordered to examine into the merits of various kinds of breech-loading rifle muskets, and report the result of such examination to the Governor. In compliance with this order the Board convened on the 7th of June, in the city of New York, having previously given public notice of their procedure.

The following arms were presented in competition:

Roberts (new),
Roberts (transformed),
Peabody,
Barnekov-Green,
Ward-Burton,
Whitney,
Berdan (slam-bang),
Berdan (Russian),
Remington, Spanish, cal. .43,
" " " .50.
Brown,
Green,
Conroy,
Wohlgenmuth,
Williamson,
Kentucky rifle,
Joslyn-Tomes,
Springfield (Allin patent),
Needham,
Broughton.

After a most complete and thorough trial of the various arms presented, the Board made a careful report, from which the following is an extract:

After careful examination and full explanation by the exhibitors of the various arms submitted, the Board selected from among them those, which in their opinion, were best adapted to the use of the National Guard, and caused circulars to be sent to them asking for proposals. * * * The representatives of the arms tested were afforded every opportunity to display the merits of their respective systems, to point out the alleged defects of competing guns, and to demonstrate by actual test the superiority claimed for each in any particular. The experiments resulted satisfactorily, and demonstrated that all the arms possess great merit in point of accuracy, durability and facility of manipulation. * * * In arriving at the recommendation embodied in this report, the Board considered primarily, the relative merits of the various systems presented, as regards strength, durability, accuracy, and simplicity of mechanism, and liability to accident in the hands of troops who might be comparatively inexpert in the use of arms; secondly, economy rendered necessary by the limitation of the appropriation for their purchase, and, in view of the urgent necessity for the immediate procurement of breech-loaders for the National Guard, the ability to finish the requisite number within a short time.

The Board, recommend, unanimously, the adoption of the Remington rifle musket of the improved model manufactured for, and submitted to this Board (loading at assimilated half-cock, locking the breech-piece in the act of loading, withdrawing the firing-pin by a positive motion, and ejecting the shell on opening the breech), as the best arm in all respects for the use of the National Guard of the State of New York.

Respectfully submitted,

JAMES McQUADE, *Brevet Maj.-Gen., Inspector General.*
SAMUEL W. JOHNSON, *Brig.-Gen., Chief of Ordnance.*
J. B. STONEHOUSE, *Colonel and Assistant Adjt.-Gen.*

Received November 1st, 1871, and approved. Issue order accordingly.

JOHN T. HOFFMAN.

GENERAL HEADQUARTERS,
STATE OF NEW YORK, ADJT.-GEN.'S OFFICE,
ALBANY, November 1, 1871.

GENERAL ORDER No. 23:

The Board appointed by General Order No. 11, Current Series, 'to examine into the merits of various kinds of breech-loading rifle muskets,' having reported to the Governor the result of such examination, and recommended the adoption of the Remington rifle musket, improved model, for the use of the National Guard, the same is hereby approved and confirmed.

By order of the Commander-in-Chief,
J. B. STONEHOUSE, *Assistant Adjutant-General.*

The introduction of the new American breech-loader in Europe dates from the autumn of 1866. During the summer of this year a special commission was appointed by the Emperor of Austria to inspect and test the various systems of the new type of small arms. The commission, under the direction of the Arch-Duke William, commenced its work on the 20th of September. With the single exception of the United States Board at St. Louis, it is doubtful if any similar body of ordnance experts has ever prosecuted a trial as thorough and severe as did this Austrian Commission. The following extract from the official report will measurably suggest the exceeding harshness of the tests imposed:

"The trials of the Remington gun, marked No. 1, had for their principal object the testing of the breech with regard to its adaptation for military purposes, and with regard to its efficiency and durability under the different circumstances occurring in warfare. The arm was fired sixty rounds with the heaviest charges present, that is, containing seventy-five grains of English powder, forty rounds with cartridges of sixty grains of powder against a target 800 yards distant, and forty rounds with sixty grains of powder fired for

13

rapidity. With these one hundred and forty rounds there was no fault of any kind. The breech acted perfectly. The accuracy, as shown by annexed target, proved very good, and in firing for rapidity thirteen shots were fired per minute."

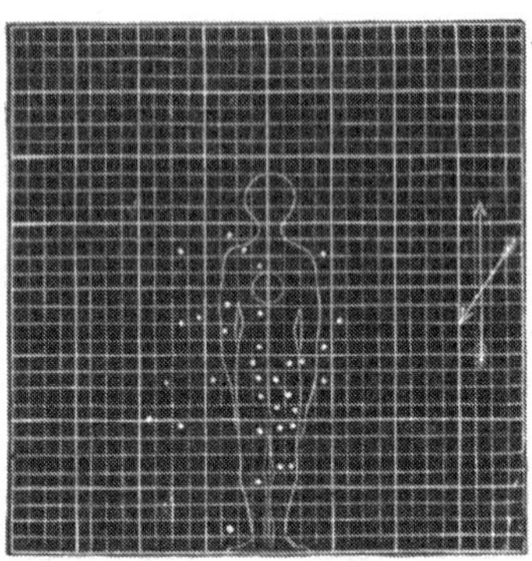

"The arm having been taken apart after this trial, showed no signs of wear in any part of the breech. It was put together without cleaning of any of its parts, and preserved for further trial. Second trial, September 21st, 1866. The firing for testing the durability of the breech was continued with cartridges of sixty grains. Eighty rounds were fired in one continuous series. One cartridge split lengthways without causing any difficulty in opening the breech and without covering the latter with dirt. The barrel having then been cooled by cold water poured through it, a further number of thirty rounds were fired, after which cartridges of forty-five grains were used, with which three hundred and four shots were fired. The barrel was cooled after each series of rounds by running cold water through it, and at last, after having fired four hundred and fourteen rounds, the whole gun, including the breech, was made wet and left in that state to ascertain the influence of rust upon the working parts. Third trial, September 22d, 1866. The gun left in a wet state on the previous day was taken apart and examined. All parts of the breech and lock were thickly covered with rust, but the working of the breech was not interfered with. The gun was put together without cleaning, and the trials continued in that state, in order to establish the influence of rust covering the breech and lock upon the firing of the gun. It was decided to fire two thousand rounds in all with this gun. Of these, six rounds were fired to measure the force of recoil in a special apparatus. The mean recoil was forty-eight pounds. Thirty rounds for rapidity without taking aim were made by an expert in one minute and fifty-two seconds, giving seventeen shots per minute. Thirty-four shots were fired in succession after the entire breech was covered with road dust, and fifty rounds after that without any difficulty occurring. The gun was thereupon covered with dust again and left exposed to the influence of damp air during one night. On the 28th of September, 1866, the gun was examined and it was found impossible to set the hammer at full cock. Having been taken apart, it was found that some sand had lodged itself between the breech-piece and the spring acting upon it, which caused the above-named obstruction. After removal of this sand, but without any further cleaning of the breech, the gun was put together and its action was again perfect. The trials were continued. Ten cartridges, which had been previously kept under water for a quarter of an hour, were fired without missing, and eight were fired at a wooden box filled with cartridges. The eighth shot hit the box, five were exploded, and the lid of the box thrown off thereby; of the rest, ten cartridges were squeezed in and spoiled; twenty-six were blackened outside;

all the rest remained intact. After completing the number of 2,000 rounds, seven cartridges having their ends purposely filed through and cut in different places, were fired, in order to ascertain the effect of the escaping gases upon the breech, in case of bursting of cartridges. The gun was for that purpose inserted in a rest. Five of the cartridges burst open and an escape of flame was observed at the breech, but the latter was not injured or thrown open. The final examination of all parts showed no perceptible wear of any of the parts of the breech and lock, the same having retained their original solidity and freedom of movement."

The determination of the Commission was an unequivocal recommendation of the system for adoption. Certain conditions affecting the first contract for 50,000 stand, and the difficulty of furnishing proper cartridges in the Imperial works, however, occasioned a delay which was permanently unfortunate. The local press took advantage of the temporary suspension to incite the prejudice of the army against the foreign invention, and to such effect, that despite the fact that the Remington was the first, and another American breech-loader the second in the preference of the Commission, an inferior Austrian system, the Wandl, was in the exigency adopted. It is hardly to be regretted that the practical Nemesis, sure to follow on such short-sighted action, has not made an exception of Austria, the Wandl having developed features of weakness and inefficiency that condemn it as a military arm.

Notwithstanding the unfortunate event of the Austrian episode, the Remington system was soon to commence a permanent European record. In April, 1867, the Kingdom of Denmark, revoking its decision previously expressed in favor of another American invention, formally adopted the Remington. The contract with this power was completed in the early part of the succeeding year, 42,000 stand having been furnished, since which time the production of the complement is understood to have been continued in the State arsenals, under royalty to the owners of the patents.

The Minister of War, in his report to the King, November 10th, 1868, in reference to the equipment of soldiers with new arms, says:

"The Battalions of the Line, the Reserve Battalions and the Life Guards, are now furnished with the Remington breech-loading rifles, and the Cavalry with the Remington carbines of the same model. These arms have been tried and have given a very satisfactory result. During the camp held last summer, eight battalions were armed with the Remington rifle, and it has answered expectations in every respect. The strength of the breech-loading system did not suffer in the least by use. The arm furnished most excellent target-shooting at 800 yards distance, and there is not the least doubt of its efficiency at 1,200 yards. The manipulation of the arm is altogether simple, the soldier rapidly learning and becoming expert in taking apart and re-assembling it. After a very short practice, the troops in camp attained, in some cases, to firing seventeen shots per minute, while fourteen and fifteen shots per minute were of common occurrence, the average rapidity of firing being 9 1-3 shots per minute, so that the Remington rifle can be confidently placed above all other known single-barrel breech-loaders."

That continued experience has not affected the original preference for this arm is evident from the subjoined passage of a recent letter written by a distinguished officer of the Danish War Department:

"COPENHAGEN, Nov. 21st, 1871.

"I do not need to say that the Danish Government is pleased with your arms, which have shown themselves to do perfect work in all respects, and are loved by all the soldiers."

The example of Denmark was almost immediately followed by the sister kingdom, Sweden, contracting the same year for 30,000 rifles, and subsequently for the right to manufacture in her royal armories. An order from the War Office, accompanying the issue of the arms, conveys the final endorsement of the Minister:

WAR DEPARTMENT, No. 282:

The Remington arm having been adopted as the new model-arm by the Swedish Government, consequent upon the most careful trials proceeded to before handing the new rifles to the army, I hereby certify:

That the said testings proved the Remington rifles to unite all those qualities that are required of a first-class arm. * * *

And that the War Department has had every reason to be entirely satisfied with the decree, in virtue of which the Remington arm was adopted for the Swedish army,

STOCKHOLM, May 31st, 1869. (Signed,) ABELIN.

In confirmation of this official *dictum*, recent letters from Stockholm report the earnest desire of the volunteers to be equipped with the arm which has become the universal favorite of the regular force.

In April, 1867, a Commission, designated by the War Secretary, was convened in England, to examine and test such breech-loading inventions as should be brought before it. The conditions, which made the Snider naval rifle a standard of maximum weight and length, and, without positively insisting, very strongly suggested the Boxer cartridge as the style of fixed ammunition, seem rather inconsistent with a simple study of the merits of systems. Of the 112 different arms entered, 74 were forthwith ruled out. The Remington, by good fortune, having a length of barrel within the limit of the ordnance conditions, was subjected with 37 others, to the test. At the first trial each gun was required to have a complement of 20 cartridges. In the immediate exigency, the representative of this system was obliged to use cartridges made in Birmingham, of miserable construction, and so illy adapted for the Remington arm, that, in frequent instances, it was necessary to force out the shell by the application of the ramrod. Notwithstanding this embarrassment, however, the arm was named as one of the nine to be subjected to a second and final trial. In the interval, each competitor being required to provide himself with 6,000 cartridges for the conclusive test, Mr. Remington had taken care to procure the necessary quantity from the United States. Upon presenting himself with ammunition thus fitted for his gun, he was informed that he must use the same with which the initial test had been conducted. An appeal to the War Office to be allowed the cartridges suited to the system was answered by a peremptory negative. Obliged to submit to a condition thus utterly inconsistent with the best development of his gun, and, it would certainly seem, with the thorough and impartial conduct of the Commission itself, the result need hardly be suggested. The issue of the prolonged trial has since been announced in the selection of the Martini-Henry for the British army, an arm thought worthy of adoption by no power in Europe except England. The remarks of a leading English army journal have a pertinent interest in this connection:

"It is not calculated to reassure public opinion that no other country endorses the estimate of merit which Lord Spencer's Committee attached to the Martini-Henry. In no country has gunnery found such a fair field and no favor, as in the United States; nor has any other country given such a stimulus to invention on this subject of breech-loading. But the American Commission place the Martini-Henry only fifth in their order of merit, and are unanimous in their recommendation of the 'Remington,' which our committee, in their first report of February, 1868, placed *eighth* on the list. In common with the Martini rifle, the Remington, according to that report, came to grief through defective cartridges, yet the committee,—goodness knows why,—never took the trouble of doctoring the 'Remington,' or any other mechanism as they did the Martini. One passage in the report of the American Commission, is worth noting. They say: 'Our investigations have been limited to the determination of the relative merits of the various systems of breech-loading small arms, without regard to questions of calibre, rifling, ammunition, etc. The main elements of excellence considered are strength, durability and simplicity of breech-mechanism; ease, certainty and rapidity of firing; and security against injury to arms, or accidents from use in the hands of troops.'

"The wisdom of this reasoning is obvious, and exhibits the blunder of our committee, who, composed almost entirely of musketry instructors and crack shots, naturally drifted into finding a first rate shooting barrel and a most indifferent breech-action. We do not consider the Remington action to be absolute perfection, but with the American officers, we consider it much superior to the Martini, and, had it been fondled and fostered with the same care, it would, like many others, have proved its title to be the better mechanism."

It is noteworthy that Switzerland, the native country of Martini, where he elaborated his principle, confessedly borrowed from the American Peabody, after an exhaustive trial, in which both the

Martini and the Remington were competitors, formally adopted the latter system. The contract for 100,000 stand required an almost immediate delivery of 10,000, which obliged the Messrs. Remington, then engaged to their full capacity upon their Danish and Swedish orders, to decline it, so that the service arm of Switzerland, with the exception of 15,000 stand, purchased during the Luxembourg excitement, in the United States, is the Vetterly instead of the Remington.

Cotemporaneously with the conclusion of the trial in England, the Government of Greece, with a view to re-equipment of its force, instituted an examination of different inventions at Paris. The result was a contract with the foreign representative of the Remington arm. A temporary suspension occurring, the officer detailed, Capt. Alexandros Fountouclis, distinguished for his professional ability, made a tour of Europe, and returning to Belgium, conducted most thorough experiments with this system, which resulted in a second report to his Government, re-asserting its superior excellence, and a new contract for 15,000 stand. From the exhaustive record of Capt. Fountouclis' series of tests, comprising the calibres and models of the arm adopted at that time by Denmark, Sweden, the Roman States, Spain and Egypt, the concluding summary is quoted:

Extracts from Report of the Hellenic Government by Captain Alexandros Fountouclis.

Advantages.

1st. The arm permits of rapid and easy firing.

2d. The working of the rifle is so simple that the most ignorant soldier becomes familiar with it in a short time.

3d. The required motions, either for opening the breech or for raising the hammer, are short and near the body, enabling the rifle to be loaded in double ranks, on horseback, or any other position.

The absence of all salient parts renders this easier. The hammer can be raised without looking away from the enemy. Without looking, and with one finger, the soldier can examine the respective positions of hammer and trigger.

4th. The extraction of the shell is easy, especially when the cartridge is greased or when it enters it loosely.

To extract the cartridge it is sufficient to elevate the muzzle a little and strike with the forefinger of the right hand, a rap on the front part on the block's chest.

5th. The mechanism is simple, stable, and very solid; not containing any part liable to get out of order, even after a prolonged firing.

6th. The rapidity of firing is very satisfactory.

7th. The arm is not liable to any important wear.

8th. A very remarkable advantage produced by the ingenious disposition of the various parts of the mechanism, is that the power tending to keep the breech-block closed during the fire, increases with that which tends to open it.

9th. The hammer can never strike the firing-pin, and consequently the cartridge cannot explode unless the breech is perfectly closed.

The arm offers, therefore, a perfect security to the soldier.

Certificate.

The undersigned, Commanding Captain of Belgian artillery, certifies having, by order of Lieutenant-Colonel, the Inspector of Weapons of War, and Director of the State Manufactory of Small Arms, united in rendering this report, and in the execution of the experiments and trials therein mentioned, carried out by Captain of the Hellenic staff, Alexandros Fountouclis.

LIEGE, 19th December, 1869. (Signed,) DELBRUYERE.

According to the instructions of the Minister of War, under date of June 1st, 1869, I have authorized the Captain of the Hellenic staff, Alexandros Fountouclis, to make at the State Manufactory of Arms, the trials and experiments contained in this report, with various models of the Remington system.

These trials have taken place according to programme established under my sanction and approval.

The Mechanical Engineer, Mr. Covin, has been charged to provide and look after all the material means, and Mons. Delbruyere, Commanding Captain of Artillery and Attaché to the Manufactory of Arms, has been appointed to assist Captain Fountouclis in the execution of the divers and numerous experiments mentioned in the foregoing report.

Lieutenant-Colonel of Artillery, Inspector of Weapons of War, and Director of the State Manufactory of Arms.

LIEGE, 20th December, 1869. (Signed,) GILLION.

The Government of Spain, whose adoption of the Remington system is the most recent foreign endorsement of the arm, conducted a trial of nearly all the inventions known to the ordnance world, which commenced before the revolution, and was finally concluded in the late summer of 1870. The Remington models, fifty in number, used in the trial, were constructed in the State Arsenals of Spain. So long and thorough an investigation of systems, engaging the earnest attention of the best professional ability of the Spanish service, it need hardly be suggested, at last produced a report upon small arms which is exemplary for the careful consideration and practical knowledge therein developed. The following summary of the decision concludes this document, which was signed the 24th of August, 1870, an interval of nearly two years having been consumed in the action of the Commission:

Extracts from the Report of the Royal Spanish Commission at Madrid.

Of all the arms entered, the Remington offers the most advantages for bayonet charges, on account of its length; is the third in weight, the second in the advantageous position of centre of gravity, and the fifth in number of parts; but if we consider the simplicity of the various parts, there can be no doubt that it offers less probabilities of getting out of order, and more facilities for examination and repairs.

In the rust trial the Remington proved superior to all, being the only one that, after the mechanism had been thoroughly rusted, was able to fire three consecutive shots; none of the others working at all.

Finally, in the defective shell trial, the Remington showed its superiority over all the others.

The greatest initial velocity was obtained by this arm, being 428 metres per second, at 30 metres from muzzle.

Its trajectory was the flattest of all, and offered a longer dangerous space than the others

The result of these lengthened trials has been to make manifest once more the superiority of the *Remington* arm over all other breech-loaders.

The results of the trials would of themselves be sufficient, without their being confirmed by the report received from Cuba, where more than thirty thousand are in campaign. This report made by a Board composed, for the greater part, of officers who had been in the field and witnessed the working of the gun, certifies in a most positive manner, the brilliant qualities of this arm, and its undoubted superiority over all others tried there,—among which are the Peabody, Sharps, Berdan (Russian), Palmer, Gallagher, Spencer, and others.

It reports the many positive advantages it possesses, and its freedom from inconveniences; and above all, the successful experience had with it in a climate much more severe and trying than our mild one.

It is, therefore, a source of congratulation to see our report of the trials in perfect harmony with the practical results obtained in Cuba.

The *Remington system is therefore approved by this Board, for the use of Infantry and Cavalry.*

MADRID, 24th August, 1870.

To His Excellency the Director-General of Artillery.

(Signed,) Brig.-Gen. CAYETANO FIGUEROA, *Vice President.*
Col. ENRIQUE BUELTA, *Secretary.*

ROYAL DECREE OF MARCH 24th, 1871.

EXCELLENCY: After carefully examining the results of the numerous experiments carried out by the Board named on the 1st of January, 1868, and the report that the Board of Directors make on their extensive trials, the King has been pleased to resolve:

That the two models of rifle and carbine Remington accompanying this, and which have been duly sealed by this Ministry, be held as the *standard models for the small arm of the various services of the army;* it being besides, the desire of His Majesty, that the Arsenal should proceed at once with the manufacture of said arms.

Which royal determination I communicate to you for your guidance.

MADRID, 24th March, 1871.

To His Excellency the Director-General of Artillery.

(Signed,) SERRANO, *Minister of War.*

During the prolonged session of the Royal Commission in Spain, the exigencies of war in Cuba had subjected the system to a service trial, imposing tests naturally severer than those which suggest themselves to an official board, in this instance rendered especially demonstrative by the character of the country and climate. Of this actual service experience with the Remington arm, the *New York Army and Navy Journal*, under date of January 13th, 1872, remarked, in a review of the business exhibit recently issued by the Company:

"The documentary portion of this exhibit is made up of abstracts and summaries of reports, issuing from Commissions of the several Governments which have adopted the arm Among the latest is the *dictum* of Spain, made through a Board of officers distinguished for scientific and experimental knowledge. This body consumed something more than two years in an inspection and trial of a very large number of inventions, including the American Peabody, Sharp's, Berdan, Spencer, Gallagher, and Palmer. The official tests were of the severest character, anticipating every incident of service. But the Remington arm was meanwhile being tried by Spain under more *exigeant* conditions than any which an official military commission could impose. More than 30,000 guns of this system had been previously to and during the session of the Commission purchased and issued to Spanish troops fighting in Cuba. Here, where the humidity of the climate exercises what may be termed a corroding influence upon any mechanism at all exposed, and where the combatants on both sides were to a large extent unused to the manipulation of breech-loaders, the arm had shown itself proof against a perspiring atmosphere, and the rough handling of untaught negroes, and raw Catalans as well. The abstract of the Cuban report to the Commission above referred to, is subjoined:

"'The Brigade or Committee of officers appointed by the General Sub-Inspector of this Military Division, composed of those mentioned in the margin, having assembled under the presidency of Brigadier-General Don Eduardo Seguera, this officer declared to them that the object of their meeting was to consider and report upon the best war arm to be adopted and selected out of those called breech-loaders, and that have been used in the present Cuban campaign.

"'In consequence thereof, the Committee proceeded at once to the study and close examination of all and every one of the weapons, taking as point of departure the proceedings of the nine different Sub-Committees that from time to time have made experiments on the Remington gun of 11 mill.; *the result of which was its adoption for the army on this Island.*

"'They likewise made trials with the Peabody, Sharps 4th, Berdan (Russian model), Miller, Palmer, Gallagher, Spencer, and other systems of repeating or single-shot guns, as well for infantry as cavalry.

"'Not only were all and every one of the above-mentioned systems closely inspected and examined and tried so as to form the best possible idea of their merits and ballistic qualities, but all the models generally known in Europe and the principal ones in North America that could be procured were also submitted to the same trials.

"'In order to ascertain the qualities of each system, it was resolved to ask the opinion of all the superior officers of infantry or artillery, who, during the last eighteen months' campaign, had had the command of troops armed with breech-loaders of whatever description, commanding them to report on the same, and to state the result of their experiments.

"'These reports having been carefully examined, independently of information gathered from other sources, the Brigade, or Committee of officers has come to the conclusion that the Remington gun of 11 mill. calibre is by common consent and the general opinion of natives and foreigners, that which unites most of the conditions requisite for a war arm, and that the same qualification is applicable to the carbine and pistol to be used by cavalry, the rifle carbine and pistol being loaded with central-fire cartridges.

"'*Experience has shown that system is not liable to get out of order, notwithstanding the rough handling to which in war it must be submitted; that shots with it never fail; that its mechanism is so simple and so perfect that several divisions of the army have voluntarily adopted it during the present campaign and made use of it with facility and without accident, notwithstanding the soldier had not time or leisure to be properly instructed in the handling of the weapon.*

"'The result of the trials has been, that though the cartridge may explode or burst, yet the breech mechanism still remains unchanged; a circumstance of the highest importance, and which makes the weapon comparatively preferable to all others of its class.

"'The firing is not only certain but precise, the sighting being so well graduated that the middling marksman invariably hits the target, to which condition of the Remington gun is owed the fact that the soldier who has once used it has unlimited confidence in his arm.

"'The Secretary of the Committee, Colonel Don Francisco Rull, says in his report, that having been in command of his battalion during *the whole year of the present campaign, his men have constantly used the Remington gun without his having experienced one single case of failure either in the system or in the gun itself.*

"'The Committee is finally of the opinion that *the Remington system is in every respect the best, and that which unites all the conditions requisite for war.*

Signed at Havana, this 25th of April, 1870.

Col. FRANCISCO RULL, Secretary, Col. ENRIQUE BARBAZA,
Col NARCISO HERRERA DAVILA, Brig.-Gen. EDUARDO SEGUERA, Pres.'"

The following documents, emanating from the Corps of Artillery and Engineers of the Spanish Regular force, and from the Chief of the Civil Guard, indicate the unanimous sentiment of the army in Cuba:

DEPARTMENT OF ARTILLERY OF THE ISLAND OF CUBA.

Don Juan de Ojeda y Alcarny, Colonel of Artillery, decorated with the grand, and also with the inferior cross of San Hermenegildo and with two of San Fernando; also Commander of Isabel la Catolica, and with other marks of honor for deeds of war; Director of the Arsenal of this Island, whose Sub-Inspector is General Antonio Venenc, decorated with the grand cross of San Hermenegildo and that of Isabel la Catolica; Commander of the, same and also twice honored with the decoration of San Fernando, and many others on account of deeds of war, &c., &c., &c.

Certify,—That the ten thousand Remington rifles, purchased from Messrs. E. Remington & Sons, of Ilion, New York, United States of America, have been received in this arsenal, in complete and satisfactory state of construction; and that in the battalions of the army, where these arms have been tried, they have proven their superior quality, both as regards precision and strength. These arms have been so favorably received by all who have had occasion to use them, that many corps of volunteers are desirous to procure them. Wherefore, at the request of these gentlemen, and by order of His Excellency, I do thus certify.

HAVANA, March 19th, 1869.

(Signed,) JUAN DE OJEDA,
[L. S.]
Approved,
(Signed,) ANTONIO VENENC,
[L. S.] *General of Artillery.*

INSPECTION OF VOLUNTEERS OF THE ISLAND OF CUBA.

I certify that the excellence of the Remington guns has been proven, not only as regards the simplicity of their mechanism and the facility of their manipulation, but likewise in respect to their precision and strength; and that the volunteers of this island have therefore hastened to supply themselves with a very large number of them. The result obtained, from practical tests, has been highly satisfactory, and these arms are much preferred to any others.

HAVANA, March 23d, 1869.

The Sub-Inspector General,
(Signed,) RAFAEL CLAVIJO,
[L. S.] *Chief of Engineers.*

CIVIL GUARD.

Eugenio Lono y Montano, Colonel of Infantry and First Chief of the Section of the Civil Guard of this Island: I hereby certify that the Remington gun, used by the companies of the Institute, is an arm of great strength in its construction; and that up to this date, notwithstanding its frequent use, not the slightest change has been observed therein. The mechanism of the gun is so simple, that the soldier can readily be taught its effective use. I am of the opinion that in battle, this gun must be far superior to any other yet known, since it can be loaded with ease and expedition, discharged with great rapidity, and besides this, the deviation of the ball is so insignificant that the marksman can acquire a precision in his aim that cannot be arrived at when using other guns, lately invented, including those of the * * * system. I base this opinion on experiments made by members of the Section, as well as on the unanimous voice of the Chiefs of the Divisions of the same. And in justice to the manufacturers of the gun (Messrs. E. Remington & Sons). I hereby sign the present in Havana, the 28th day of March, 1869.

(Signed,) EUGENIO LONO,
[L. S.] *Chief of Civil Guard.*

The foregoing record of Spanish experience with the Remington system of arms is happily endorsed by a distinguished American soldier, holding a high command in the Patriot Army. The communication which follows seems to have been specially suggested by the points of the Spanish-Cuban report:

NEW YORK, December 1st, 1871.

To Messrs. E. Remington & Sons, Ilion, N. Y.:

GENTLEMEN: My attention having been called to the published report of a board of Spanish officers of the experience of their service in Cuba with the Remington fire-arms, I take pleasure in saying that my experience upon the same field, both in the use of and in collision with the same arms, warrants me in confirming all that those officers say of the efficiency and admirable qualities of your rifles and carbines as weapons of war.

The rifle used in the Spanish army in Cuba is of the caliber .43, and is, above all the weapons I ever met, most notable for its precision and certainty of aim. It is, *par excellence*, the arm of precision. Frequently the Cubans used to capture this arm, which was much dreaded in the hands of their adversary, and the capture was always a matter of peculiar satisfaction, because of the highly-prized character of the gun.

The rifle and carbine, which had been purchased in this city for the Cubans, were altered arms, and cheaper, being of the caliber of .58. These were thoroughly tested under my own eyes for a period of eleven months, under every disadvantage, and throughout the excellence of the arm was demonstrated. Nowhere else, in active service, in my belief, has any fire-arm been subjected to such trying tests as the Remington rifles in Cuba, both by Spanish and Cuban troops, taking into consideration the warm, damp, corrosive climate and the character of the men who handled them — very often negroes, who had never before been used to handle a gun of any sort. The mechanism proved as strong and enduring as simple and easy working. Scarcely any sort of hard usage or any degree of moisture impaired its efficiency. Other breech-loading arms were in use both by Cubans and Spaniards, but none gave the same degree of satisfaction.

In close observation of the Remington arm, under circumstances daily of the keenest solicitude, when a single fire-arm in thoroughly effective condition, more or less, was a matter of great importance to me, I could discover no defect in it.

Respectfully, your obedient servant,
THOMAS JORDAN.

Previously to the adoption of the Chassepot by the French Government, in August, 1866, initial trials of a satisfactory character having been made with the Remington system, a sufficient number of arms were ordered to be made in the United States to admit of such exhaustive tests as could warrant a determination of the matter. The unavoidable delay, however, in the delivery of the arms, necessitated the decision of the Government in favor of the Chassepot, a conclusion probably likewise affected by the existing difficulty in the production of suitable metallic ammunition. A distinguished French officer of ordnance, in a little work criticising the defaults of the national armament, published about the commencement of the Franco-Prussian war, observes of this circumstance: "This last arm, known too late to the Emperor, through trials at Biarritz and at Compiegne, balanced for an instant the fortune of the Chassepot; but the latter, backed by influential partizanship, was, after all, the final victor." In a foot-note the writer thus refers to the success of the Remington in the Vienna trials: "A characteristic anecdote was first at this time current, for the truth of which, however, I cannot vouch: 'Very well, Prince,' said the Emperor one day to M. De Metternich, 'what is going on in Austria?' 'Your Majesty,' replied the Minister, 'we are trying the Remington!' 'The Remington; pardon me, what is that?' Inquiry having thus been suggested, it was discovered that this arm had been for some months at the Artillery Bureau, but that no one had spoken of it to the Emperor.

So far as the general preference of the French Government has been manifested, with the single exception above noted, it has been strongly in favor of the Remington system. Its repeated endorsement by the ordnance officers in view of a Grecian re-armament, has been already stated. About the same time a committee of English, Belgian and French officers, proposing to raise a fund to equip the troops of the Papal States, consulted the French Government, which again strongly recommended this arm. To the application of a Chinese Commission, the same favorable report was made.

In 1868 the Vice-Royalty of Egypt requested the French Minister of War to select a board of experts from his command to aid the Egyptian General-in-Chief, who had been sent to Europe to determine upon an arm. This Commission was organized under the direction of Col. Nessler, an accomplished officer of infantry, and prosecuted its investigation of the merits of various inventions for more than six months, in the presence of the Egyptian envoy, General Ratib Pasha. The Remington was the arm finally selected from a large list of competitors, conspicuous among which were the Chassepot, the Martini-Henry and the Peabody. The Viceroy thereupon visiting Europe in person, efforts were made on the part of several parties interested in the competition, to have the trial resumed; but the Egyptian ruler concluded to defer to the action of the Commission and the opinion of his son. On the 30th of June, 1869, a contract was signed in England for 60,000 Remington rifles, which were delivered during the succeeding twelvemonth. The construction of this complement was superintended in the United States by Colonel Minie. This distinguished officer, occupying a responsible position upon the Egyptian Military Staff, has repeatedly communicated to

Messrs. E. Remington & Sons the general satisfaction with which the system is regarded by the rank and file of the Viceroy's army.

It has been observed from the foregoing relation of the facts regarding the re-armament of several powers that have applied to France for advice, that the sentiment of the professional authorities of that nation has been invariably favorable to the Remington. The adoption of the Chassepot in 1866 was the incident of an apparently imperative exigency, and the choice was actually made out of no competition at all, there being but two other entries, one of which was an improvised modification of the successful arm. In every subsequent trial, the results have been highly favorable to the American breech-loader, the last one, conducted just before the late war, concluding in a recommendation of its adoption for the mounted force of the French army. The names of Nessler and Minie are too well known, to necessitate any suggestion of the value attaching to their endorsement of the system. There may be added, however, to these names of practical and thorough military scientists the more conspicuous one of a French Marshal.

At the Imperial Exposition of 1867, the United States, and several European countries, were represented by large contributions of war material, comprising not only siege and field ordnance and general munitions, but the latest types of small arms. The sentiment of the Commissioners controlling the Industrial Palace was adverse to any consideration of this feature of the exhibition — it has been suggested on account of the paucity of the French contribution. "The fruit of peaceful civilization, it was designed that the Exhibition should remain true to its object. Founded upon progress in peace, it was not thought proper to extend a friendly hand to engines of destruction." Against this rather narrow construction of the purposes of the gathering of a whole world's resources, the Governments represented protested with such force of argument, urging the cost incurred by inventors and manufacturers in the preparation of models as well as the fallacious inspiration of the International Jury, that the Emperor decided to form a High Commission, under the presidency of Field Marshal Canrobert, and composed of general officers of different nations, to whom was assigned the duty of examining, classifying and reporting upon the army material sent to the Exposition. In accordance with the Imperial order, the Ministers of War and Marine named the following members:

MM. DE FAILLY, General of Division, Aide-de-Camp of the Emperor.

FORGEOT, General of Division, Member of Ordnance Board.

GUIOD, General of Division, Member of the Ordnance Board.

LABROUSSE, Vice-Admiral.

FRÉBAULT, General of Division, Chief of Ordnance of the Navy.

VIGO-ROUSSILLON, Military Intendant, Professor in the Imperial Staff School.

RIBOURT, General of Brigade, Superintendent of the Imperial Staff School, Secretary.

And the following foreign officers, sent by their respective governments, were added :

ENGLAND.—Col. Younghusband, of the Royal Artillery.

AUSTRIA.—Col. Von Ebner, of the Engineers.

BELGIUM.—Capt. Vautier, of the Artillery.

SPAIN.—Gen. De Elorza, of the Artillery.

ITALY.—Col. Mattei, of the Artillery.

HOLLAND.—Major Van Sousbeeck, of the Artillery.

PRUSSIA.—Major Von Burg, Military Attaché of the Prussian Embassy.

RUSSIA.—Gen. Gadolin, and Col. De Novitzky, Military Attaché of the Russian Embassy in London.

SWEDEN.—Major Staaf, Military Attaché of the Swedish Legation.

Thus was constituted a sort of International Military Jury, on the pattern of the Jury of the Exposition.

The war contribution, thus recognized as a legitimate feature, was divided into twenty-one classes, the first class including small arms under the title *Armes Portatives.* The collection under this class was very comprehensive, England having sent, among other inventions, the Medford carbine, the new Whitworth rifle, and the Martini-Henry ; Austria the Wandl ; Belgium the Albini ; and the United States the Joslyn, Peabody, Spencer, Wesson and Remington. The report of the Commission, a very large volume of 630 pages, presents a most thorough study of the progress of destructive invention. Its determination of the relative merits of the small arms entered was in favor of the Remington.

" This arm, very remarkable for its accuracy at long ranges, its strength, and the almost unalterable working of its parts, enjoys like the preceding (another American system), and perhaps to a much greater degree, general favor. The action of the extractor is sure and efficacious; it may be fired twelve times per minute."

As a material evidence of this official endorsement, the European representative of the arm received for the Messrs. Remington, from the hands of the Marshal, the silver medal of the Exposition, the trophy of the highest class awarded to military and sporting arms.

In the summer and fall of 1870, the terrible exigency of France demanding an immediate reinforcement of her armories, a contract was concluded between the Provisional Government and E. Remington & Sons for the construction of 50,000 stand of rifles, speedily followed by an order for their entire production. The extraordinary resources of the establishment were exercised to their extreme capacity, and a result was attained which, it is belived, has no precedent in the record of arms manufacture. A leading industrial journal,* alluding to this episode in the history of the Remington enterprise, embodies the following facts of practical interest:

"The fall of 1870 doubtless witnessed in the Ilion armory a larger number of men employed, a greater daily production and a more earnest concentration of thoughts and energies upon one object, than the small arms business in this or any other country had ever known. The contract with the French Government was commenced about the middle of September. The final installment was shipped in the first week of the succeeding May. During the seven months inclusive, from September 21st to the latter date, the number of service arms of its own production furnished and shipped to French ports from the Ilion armory, was about 155,000, a total result altogether unprecedented in the history of similar transactions. The arms composing this total were divided among the following classes: 130,000 rifles of .43 calibre; 5,000 carbines, and 20,000 transformations. The *Army and Navy Journal* remarks of this great industrial achievement, 'the resources of the great armory have, of course, been taxed to the utmost. The buildings devoted to small arms manufacture have, for twenty hours of each working day, been crowded with workmen, from 1,300 to 1,400 employees having been all the time engaged. The largest daily production has been 1,400 rifles (our contemporary's figures are not large enough, each of the last three day's product having been 1,530 stand of rifles, with 1,300 stand on each of the fifteen working days preceding), "and about 200 revolvers, and the monthly pay roll amounted to from $138,000 to $140,000.'"

"In September, at the reception of the order from France, the capacity of the armory, working double gangs, was equal to the production of a little over 500 stand of new arms and 200 transformations. Thenceforth the effort was general not only to sustain the original figures, but to provide machines and tools for a much larger production. Three months saw the daily total handsomely enlarged. By the end of five months the number of new arms turned out in each twenty hours reached 1,000. We have already noted the culminating daily results at the close of the contract."

---

* *The Iron Age*, New York, March 7th, 1872.

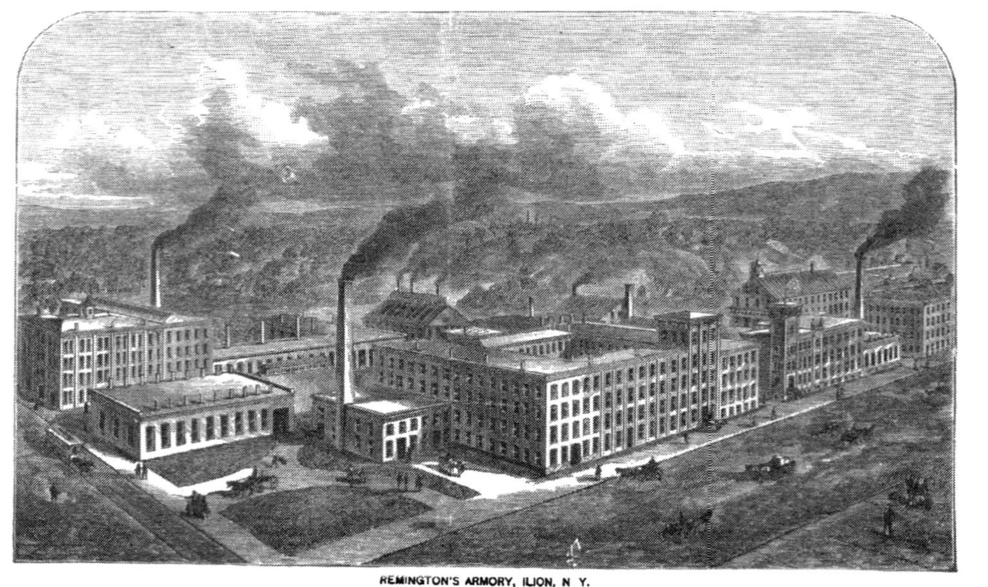

REMINGTON'S ARMORY, ILION, N Y.

The present establishment at Ilion, a thriving village of some three thousand population, located on the line of the New York Central Railroad, in Herkimer County, about eighty miles west of the State capital, Albany, was originated in 1825 by Mr. Eliphalet Remington. In 1816 the singular good fortune which had succeeded the crude essay of the founder, then a youth just reaching maturity, at the construction of a barrel for a fowling-piece, with only the simple appliances of a disused farm-forge, inspired him to enter upon the manufacture of small arms as a life occupation. Pursuing his humble work for nine years as a handicraft at the starting point upon his father's farm, the excellence of his gun-barrels having meanwhile secured a reputation throughout the country, he in the year 1825 was able to purchase a large tract of land and erect the first structure of the present armory. The journal previously quoted, narrates the subsequent progress of the industry:

"In 1825, the Erie Canal having been made through the valley of the Mohawk, Mr. Remington, after a few years' hard experience of the difficulty of conducting his growing business at so considerable a distance from that thoroughfare, with wise prevision of the future, purchased a large tract of land where now stands Ilion. His first erection, a low one-story building, is included in the present forging-shop. The variety and capacity of plant for some years was not increased to any great extent, though the distinct business of barrel-making experienced a natural and healthy growth. In 1835, the establishment of Ames & Co., of Springfield, Mass., which had a United States contract for a number of thousands of carbines, wishing to dispose of a portion of its award then uncompleted, and of its gun-finishing machinery, Mr. Remington became the purchaser of both contract and plant. At this time, his first government contract necessitating an increase of shop capacity, he erected a frame building of considerable size for that day, which is still standing, and known as "the old armory." Before finishing the carbine order, the enterprise of the rising establishment was encouraged by the reception of another contract—this time for 5,000 Harper's Ferry rifles. Tools were forthwith made or bought, and the work proceeded with, still another contract for 5,000 similar arms coming before the first was finished. At this date (1835 to 1840), the machine plant amounted to four milling machines, one stocking machine and one turning lathe, the fixtures or tools having to be changed as occasion demanded. About 1840, two of Mr. Remington's sons coming of age, became active in the enterprise.

"The accession of his two elder sons to the business gave the founder a temporary respite, grateful enough, we may well believe, after such a quarter of a century of endeavor and achievement.

"The award of a third contract—this time for 2,500 Harper's Ferry rifles and for a quantity of Maynard's magazine locks—was the first fruits of the new management and an initial trip to Washington.

"In 1847 the Remingtons commenced the construction of pistols, their first effort being a pocket revolver, which from its simplicity and general efficiency, secured a market at once. A short time anterior to the rebellion in 1861, they began to produce their well-known army and navy revolver, since adopted for both branches of the United States service. The company now turns out eighteen different sizes and patterns of holster and other pistols, from the terribly effective single-shot arm of .50 calibre, of a breech-loading system similar to the rifle, to the vest pocket companion, a toy weighing but three and a half ounces, yet in the hands of an expert marksman true enough to kill a squirrel at fifty feet.

"The establishment of E. Remington & Sons (Mr. Remington, the founder, died in 1861), exclusively devoted to the production of small arms, has, of course, very largely increased in capacity since the Danish and Swedish contracts first brought the new military arm into prominence. The structures in which this branch of the business is pursued, though erected at intervals, present an architectural *ensemble* far from disagreeable to the eye, an effect by no means lessened by the pleasant village surroundings in the midst of which they stand. They cover, including the pistol department, from three and a half to four acres of ground. The motive force is furnished by three principal engines, aggregating 400-horse. The number of operators averages about 1.000, though the machine plant as now perfected would probably provide work for double this number. The superficial area of the armory, estimating the floor space of the immense four-story buildings that constitute it, is very nearly equal to fifteen acres. A detailed description of the several departments, though practically interesting, is not within the scope of this article. It may be said, however, that every feature of construction has here subsidized all that scientific and mechanical achievement can contribute, each operation, from the first subjection of the steel mould in the rolling-mill, to the ultimate equipment of the barrel with stock and breech-system in the assembling-room, being effected by the most improved artificial device, the direction of the most thorough skill and experience. It need hardly be suggested that such extraordinary results as are above recorded, results absolutely unique in the history of manufacture, required not merely organization, but earnest individual co-operation on the part of all engaged, whether principals or employees. We do not know that the organization at the Remington armory is oppressively exacting, that a grinding discipline absorbs every breath of labor—in fact, we fancy there are many large es'ablishments in which the workmen are much more enslaved by system and supervision. There is, however, sometimes a something more exacting than organization, or system, or supervision. In this instance, indeed, it is a something infinitely more creditable to the humanity of labor than either or all of these forces. The great armory at Ilion, is, in fact, but a great family--and this, indeed, may be truly enough said of the whole busy village, every member, every citizen of which owns an interest, at least of good wishes, in the general prosperity. While the Remingtons are sole owners of buildings and machinery, the work is given out by contract. Each contractor, of whom there are more than thirty in all, has his particular job, hires his own gang of men, and executes his work, whether it be on the barrel, the stock or some part of the system, to exact gauges, of which one set remains in the hands of the company, and the other is kept carefully in his own little office, his sole care being to sustain his branch of production upon a base with the general result. The direct issue of such a division of labor is that it equalizes or disseminates interest, and is a constant spur to endeavor in its various shapes, every little while bringing out of some clever brain a tool or a process by which operations may be reduced in number, or helping the enterprising *sub* to realize better results from his gang of artisans.

The system of labor as above suggested is certainly better calculated to answer such imperious exigencies as that of France in 1870, than any other could be. It does not turn out an individual arm as speedily perhaps as a single expert gunsmith might, but it turns out a thousand in less time by far than the same number of smiths, separately employed, would dare to think of doing. Thus, while it would be possible to take one of the molds of excellent steel, piled up in the rolling-mill, and have the gun-barrel completed in three hours, a careful estimate gives thirty-three days as the average time in which the mold goes through its eighty-three distinct operations and reaches the assembling-room in the shape of a gleaming tube of .50 calibre ready to be issued to the National Guard. It is, however, not the single mold but the pile of a thousand, more or less, that the barrel-making gang, in all its various branches, has to consider, and both long experience and wise economy show that this dissemination of work and multiplicity of operations effects the quickest aggregate at the smallest cost.

From 1835 to 1840, we find, by recurring to the early part of our sketch, that the entire machine stock of the Remington establishment comprised one turning lathe, one stocking and four milling machines, and that the fixtures and tools had to be changed about as occasion demanded. In those days barrels were forged and welded into shape. Now in the rolling-mill each furnace turns out from 300 to 350 barrels per day at the hands of four men. If we follow the barrel department through, we shall find that this branch of the establishment alone, when at full head, has at work about a score of milling machines, forty-six drilling machines of various capacity and speed, thirty-one lathes and nine rifling machines, not to mention a legion of other labor devices, whose names have escaped our memoranda. A hasty estimate gives the number of milling machines alone, used in the establishment, at over four hundred.

"As in most large workshops, there are in use at the Ilion armory several processes special to the establishment. The courtesy due to the company which has furnished us the means of giving our readers a general idea of the extent and organization of this representative American industry, forbids a particular description of mechanical resources, the origin and uses of which are private property. Suffice it that the long and intelligent experience of the Remingtons and of their artisans, many of them a second generation of the same family in the employ of the company, has achieved large results in the mechanical features of their work, as well in the economizing of operations as in the lessening their number. There are especial features of the Ilion work which we can not err, however, in noting particularly. The excellent shooting qualities of the barrels made at their establishment, have been from the era of the founder a proverb in mouths of wisest censure. This superiority has been, moreover, quite as generally observed in the barrels of the military as of the sporting rifles. It is possible that a degree of this excellence may be due to choiceness of material, but the extraordinary care given to the interior finish, the delicate gauging of the chambers, and the exact turning of muzzles, and, more than all, the patient and faithful straightening process, which is never neglected, are probably the general claimants in this instance. The operation of straightening a barrel, an achievement as yet unattained by mechanical process, is one of the most difficult in the manufacture of a gun, an art so rare in fact that accident has often produced a guinea Brummagem fowling-piece that would outshoot a Wesley Richards, or Greener, in the same field. The Remingtons, with an honorable pride in the excellence of their productions, and correctly estimating the superlative importance of this quality in a barrel, have omitted no care, whether it concerns the experience and skill of artisans, or the severity of intermediate and final inspection, that will secure the merit of precision for their work."

In 1864 the business at Ilion had attained such proportions as to render a new organization imperative, as well for the purpose of perpetuating it, as of more easily controlling the multiplicity and extent of its operations. The private firm, still including only the sons of the founder, was accordingly made into a company, under the general law of the State of New York. The incorporation, legally known as E. Remington & Sons, dates from January 1st, 1865. The first officers were Philo Remington, President; Samuel Remington, Vice-President, and Eliphalet Remington, Secretary and Treasurer. In 1866, in anticipation of Mr. Samuel Remington's going to Europe, he was chosen president in order to more fully represent the company in the Old World. At this time Mr. Philo Remington became Vice-President. In the summer of 1870, Colonel

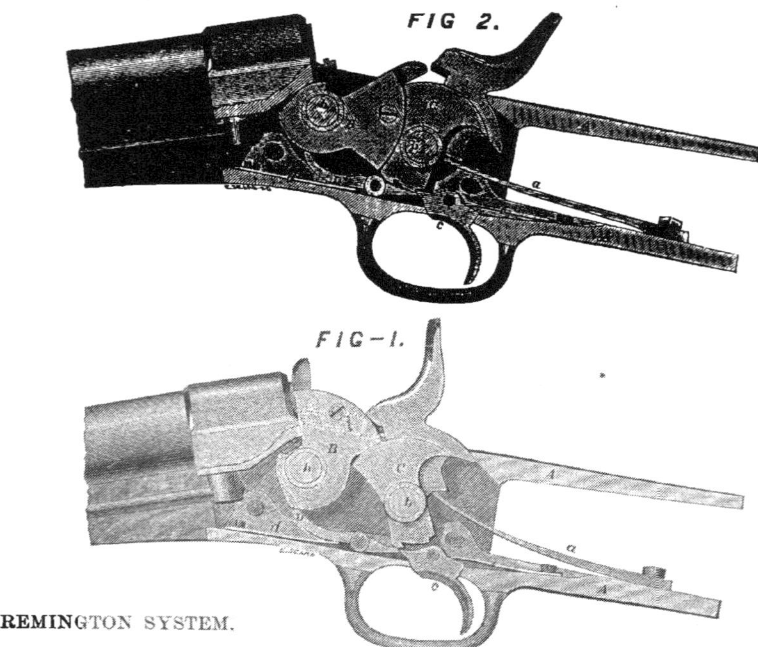

REMINGTON SYSTEM.

W. C. Squire, to whose large executive ability and fine business tact are due no small measure of the more recent triumphs of the establishment, was elected secretary of the organization. This gentleman being a son-in-law of Philo Remington, all the offices are retained in the family. The nominal capital of the company was named at $1,000,000, the value of the buildings, machinery and stock in progress having been moderately estimated at $1,500,000. The entire stock of the company at the date of incorporation was—and still is—owned by the different individuals of the Remington family, with the exception of a few hundred dollars in amount, necessary by law to qualify the three other members of the board of seven trustees, all of whom are residents of Ilion. The present valuation of buildings, machinery and stock ranges from $2,750,000 to $3,000,000.

DESCRIPTION OF SYSTEM.

The mechanical construction of the breech-system of the Remington arm is plainly shown in the accompanying wood-cuts, figure 1, exhibiting the system with breech-block and hammer closed, and figure 2 with those parts open in position for loading. The simplicity of the system, the largeness of its parts and their peculiarly natural operation, it is thought, avoid the necessity of more elaborate and distinct illustration.

The receiver, composed of frame and guard-strap (AA), is a substantial housing of wrought iron, case-hardened, the sides of which are 28-100 inch in thickness. This frame, containing the lock and action, is closed at the bottom by the guard-strap, which is firmly secured in its place by two screws. The butt-stock is morticed for the reception of the end of the guard-strap (lower A) and tang of frame (upper A), tenoned into the receiver, and fastened by a tang-screw passing through the stock vertically from tang to guard-strap. The front part of the receiver is the chamber, 1½ inches in length, into which the barrel is screwed. The fore-stock is secured to the barrel by a recoil-stud upon the under side of the latter.

The constituent parts of the action are the breech-block (B) and pin (b); hammer (C) and pin (b); main-spring (a) and screw; trigger (c), trigger-spring (e) and screw; locking-lever (D), locking-lever spring (d) and screw; firing-pin (f) and screw. The extractor, not indicated by a letter, is seen in figure 2, engaging in a slot in the shoulder of the breech-block. The end of the ramrod screws into a ramrod-stud, similarly shown in the cuts.

The breech-block and hammer are solid pieces of fine steel, 69-100 of an inch thick, pivoted upon pins of the same material 46-100 in diameter. These pins pass entirely through the sides of the frame, and are held in place by the button screwed on to its left exterior side. The main-spring, trigger-spring, locking-lever and locking-lever spring are all of steel, the springs having the simplest possible curves, and the action of the main-spring upon the hammer being direct. The function of the locking-lever is two-fold, one of its offices being to lock the trigger, so that it cannot escape from its notch in the tumbler, when the breech-block is opened, and a second to secure the breech-block when closed by the force, directly transmitted, of the lever-spring (d). It should be remarked that the whole of the lock work of this system, with the exception of the hammer, is attached to the guard-strap, which is thus by a very ingenious construction made to subserve the double purpose of guard-strap and lock-plate.

The extractor works in a recess cut in the left interior of the chamber, and is operated by means of a projection on its lower face, which engages with the shoulder of the breech-block, so that the act of swinging back the block withdraws the empty cartridge-case by an entirely positive motion, independent of spring or indirect agent, a mode of extraction distinguished for its simplicity, smoothness and certainty of operation.

The firing-pin works through the breech-block, as indicated by the dotted lines at *f*. It is forced against the primer by the sudden shock of the hammer, which is imparted through the direct action of the strong and very slightly curved main-spring, so that a misfire is impossible with cartridges properly made and fitted to the chamber.

The operation of this arm is especially simple. To load the piece, the hammer is first brought to full cock, and the breech-piece swung back by pressing the thumb-piece with the thumb of the right hand. The backward motion of the breech-block withdraws the discharged shell from the chamber, and if this motion is executed quickly, with the muzzle of the arm slightly elevated, the case will fall out without necessitating the use of the fingers. The fresh cartridge is then inserted, and the breech closed in one continuous motion. The arm is then ready to fire.

The successive stages of improvement by which the present excellence of this breech-system has been reached, are indicated in the opening pages of this chapter. In the carbine first tried at Springfield, in 1865, the motive of the invention was apparent, though crudely considered and very imperfectly adapted. The successful result witnessed in the improved arm, so far from being an initial triumph, has been wrought out only through patient study and thorough experiment. And now that the award of so many official trials has been honorably certified by the crucial test of actual service, beneath different flags and under conditions of climate, military organization and individual usage, more extreme and varied than any other modern arm has been subjected to, the theory upon which this system is constructed may justly claim attention.

FEATURES OF CONSTRUCTION.

The mechanical characteristics of the system are its simplicity, manifest in the small number of parts and their direct action; its solidity and strength, due to the extraordinary size of parts and the relation of each part to its fellows and to the whole action; durability, secured by the foregoing features and by the general design, which in the highest degree prohibits the entrance of gas to the action, offers the least possible frictional surface to the rusting effect of humidity, and, if sand or dust is admitted, ejects it freely from the working principle.

SIMPLICITY.

The simplicity of the system, so far as it consists in the number of parts, may be appreciated, in its comparative importance, by a study of the official reports of the United States Commission of 1870. Of the various arms represented at St. Louis, the entire number of mechanical details in each one of the most prominent, is thus stated:

			No. of Parts
Remington,		carbine,	51
"	(U. S. .50)	rifle,	55
"	(Spanish .43)	"	55
"	(Schofield's half-cock)	"	55
Peabody (Wessely)		"	66
"	(Spanish)	"	60

		No. of Parts.
Peabody (U. S. transformed)	"	64
" (Roumanian)	"	59
" (self-cocking)	"	67
" (Wessely)	"	65
Allin (U. S.)	"	62
Sharps (Hartford)	"	78
Martini-Henry,	"	61
"	"	62
Ward-Burton,	"	59
"	"	57

It is worthy of remark that this relative superiority has not been attained by the sacrifice of a single mechanical incident essential to the effectiveness of the organization, nor has it been the mere purpose of designer and fabricant to construct a system which the veriest dolt, blindfolded, can take to pieces and assemble at first sight. The fact of fewness of parts in a breech action is valuable in the degree that it contributes to ensure the reliability and efficiency of the weapon. In considering such simplicity, it should always be kept in view that the mechanism of a service arm* should be of a "simple, strong and durable character, free from risk of derangement, either by accident, long wear and tear, rough usage in active service, exposure to wet or sand, or fouling from long continued firing. In the case of military guns, the latter requirements are of especial importance, as the whole value of a breech-loading gun, on account of increased rapidity of fire, would be outweighed by any increased liability to failure in action." The justice of this observation, of a very clever inventor and artisan, has been illustrated by the fate of more than one system, which by the elimination of necessary parts, has been made, in the hands of an expert, to show exceeding hability of discharge when tested a few minutes for rapidity, yet when undergoing the ensuing test of 500 rounds, soon exhibited the effect of fouling and clogging, and afterward, tried with filed cartridges or an excessive charge, at once became disabled.

The simplicity of the Remington system is happily characterized by Captain Fountouclis : "the mechanism is simple, stable and very

* Essay of Mr. Wm. P. Marshall, of Birmingham, British Association of Mechanical Engineers, May, 1871.

solid, not containing any part liable to get out of order, even after a prolonged firing." So far as has been consistent with the permanent effectiveness of the action, the number of details has been reduced to the extreme limit. The guard-strap secures by direct attachment every part of the lock with the single exception of the hammer. The action of each part is, moreover, natural and direct. Especially is this general character of the system observable in the EXTRACTOR, which, avoiding the use of a spring or irregular cam motion, executes its work by a direct and positive withdrawal of the shell.

STRENGTH OF THE SYSTEM.

Strength and stability are necessary results of the general design of this system. The breech-piece and hammer of the best obtainable material, and forged into shape with the most severe inspection, are of very large size, and secured in position beyond a possibility of derangement. The parts of the lock, each firmly attached to the heavy guard-strap, are in weight, formation and material, equally calculated to withstand the most sudden or harsh shock. The whole action is so securely protected in the solid frame as to remain serviceable even after the entire destruction of the stock. In the course of the trial of breech-loaders, conducted at Washington Navy Yard, in 1869, by the United States Official Naval Commission, this extraordinary stability of organization was demonstrated by actual test, as follows: "*the butt-stock (wood) was then removed from the piece, and the exhibitor fired eighteen* (18) *shots at a distant mark on the river, with a fair aim, and with tolerable accuracy, showing the independence of the lock and barrel parts from the butt-stock.*

The obvious material strength of the system requires hardly more than a suggestion, to be appreciated, the reader having already *data* as to size and proportion of parts. The distinct merit of this system, however, derivable apparently from these material features, is to be discovered by a careful study of its arrangement of parts, rather than of their individual solidity. While the success of the arm may seem certain from its avoidance of complex detail and the intrinsic strength of each constituent of its action, its actual merit exists in the design itself. It would be perfectly easy to dispose the same weight and strength of metal that are collected in this system, so that a comparatively weak shock would throw them out of relation, and consequently disable the action.

The inventor has, however, aimed to arrange its details so that the individual strength of each is brought into play, in every case supported by its fellow.

The elaborate paper from which quotations have already several times been made in this article, after noting with extreme fairness the defaults of previous inventions, observes of the necessary scientific relation of the parts of a breech system to each other, as follows:

"If our analysis of other popular, or once approved models, has been of adequate clearness, the reader will have deduced from it the truth that mere mechanical design and execution are not the only requisites to the endurance and reliability of a system. While the mechanism must be of the very best to insure efficiency, the constructive design must be based upon correct science to make safety certain. It is the unique claim of the patentees of this arm that no accident has ever occurred with one of their productions. The reason of this alleged security is to be found in the perfectly scientific design of the system. The relation of the parts to each other and to the whole organization, the relative strength of each part, the directly parallel planes of recoil and resistance axes, are the characteristic merits of this system, without which no system, however excellent its mechanical execution, can be depended upon against extraordinary incidents.

"It will be observed that at the moment of discharge the breech-piece is immediately supported by the front portion of the hammer, which forms a superlatively powerful recoil tumbler. Both of these pieces are of considerable weight and thickness, and of the choicest metal—as substantially designed and constructed, in a word, as the largest capacity of frame will permit. The metal in these parts, and in the pins upon which they move, is so located as to equalize their power to absorb the recoil shock. The result, indeed, is that the recoil shock is practically co-operative in the stability of the system, a fact due to the scientific relation of the two sectors of circles, the hammer and breech-piece, between which there is a constant interlocking and bracing connection. Thus the greater the recoil, the more securely the hammer is locked, and the shoulder of the hammer becomes of necessity a fulcrum, acting upon the bearing of the breech-piece in such a manner that the entire strain upon its axis is taken up by the part in the rear of the forward pin. This theory of correlation of forces in a breech system was admirably illustrated at Washington, where, says the official report of the naval commission:

"'The exhibitor fired four shots with a wooden pin (hickory) substituted for the front recoil pin. No derangement of the piece; no marks on the pin; and then fired four shots with two wooden pins in place of both steel recoil pins. No derangement of the piece or impressions on the wood pins.

"'*A breech-piece, filed away to nothing, in front of forward pin, was then substituted in place of the ordinary breech-piece, and the gun fired seven times without jar or injury to any of the parts.*'

"No more pertinent demonstration of the valuable relationship of science to mechanism could be furnished than the foregoing, yet, as a further proof of the extraordinary strength of the system we are describing, the fact may be adduced that on several occasions it has been subjected to charges which filled the entire barrel of the piece, from breech-chamber to muzzle, without effect upon its action or efficiency, a statement which, we believe, can be made of no other breech-loading arm."

A conspicuous instance, above referred to, was furnished at the Belgian trial, in 1869, and is thus certified by the Director of the Proving-house:

The undersigned, Director of the Proving-house for firearms at Liege, certifies having proved on behalf of Messrs. E. & L. Nagant, manufacturers of arms at Liege, a Remington rifle, 50 cal., as follows:

1st proof, 90 grs. powder, 1 ball, 2 wads,
2d " 750 " " 40 " "

This rifle has received the two corresponding stamps.

The Director,
(Signed,) ALPH. POLAIN.

LIEGE, Sept. 29, 1869.

The barrel could not receive a stronger charge, as the last one filled its entire length, 750 grains of powder and 40 balls, occupying 36.31 inches.

(Signed) EM. & L. NAGANT.

As a further demonstration of the strength of this breech system, the report of Captain Fountouclis, who conducted experiments with the arm at Liege, with the co-operation of the Director of the State manufactory, furnishes the following tests:

"A Belgian cartridge-shell has been introduced into the Grecian gun, and the loading has been completed through the muzzle as follows: ten grammes (a double charge) of powder, a strong paper wad, rammed by two blows of ramrod, and a forty-four grammes slug wrapped in paper and upset by the ramming home.

"*Nothing extraordinary was noticed.*

"The *same* rifle has again been loaded in the same manner with twelve and one-half grammes of powder, wad, ten spherical balls of .43 calibre and another wad.

"*Nothing remarkable took place.*

"Again the *same* rifle has been loaded with six grammes of powder, wad, twenty-five spherical balls of .43 calibre, and a wad.

"*Nothing occurred; the barrel and system uninjured.*

"The Egyptian rifle has been loaded with its own cartridge, but with the shoulder of the head filed off, the ramrod left in the barrel so that its head should be ten centimetres from the ball. After firing it was discovered that the ramrod had been ejected against the target, but that its head as well as the bullet had remained wedged at thirty-three centimetres from the muzzle of the barrel, which experienced a considerable swelling at the original position of the ramrod head, and was also split below that point lengthwise a distance of fifteen centimetres, with two transverse cracks at the point of swelling. The stock at this place had been shattered, but the barrel, though weakened by the sight-base screws, did not burst at this spot.

"THE CARTRIDGE WAS INTACT, AS ALSO THE MECHANISM."

More severe tests of the stability of an arm could not be devised. The admirable arrangement of the parts in the Remington is, however, more satisfactorily proven by trials less dependent for severity upon the exaggeration of charges than upon conditions affecting the pivotal action. The curious experiments conducted at the United States Naval trial, introducing wooden in place of the steel pins, has been already noted. At Liege, under the class of tests termed "Facility of Service," and reported in Captain Fountouclis' report, the following conditions were prescribed:

"To fire one shot, the block-pin being pushed out of one of its bearings.

"To fire two shots, the block-pin being of oak (*chêne*) in one instance and of beech (*hêtre*) in the other.

"To fire one shot, the block-pin being removed.

"To fire two shots with the Danish rifle, the block-pin being cut in two through the centre.

"Under the first condition, no effect upon the working of the system was observable.

"Under the second, though the oaken substitute was broken by the block in three parts, so that the firing-pin was bent, the cartridge-head blown off, and the lower part of the countersink of the chamber slightly dented, after a few taps of the armorer's hammer upon the affected parts, *the steel pivot being replaced, the mechanism worked perfectly well, and was not injured in the least degree.*

"In the succeeding tests, the breech-pin was slightly indented, allowing the block to fall back upon the cam of the hammer, and the cartridge-head was blown off with, however, but a very slight leakage of gas. A momentary application of the hammer handle upon the block, to make it assume its place, with a re-insertion of the steel pin, set the action in order again, and *the mechanism worked perfectly well.*

"With the front pivot entirely removed, the block was ejected vertically out of the frame, firing-pin broken, countersink of chamber bent and cartridge-head blown off, with large escape of gas as a matter of course, yet the mechanism remained perfect.

"In the concluding trial, with front pin cut through the centre, the first fire being made with the regular service charge, five grammes, and the second with fourteen grammes of powder and a forty-four grammes weight bullet, *nothing noteworthy was observed; the pin resisted well; the mechanism as before. Therefore no danger could exist for the soldier, even if, through defect, or any other cause, the pin should break in two.*"

If the result was in no other degree noteworthy, it certainly may be justly cited as demonstrating a very considerable superfluous solidity in the breech-block pivot and its bearings.

The strength of the Remington breech-system has thus been demonstrated under conditions of a character that may seem absurdly severe to all but experts in mechanism and material. Taking into consideration, however, the inadequacy of the most thorough and honest inspection, and of the most carefully conducted proving-house, and the actual impossibility of the best artisan detecting hidden faults in the metal he is fashioning into shape, trials that discover the inherent weakness or the essential strength of an organization are undeniably valuable. A more extended analysis of the system now under view is not within the scope of this paper, nor should it be necessary. It should be remembered that this system is actually the last invention in its line, although distinct in character from all others, and that in its construction regard has been had to the defaults of its predecessors. In practical simplicity it is manifestly an improvement, as this simplicity abides in the direct action and plain formation of the parts composing it, as well as in their relative fewness. In stability and solidity it possesses a kindred claim to superiority. A carefully conducted series of experiments, with proper instruments, that could show with mathematical precision, the degree in which each part of its organization contributes to the strength of the whole, how far the recoil shock is taken up by the tumbler, and how much of it is diverted by the inertia of the breech-block, would be of hardly less value to the patentees than of interest to the profession. It is a fact that whatever accident may happen to the details of this system from defects that are attributable to occasional flaws or weakness of material, never one has been due to the force of recoil, nor has an arm ever been injured beyond the power of an ordinarily clever armorer to render it again available in a few minutes. That this is due to the admirable capacity of the design to distribute the shock of an excessive charge or of a defective cartridge among its parts, and to the perfect locking of the breech* at the moment of firing and by the recoil itself, is assumed to be obvious enough. A glance at other systems, which, however well mechanically constructed and easily manipulated, take the recoil upon an indirect plane, or permit it to be diverted and altogether thrown upon a single point, has a present pertinence in this connection. In guns of the bolt class, it is obvious that the recoil must be finally expended upon the shoulder of the bolt which secures it in the frame or housing. The experience of the Franco-Prussian war has shown the serious character of this default, large numbers, both of needle-guns and Chassepots, having been collected upon the field, disabled by expansion of frame through a recoil at the point suggested.

Where the bolt is secured by a screw-thread entirely surrounding it, or engaging both its sides, the default is hardly less liable. At the St. Louis trial, the disabling of a bolt gun in the test of 500 rounds for endurance is thus recorded:

"Second 100 rounds: time, nine minutes for ninety cartridges; thirty-eight cases were puffed in front of rim; dispersion of balls, 20 by 15 1-2 inches. The arm could not work any further without removing the stock, several times the rear end of the sleeve cover slipped over the threads of the locking-screw, and the breech could not be closed without pushing the cover back with the hand. The shell extractor slipped in several instances over the rim of the case in opening the breech.

"After the parts had been put in proper position, the third 100 rounds were fired: time, ten minutes fifty-five seconds; dispersion of balls, 37 by 16 1-2 inches. In extracting the third case, the sleeve cover slipped over the threads of the screw, and was forced back to its place by slight blows; cartridges were forced home with difficulty; the sleeve cover slipped over the threads of the locking screw four times in this 100 rounds; the extractor slipped over the base of the cartridges several times.

"Arm removed. No further tests made with this arm."

* "The locking of the breech by the tumbler commences as soon as the hammer is relieved from full cock, and is perfectly secure at half cock or down."—*United States Naval report, Remington system.*

This diversion of recoil in systems having the breech-block pivoted at the rear above the axis, and swinging longitudinally through the frame by the operation of levers, is equally a result of over-charge or of bursting cartridge-head. Of systems of this nature the trial above referred to disabled nearly all the arms entered, the shock naturally departing from the plane of resistance and seeking the weakest point, with the effect, in one instance, of blowing away the stock beneath the breech-block, in a second of raising the breech-block and bending the lever upward, and in a third of bending the hinge-screw and cracking the adjacent receiver; in each case the piece being disabled. In this class of systems, moreover, the long swing of the breech-block necessitates a difficulty of locking it by mechanical device, which, as has been seen, is avoided by the very organization and operation of the Remington action, in which, to follow the *dictum* of Captain Fountouclis, "the power tending to keep the breech-block closed during the fire increases with that which tends to open it."

DURABILITY AND ENDURANCE OF THE SYSTEM.

The design of this arm is such as to ensure durability, so far as simplicity and strength are agents in this result. Primarily the very least frictional or bracing surface is attained, stability of the system having been secured, not by the *extent*, but by the *relation* of contiguous surfaces. Compared with the long sleeve-encased cylinder of the bolt, or the broad sided breech-block of the lever action system, the surfaces meeting in the Remington action are obviously small. This feature originating in the design itself, is, moreover, fully appreciated in the mechanical execution. Thus the greatest care is taken that the action and frame shall not have too close relation. The breech-block and hammer tumbler have delicate bosses raised up on their lateral faces, through which the pivot pins pass, in such a manner that those parts cannot wear against the corresponding area of the frame. The action is likewise so open and free internally that both the clogging attrition of sand and the corrosion of salt water tests have been found inefficient to stop its working. Consequently there is hardly a possibility of rust from humidity, a fact singularly proven by the favorable experience of both Spanish and Patriot officers in the damp atmosphere of Cuba. The absence of spiral springs, which have been found practical objections to the reliability of the Martini-Henry and of bolt-guns generally, should also be noted as a distinct merit in this direction. Another important feature of the system is the perfect closing of the lower part of the chamber by the breech-block, at the moment of discharge, thus entirely preventing the entrance of gas into the lock mechanism, and the presence of deeply grooved channels on the inner surface of the frame, which conduct the fouling agent away from the system into the open air. By this mechanical device, the serious defect of admission of gas to the action, a necessary evil in the systems above suggested, has been effectually avoided. A farther advantage of this breech construction exists in the fact that the main part of the action is not entirely enclosed by the frame, as in other arms, but projecting out of it, and swinging back from the chamber in a manner not only to offer easy exit to gas, but to facilitate the removal of a shell or any occasional obstruction. Still another concomitant of durability is found in the peculiar action of the extractor, which, operating without spring, cannot possibly slip over the cartridge-head, but, immediately actuated by the movement of the breech-block, performs its office positively and directly.

One of the tests conducted at the Liege trial of the Remington arm was:

"To fire 2,500 shots with the Grecian model, and an equal number with the Egyptian, without cleaning the guns or lubricating the mechanism during this trial. The Hellenic report states the result thus: 2,500 shots have been fired with the Grecian gun, having already fired 3,000 other shots and having stood the severe tests of bursting charges and several bullets. A like number of shots were fired with the Egyptian rifle that had also already fired 2,500. During this experiment the arms were in no wise cleaned or greased. *The arms have stood the test as usual, the tips, however, becoming detached from the stocks on account of the heat of the barrel.*"

At the Washington trial, which resulted in the adoption of the Remington arm for the United States Navy, the official record states as the result of a firing test of 500 rounds, with the Spanish model of .43 calibre, average time for each 100 rounds four minutes, fifty-five seconds:

"*At conclusion of the 500 rounds, the gun was carefully examined, cooled, and cleaned. Not a trace of leading was to be seen in the barrel, and very little fouling, which was removed by washing. Barrel and stock greatly heated. No injury to the breech parts. Gun worked well.*"

In this connection the record of the following tests at the same trial may properly be quoted:

"FIFTH TEST.—Simplicity of mechanism and liability to derangement in ordinary service.

"It seems to be reduced to the *minimum* as to both conditions.

"ELEVENTH TEST.—Effects of the introduction of the extraneous matter, sand, etc., into the open breech.

"Five shots were fired, without any difficulty or obstruction, after throwing a handful of sand in the open breech parts, and removing it partially by the hand and by shaking.

"TWELFTH TEST.—Effects of moisture upon the action of the breech-piece.

"After steeping in salt water of somewhat greater density than that of ordinary sea water, from noon until 3:30 P. M., and then being exposed to the atmosphere until the next day at noon, the piece was examined and found to be very fairly coated with rust about its breech-loading parts.

"Five shots were fired without obstruction or difficulty; after oiling and cleaning the piece, it was found to be uninjured, and in good serviceable order."

The accomplished author of the Hellenic report, concluding his summary of the qualities of the Remington arm, observes:

"It should be remarked that the whole mechanism does not contain any part liable to get out of order, and that no main-spring vice is necessary to pull to pieces or to put up the system. The occurrence of any repair of importance is very rare, as has been observed in the course of these trials, and those repairs that might be needed would be of such a nature as to come within the scope of the regimental armorers."

FACILITY OF DISCHARGE AND MANIPULATION.

The official documents, from which copious extracts have been made in this article, are ample endorsement of the justice of any claims set forth for rapidity of fire and natural ease of handling. The Danish report, observing that the soldiers, after very little practice, get 17 shots per minute, adds: "The manipulation of the arm is altogether simple, the soldier rapidly learning to become expert in taking apart and assembling it." This language is very nearly repeated by Capt. Fountouclis, and by the several Spanish experts and professionals. The expression of the Cuban commission is especially strong:

"*Experience has shown that this system is not liable to get out of order, notwithstanding the rough handling to which in war it must be submitted; that shots with it never fail; that its mechanism is so simple and so perfect that several divisions of the army have voluntarily adopted it during the present campaign and made use of it with facility and without accident, notwithstanding the soldier had not time or leisure to be properly instructed in the handling of the weapon.*"

The following illustration of the availability of the system, in the features suggested, is the record of an award of a prize trial for rapidity of fire, including dismounting and re-assembling the mechanism, conducted before a Belgian jury:

The following conditions were established:

1. The competitors will perform a series of fifteen shots, the gun at the hip.

2. Will dismount the mechanism of their arm, placing on a table and separate from each other the parts that close the breech, the hammer, percussion springs (main), and those of the closing block, if any. (The trigger may remain in its place.)

3. Will assemble the mechanism, and will then fire another series of fifteen shots, with the gun at the hip. The ammunition may be taken from a table within reach of the person firing. Time occupied (in these operations) will be measured by the *sachimetre*, as follows:

1. Between the first and fifteenth shots of the first series of firing, for rapidity.
2. Between the fifteenth shot of the first series and the first of the second series.
3. Between the first and fifteenth of the second series.

The prize will be awarded in favor of the gun with which these three operations are completed in the shortest time.

The guns intended to compete will be presented the eve of the trial to a jury, composed of three members. The jury will determine the number of parts that will have to be dismounted to conform to the preceding condition.

FIRST PRIZE.—The Remington system * * * * * * has satisfied the conditions of the trial in one minute, thirty-nine seconds, - - - - - - - 500 francs.

The Secretary,	The President of the Jury,
F. RAICK,	ALPH. POLAIN,
LIEGE, October 25th, 1869.	*Directeur du Banc d'Epreuves.*

The value of the above decision is appreciable from the fact of fairness with which the trial was made. The test of rapidity, conducted by an expert used to the manipulation of a particular arm, affords anything else than a relative demonstration that can be relied upon.

The best firing for rapidity with the Remington arm, made at the naval trial, is recorded as follows:

"THIRD TEST.—Rapidity of fire from the shoulder at a target at a distance of 100 feet. *Accuracy* of fire will also be considered in this test.

"*Result.*—First round of 16 *fires in one minute; 14 shots striking the figure of an ordinary-sized man on the target in vital parts, and two* (2) *striking the arms of the figure. Regard to aim was paid in this round.*

"Second round of 19 *shots in one minute was had; 6 shots striking the figure in vital parts, 4 outside and 9 wild.* This round was fired with less regard to aim than during the first round."

At the St. Louis trial, soldiers from the barracks having been detailed for firing, the test being "twenty-five shots to be fired from the shoulder; fair aim to be taken at the target; distance 100 yards," the relative result is thus reported:

Remington,	rifle,	cal.	.50,	2 min.	51 sec.		
"	"	"	"	2 "	11 "		
"	"	"	.44,	2 "	20 "		
"	"	"	.50,	2 "	8 "		
"	"	"	.43,	2 "	21 "		
"	"	"	.50,	2 "	38 "		
"	"	"	"	2 "	3 "		
"	"	"	"	2 "	55 "		
"	carbine,	"	.43,	2 "	1 "		

Peabody	rifle, cal. .42,	. . . . . .	3 min.	40	sec
"	" " "	. . . . . .	4 "	—	"
"	" " .50,	. . . . . .	2 "	55	"
"	" " .45,	. . . . . .	3 "	15	"
"	" " .42,	. . . . . .	3 "	40	"
"	" " "	. . . . . .	2 "	51	"
Ward-Burton,	" " "	. . . . . .	3 "	—	"
"	" " .45,	. . . . . .	2 "	8	"
"	" " .50,	. . . . . .	2 "	21	"
Springfield-Allin,	" " "	. . . . . .	2 "	33	"
Martini-Henry,	" " Boxer .45,	. . .	2 "	38	"
"	" " " "	. . .	6 "	"	"

The foregoing trial for rapidity, made by soldiers presumed justly to have no habitude for any particular system, was doubtless as fair an exhibition of relative superiority as could be anywhere secured. While a considerable usage of any arm is indispensable to a perfect command of its powers, the superior ease and simplicity of a system are most honestly developed under such conditions as governed the St. Louis tests. To recur again to the thorough essay of the *Iron Age:*

"Externally, the Remington gun is in all respects an admirable military weapon. Its manner of loading is so easy and of discharge so natural, that raw recruits and untaught Africans, according to the testimony of the Spanish leaders on one side and of the patriot commander, Gen. Thomas Jordan, on the other, need no drillmaster to instruct them in its use. In sharpshooting contests or in close engagements, where the arm is handled closely parallel to the ground, top of breastworks or level of rifle-pits, it can be charged and fired without exposure of the hand above the line of the barrel and without raising the gun, while it has the same facility for loading with muzzle elevated as in the old position for priming, thus favoring its use in two-rank formation of troops. For rapidity of fire, its simplicity of mechanism and ease of handling give it such advantages that at the prize trial in Belgium a few years since it won the first award in a general competition of the most approved systems. The expert at the 'works,' with a little practice, gets from 25 to 28 shots per minute out of the arm, while the Danish soldiers, with no practice at all, were reported, in 1868, as firing their new arms 17 shots per minute."

The suggestions embodied above are of the greatest importance as regards a military arm. The unnatural movement of the bolt-system in opening and closing the breech by an eccentric and forced manual, and the awkward lever action of the Martini-Henry type, always uncomfortable to and frequently wounding the hand of the soldier, have become serious objections to those arms after practical service trials. Less serious, but still of considerable detriment to the usefulness of the gun, is the necessity of a forward motion in throwing up the block, in systems having the breech opening upon the upper surface and hinged at the rear or on either side, in which class experience has demonstrated the great danger of breaking the fastenings of the block as well as the difficulty of loading with the muzzle raised at any considerable angle. In the Remington system the motions are all toward and near the body (the breech-block being closed by the thumb), and so natural that the constant surveyance of the eye is entirely unnecessary; the arm can be loaded and discharged without changing its elevation or direction; not only "without looking and with one finger the soldier can ascertain the relative positions of hammer and trigger," but there is no danger of accident from ignorance of the contents of the gun as would be in the case of an "enclosed chamber," or "concealed hammer." The motions for loading being all performed from the wrist, by the thumb and finger of a single hand, the carbine of this system is an especially available weapon for cavalry.

The subjoined formula for dismounting and assembling the parts of the arm may be of use to those entirely unacquainted with its construction:

To REMOVE THE BREECH-PIECE AND HAMMER.—Loosen the Button screw until the Button can be removed from the heads of the Breech and Hammer Pins. Cock the Hammer, push out the Breech-pin, take out the Breech-piece, let down the Hammer as far as it will go (which leaves the Main-spring resting upon a stationary pin, and obviates the necessity of using a Main-spring vice in re-adjusting the parts). Remove the Hammer-pin and take out the Hammer.

To REPLACE THE HAMMER AND BREECH-PIECE.—Lay the arm down on the right side, press upon the Trigger, at the same time replacing the Hammer with the Thumb-piece forward and downward, until the hole in the Hammer and Receiver correspond. Replace the Hammer-pin, cock the Hammer, replace the Breech-piece, insert Breech-pin in Receiver, and by pressing on the pin, at the same time pressing down the Breech-piece and working it back and forth slightly, the Pin will enter. Adjust the Button and tighten the Button-screw.

To TAKE THE ENTIRE ARM APART.—Take out the Extractor screw, open the Breech, remove the Extractor, take out Breech-piece and Hammer as above described. Remove the Wiping-rod by unscrewing the same, remove the bands, separate the Tip-stock from the Barrel at the muzzle until it is liberated from the stud upon the under side of the Barrel, when it may be withdrawn from the Receiver, take out the Tang screw, remove the Butt stock. To detach the Guard-strap, take out the two side screws which pass through the Guard-strap, always removing the rear screw first. Unscrew the Barrel from the receiver, taking care that the Extractor has been removed before unscrewing the barrel.

To ASSEMBLE THE ARM.—Screw the Barrel in the Receiver until the mark on top of the Barrel and Receiver correspond. Replace the Extractor and Screw, place the forward end of the Guard-strap in the Receiver, putting in the screw. See that the Main-spring is in the centre of the Guard-strap. Press the rear end in until the screw will enter. Replace Hammer and Breech-piece as previously described. Replace Butt stock and Tip. In putting on the Bands, see that the letters upon them are on the same side with the Band-springs. Replace the Wiping-rod by screwing it in.

It has already been suggested that the original success of the Remington enterprise was due to the exceptional quality of the barrels produced, which at once became recognized by military and sporting men. The tradition of the founder has not been forgotten, and in the construction of the small arms made at Ilion the most thorough finish of the barrel interior is an imperative rule of the establishment. The straightening process, an operation as yet impracticable by mechanical appliance, at the Ilion armory is conducted with the most rigid care and under the severest inspection. The legitimate result is found in the singular unanimity with which official commissions and experts report the shooting powers of the Remington arm. While a certain degree of the relative excellence of targets made by breech-loading arms is to be credited to the character of ammunition used, the fact should not be lost sight of that, in the largest measure, superiority of precision, attained by fixed-rest firing, is a just claim of the gun itself.

Fac-simile of ten-shot target made with Remington Military Rifle, calibre .50, United States model, range 100 yards.

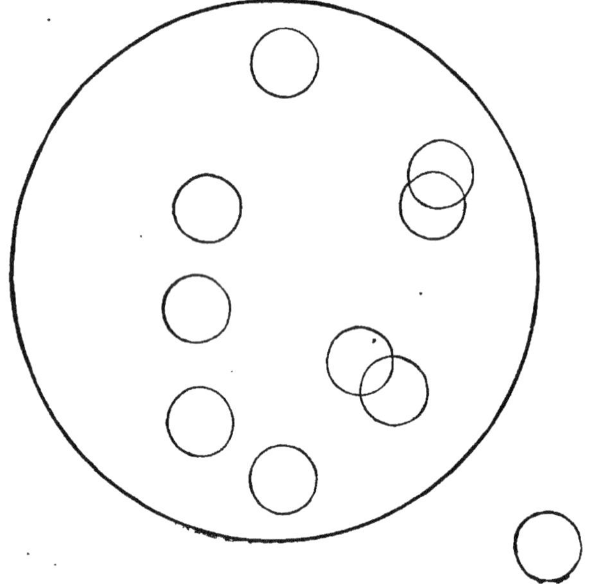

The firing test for accuracy at the United States naval trial was particularly thorough. The succeeding targets are copied from the official report of the Commission:

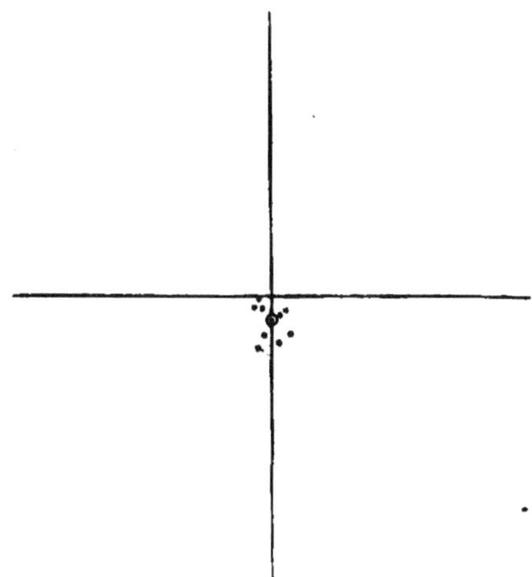

⊙ Denotes Centre of Impact.

TEST OF REMINGTON (U. S. ORDNANCE) RIFLE FOR ACCURACY, AT WASHINGTON NAVY YARD.—DISTANCE 100 YARDS.

No. of shots.	Distance in Inches from Centre of Target.				Distance in Inches from Centre of Impact.				Missed.	Remarks.
	Vertical.		Horizontal.		Vertical.		Horizontal.			
	Above.	Below.	Right.	Left.	Above.	Below.	Right.	Left.		
1	......	6.00	4.00	....	....	2.28	3.65	....	..	Size of the target, 80"x80".
2	......	3.00	1.25	....	0.72	....	0.90	....	..	
3	......	5.00	....	1.00	...	1.28	....	1.35	..	U. S. cartridges, cal. .50. Sighted for 100 yards.
4	......	3.00	1.25	....	0.72	....	0.90	....	..	
5	......	2.25	3.00	....	1.47	....	2.6·	....	..	
6	......	6.00	2.00	....	....	2.28	1.65	....	..	
7	......	7.50	....	2.00	....	3.78	....	2.35	..	
8	......	0.50	....	1.75	3.22	....	...	2.10	..	
9	......	2.00	....	2.25	1.72	....	....	2.60	..	
10	......	2.00	....	1.00	1.72	....	....	1.35	..	
	......	37 25	11.50	8.00	9.57	9.62	9.75	9.75	..	
	3.72		0.35		1.92		1.95			

Absolute — 2.78.

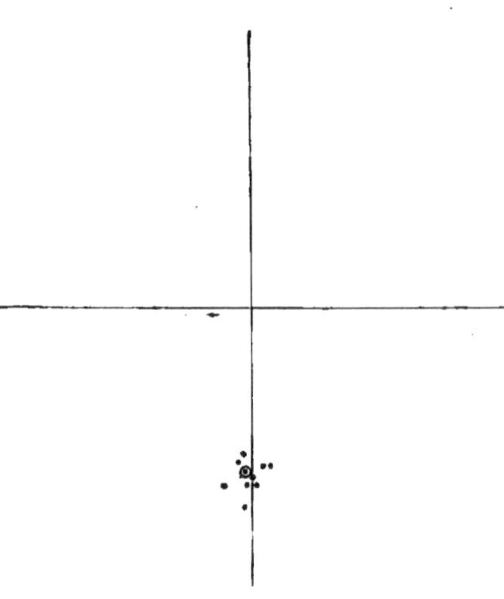

⊙ Denotes Centre of Impact.

TEST OF REMINGTON (SPANISH) RIFLE FOR ACCURACY, AT WASHINGTON NAVY YARD.
DISTANCE 200 YARDS.

No. of shots.	Distance in Inches from Centre of Target.				Distance in Inches from Centre of Impact.				Missed.	Remarks.
	Vertical.		Horizontal.		Vertical.		Horizontal.			
	Above.	Below.	Right.	Left.	Above.	Below.	Right.	Left.		
1	......	20.00	....	2.00	3.4	...	....	1.42	..	Target 80x80.
2	......	24.50	....	0.50	....	1.1	0.08	....	..	Sighted for 200 yards. Brass-case cartridge, cal. .42, used for this test. Bullets patched. Calibre less than bore.
3	..	24.50	0.50	....	....	1·1	1.08	....	..	
4	......	22.00	2.25	...	1.4	....	2.83	....	..	
5	......	23.5	....	....	....	0.1	0 58	....	..	
6	......	21.5	....	2.25	1.9	....	....	1.67	.	
7	......	22.2	2.00	....	1.2	....	2.58	....	..	
8	......	23.2	....	0.25	0.2	....	0.33	....	.	
9	......	28.2	....	1.25	....	4.8	....	0.67	..	
10	......	24.7	....	4.25	....	1.3	....	3.67	..	
	......	234.3	4.7	10.50	8.1	8.4	7.48	7.43	..	
	23.43		0.58		1.65		1.49			

Absolute — 2.21.

The seven following targets were made upon the trial ground at Ilion. The gun used was the Danish model of .45 calibre; length of barrel, 33 inches; rifling, 7 grooves, 5-1000 of an inch deep; twist, one turn in 22 inches; weight of gun, 9 pounds 9 ounces; charge, 70 grains of powder, 450 grains projectile.

Scale of Cuts. ⅛ of an inch to the foot. Size of Target 12x12 *feet.*

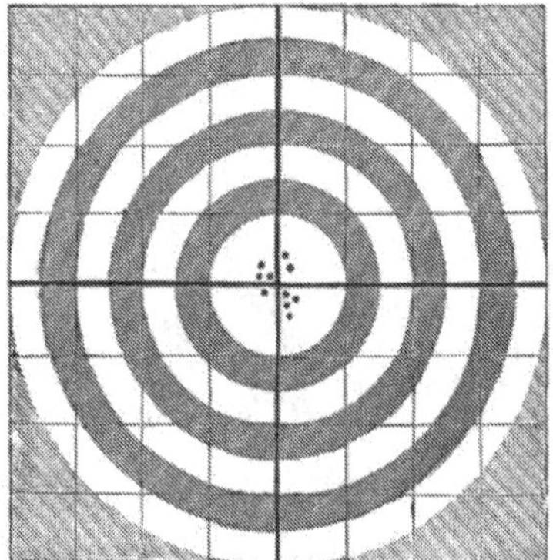

Target No. 1. 10 Shots. Distance 200 yards.

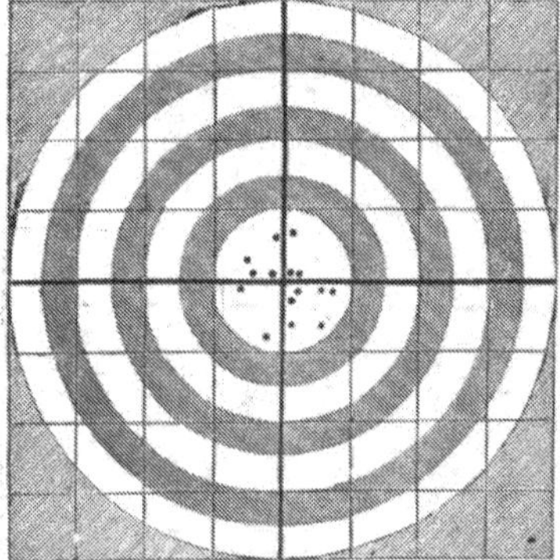

Target No. 2. 15 Shots. Distance 300 yards. Windage 30 degrees to the right.

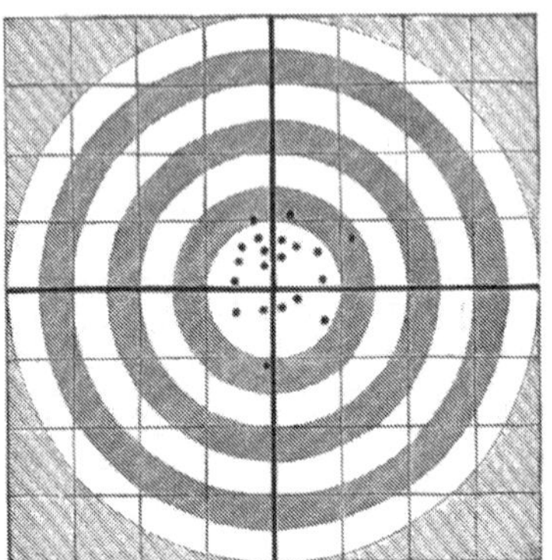

Target No. 3. 20 Shots. Distance 400 yards.

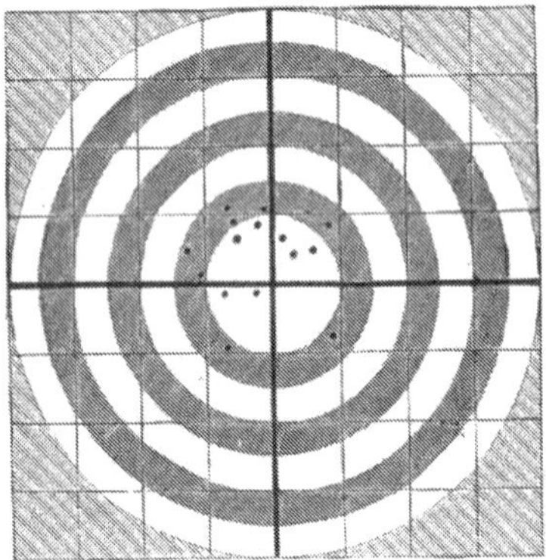

Target No. 4. 15 Shots. Distance 500 yards. Windage to the left **at 45 degrees.**

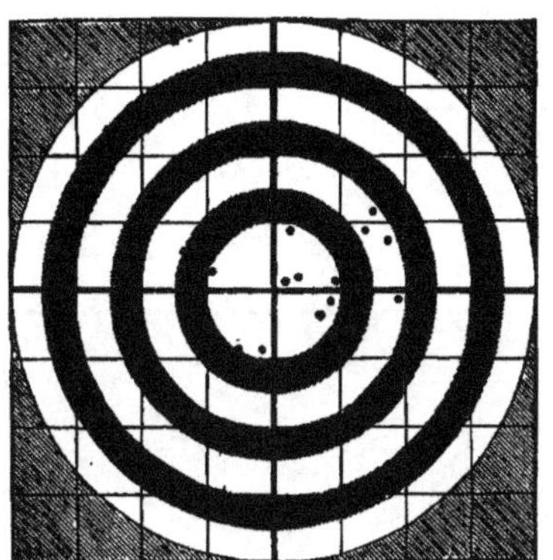

Target No. 5. 15 Shots. Distance 600 yards. Windage to the right 45 degrees.

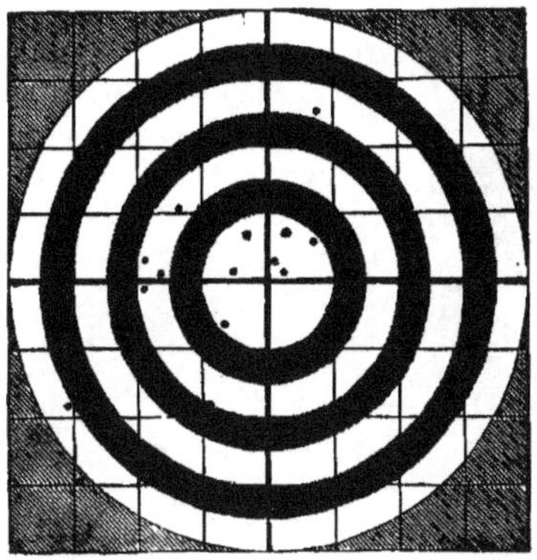

Target No. 6. 15 Shots. Distance 700 yards. Windage strong to the left at 90 degrees.

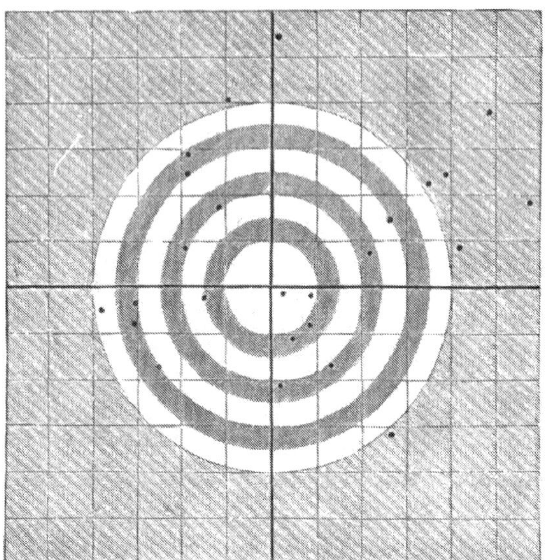

Target No. 7. 25 Shots. Distance 1,000 yards.

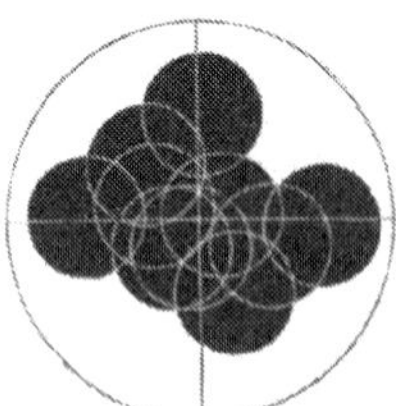

The succeeding cut is *fac-simile* of a target made by Mr. Gove, of Denver City, Colorado, with a Remington sporting rifle of .44 calibre, or 60 round balls to the pound. The ten consecutive shots were made with the rifle in a fixed rest, at a range of fifty yards.

Arms of this system, including rifles, carbines, and pistols, as has already been stated, have been issued to troops in larger numbers than any other breech-loader, with the single exception of the needle-gun. The subjoined summary is interesting, as it shows not only what countries have adopted the invention for service, but will suggest the different models now in use. Arms have been furnished or are being issued to governments or private parties as follows:

Denmark	42,000,	
Sweden..................	30,000,	
U. S. Navy..............	28.000,	including rifles, carbines and pistols.
Spain, for Cuba	75,000,	
Rome	10,000,	
France..................	155,000,	
Egypt...................	60,000,	
Japan	8,000,	
U. S. Army..............	16,500,	
South America..........	10,000,	
New York................	15,000,	model of 1871.
South Carolina..........	5,000,	Springfield muzzle-loaders, transformed.
Miscellaneous............	100,000.	

It should be stated that the details of the system, as described in the foregoing pages, have been more or less modified in the different models. In all, with the exception of those being issued to the State of New York, and those now in course of construction for the United States army, the original plan of simple cartridge extraction and full-cock loading has been adhered to, not because a mode of cartridge ejection as well as of loading at half cock was inconsistent with the design of the arm, but in deference to the judgment of the accomplished professional experts who have superintended the conduct of trials and the completion of the contract for foreign States, and to that of the best mechanics as well. It is believed that the expression of the United States Naval Commission and of the Hellenic inspector, in declining, after serious consideration, a model which loaded at half cock, on the ground that such a faculty was practically unnecessary, will yet be fully justified by experience. The decision of the United States Army Commission, however, was imperative in this respect, and has since been followed by the official commission of the principal member of the Union of States in the re-armament of her militia. In accordance with the views of the latter body, the arms which have been manufactured for the State of New York have, in addition to the distinct features of the system, the faculty of loading at half cock, the introduction of an improved device for ejecting the shell after firing, and another of withdrawing the firing-pin, out of any possible contact with the cartridge, by a positive motion. In the New York model, the relation of the sear and hammer is such that the arm is always left at half cock, and the breech-block firmly locked after loading. A necessary result of this

Fig. 1

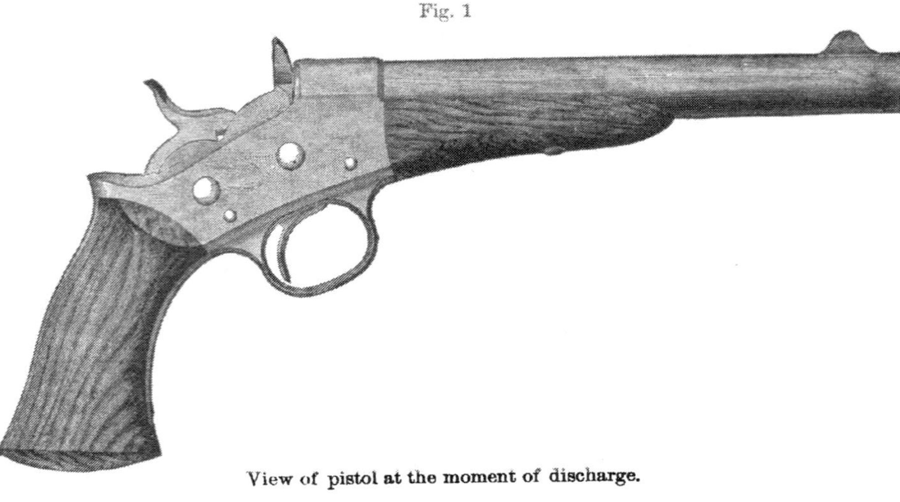

View of pistol at the moment of discharge.

construction is that the soldier must always go through the same motions. In order to charge the piece the hammer must be pulled back to its extreme limit, the breech-block being opened by pressing on the thumb-piece. This latter motion disengages the sear from the full cock and the hammer advances to a safe position, from which, after the breech is closed, it cannot be moved except to draw it back to the firing or full cock point again. The result of safety is mechanically assured by this modification. Yet under no circumstances is a gun as innocent an affair as a walking-stick and, however strong may be the arguments in favor of a half cock loading mechanism, experience has developed the fact that soldiers in action rarely avail themselves of it, it being the most natural act to draw the hammer back to its utmost tension.

Among the several recommendations of the United States Board of 1870 was one in favor of the single shot, breech-loading pistol, of the Remington system, for cavalry. To determine upon a proper holster weapon was a distinct portion of the order directing the organization and action of the Board. Its decision is embodied in the subjoined extract from the report, as published in *Ordnance Memoranda, No.* 11:

"Of the breech-loading pistols submitted, the Board have selected the following six in the order of relative merit:

"*First.*—The Remington single-barreled pistol, with guard, centre-fire,

"*Second.*—The Smith-Wesson revolver,

"*Third.*—The Remington revolver, No. 2,

"*Fourth.*—The Remington revolver, No. 5,

"*Fifth.*—The Remington revolver, No. 3,

"*Sixth.*—The Remington revolver, No. 4.

"The Remington is the only single-barreled pistol submitted. It is an excellent weapon, but should be so modified as to load at half cock. The main-spring of the Remington

Fig. 2.

Sectional view of pistol when open to receive cartridge.

should be strengthened so as to increase the certainty of fire; also the plunger should be made to strike more accurately the centre of the base of the cartridge. Pistols and revolvers should have the 'saw-handle' so shaped that, in bringing the weapon from the holster to an aim, it will not be necessary to change the first grasp or bend of the wrist."

By a reference to the antecedent record of this system, it will be seen that a complement of single-shot pistols was, in 1867, furnished to the United States Navy. In his communication to the Secretary of War, accompanying the report of the Board, General Dyer recommended that 1,000 arms of this type be purchased for trial. This number was in due time secured, and since the original order, 5,000 pistols of the same model have likewise been ordered for, and will soon be issued to, the army.

The cuts which follow are illustrative of the style, entire action and mechanical details of the

REMINGTON BREECH-LOADING, SINGLE-SHOT PISTOL, MODEL OF 1871.

This new holster arm in construction conforms to the suggestions of the St. Louis Commission, in so far as that body recommended a change of handle and a modification of the firing-pin. The "saw-handle," as applied to the new model, renders it an almost perfect weapon in simple ease of manual, as it "brings up" in the most natural manner possible. A second improvement is the introduction of a *positive firing-pin retractor*, in lieu of the spring heretofore filling that office, by which the clogging or fastening of the firing-pin by rust or dirt is rendered an impossibility.

The length of barrel of the improved model,—eight inches,—and the admirably adapted degree of rifling twist, secure not only almost a carbine's range, but remarkable precision for this pistol. The exceeding ease with which it is loaded and its natural grasp, make it also capable in practical hands of a rapidity of consecutive discharge, per minute, greater than that of any revolving or repeating arm. In addition to such shooting qualities and facility of manual, possessing the calibre of .50, it is, beyond a doubt, the most formidable weapon known to any service or as yet produced.

The weight of the model of 1871 is but slightly over two pounds.

The parts of the improved system are fully shown in cuts 3, 4, 5, 6 and 7. Cut No. 1 represents the pistol with breech closed and ready for discharge. Cut No. 2 is a sectional view of the system open and in a position to receive the cartridge.

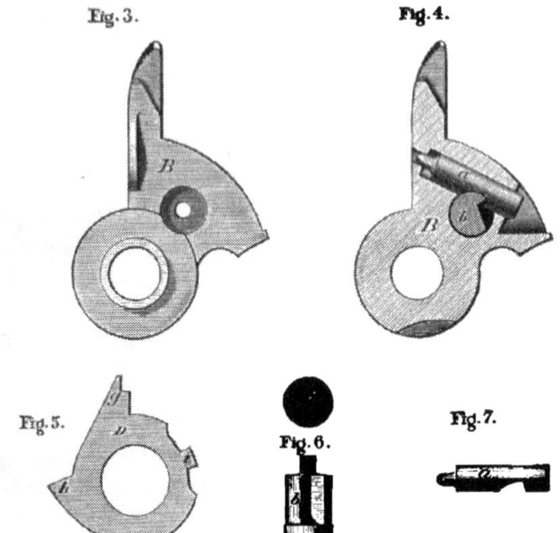

AA. Receiver, consisting of Frame and Guard-Strap, connected by three screws.

BB. Breech-Block.

C. Hammer.

D. Cartridge retractor.

EE. Hammer and Breech-Block Pins.

aa. Firing Pin.

b. Firing Pin Retractor.

c. Sear.

d. Trigger.

e. Main-spring.

f. Sear and Breech-Block Spring.

The Frame and Guard-Strap are made of wrought iron, case hardened. The barrel and lock work are of steel.

The breech-block, Fig. 3, is formed with an annular groove for the reception of the cartridge retractor, *D*, which serves the double purpose of withdrawing the empty cases from the chamber and operating the firing-pin retractor, *b*, to effect a positive withdrawal of the firing-pin. Fig. 4 is a longitudinal section through the breech-block, showing the engagement of the firing-pin and firing-pin retractor. Figs. 5, 6, and 7, show these several parts in detail. Shoulders *k* and *l* are formed on the breech and hammer, which *prevent* the closing of the breech if the trigger is accidentally pulled while the breech is open.

The sear, *c*, and trigger, *d*, are pivoted to the guard-strap. The sear-spring, *f*, rests in a slot in the trigger, and is held in place by the trigger-pin. One end of the sear-spring rests upon the sear, and the other against the breech-block, serving to keep it closed.

DIRECTIONS FOR USE.

Bring the hammer to full cock, open the breech by pressing back the thumb-piece. The backward movement of the breech carries with it the cartridge retractor and withdraws the empty cartridge case from the chamber. After the cartridge retractor has moved back a certain distance the shoulder, *h*, comes against the frame and arrests its movement, while the backward movement of the breech is continued to permit the insertion of a cartridge. The firing-pin retractor, *b*, is thus caused to roll over and receive a slight angular movement from the tooth, *i*, on the cartridge retractor, which angular movement serves to retract the firing-pin as shown in Fig. 4. A cartridge being then placed in the chamber and the breech closed the arm is ready to fire.

Care should be taken to keep the chamber clean and free from sand or dirt, which would cause the cartridges to extract with difficulty. The hammer should be carried at half cock.

As this new holster arm is already fast gaining precedence "on the plains," and wherever buffalo or other large game is to be encountered in the saddle, the following directions for dismounting and assembling the parts of the system will be of general service:

To REMOVE THE BREECH-PIECE AND HAMMER.—Loosen the button-screw until the button can be removed from the heads of the breech and hammer-pins; cock the hammer, push out the breech-pin, take out the breech-piece, let down the hammer as far as it will go (which leaves the main-spring resting upon a stationary pin, and obviates the necessity of using a main-spring vice in re-adjusting the parts); remove the hammer-pin, and take out the hammer.

After the breech is removed from the frame, the cartridge retractor may be removed, and the firing-pin and firing-pin retractor taken out. As the last mentioned parts are held in place by the cartridge retractor, care should be taken not to lose them out when that is removed.

To REPLACE THE HAMMER AND BREECH-PIECE.—Lay the arm down on the right side; press upon the trigger, at the same time replacing the hammer with the thumb-piece forward and downward, until the hole in the hammer and receiver correspond; replace the hammer-pin, cock the hammer, replace the breech-piece, insert breech-pin in receiver, and by pressing on the pin, at the same time pressing down the breech-piece, and working it back and forth slightly, the pin will enter. Adjust the button, and tighten the button-screw.

To TAKE THE ENTIRE ARM APART.—Take out the breech and hammer, as above described. Take out the tang-screw, and remove the butt-stock. To detach the guard-strap, take out the two side-screws which press through the guard-strap, always removing the rear screw first. Unscrew the barrel from the receiver.

The virtual adoption of the single-shot pistol for the United States service,—since the recent order of the Chief of Ordnance that 5,000 pistols of this class, altered and improved in accordance with the recommendations of the Commission which named it "first in order of merit," is equivalent to its adoption,—suggests a most important official endorsement of the Remington system, which, though appropriate enough in this place, with perfect regard to the consecutive unity of the chapter should have been quoted in an earlier connection. In his annual report to the Secretary of War, dated Nov. 10, 1870, General W. T. Sherman observes of the administration of ordnance affairs during the year:

"The board of officers assembled at St. Louis, Missouri,* by virtue of General Orders Nos. 60 and 72, of 1869, has reported that their labors have been substantially concluded, and although not yet in possession of the text, I desire to express my opinion of the importance of their work. This board, composed of officers of great experience, was required to report on the best small arms and equipments for the army, and also to prepare a system of tactics for all arms of service. Their conclusion on the first branch of the subject has heretofore been laid before the Secretary of War, who has ordered a supply of the arms recommended by the board to be distributed to the army for further practical tests. But I observe that the Chief of Ordnance, in his annual report, advises that another 50,000 of

* *Since the pages, in which the announcement should have been made, have been stereotyped, Gen. A. B. Dyer, Chief of the Bureau of Ordnance, has directed the construction, at the United States Armory, of* 10,000 *stand of the Remington rifle, improved model of* 1871, *embodying the features of the arm issued to the National Guard of the State of New York.*

the Springfield musket should be altered according to the ordnance pattern, the one now in general use by our infantry. This would imply a selection of that form of musket before the practical tests already in progress are completed. The recommendation of the board was strongly in favor of the Remington system, and I concur with it entirely, and therefore suggest to the Secretary that he await the result of the tests he has already ordered before incurring the expense of alteration of the second 50,000. All officers agree that the present musket is an admirable weapon, but the breech-block is not suited to a carbine and entirely out of the question for the pistol, whereas the Remington system is equally suited to all, so that we could have identically the same calibre and cartridge for all arms, a matter of infinite importance in action, and especially so for our troops, who are often detached from their own baggage for months, and come in for a re-supply of ammunition at posts where they often find no cartridges suited to their special weapon. The Remington is already adopted by the navy, and this is an additional good reason for its adoption in the army, for, in combined operations, both arms and ammunition could be mutually interchanged.'

No higher or more impartial authority could add its weight of credit to the mass of testimony collected in the preceding pages, than this official commendation of the Remington system as the best for all uses of war on land or sea, for infantry, cavalry, or boat service, from the General of the army of the United States.

EXPOSITION UNIVERSELLE DE 1867, À PARIS.
LE JURY INTERNATIONAL DÉCERNE UNE MÉDAILLE D'ARGENT À E. REMINGTON AND SONS, (ILION, ÉTATS-UNIS).
Agriculture et Industrie,
Groupe IV, Classe 37, Armes de Guerre.

PARIS, le 1er Juillet, 1867.

Le Conseiller d'État, Commissaire General,
F. LEPLAY.

Le Ministre, Vice-Président de la Commission Impériale,
M. DASSAU.

THE REMINGTON MAGAZINE GUN.

Keene's Patent.

ARMY MODEL.—Number of shots in magazine 8. Length of gun 51 inches. Length of barrel 32 inches. Weight without bayonet 9¾ pounds.

NAVY MODEL.—Number of shots in magazine 9. Length of gun 48½ inches. Length of barrel 29½ inches. Weight without bayonet 9½ pounds.

THE REMINGTON MAGAZINE GUN, KEENE'S PATENT.

This gun is now being made for the United States military cartridge, forty-five calibre, seventy grains powder, but can be adapted to the use of other forms of military cartridge, such as the Spanish and Russian. The magazine is located under the barrel, thereby enabling it to carry the greatest possible number of cartridges within a given weight and length of barrel. It is believed that this is for many reasons the best position in which to carry the cartridges of a magazine gun.

All of the motions are direct and positive. The cartridges are held securely in position while passing from the magazine over the carrier to the chamber in the barrel, in which respect it has a decided advantage over other magazine arms. The cartridge does not pass on to the carrier until the gun is opened for the purpose of loading, so that there is no danger of a cartridge being exploded in the carrier in case a defective cartridge is fired in the gun.

The arm is always left at half-cock and the breech locked so that it cannot be jarred open and the cartridge lost out. From the half-cock it can be brought to the full-cock readily and quickly while the arm is being carried to the shoulder and without *removing the finger from the trigger;* in this last respect differing from other magazine guns which can only be cocked by removing the hand from the trigger.

The parts are all large and strong, and can be readily removed and replaced for the purpose of cleaning or inspection. The magazine is so arranged that it can be charged while the breech is closed, thus avoiding the entrance of dirt into the working parts of the gun. The gun may be held either barrel up or reversed for this purpose.

The importance of the advantages above mentioned has been so evident, that although the gun in its present form has been perfected since the completion of the trials made by the United States Government, an order has been given for a number to be used in the United States navy.

DIRECTIONS FOR USE.

To charge the magazine.—Hold the arm in the left hand, the butt stock under the right arm. Grasp the cartridge between the thumb and forefinger of right hand, and press it forward, bullet first, into the magazine with the end of the thumb, which may be held sideways for that

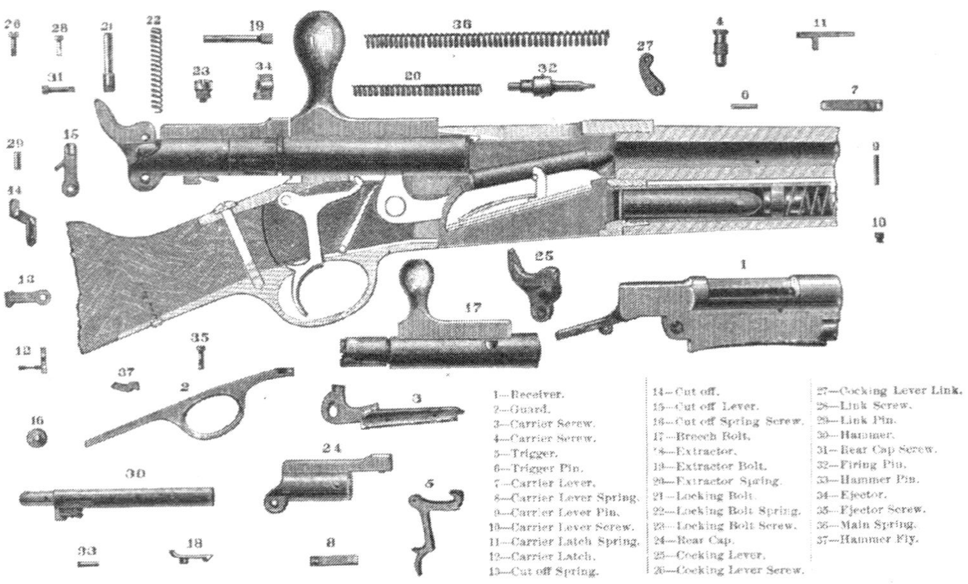
1—Receiver.
2—Guard.
3—Carrier Screw.
4—Carrier Screw.
5—Trigger.
6—Trigger Pin.
7—Carrier Lever.
8—Carrier Lever Spring.
9—Carrier Lever Pin.
10—Carrier Lever Screw.
11—Carrier Latch Spring.
12—Carrier Latch.
13—Cut off Spring.
14—Cut off.
15—Cut off Lever.
16—Cut off Spring Screw.
17—Breech Bolt.
18—Extractor.
19—Extractor Bolt.
20—Extractor Spring.
21—Locking Bolt.
22—Locking Bolt Spring.
23—Locking Bolt Screw.
24—Rear Cap.
25—Cocking Lever.
26—Cocking Lever Screw.
27—Cocking Lever Link.
28—Link Screw.
29—Link Pin.
30—Hammer.
31—Rear Cap Screw.
32—Firing Pin.
33—Hammer Pin.
34—Ejector.
35—Ejector Screw.
36—Main Spring.
37—Hammer Fly.

REMINGTON MAGAZINE GUN, Keene's Patent.

purpose. The magazine may be charged with the breech either open or closed, and with the cut off lever in its forward or backward position, but it is more convenient to do so with the breech *closed* and the cut-off lever *back*.

To load from the magazine.—*First. If the arm has been fired or the hammer is down.*—Unlock and draw back the breech bolt *quickly* and with sufficient force to bring it *clear back*, thereby raising and locking the carrier and bringing up a cartridge. Shove the bolt forward and lock it, the hammer will remain at half-cock. If it is desired to fire, the hammer may be brought to full cock while the arm is being lifted to the shoulder, the forefinger remaining on the trigger. *Second. If the arm has been closed and left at half cock.*—Lower the hammer, and then proceed as before.

After the cartridge has been transferred from the magazine to the chamber, it should either be fired or removed from the gun before another cartridge is passed through the carrier.

To use the arm as a single loader with the magazine in reserve.—Push the cut-off lever forward. This cuts off the passage of the cartridge from the magazine. The arm may then be used as a single loader.

TO TAKE THE GUN APART.

To remove the breech.—Turn the large screw at the right hand side of the stock below the hammer to the right, until the carrier (which should be in its lower position at the time) drops free of the bolt and allows it to be withdrawn.

Note.—The screw referred to is cut with a left hand thread.

To separate the rear end of the bolt and firing-pin from the front end, bend back the hammer and twist it around to the right until the shoulder on front end of rear cap slides back in the groove in breech bolt. To re-assemble it, reverse the operation described.

To remove the stock.—Take off the bands; take out the screw at the end of the metal tip, and remove tip stock by slipping it forward over the magazine tube. Unscrew the magazine tube, take out the tang screw, remove the guard bow, and take off the butt stock. The barrel should never be unscrewed except by an experienced armorer and with proper appliances to avoid injuring the receiver.

THE REMINGTON IMPROVED NO. 3 RIFLE.

To re-assemble the parts reverse the operations described, taking care in screwing in the magazine tube that the follower does not catch against the cut-off and interfere with replacing the tube.

THE REMINGTON IMPROVED NO. 3 RIFLE.

Solid breech, rebounding lock, side lever (Hepburn's patent, October 7, 1879). This rifle is designed especially for long range target shooting, and for general use as a sportsman's and hunter's rifle, being constructed with special reference to the use of a reloading shell. It has a solid breech block, with direct rear support, side-lever action and rebounding hammer; so that the arm always stands with the trigger in the safety notch, thus rendering premature discharge impossible, and is believed to be the best in use, for the purpose described.

They are all made with pistol-grip stocks, which have heretofore been furnished only with the higher priced rifles, and are chambered for the straight forty calibre and forty-five calibre shells, using either a patched or cannelured bullet.

20

Directions for taking apart.—Remove the upper screw in the left hand side, and the breech block may be taken out. To take out the hammer, remove the next upper screw and slip the hammer forward into the breech block hole. To take out the extractor, remove the forward screw on left hand side.

The lever which operates the breech block passes through the rocker sleeve with a square stud and is held in place by a set screw directly under the fore stock, which must be removed if it is ever desired to take off the lever.

If necessary to remove the guard it can be done by taking off the butt stock and taking out the side screws in the usual way.

The barrel should not be unscrewed from the frame except by experienced hands and with proper appliances.

When necessary to unscrew the frame the extractor should be taken out, the breech block and guard put back in place, before putting on the wrench.

NEW HAVEN, CONN.

CHAPTER V.

THE WHITNEY SYSTEM—THE BURGESS SYSTEM—THE KENNEDY SYSTEM.

THE name of Eli Whitney has for many years been connected with an invention which, of the greatest value to mankind, has not in half a century been improved upon. This invention will be recognized as the Cotton Gin. It is not so well known, however, that to the ingenuity and inventive genius of Mr. Whitney are also due great improvements in the machinery for the manufacture of small arms. His establishment for this purpose was originally started in 1798, thus making Mr. Whitney the pioneer in this line of manufactures. He was the first to invent and develop the system known as the American or interchangeable system, carried out by the use of hardened jigs or forms of the same shape as the part to be produced, thereby turning out every piece for each particular part of the same form and dimensions. He also introduced the use of milling, by means of revolving cutters, those irregular and intricate forms necessary to be produced in making a gun. At the special request of President Jefferson when Secretary of State in Washington's administration, Mr. Whitney undertook the manufacture of muskets for the United States, taking as a model the French Charville flint-lock, that being the most approved arm in use in Europe. In presenting his views to Mr. Jefferson in reference to the feasibility of making all arms interchangeable, Mr. Whitney met with most violent opposition, both English and French ordnance officers ridiculing the idea as an impossibility, and claiming that each arm would be a model and would cost at least one hundred dollars. Supported by government, Mr. Whitney prosecuted his labors, and established an armory where the most perfect uniformity of parts was secured to the great satisfaction of his friend, Mr. Jefferson. The Springfield armory was established in the year 1800, and the system invented by Mr. Whitney was put in force there, and has been in use in all Government works

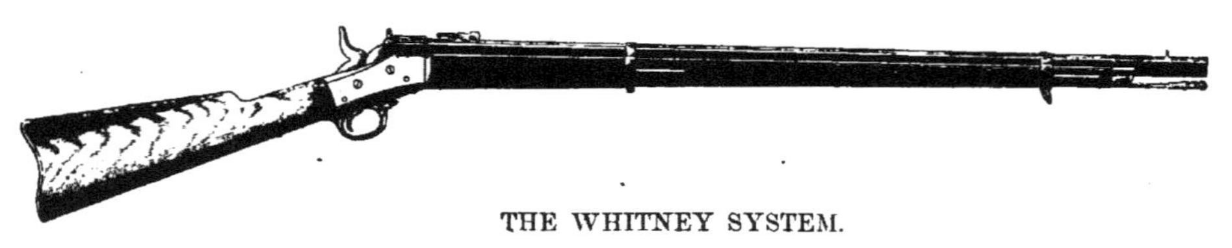

THE WHITNEY SYSTEM.

ever since. The English War Department was forced to adopt the same system, and put it to practical use in 1855 by importing a large amount of American machinery. Since that date other European governments have adopted the same general system, which is made specially necessary in the proper manufacture of breech-loading small arms. The admirable series of inventions used in this system of Mr. Whitney's remains now, like the Cotton Gin, the same as when first invented, no practical change taking place in eighty years, notwithstanding the inventive genius which has been at work during that period of time. No patents have ever been taken out for the Whitney inventions, but they have been freely given to the public, and have saved the United States Government large sums of money by lessening the cost and perfecting the manufacture and repairs of fire-arms.

The Whitneyville Armory, property of the Whitney Arms Co., is now one of the largest in the United States. It is located near New Haven, in the State of Connecticut, and has a capacity for employing over 500 men, being supplied with all the modern improvements in machinery, and now under the control of the son and grandson of the founder, who have added many valuable improvements. Polishing the outside and inside of gun barrels by machinery, straightening the barrels while in the process of boring by the shade in place of the imperfect method of a string; also an automatic machine for smooth or finish boring barrels were invented at this armory.

The system of breech-loading small arms, now known as the Whitney system, has its foundation in the invention of that experienced officer, Colonel T. T. S. Laidley, of the United States Ordnance Bureau, and was first patented in the United States in 1866, at which date foreign letter patents were also obtained. In its original form it was put to the severest tests by United States and foreign military boards, and was almost universally pronounced by them an excellent arm for military service. It has been remodeled and greatly improved by the present owners, who have carefully endeavored to meet every objection, and is now presented as the Whitney system. The claims made for this arm are very strong, the most prominent being as follows:

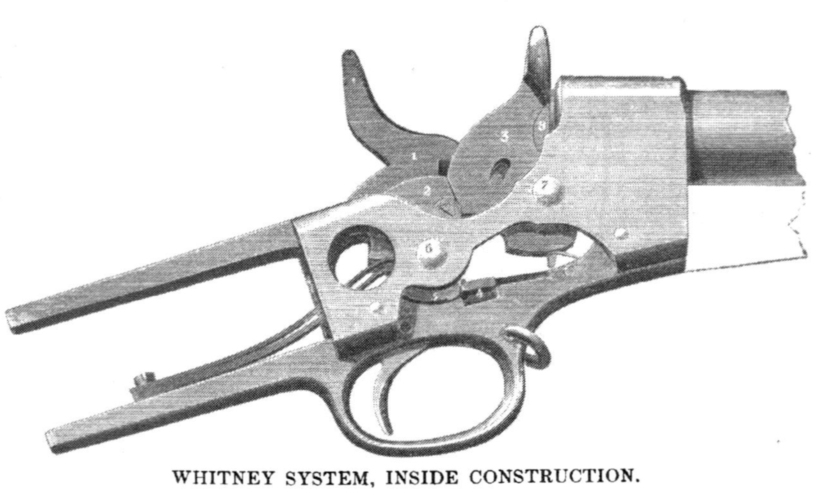

WHITNEY SYSTEM, INSIDE CONSTRUCTION.

Rapidity of Firing.

This arm can be loaded and fired with a rapidity equal to that of any other single breech-loader, and it is claimed that in continuous firing, its rapidity cannot be excelled by any repeater or magazine arm.

Weight, Force and Accuracy.

The weight of this arm varies from 8 to 9½ pounds, according to the calibre and length of barrel. The best system of rifling is employed in manufacturing, and barrels of any calibre can be adapted and fitted for any ammunition.

Transformation.

Arms of other systems can be transformed upon the Whitney system at very small expense comparatively.

Since the publication of "The History of American Breech-Loading Small Arms" in 1872, the Whitneyville armory has been kept constantly busy not only in the regular manufacture of arms already established, but also in the production of new improvements that have been made in the Whitney system. Thousands of these arms have been made and sold in our own and foreign countries and gone into actual service in the field, thereby being put to every possible test, and with the most satisfactory results. The Whitney arm has been fired on the first trial by a novice, twenty-three times in one minute with an additional cartridge in the chamber. The specially novel systems of arms introduced by the Whitney Arms Company, are known as the Burgess and Kennedy systems of repeating rifles, and are manufactured in all the various styles for military and sporting service.

THE BURGESS is a repeating or magazine rifle with the magazine placed under the barrel, and is operated by a lever, the backward and forward movement of which cocks the hammer, opens the breech, throws out the empty shell, and brings a new cartridge into place, ready for discharge.

It has all the requirements requisite to a first-class magazine gun.

It is of simple construction, and has fewer parts than any other magazine rifle operated by a lever.

It is strong. The parts are of such size and form as not to be liable to break or get out of order.

It is made of the best material—wrought iron or steel, as is most suitable for each part.

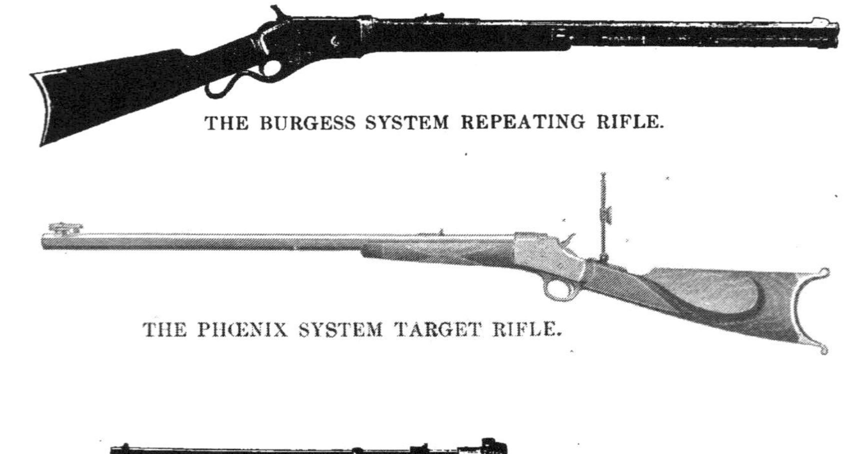

THE BURGESS SYSTEM REPEATING RIFLE.

THE PHŒNIX SYSTEM TARGET RIFLE.

THE PHŒNIX SYSTEM, CAVALRY CARBINE
WITH BREECH OPEN.

The workmanship is superior throughout.

It is very easily manipulated, and can readily be understood by any person who is at all familiar with fire-arms.

It is safe, accidents from premature discharge being impossible.

The resistance to the discharge is in direct line with the bore of the barrel.

The firing pin cannot reach the head of the cartridge until the breech is fully closed—consequently,

The piece can only be fired when the breech is locked.

It has been thoroughly tested by firing many hundreds of rounds successively, by excessive charges, by defective cartridges, etc., and has stood every test.

It meets a want long felt, for a magazine rifle, that, while of lighter weight and less cumbersome than those now in use, would carry a sufficiently heavy charge to make it reliable for large game, target practice at long range, and military service.

The cartridge used is the 45-calibre center-fire, United States Government standard, containing 70 grains of powder and 400 grains of lead.

When a lighter charge is desired, the United States carbine cartridge —the same length as the above—but loaded with only 55 grains of powder, may be used.

The shells can be reloaded.

The magazine is charged through the side of the receiver when the breech is closed.

The rifle can be used as a single loader, the charged magazine being held in reserve.

The prices are reasonable.

The musket weighs 9 lbs. 4 oz. The barrel is 33 inch. It carries when loaded, 11 cartridges.

The carbine weighs 7 lbs. 8 oz. The barrel is 22 inch. It carries when loaded, 7 cartridges.

The sporting rifle weighs 9 to 10 lbs. The barrel is 28 inch. It carries when loaded, 9 cartridges.

The Kennedy is similar to the Burgess in general outline, and the manipulation is the same with the exception of its being necessary to open the breech before charging the magazine through the side of the receiver.

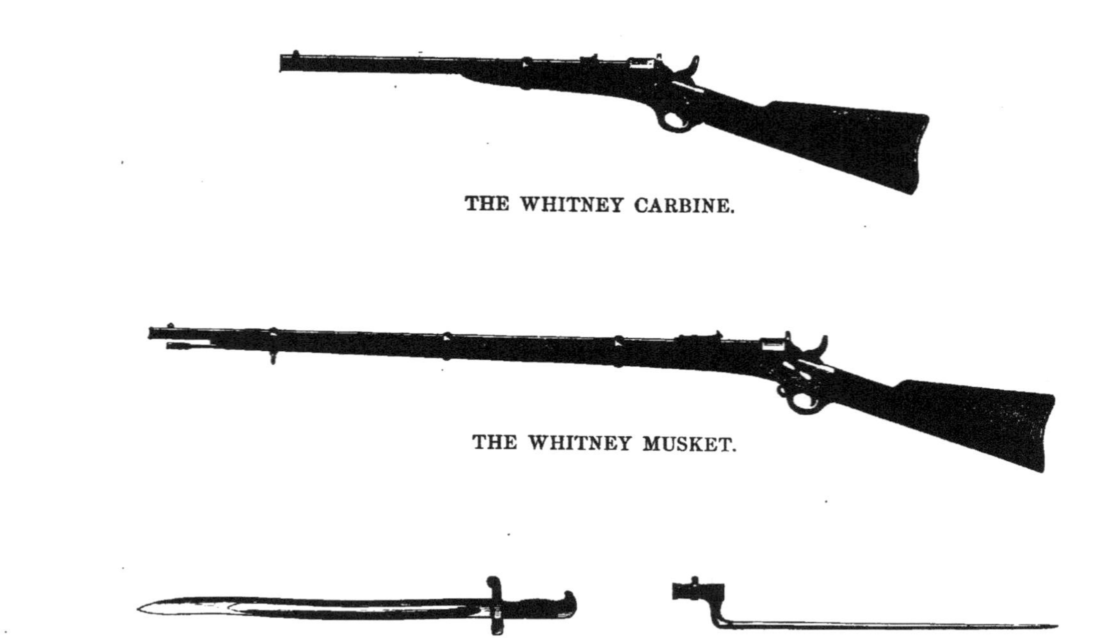

THE WHITNEY CARBINE.

THE WHITNEY MUSKET.

The difference consists in the arrangement of the carrier block, and other parts whereby it is adapted to a cartridge of different calibre from, and lighter weight than that used in the Burgess.

The cartridge used is that known as the "Winchester model of 1873."

It is 44 calibre center-fire, containing 40 grains of powder, and 200 grains of lead.

The shells can be reloaded.

The musket weighs about 9 lbs. The barrel is 30 inch. It carries when loaded, 17 cartridges.

The carbine weighs about 7¼ lbs. The barrel is 20 inch. It carries when loaded, 12 cartridges.

The sporting rifle weighs 9 to 10 lbs. The barrel is 24 inch. It carries when loaded, 15 cartridges.

In addition to the above, the Phœnix system breech-loading rifle is manufactured by the Whitney Arms Company.

These arms possess all the elements of the best breech-loading rifles. They are very simple of construction, and perfectly strong, safe and durable, while the ease of manipulation in opening and closing the breech, and extracting the shell or cartridge cannot be surpassed. They have less parts than any other breech-loading rifle in use, and the parts are of such form as to render the arm strong and safe as a rifle can be made. They have short top action, and are symmetrical in form. On this system are made military arms, sporting and target rifles of both rim and central fire of the different calibres, and single barrel shot guns, which are considered the best and cheapest breech-loading single barrel shot guns in market. Every part of the gun is made from the best of steel or wrought iron, by the most approved machinery and skillful workmen.

These guns have been fired 1400 successive shots, with no signs of failure of any part.

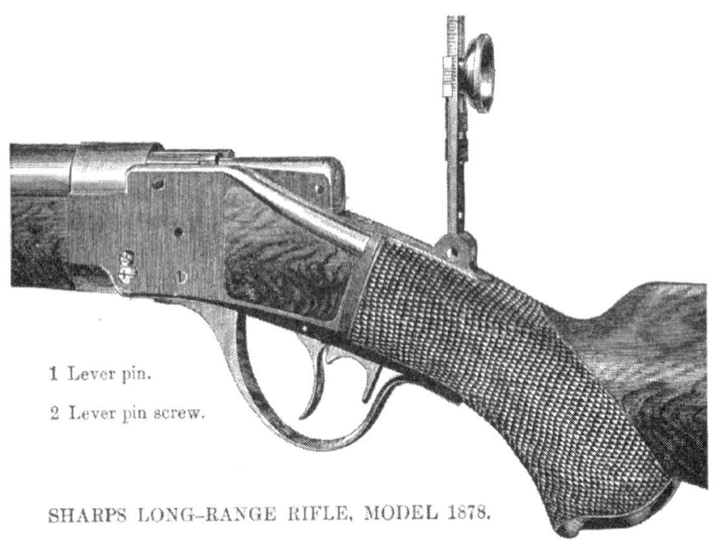

SHARPS LONG-RANGE RIFLE, MODEL 1878.

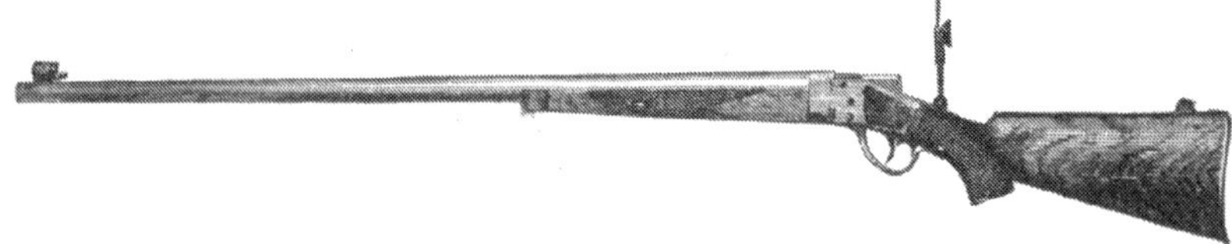

SHARPS LONG-RANGE RIFLE, MODEL 1878.

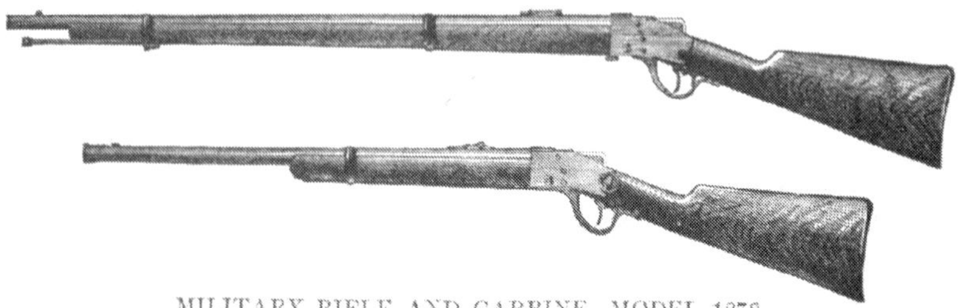

MILITARY RIFLE AND CARBINE, MODEL 1878.

CHAPTER VI.

THE SHARPS SYSTEM—THE LEE MAGAZINE SYSTEM.

Sharps rifle is perhaps better known as an American rifle than any other up to the present time. It was invented, in 1848, by Christian Sharps and with the improvements and new inventions, made by him, was produced in 1857 as the *first* practical breech-loading rifle, and during what is known as the Kansas struggle, secured for itself permanent fame for its rapidity and accuracy of fire. The inventor continued his improvements up to 1873, and in 1875 a company was formed under the name of Sharps Rifle Company, a large armory erected at Bridgeport, and the manufacture carried on upon a scale commensurate with the increased and growing demand for this arm which had become exceedingly popular. The certainty of the results with the Sharps Rifle have led to its receiving the familiar cognomen of "old reliable," which it retains to the present day.

For safety, accuracy, penetration, range, ease of manipulation, rapidity and certainty of fire, strength, durability, and lightness of recoil, they are claimed to be unexcelled by any military rifle made.

The safety-catch is so located behind the trigger, and under the trigger-guard, that it can be instantaneously, but in no case accidentally, released.

When great rapidity of fire is desirable, as in battles, the safety lever may be quickly removed, so that the piece can be discharged immediately upon closing the breech, and thus save one movement.

U. S. cartridges 45 calibre, length of shell, 2$\frac{1}{10}$ inches, with 75 grains powder and 420 grains lead, can be used. The length of barrel is 32 inches, length of rifle 48½ inches, weight without bayonet, 9 pounds. For carbines U. S. Government cartridges 45 calibre, length of shell, 2$\frac{1}{10}$ inches, and 70 grains powder, can be used, length of barrel, 24 inches, weight about 7½ pounds. Double triggers can be applied to both military rifle and carbine. During the war of the rebellion, nearly one hundred thousand of Sharps Rifles were ordered by the Government for use by the army of the United States, a large majority of them being issued to mounted troops, and the general result of their use proved highly satisfactory. The reports of the Secretary of War and Chief of Ordnance in 1869, fully indorse the opinion already formed by officers and soldiers in the field. The Adjutant-General of the State of Michigan, who has made a very complete and learned report on the introduction of breech-loading small arms, states as follows in his report for 1878.

*"After full consideration by the State Military Board, the State Arm has been changed from the Springfield Breech-Loading 50 calibre Rifle, to the Sharps Military Rifle, calibre 45, a breech-loader with the latest improvements. This exchange is not only made on account of the great superiority of the Sharps, but that the Government has adopted the 45 calibre. * * * * The Sharps is an arm of fine finish, great durability, perfectly safe in use, of comparatively light weight, with rapidity and certainty of fire, light recoil, and for accuracy, at either short or long range, is considered to be unsurpassed, perhaps unequaled. * * *"*

The following has also been received:

STATE OF NORTH CAROLINA, OFFICE ADJUTANT GENERAL,
RALEIGH, June 21, 1879.

The Sharps Rifle Company, Bridgeport, Conn.:

GENTLEMEN:—I desire to say, that I regard your gun, as "The Military Rifle," perfect and simple in its mechanism; it is the quickest and easiest loaded of any arm I ever fired, while the locking trigger gives perfect safety. The absence of a hammer is another advantage. In its qualities as a hard and close shooter, it has not a superior, and may always be depended upon for sure work.

Respectfully,

FRED. A. OLDS, *State Ordnance Officer.*

In computing percentages made in the great International Match of 1876, with forty competitors in the field, using rifles of six different makers, including all the *crack* British muzzle loaders, it was found that Sharps headed the list with .877, the next highest scoring only .867. (See official report in *Rod and Gun*, September 30, 1876.) In the International Match of 1877, America against best marksmen of England, Ireland, and Scotland, Sharps is found still in the lead with an average of 420 per man against 414 by any other rifle, and a percentage of .933, the next highest being but .920.

In Fall Meeting, 1878, of N. R. A., at Creedmoor, Sharps rifles entered in *sixteen* matches, took first prize in twelve of them, and good prizes in the other four. Among them the

INTER-STATE MILITARY MATCH.

The New York State Team, using Sharps Military Rifle, won with a score of............974
Best score with other rifles............960

THE INTERNATIONAL MILITARY MATCH.

New York State Team, with Sharps Rifles, won with a score of........................1044
Best with other rifles.. 903

THE INTER-STATE LONG-RANGE MATCH.

Average per man using Sharps Rifles.. 213
Other rifles used, averaged...193 and 197

THE WIMBLEDON CUP.

Won by Mr. Frank Hyde, with a Sharps Long-Range Rifle, with a score of 143 out of 150, at 1000 yards. (The LEECH CUP with same rifle at Spring Meeting, was won with a score of 205 points against best score by any other rifle of 197.)

For the grand aggregate prize, three competitors, Mr. F. Hyde, Col. H. F. Clark, and Capt. W. H. Jackson, all using Sharps, tied on a score of 300.

THE LONG-RANGE MILITARY CHAMPIONSHIP.

First prize won by J. S. Barton with a Sharps. *All prizes in this match were won with* SHARPS *Rifles.*

INTERNATIONAL LONG-RANGE MATCH.

J. S. Sumner made, with a Sharps Long-Range Rifle, the extraordinary score of 221, out of a possible 225, at 800, 900, and 1000 yards.

For hunters and sportsmen Sharps Rifle has proved most serviceable, coming into satisfactory competition with the best known and most expensive of the English sporting rifles. The operation of this system as adopted in 1878, is remarkable for its simplicity and ease of manipulation as a glance at the illustrations herewith given will indicate.

Throwing down the lever (which serves also for a trigger guard) ejects with certainty the exploded shell, and cocks the rifle; the same motion automatically moves the safety-catch and locks the trigger, so that accidental discharge is impossible. The cartridge is now inserted and the lever returned to its position. The rifle, although now loaded, may be carried and handled in any manner with perfect safety; there is nothing to catch in bushes; it may be pulled out of boat or wagon by the muzzle, or handled in any manner, however carelessly (for other rifles), and it cannot be discharged, except by intentionally releasing the safety-catch and pulling the trigger.

The safety-catch is so located behind the trigger, and under the trigger-guard, that it can be instantaneously, but in no case accidentally, released.

When great rapidity of fire is desirable, the safety-lever may be quickly removed, so that the piece can be discharged immediately upon closing the breech.

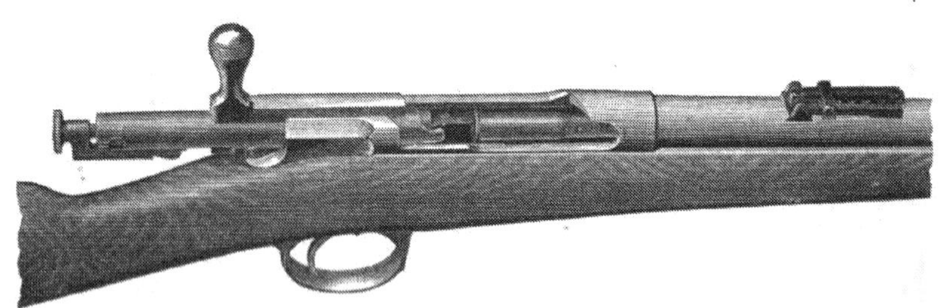

LEE SYSTEM OPEN, WITH MAGAZINE DETACHED.

LEE MILITARY RIFLE, WITH MAGAZINE IN PLACE.
Weight, nine pounds.

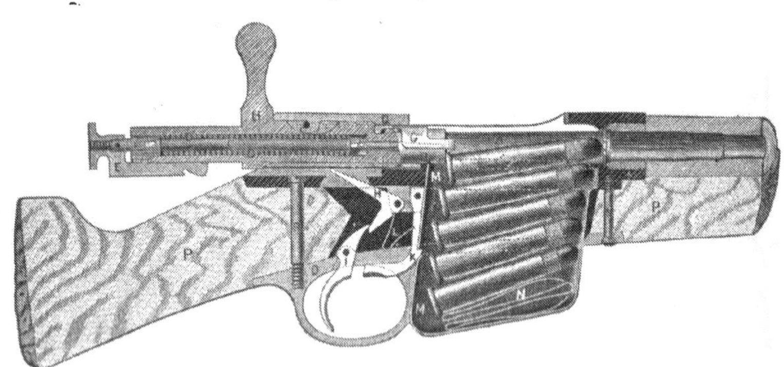

SECTIONAL VIEW OF LEE SYSTEM, WITH MAGAZINE IN PLACE.

A. Receiver.
B. Bolt.
C. Firing Pin.
D. Main Spring.
E. Thumb Piece.
F. Key Sleeve.
G. Extractor.
H. Sear.
I. Trigger.
K. Magazine Catch.
L. Sear Spring.
M. Magazine.
N. Magazine Spring.
O. Trigger Guard.
P. Stock.
R. Tang Screw.
S. Guard Screw.

THE LEE MAGAZINE SYSTEM.

All magazine guns, hitherto made and in use, have been constructed with a tubular receptacle for containing the cartridges, placed either under or above the barrel, or in the butt stock. In this tube or magazine the cartridges ride lengthwise, one following another; the bullet of one coming directly in contact with and resting on the primer of the cartridge next it. All of the cartridges are forced toward the breech mechanism by a spiral spring which spring must be of sufficient strength to support the weight of the column of cartridges, and force them into the receiver or breech of the arm as fast as required, and of necessity it must have very considerable stiffness or strength. A French army cartridge, which is about the average weight of military cartridges in use, weighs more than $1\frac{4}{10}$ ounces. The weight of a column of five such cartridges would be seven ounces, four-fifths of which weight would, in a tubular magazine, rest upon the point of the bullet of the last cartridge, and which bullet comes directly in contact with the primer of the cartridge in advance of it.

The Lee Magazine System, patented in 1879 in Europe and America, is claimed to be entirely novel in principle, obviating all the objections found in tubular magazine systems, but possessing numerous and marked advantages peculiar only to itself.

As will be seen, the Arm is of the bolt class, which years of use in the armies of many of the great powers of Europe, has proved to possess all the essential qualities of a military weapon.

The Lee Bolt System (not referring to its magazine attachments) has fewer parts than any other in use, there being in all

1. Receiver A.
2. Bolt B.
3. Firing Pin C.
4. Main Spring D.
5. Thumb Piece E.
6. Key Sleeve F.
7. Extractor G.
8. Sear H.
9. Trigger I.
10. Sear Spring L.
11. Trigger Guard O.
12. Extractor Spring Q.

together with Tang and Guard Screws R and S, and four pins, two of which are shown in lower part of Receiver A.

In this system the resistance is direct, and is taken on both sides of the receiver; a lug being constructed on the lower side of the bolt and opposite the shoulder on the bolt handle, which locks itself firmly into a recess made for that purpose in the receiver, thereby affording an equal bearing on each side instead of on one side only, as in most other bolt systems ; the extractor is of new design, having direct action and great power.

The main-spring D is made of best steel wire, five feet in length, coiled, and having only three-fourths of an inch movement or thrust (being about 1 to 80) the metal is subjected to but slight strain, and all danger of breakage is obviated.

The arm can be carried while loaded with perfect safety by withdrawing the thumb piece E to the half-cock notch, which operation fixes the bolt firmly to its closed position, and locks the firing pin backward clear from the cartridge until the thumb piece is drawn back to full-cock, when the piece may be fired.

The ease and rapidity with which this arm can be dismounted and assembled is noticeable. By inserting the point of a knife or screw-driver into the notch cut on the extractor spring next the shoulder of the bolt handle the extractor spring Q is pressed forward, releasing the hook on its under side, from the pin with which it engages when in place. This releases the extractor spring and the extractor, and the bolt may then be drawn out of the receiver. By pressing forward and downward on the lug of the key sleeve F it is released from the bolt, together with the thumb piece E, the firing pin C, and the main spring D. To assemble the bolt and its parts, the pieces E, C and D are placed in their proper position, and the lug of the key sleeve F is pressed upward into its locking notch in the bolt. Returning the assembled bolt into its place in the receiver, lay the extractor in its notch on the bolt and place the extractor spring in position, giving the bolt a sharp push forward, and the hook will engage itself on the pin on the bolt-rib created for the purpose, and the arm is ready for use.

For simplicity, strength, ease of manipulation, rapidity and certainty of fire, this system is not excelled as a single-fire breech-loader by any other in use, the weight of the Lee Army Musket not exceeding nine pounds.

To change this single-fire breech-loader to a magazine arm, consists simply in introducing through a slot or opening cut through the stock and receiver, forward of the trigger guard, a magazine made to contain five (more or less) cartridges, which insertion or removal can be effected more quickly than a single cartridge can be loaded into or ejected from any ordinary single breech-loader. The magazine is held in place by the magazine catch (K), which engages into a notch or depression in the rear of the magazine, and can be released in a moment by an upward pressure on the magazine catch K at its lower end, where it projects downward into the trigger-guard.

The magazine is retained so firm and secure in position that it is impossible for it to become accidentally released, no matter how roughly the arm is used or how severe a shock it may receive. These magazines are pressed into shape from one piece of metal, and are strengthened by a rib formed on their rear and bottom interior, which renders them, although weighing but about three ounces, strong and rigid enough to endure without injury any shock or blow liable to be received in rough service. They may be adapted to cartridges of any length. The cartridges are held in a nearly horizontal position, the flange or head of each being in advance of the one below it, rendering it impossible for anything to impinge upon the primer of either cartridge, and thus obviating every possible danger of premature discharge in the magazine.

The cartridges are fed upward into the system by the magazine spring N as fast as required, and being held strongly in position, no deformation of the bullet is possible. By actual experiment, the bullet of cartridges so held, and exposed to the recoil received from one hundred shots fired in the arm, showed no diminution in length.

The simplicity of the magazine mechanism proper, of this arm is unequaled and remarkable, consisting of only three pieces, the Magazine M, the Magazine Spring N, and the Magazine Catch K, and, *incidentally*, the Spring W, which operates in a slot in the side of the receiver, and projects over the opening through which the cartridges pass upward from the magazine, forming a bottom to the receiver, while the arm is being used as a single loader. The lower part of this spring is beveled, so that on introducing the magazine into the system, the spring is forced back into its recess in the side of the receiver, and out of the way. The complexity of the magazine mechanism of repeating arms hitherto produced, with the consequent liability to breakage or derangement, has been one of the objections offered to their adoption for

POSITION OF SOLDIER WHILE INTRODUCING OR REMOVING MAGAZINE FROM THE LEE MAGAZINE RIFLE.

military purposes. Here are, at most, *four pieces*, each simple and strong, and whose place and purpose are so apparent that the least intelligent recruit cannot for a moment be puzzled as to their proper use.

The cartridges contained in charged magazines (while the magazines are not in the arm) are retained in position by sliding forward the upper cartridge until the point of the bullet rests in the hemispherical depression formed in the front and upper part of the magazine. The upward pressure of the spring N holds the head of this upper cartridge against the projecting inclined flanges on the upper and rear part of the magazines so tightly, that the filled box may be carried, handled or dropped without displacing the position of the ammunition.

The charge magazine should only be inserted into the arm when the system is closed. When the magazine is put into place (accomplished either by pressure or by a sharp tap of the hand), the head of the upper cartridge is relieved of its tension against the inclined flanges on the rear and upper part of the magazine, by its pressure against the under side of the bolt B (the upper edge of the rear wall of the magazine being slightly hollowed to the shape of the bolt). The rearward motion of the bolt in opening the breech, draws back the upper cartridge, relieving its front end from the hemispherical depression in which it rested; the spring N lifts the bullet end of the cartridge upward, and free from the magazine, the bolt moving backward just far enough to allow its front end to pass in rear of the head of the cartridge, which head, thus relieved, rises by the pressure of the spring N sufficiently to engage the end of the bolt. The forward movement of the bolt then carries this cartridge into the chamber of the barrel.

On opening the system and withdrawing the bolt, the extractor ejects with certainty the exploded shell, and the same operations apply until the magazine is exhausted.

It is intended that two or more magazines shall be furnished with each arm, which are to be carried, charged, in the cartridge box or pocket of the soldier. The magazines can be charged with cartridges (five is the number recommended that they shall contain), each in less than five seconds. It is quite practicable that all ammunition issued to troops be contained in these magazines, which may be made, if required, very light, of skeleton form, and of such cheap construction, as will admit in action of their being dropped and left on the field, as are the exhausted shells of expended cartridges.

The arm can be used as a single loader until the need of rapid firing becomes apparent, when, at the word of command, the charged magazines may be inserted and used. The least intelligent soldier can obey this order without looking at the arm. While removing or inserting the magazine, the arm should be held at the grip by the soldier's RIGHT hand, in the position illustrated.

It is believed that the feature of *detachability*, as arranged in the Lee System, will particularly commend itself to the minds of military authorities. The ease, rapidity, and certainty with which the charged magazines can be inserted into or removed from the arm, places it in the power of the officers of disciplined troops, to positively control the expenditure of ammunition. The soldier may use his arm as a single loader until the vital moment when a rapid fire is needed. At the order a loaded magazine can in an instant be inserted, and a volley of five, to be immediately succeeded by five, ten, or fifteen more shots (if as many as four magazines be supplied), rapidly delivered. It will require but little drill to teach the ordinary soldier to deliver twenty-one well directed shots from a Lee Magazine Gun in forty seconds. Experts at the Armory fire that number easily in *thirty* seconds. Using the *detachable magazines*, the necessity of all *cut-off* appliances is obviated, and the danger of soldiers becoming so confused in the heat and excitement of action as to err in the proper adjustment of the cut-off, need not be feared. It is, however, quite practicable to construct and use the Lee System, as a FIXED MAGAZINE ARM. By a very simple device the cartridges contained in a magazine of similar construction, *but permanently attached to the arm*, may be carried in reserve, or otherwise, as desired. The magazines so affixed, can be as conveniently and quickly refilled, as those of any other repeating rifle. The Company do not recommend such fixed attachment, believing the adjustable form to be far preferable, but are prepared to manufacture them, if ordered in quantities.

The originator of the Lee Magazine System had not sufficiently developed his invention to submit it to the Board of U. S. Ordnance Officers, appointed in 1878 to examine and test the various magazine arms presented before them, and consequently no examination was had, or report made, by that Board as to its merits.

The "Equipment Board," selected, as the General of the Army has written, "by reason of their fitness, and their large experience with the wants of the troops in actual service on the plains, and in the mountains of the interior of the continent," of which Gen. N. A. Miles, U. S. A., was chairman, by order of the War Department issued May, 1879, made an examination and the following report on the "Lee Magazine Gun."

"This Gun, which was referred to the Board by the Honorable the Secretary of War, may be briefly described as belonging to the class of breech-loading bolt guns. The peculiarity consists in the application of the magazine principle. In other breech-loaders the magazine is permanently attached, and placed under the barrel, over the barrel, or in the butt or stock. These magazines are all tubular, the cartridges being placed one behind the other, so as to be in dangerous contact when the gun is fired. The magazine of the Lee Gun is a small metallic case containing five cartridges, which can be attached or removed at pleasure, and in the time required to load a single cartridge. The cartridges are side by side, and the magazine, when in position, is just below the receiver in front of the guard, and the weight of the cartridge is therefore in the center of the piece. When detached the gun may be used as a single loader. In the breech mechanism there are but 22 parts. The recoil is taken upon both sides of the bolt, and the gun can be fired with accuracy 20 times in 30 seconds.

The comparative simplicity of the mechanism, and the ease with which the magazine can be applied, make it a valuable and destructive weapon. The trials made with this Rifle in the presence of the Board were most satisfactory."

The commander of the large force recently sent against the hostile Indians in the Northwest, an officer of great experience and high reputation, being impressed with the superiority of the Lee Magazine Rifle, has made request of the U. S. War Department that his command shall be armed therewith.

The marked favor and high commendation which the Lee System has received from all the many eminent military authorities and mechanical engineers to whom it has been shown, but strengthens the confidence with which the Company claims that this Magazine Rifle is in many if not all essential points, *the best that has been produced.*

ARMORY OF SHARPS RIFLE COMPANY,
BRIDGEPORT, CONN.

Fig. 1.

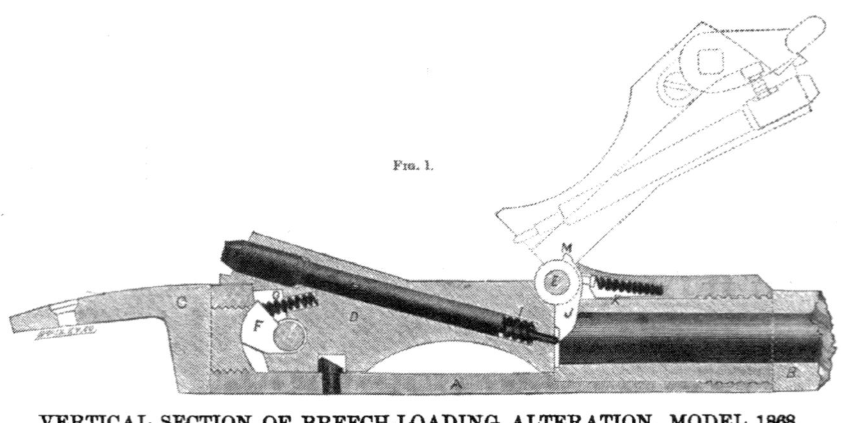

VERTICAL SECTION OF BREECH-LOADING ALTERATION, MODEL 1868.

Springfield Model.

CHAPTER VII.

SPRINGFIELD BREECH-LOADING RIFLE MUSKET,—MODEL OF 1868. —MODEL OF 1879—BENTON'S ELECTRO-BALLISTIC PENDULUM.

THE arm known as the Springfield breech-loader is derived from a model submitted in 1865 by Mr. E. S. Allin, Master Armorer of the United States Armory. A few guns made in accordance with this model were issued to the troops in 1866, but they were not found to answer the requirements of the military service. Extensive changes were made in it from time to time, constituting the models of 1866, 1868 and 1870. These changes were the results of suggestions made by officers and workmen of the Springfield Armory. The arm, as thus improved, has been issued to troops in the field in competition with other systems, and reports will soon be made as to its value. The following description has been prepared by the Ordnance Bureau for the use of troops:

I. The rifle musket adopted for the United States Army in 1868, is the muzzle-loading rifle musket, model 1863, altered to a breech-loader. The following are the principal changes, viz.:

1st. The substitution of a new barrel, 36 in. long (32.75 in. in the bore), and one-half inch (0.5) calibre. The rifling is the same as in the altered gun of 1866, viz.: three grooves equal in width to the lands, 0.0075 in. deep, and 42 inches twist.

2d. To the barrel is screwed a *receiver*, or breech-frame, in which the breech-block swings upwards and forwards as in the model of 1866.

3d. The ramrod is reduced in size and is secured in its bed by a shoulder, about 4 inches below the head, which rests against a *stop* inserted in the stock just below the tip.

4th. The middle band is omitted, and the swivel is attached to the upper band. The bands are held in place by springs.

5th. The short-range leaf sight is replaced by a long-range sliding-sight, secured to the barrel by a dove-tail mortice and screw.

other fingers in front of the breech-block—and close it down; the breech-block will press the cartridge home. The cam-latch will spring into its place and lock it; but to make sure of this, it may be well that the soldier acquire the habit of pressing the thumb on the thumb-piece as the hand is withdrawn to its place. Should there be any difficulty in pressing down the thumb-piece, it is probable that the rim of the cartridge is too thick; it should be withdrawn and another tried.

II. The surface of the cam-latch and that of the recess in the breech-screw should be kept free from dust and rust, to prevent sticking in opening the breech after each discharge; these surfaces should be oiled occasionally. Should the cam-latch spring break, or impede the operation of the cam in any way, unscrew the cap screw and remove the cam-latch, which will enable the soldier to renew or adjust the spring. The force of the discharge is exerted against the rear of the cam-latch, and to ensure this the arbor and body of the cam-latch shaft are made purposely to fit their bearings loosely.

III. The hammer should habitually be carried at half-cock, and care taken that the motion of the firing-pin be not obstructed by dust nor rust.

IV. Should the extractor cut through the rim of the shell, and thereby fail to withdraw it, draw the ramrod and drive the shell out.

V. The chamber should be kept clean, and great care should be observed to prevent cartridges fouled with dirt, and particularly sand, from being inserted or discharged in the piece, as the expansion of the shell presses the sand into the metal and mars the surface of the chamber, and thus causes the shells to stick. Care should also be taken in cleaning the chamber for the same reason. The shell of an exploded cartridge should not be allowed to remain in the chamber any length of time for fear it may adhere by corrosion.

Fig. 10.

CAM LATCH SPRING.

Fig. 11.

FIRING PIN SPRING.

Fig. 12.

RAMROD.

"Fig. 10 is the Cam Latch Spring.

Fig. 11 is the Firing Pin Spring. The firing-pin is shown in Fig. 1. It is kept in place by a small screw which projects into a slot on its under side. This screw is shown in the broken lines representing the raised position of the breech-block. See Fig. 1.

Fig. 12 represents the end of the Ramrod. A is the *shoulder* which rests against the stop; B is the *head*, converted into a *wiper*.

Fig. 13 represents the Ramrod Stop. A is the *body* of the stop; B, the body which fits over the shoulder of the ramrod; C is the *groove* which fits against the barrel.

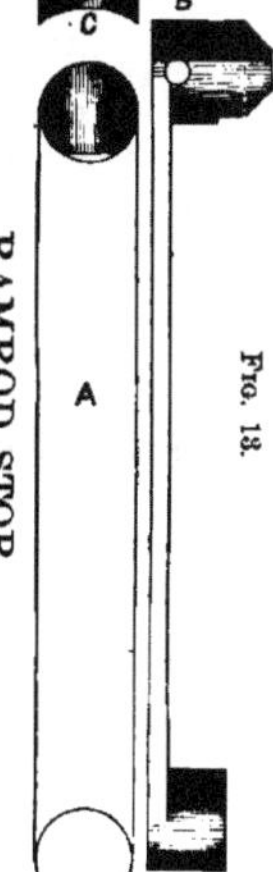

RAMROD STOP.

Fig. 13.

DIRECTIONS FOR USE.

I. Raise the breech-block by pressing against the thumb-piece upwards and forwards till the breech-block rests on the receiver; if there be an empty shell in the chamber, it will be loosened from its place by the extractor and thrown out by the ejector-spring. Place the cartridge in the chamber with the thumb and two fore-fingers; seize the thumb-piece with the thumb and forefinger—the

Fig. 6. Fig. 7.

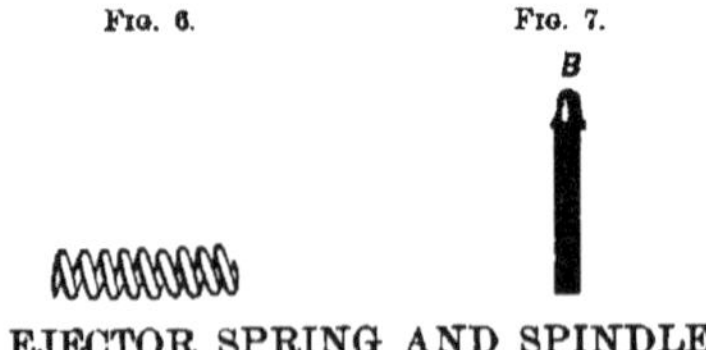

EJECTOR SPRING AND SPINDLE.

Figs. 6 and 7 represent the Ejector Spring and Spindle. The spring presses against the shoulder of the spindle, and the point of the spindle presses against the extractor.

Fig. 8.

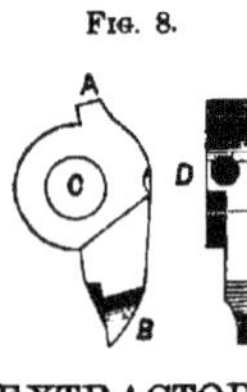

EXTRACTOR.

Fig. 8 represents the Extractor. A is the part against which the breech-block presses in opening; D is the countersink to receive the point of the spring spindle; B is the portion which projects through to the inner surface of the barrel. The surface of this part is shaped to fit the under side of the head of the cartridge-shell.

Fig 9.

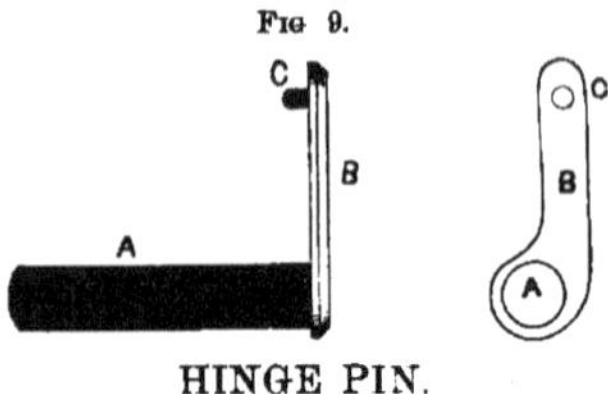

HINGE PIN.

Fig. 9 represents the Hinge Pin. A is the body of the pin; B is the arm; C, the stud which projects into the receiver to prevent the pin from turning.

FIG. 3.

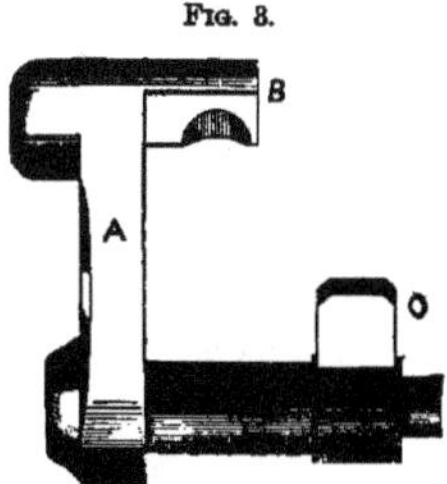

CAM LATCH AND THUMB PIECE.

Fig. 3 represents the Cam Latch and Shaft and *Thumb Piece* combined. A is the body of the thumb-piece; B, the *firing-pin guard*, cut away to allow it to pass freely over the head of the firing-pin. The thumb-piece is secured to the shaft by riveting the end of the latter.

FIG. 4.

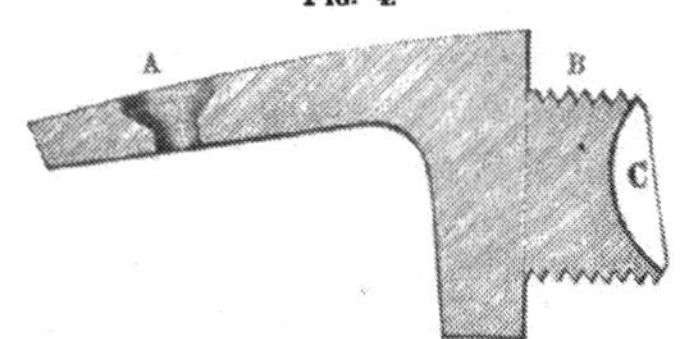

BREECH SCREW.

Fig. 4 represents the Breech-screw. A is the tang-screw hole; B, the screw thread; C, the *cam-latch recess*.

FIG. 5.

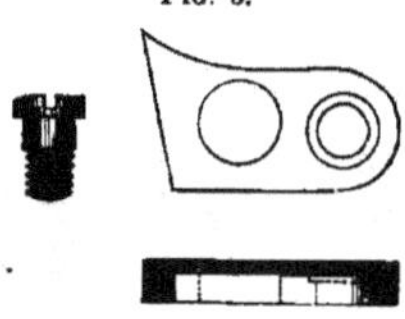

BREECH BLOCK CAP AND SCREW.

Fig. 5 represents the Breech Block Cap and Screw. The object of the cap is to support the cam-latch shaft, and the screw keeps it in place.

6th. The cupping of the hammer is removed and the main spring swivel is shortened.

NOMENCLATURE OF ALTERED PARTS.

II. Fig. 1 represents a vertical section through the axis of the Receiver, with the several parts projected thereon, showing their relative position.

A, the bottom of the Receiver: B, the *Barrel*, with its *screw-thread;* C, the *Breech-pin*, with its *circular-recess* to receive the cam-latch ; E, the *Hinge-pin*, around which the breech-block turns ; F, the *Cam-latch*, which locks the breech-block in place; G, the *Cam-latch Spring*, to press the cam-latch into the recess; H, the *Firing-pin*, which transmits the blow of the hammer to the priming of the cartridge ; I, the *Firing-pin spring*, to press the firing-pin back when the hammer is raised ; J. the *Extractor*, to withdraw the empty cartridge-shell after firing ; K, the *Ejector Spring*. When the breech-block is closed, the point of the ejector-spring presses against the extractor above the position of the axis of the hinge-block, and no motion takes place ; when the breech-block is raised so as to press against the point M of the extractor, the point J moves to the rear, withdrawing the shell, and when the point of pressure of the spring passes below the centre of the hinge, the extractor moves rapidly and throws the shell clear of the receiver. L, the *Ejector Stud*, which serves to deflect the shell upwards and thereby clear the *well* of the receiver.

FIG. 2.

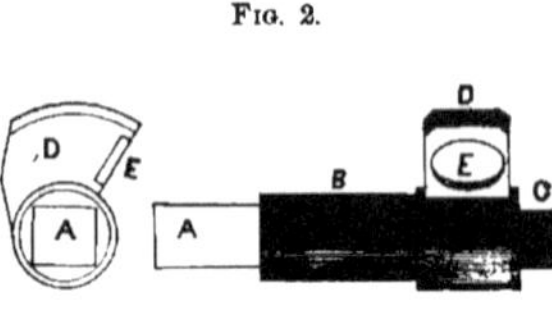

CAM LATCH AND SHAFT.

Fig. 2 represents the Cam Latch and Shaft. The portion A is the *square* upon which the *thumb-piece* is fitted ; B is the *shaft;* C is the *arbor ;* D is the *cam ;* E is the *spring recess.*

SPRINGFIELD RIFLE AND CARBINE SIGHTS, MODEL 1879.

The Springfield Rear Sight, known as the Model of 1879, differs from those of previous models in having a *buckhorn* shaped eye-piece attached to the slide; and also that the slide can be moved sidewise, to enable the marksman to correct his aim for *wind*, *drift*, and *errors of construction of piece*. The only exception to side motion is at the lowest,—or 100 yards elevation,—where the sight notch is intended to be always over the axis of the piece.

The *front sight* of the arms to be made hereafter will be thinner at the base, the rear edge will be vertical, and the top will be slightly rounded and polished, to give a brilliant point or "bead" in service firing.

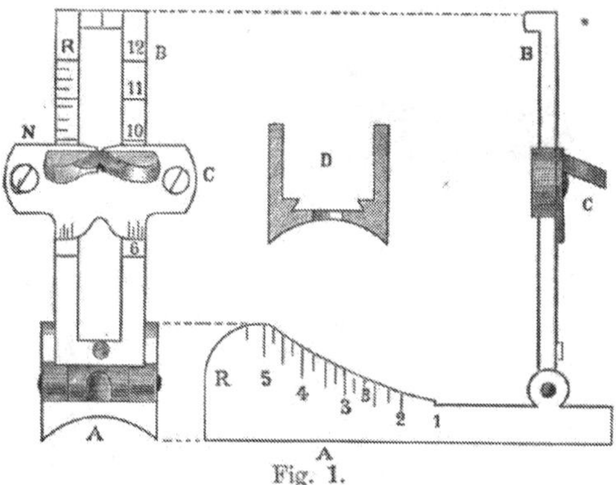

Fig. 1.

DESCRIPTION.—Fig. 1 represents the face and side elevations of the rear sight complete. (A) is the *base;* (B) the *leaf;* (C) the *slide;* and (D) the cross section through the base, showing the thickness of the sides, the front screw hole, and the under cut slot for the *base spring*. The upper edges of the sides of the base are *knurled*, leaving minute offsets to prevent the slide from moving forward when the piece is fired.

The rifle and carbine sights are distinguished by the letters R and C respectively. The figures denoting ranges are stamped as follows, viz.: for the rifle sight, from 100 to 550 yards on the left side of the base;

from 550 to 1,300 yards on the face of the leaf; from 1,300 to 1,600 yards on the back of the leaf. The 550 mark is in front of the 500 mark, and the elevation is determined by placing the front edge of the slide immediately over the 550 mark. The top line of the leaf gives, when elevated, 1,300 yards; to obtain elevations above this, the aim is taken over that part of the slide which projects from the left edge of the leaf and the fore end of the tip of the stock. The upper left hand corner of the leaf and fore end of the tip give 1,600 yards.

The letter B opposite the 260 yards mark indicates the most suitable elevation for firing at an enemy's line of battle within a range of 400 yards, "aiming low."

In the carbine sight the graduation marks from 100 up to 800 yards are on the base; from 800 to 1,500 yards, on the face of the leaf.

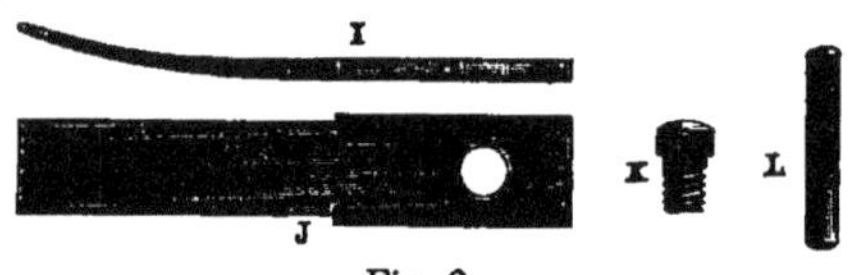

Fig. 2.

Fig. 2 represents the *base spring.* (I) is the side and (J) the top view; (K) is the *base screw,* two in number; and (L) is the *joint pin.*

Fig. 3 represents the *buck-horn plate,* rear and top views. The V shaped notch in the lower edge embraces a pin projecting from the lower part of the leaf, for the purpose of centering the slide when at the 100 yards elevation. The graduations on either side of the notch are for the purpose of regulating the side motion of the slide. The slide is central when its vertical edges conform to the outer edges of the leaf. The other parts are as follows, viz.:

Fig. 3.

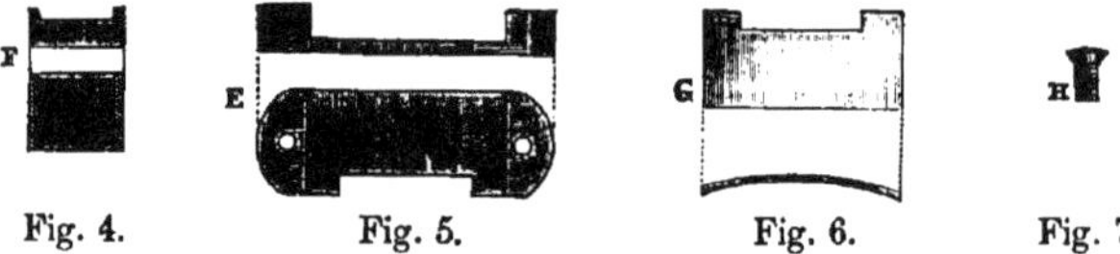

Fig. 4. Fig. 5. Fig. 6. Fig. 7.

Fig 4, the *slide block;* Fig. 5, the *slide plate;* Fig. 6, the *slide spring;* Fig. 7, *slide screw*, two in number. The points of these screws are riveted, and no attempt should be made to turn them out.

New sights issued to replace old ones in the field will have base screws with slotted heads, so that they may be turned in with a common screw-driver. The old sights may be removed by slotting the heads of the base screws with a three cornered file, and turning them out with a screw-driver with a handle. As far as practicable, special files for this work will be issued with the sights, until the change is complete.

INSTRUCTIONS FOR USE.

In the preliminary (or sighting) shots at any range above 100 yards, the slide will be supposed in a central position. If in this position the ball be found to carry to the *right*, either on account of *drift* or a wind from the left, then the plate must be gently tapped to the *left* (an empty cartridge-shell will serve) until the deviation is found by trial to be overcome. If the ball be carried to the *left*, tap the plate to the *right*, etc. Each space between the lines on the buckhorn plate is .02 of an inch, and a side motion of the plate through one of these will correct a deviation of $5\frac{1}{2}$ inches at 200 yards, $8\frac{1}{3}$ at 300, $13\frac{9}{10}$ at 500, $21\frac{2}{10}$ at 800, and $26\frac{1}{2}$ at 1000 yards for the rifle. With the carbine a movement through one space will correct a deviation of $8\frac{4}{10}$ inches at 200 yards, $13\frac{1}{2}$ at 300, and 23 at 500 yards. This gives approximately the side distance through which the plate should be moved to overcome an observed deviation at a known range.

The values given result from the proportion, viz.:

Distance between sights (d) : .02 : : range (r) : deviation (x). Or $x = .02\frac{r}{d}$, r and d expressed in inches.

The spaces being equal to each other, the value of 2 is twice that of one, and so on.

When the aim is taken with the leaf resting on the base, care should be taken to bring the upper edge of the slide into a horizontal position; this will make the plane of sight vertical. When the leaf is raised, the same end is accomplished by making the edges of the leaf vertical.

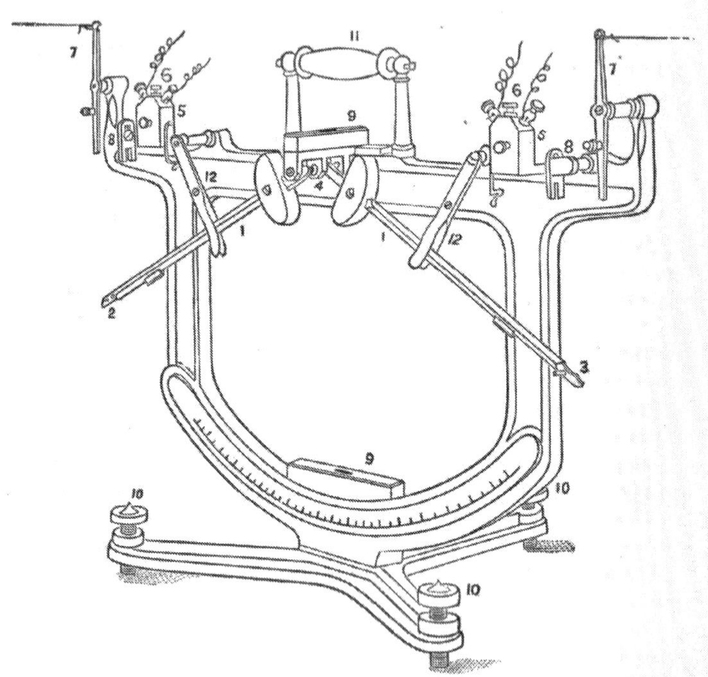

BENTON'S ELECTRO-BALLISTIC PENDULUM.

National Armory, Springfield.

The following articles, having relation to tests made with the Springfield rifle, are published in connection therewith.

BENTON'S ELECTRO-BALLISTIC PENDULUM.

This pendulum was invented at West Point in 1859 by Colonel J. G. Benton, Ordnance Department, U. S. A., for the purpose of determining the velocity of projectiles. It belongs to the Navez class of machines in which the error arising from variation in the power of the electro-magnets is eliminated by means of an instrument called the disjunctor.

The accompanying figure shows a front view of the pendulum in perspective. It is simply a time-keeper capable of measuring accurately intervals of time as small as one-thousandth part of a second. It is essentially composed of an upright cast-iron frame which supports two pendulums having a common axis, a graduated arc to measure their vibrations, and two electro-magnets for holding them suspended in a horizontal position until the galvanic currents actuating the magnets are broken by the movement of the projectile, the velocity of which is to be determined.

The time of the falling of both pendulums through each degree of the arc is known from a computed table. If the pendulums begin to fall at the same instant they will meet opposite to the zero point; if one pendulum starts before the other, the arc described by it will be longer than that of the other, and the difference in the times of starting will be equal to twice the time corresponding to the arc measured from the point of meeting to zero of the arc. The time thus obtained will be that which the projectile has taken in passing between the two targets to which the galvanic currents are attached. *The distance between the targets divided by the time is approximately equal to the velocity of the projectile at the middle point.*

The three thumb screws (10, 10, 10,) of the figure, support the frame, and with the assistance of the two spirit levels (9, 9), afford the means of giving it the necessary vertical position. The two pendulums are shown at 1, 1; the bobs of these pendulums are placed near the suspension frame (4) to make their fall rapid; and are so adjusted as to make the velocities of their fall equal.

Two spring clamps (12, 12) are arranged to catch and hold the pendulums after they have passed each other. Two horse-shoe magnets (5, 5) are inclosed in brass boxes which are attached to the upper edge of the frame, the poles of the magnets projecting through the bottom. Each of these boxes has attached to it three thumb screws; the central screw (6) is for the purpose of moving the magnets up and down, or to and from, the armature of soft iron attached to the suspension rod of each pendulum, and thereby to increase or diminish the attractive force with which the pendulums are held in suspension. The pendulums do not begin to fall instantaneously with the rupture of the galvanic circuits; the stronger the current, the longer will it take for the magnets to let go of the pendulums; the screw (6) affords the means of making the time of starting the same for both pendulums by varying the distance of each magnet from the armature of the pendulum.

The point at which the two pendulums pass each other is marked on the graduated arc by means of a bent lever attached to the lower end of one of the suspension rods; the point of the lever is covered with printers' ink and is pressed on the arc by the end of the rod of the other pendulum when the axis of the pendulums are opposite to each other.

The two binding screws in the oblique surfaces of the magnet boxes are for the attachment of the galvanic wires which pass to the targets, over which they are arranged in such manner as to be cut by the projectile when the piece is fired.

The projecting pieces (8, 8) are attached to the upper edge of the frame and are designed for guides to the suspension rods when the pendulums are held in a horizontal position before falling.

The disjunctor is an additional instrument used for the purpose of breaking both of the galvanic currents simultaneously. By means of it and the thumb screws (6, 6) both pendulums should be made to reach the zero point at the same time, proving thereby that they start at the same time.

Owing to the variations in the strength of galvanic batteries, it is important that this adjustment or "disjunctor observation" should be made shortly before every shot is fired for determining its velocity. No results can be considered reliable without it, and with it there is seldom a failure to get a good result.

The *modus operandi* for determining the velocity of a projectile by this pendulum is as follows:

Place two targets at a certain distance apart, generally one hundred feet; arrange a small copper wire on each target in such a manner that some part of the wire shall be cut by the projectile in its passage; from each target the wire passes to the disjunctor to which it is attached by binding screws, and thence to the binding screws of the magnet; each wire forms a complete galvanic current by means of one cup of a Bunsen battery; the piece being loaded, one or more "disjunctor observations" are made and the strength of the magnets is adjusted as before explained until the point of meeting of the pendulums is at zero of the arc; when this is accomplished the disjunctor is again closed, the pendulums are again raised, and the piece is fired; the reading of the arc giving the position of the point of meeting of the pendulums is referred to a computed table which gives the required velocity of the projectile.

Each target is generally composed of two upright pieces of wood placed a short distance apart, and the wire is stretched back and forth between them without touching to make it sure that some portion shall be broken by the projectile.

The pendulum should be placed about 100 feet from the piece to avoid the effect of the shock of the discharge; the first target should be placed sufficiently far from the muzzle of piece to prevent rupture of the wire by fragments from the discharge.

The following statements in regard to experiments recently made at the National Armory at Springfield with reference to range and the use of the Telephone will be found of interest:

SPRINGFIELD RIFLE—RANGE.

A very interesting series of experiments have been recently carried out by Captain Greer at the National Armory in reference to the increase of range in arms now in service. These experiments have proved the rather singular fact that by an increase of the weight of bullet an increased range is obtained, the difference being over 700 yards in favor of a bullet weighing 500 grains over one weighing 400, the charge of powder being the same in both cases. The explanation of this fact is due to the great ability of the heavy bullet to overcome the resistance of the atmosphere. The advantages of heavy charges of powder are to flatten the trajectory and increase the danger space, that is the position in which troops are likely to be hit, this applying specially to short ranges because at all long ranges the bullet is too high in the air to endanger troops except at the falling point. The heavy bullet also goes more rapidly as shown herewith :

405 grain bullet, ...	9¼ seconds,	2,000 yards.
405 grain bullet, ...	17¾ seconds,	2,500 yards.
500 grain bullet, ...	$11\frac{4}{10}$ seconds,	2,500 yards.
500 grain bullet, ...	15½ seconds,	3,000 yards.
500 grain bullet, ...	$21\frac{3}{10}$ seconds,	3,500 yards.

The light bullet starts more rapidly but slows up, while the heavy bullet starts with a slower velocity, yet loses less rapidly and reaches the point of impact much sooner.

TIME OF FLIGHT OF BULLETS AS DETERMINED BY THE TELEPHONE.

Hitherto the accurate determination of the time of flight of small arm projectiles has been practically impossible at long ranges owing to our inability to see them strike even when firing over water. The discovery of the telephone has opened up to us a simple as well as novel means of obtaining the time desired, and has also afforded us the means of verifying the formulas by which these times were formerly deduced.

In these experiments two telephones provided with Blake transmitters were used. One was placed within a few feet of the gun and left open to receive and transmit the sound of the discharge. The other was in the shelter-proof which was but about thirty feet in front of the right edge of the target. A stop-watch beating fourths of a second was used in connection with it. The telephone being at the ear, the instant the sound of the discharge was received at the target, the watch was started, and on the bullet striking was stopped

A mean of a large number of observations, which rarely differed more than a quarter to a half of a second from each other, gave the time of flight. Of course there is a slight delay in starting the watch, but this is neutralized by a similar one in stopping it. The times given may therefore be accepted as strictly correct. It is worthy of notice that the times vary on different days, being shortened by a rear and lengthened by a head wind.

The velocity of sound may be readily obtained with the telephone in the same manner. The time for the sound of the discharge passing through the air was always shown by the watch, but as it was not desirable for my purpose to stop the watch until the bullet reached the targets these times were not taken.

Note.—Since the above extract was written, Captain Greer informs me he has learned that the same method had been previously used by Captain Starring, Ordnance Department.

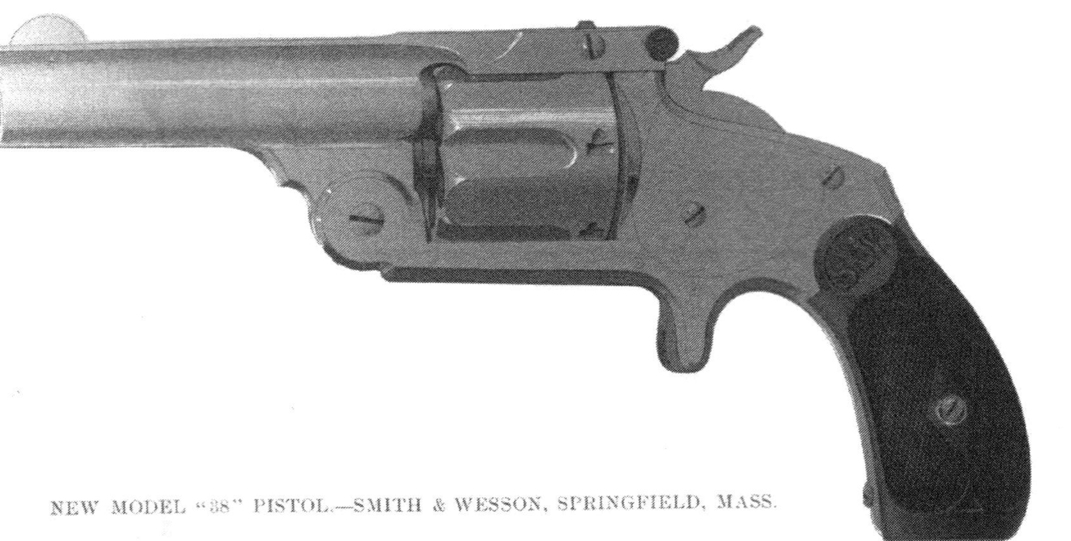

NEW MODEL "38" PISTOL.—SMITH & WESSON, SPRINGFIELD, MASS.

CHAPTER VIII.

SMITH & WESSON REVOLVERS—COLT'S REVOLVERS—MERWIN, HULBERT & CO'S PISTOLS—THE EVANS MAGAZINE GUN.

This arm, of which two distinct styles are now made, was first introduced by this well known firm about 1859. Up to that time, no arm had been used in this country in which any form of metallic cartridge was fired other than the "Flobert" French cartridge, which consisted of a small copper shell containing fulminate, and a small ball, only used in the so-called "Saloon" pistol, a single-barreled arm made in France and sold occasionally in this country. On the 8th of August, 1854, this firm patented a central-fire, metallic cartridge, which not only contained the requisite charge of powder, but which also had the lubricant placed within the case and between the powder and the ball. About the same time they conceived the idea of constructing a revolver that should use this style of cartridge, or one similar; and they immediately proceeded to make such an arm, on which they obtained patents July 5, 1859, and December 18, 1860.

About this time, they learned that a patent had been issued to Rollin White, April 3, 1855, on a revolver, which covered one feature used by them, viz.: the cylinder having its chambers bored entirely through from end to end, so as to permit the charge to be inserted through the rear end of the same. White, however, in his patent, had not contemplated the use of metallic cartridges; but instead, intended to load the chambers with loose powder and ball, or ordinary cartridge, and then close the rear end of the chambers with a wad having a hole at its centre, through which the fire from a cap placed on a single nipple located in the frame of the arm, was to pass. This arrangement, of course, required a fresh cap to be applied each time a chamber was discharged; and moreover, the fire from one chamber would tend to pass to the adjoining chambers at the rear, and thus cause a premature explosion of the others at the same time. Hence the arm was never made as patented by White.

Fig. 1.

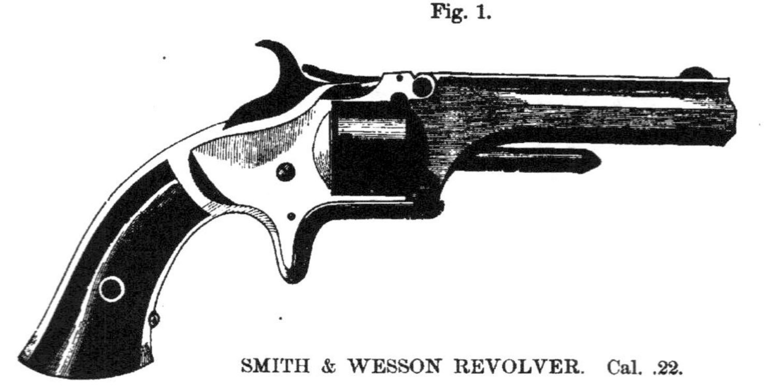

SMITH & WESSON REVOLVER. Cal. .22.

Smith & Wesson, however, bought of White the exclusive right to the use of the open-ended cylinder, and thus secured control of the new revolver they had devised, using the metallic cartridge. In the meantime, April 17th, 1860, they also obtained a patent upon an improved rim-fire cartridge specially adapted to these arms.

The arm as then introduced is represented by the frontispiece, Fig. 1, of which style two sizes were made. The smaller size, No. 1, of which the cut opposite is a full-sized representation, has seven chambers, and uses a cartridge of .22 calibre, with conical bullet, weighing thirty-four grains, and three grains of powder.

The largest size is of the same pattern, but has a barrel

Fig. 2.

six inches long, with six chambers, and uses a cartridge of .32 calibre, weight of bullet 103 grains, with 13 grains of powder.

Subsequently, a new pattern of the same arm was introduced by them, which, while using a cartridge of .32 calibre, was much lighter, and still more graceful in style and appearance, as is represented by Figure 2.

This arm, as shown in the cut, has its barrel hinged to the top strap of the frame, at the front end of the cylinder, and is locked to the lower limb of the frame by a spring catch, which locks automatically, when the barrel is swung into position. The cylinder is mounted on a centre stem, secured rigidly at its rear end to the recoil shield or breech-piece of the frame, and bearing loosely at its front end in the projection under the barrel, so that, to remove the cylinder, it is only necessary to unlock the barrel and swing the latter upward, when the cylinder can be slipped forward off from its stem. A pin is attached permanently to the front part underneath and parallel with the barrel, as shown in the cuts, by means of which the shells can be readily pushed out of the chambers after the cylinder is detached, thus avoiding the necessity of any separate rod or movable device for that purpose.

Fig. 4.

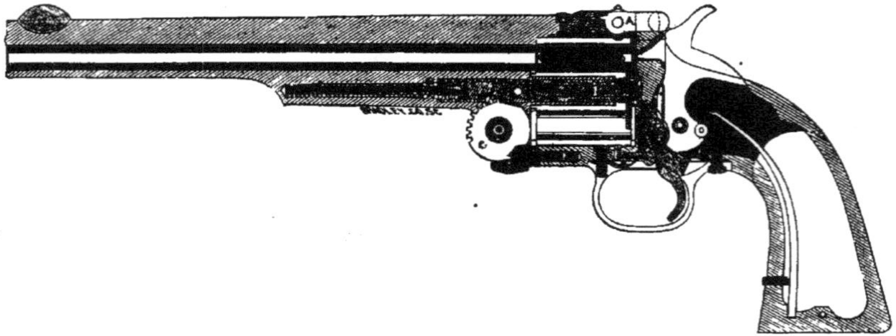

A Latch for locking barrel and breech when closed.
B Stem of extractor.
D Extractor for extracting shells.
C Ratchet wheel operating extractor.
H Pawl, holding and releasing wheel C.
n Tubular centre-pin on which cylinder revolves.

Up to the beginning of the recent war, no revolver had been adopted by the military authorities in which metallic cartridges were used; but the advantages of this new arm were so apparent that thousands of these revolvers were bought by officers in the army and navy, and so great was the demand for them that orders were upon the books of this firm for all their possible production for two years in advance.

The demand for these arms in the United States was such that up to 1867 Smith & Wesson made no effort to sell them abroad. At the Paris Exposition, a case of their various models was exhibited, which at once attracted attention, and from that time a demand arose which has constantly increased, resulting in large shipments to Japan, China, England, Russia, France, Spain, Peru, Chili, Brazil, Cuba, and to almost every nation on the globe.

The arm as thus described was manufactured without alteration until within a year or two past. Since then, however, other improvements have been added, resulting in the production of one far superior,—especially for military purposes,—to anything of the kind ever before made.

About the beginning of the war in the United States, in 1861, W. C. Dodge, then an Examiner in the United States Patent Office, turned his attention to the subject of breech-loading arms, with a view of convincing the Government of their superiority as a military weapon, and securing their adoption for the troops. While thus engaged, his attention was attracted to the revolver, and he at once conceived the idea of remodeling the same, whereby it should be rendered still more effective as a military weapon.

To accomplish this, he assumed two things as being requisite: *First*—A means of extracting all the cartridge shells simultaneously; and, *Second*—so constructing the arm, that while doing this, neither the cylinder nor any other part should be detached, thus enabling the arm to be speedily reloaded and repeatedly fired by mounted men, as well as others. He soon perfected his invention, but as the law did not permit a person employed in the Patent Office to acquire any interest in a patent, it was not patented until January 17th and 24th, 1865, he having resigned his position in the meantime for that purpose. He also patented it in Great Britain, France and Belgium about the same time.

In the spring of 1869, Mr. Dodge sold his patents to Messrs. Smith & Wesson, who immediately proceeded to get up the new revolver. In so doing, they embodied also another feature patented by C. A. King, August 24th, 1860, by means of which the extractor is operated automatically in the act of opening the arm.

This new arm is accurately represented in the illustration, Fig. 3, which shows the arm closed ready for use.

Fig. 3.

The construction of the arm is shown in Fig. 4, and is as follows:

The frame, with its handle and lock, is made as heretofore, except that the frame has but a single limb projecting forward from the under side of the recoil-shield or breech. To the front end of this limb the barrel is hinged, so as to tip forward and downward in opening, as shown in Fig. 5. The barrel, with its hinge-arm or projection, is formed from a single solid piece of steel, and it also has a solid arm or strap at its upper side, which projects back over the cylinder when closed, and is locked to the breech by a spring latch A, which operates automatically when the barrel is swung into position, as shown in Fig. 3. The cylinder is mounted on a tubular centre pin, *n*, which is screwed into the rear end of the projection under the barrel, so that the cylinder is attached to, and swings with the barrel, when opened and closed, as shown in Fig. 5. This center-pin *n* is made a little shorter than the cylinder, as shown in Fig. 4, and the central hole through the cylinder is bored out round as far as the pin *n* extends; but in rear of the extremity of the centre-pin, the hole in the cylinder is made rectangular in form, for a purpose which will be presently explained.

The arm is provided with an extractor, *D*, which consists of a plate fitted into a central recess in the rear end of the cylinder, and which extends radially to near the centre of the chambers—it, of course being cut away at its edges, so as to conform in shape and size to the chambers, thus leaving them unobstructed, so that when the extractor is in its seat, the rear end of the cylinder has the appearance of an ordinary solid cylinder, with the chambers simply bored through it. The extractor, *D*, is provided with a stem made in the form of a square bolt, and of a size corresponding with the rectangular opening in the rear end of the cylinder, previously referred to, so that when the extractor has its stem inserted into or through this opening, it is free to slide back and forth therein, but must turn with the cylinder, thus keeping the extractor always in place in relation to the chambers. The square stem is nearly as long as the cylinder, so that, when the extractor is shoved out in the act of extracting the shells, it will not pass out of the square opening, and is of such a diameter externally, as to permit it to turn freely within the tubular centre-pin, *n*, while the cylinder turns upon the centre-pin, the cylinder and extractor thus always turning together. To this square stem of the extractor, there is secured a round stem or bolt, *B*, which extends forward through the centre pin and for some distance into a hole bored longitudinally from the rear end forward, into the lug or projection underneath the barrel, as shown in Fig. 4. This stem *B*, is reduced in diameter towards its front end, to afford room for a spiral spring, which being mounted on the stem serves to draw the extractor back to its seat after it has been operated to expel the shells. This stem *B*, directly over the point where the barrel is hinged to the frame, and from thence forward to the spring, is provided with a series of teeth, which are cut entirely around the stem and which engage with corresponding teeth on a ratchet-wheel *C*, that is located vertically at the centre of the front end of the arm to which the barrel is hinged; this ratchet-wheel being inserted in a slot formed in the front end of the arm, and pivoted upon the same screw which forms the

Fig. 5.

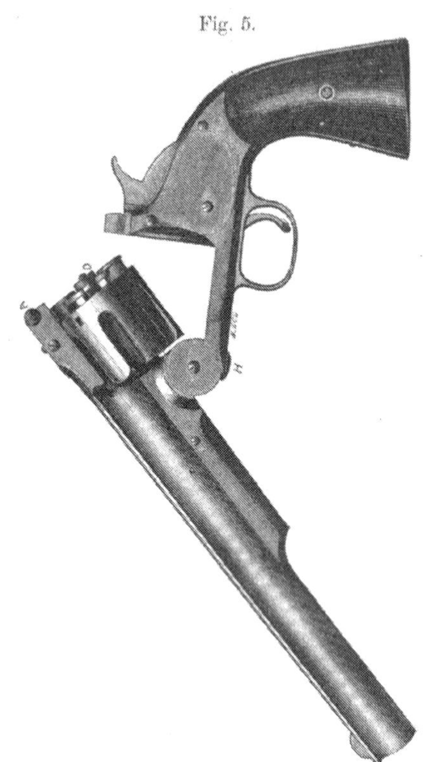

axis of the joint—the front end of the arm being made of a size and shape to correspond with this wheel, whereby also a large bearing is afforded for the joint, which tends to prevent wear and keeps the parts snug and firm. A pawl *H*, is fitted in a recess bored for it in the arm of the frame, and is so located as to engage in a notch cut in the rear edge of the ratchet-wheel *C*, by which said wheel is locked fast, and thus prevented from turning when the barrel is swung over forward—a spiral spring at the rear end of the pawl *H*, serving to press it forward and hold it in contact with the wheel, and also to cause it to automatically engage therewith again, after it has been released. This pawl *H*, also has a roughened projection at the under side of the arm near its front end, by pressing back on which, the pawl can be at any time disconnected from the ratchet-wheel, when of course, the latter will not act on the extractor.

The operation is as follows: The arm is held by the handle in the right hand, while with the thumb of said hand, the latch *A*, is raised, thereby unlocking the barrel from the breech. The barrel is then swung over forward, either by the left hand, or if that be engaged, by pressing the top of the barrel against any object. Now, as the ratchet-wheel is held from turning by the pawl *H*, it follows that the teeth of said wheel engaging with the teeth on the stem *B*, as the barrel swings forward, causes the extractor *D*, to protrude from the rear end of the cylinder, carrying the shells out with it. The size of this wheel *C*, is such that the extractor is caused to move far enough to push the shells *entirely out of the chambers;* and just as this operation is completed, the shoulder of the pawl *H*, comes in contact with the projection on the under side of the barrel, by which means the pawl is shoved back, and thereby disconnected from the ratchet *C*, when the spring on the stem *B*, immediately returns the extractor to its seat while the arm is still open, ready to be reloaded. When loaded, it is only necessary to swing the barrel back to its position, when the latch *A*, automatically locks the parts together, and it is ready for firing. Figure 5, on the opposite page represents the arm in position for loading.

It will thus be seen that while the arm is strong and consists of comparatively few parts, it accomplishes far more than any revolver ever before invented; and that its operations are automatic to a greater extent than any similar arm in existence. As a military revolver it has no equal, and the demand for it is already very large. As evidence of its superiority, it may be stated that it was recommended for adoption by the United States troops, by the Commission of which General Schofield was President, and has been extensively adopted by the Russian Government for its cavalry.

Its accuracy and penetration are shown by the accompanying diagrams of targets made with it at their factory, at Springfield, Massachusetts, at forty yards distance; the penetration of the ball was through five inches of pine boards:

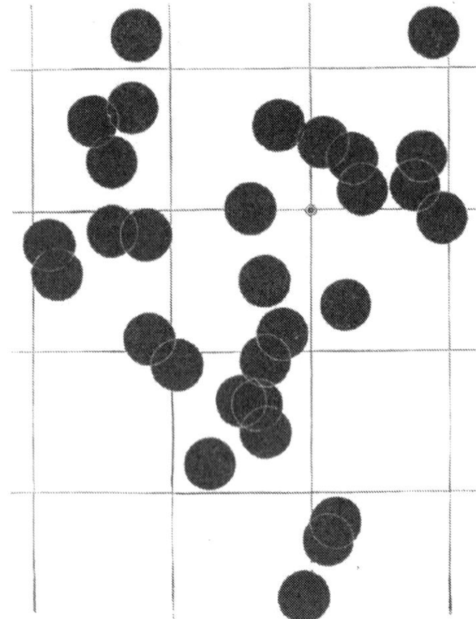

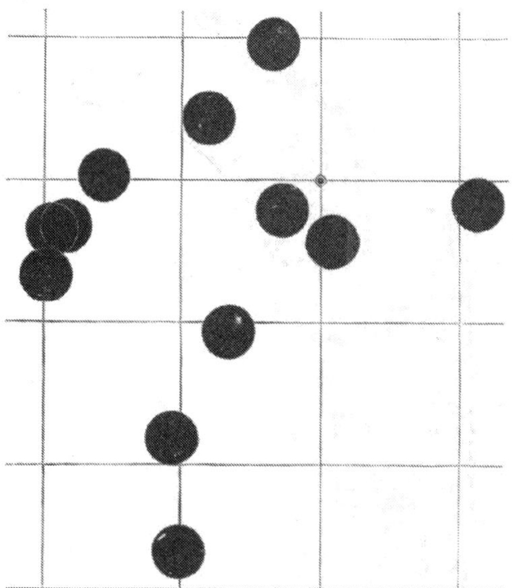

The United States use this arm for Cavalry, and the Government of Russia have adopted the same model for their Cavalry service, an order for 20,000 being now in process of execution.

The barrels, cylinders, and all the small parts are made of the best quality of cast steel, while the frame or body of the pistol is of the best quality of wrought iron, being the same brand as that used by the United States Government.

The system of inspection adopted by Smith & Wesson is such that the least imperfection in material or workmanship is detected, and for which the piece is condemned.

The facilities for manufacturing are such that 150 per day of this size alone are made, while of the other sizes 140 are turned out daily.

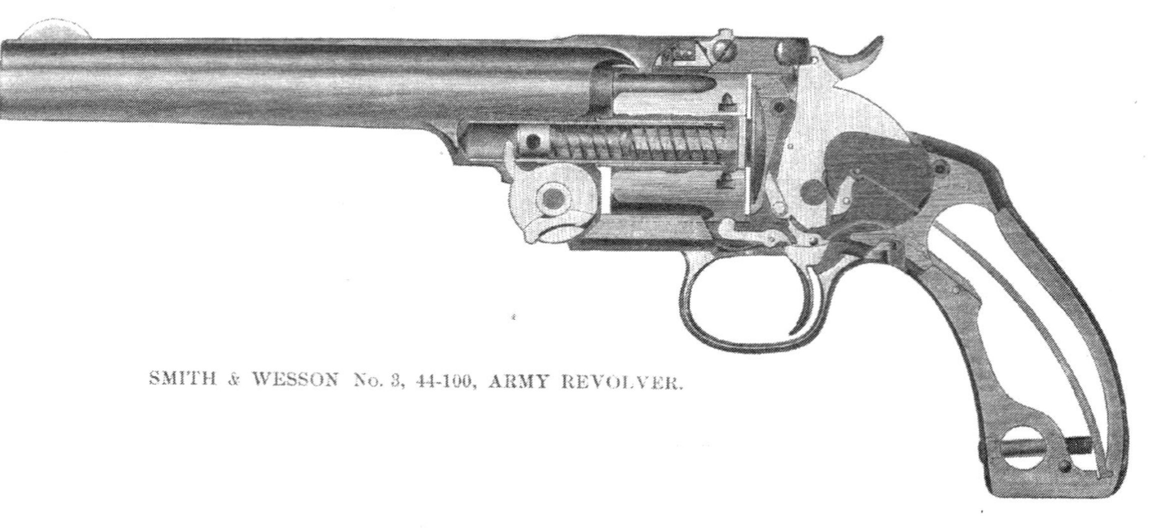

SMITH & WESSON No. 3, 44-100, ARMY REVOLVER.

1880.

During the past ten years Smith & Wesson have, by constant experiments and attention to details, largely improved their arms, and have succeeded in introducing their new army model into the armies of foreign nations, where they are used to entire satisfaction. One of the special improvements effected in the new model for the better protection against accidents is a rebounding lock. Although this feature has been adopted in connection with shot-guns, and now universally used, it has never before been applied to revolvers. These arms, more than any other class, are liable to premature discharge, caused by a chance blow upon the hammer when left, by carelessness, resting upon the cartridge head. By this new improvement the hammer is made to rebound automatically to a safety catch where it is held without the addition of a single piece for that purpose. The construction of this improvement can be seen in the Plate. The pistol is by this means *absolutely safe* in the hands of a soldier, as it cannot under any circumstances from a blow or jar be unexpectedly discharged. The change made in the form of the handle of this pistol can be readily seen by a comparison with the plate representing the model of 1872, and will be found of great advantage. By these changes nine pieces have been dispensed with, and the arm materially improved, at the same time the cost being reduced to a very considerable extent. Nearly all these improvements have been patented by Smith & Wesson in this country and Europe, and are all owned by the firm.

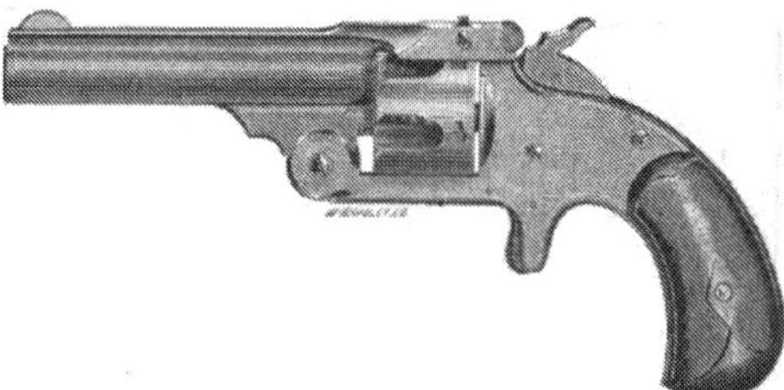

Smith & Wesson 32 Calibre Pistol, made Specially for the Pocket.

SMITH & WESSON DOUBLE-ACTING REVOLVER, Cal. 38.

For the purpose of securing a perfect interchangeability of all parts of every arm made at this establishment, a system of inspection has been adopted of the most rigid character. Only the very best wrought steel is used, and great attention is paid to the smallest details. It is one of the objects of this firm to take advantage of all new inventions or suggestions, and to that end the use of hard rubber has been adopted for the construction of the handles, especially of the smaller grade of pistols. The great improvement in range and accuracy, can best be seen by a comparison between the targets shown in 1872, and the one now published, plate —, for the first time. The works of Smith & Wesson have been largely increased, and when fully occupied with orders, over six hundred hands can be profitably employed.

Of late a demand has sprung up for a more rapid firing arm than the one regularly made by Smith & Wesson, and to meet this demand a new arm has been designed and manufactured, of which a cut showing the details is given, Plate —. There is a slight difference in the form which will be recognized in comparison with the earlier model. Upon an examination of the details in this drawing, however, it will be seen that the new arm is very simple in its construction, and that special attention has been paid to securing for it the utmost safety possible. This arm retains the distinctive feature of the Smith & Wesson System, viz.: The automatic extractor. One of the most important advantages of this pistol over ordinary double-acting pistols is, that instead of being made as heretofore in such a manner as to permit the cylinder to revolve after discharge of cartridge, which releasing it, admits of the possibility of snapping upon the cartridge already discharged. It is arranged with a cylinder stop so constructed as to firmly hold the cylinder in position except when being revolved for the act of cocking. This is accomplished by the action of the cylinder stop, as shown, placed upon the trigger pivot, the rear end of which rests in one of the stop notches shown in the drawing, while the trigger is drawn back in the act of firing, the front end of the stop resting in one of the recesses of the cylinder shown in the drawing while the trigger is forward. Special attention has been paid to reducing the number of parts comprised in the lock of this pistol. There being but seven in all, viz.: Hammer, front and rear sears, hand-trigger, cylinder-stop, two springs. The extractor cam, D, and the extractor catch, E, differ from those used in former pistols made by Smith & Wesson, being much stronger and more simple.

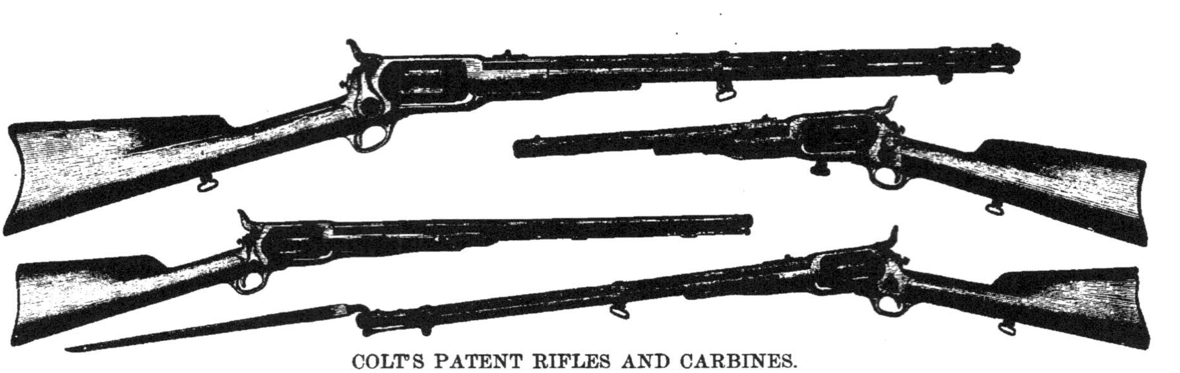

COLT'S PATENT RIFLES AND CARBINES.

COLT'S BREECH-LOADING SMALL ARMS—DESCRIPTION—INITIATORY—NATIONAL DERRINGER PISTOL—NEW MODEL ARMY—NEW DOUBLE ACTION.

THE name of Samuel Colt will be forever connected with the early invention of breech-loading small arms, although his attention was directed specially to the revolver. His first idea in connection with this subject assumed form in 1830 in a device "for combining a number of long barrels so as to rotate upon a spindle by the act of cocking the lock." In 1836 he obtained a patent for an improvement upon this plan, using a rotating cylinder containing several chambers, all of which discharge through one barrel. This weapon was the first ever made not revolving by hand which could be used. The patent in England was taken out in 1835. After a most careful test of this arm by the United States Government, he received his first order for one thousand pistols. With the capital thus furnished him, an armory was established at Hartford, Connecticut, which has since become world-renowned, not alone for the manufacture of the Colt's arms, but for the success achieved in the production of various systems of small arms, the Gatling gun, etc., etc. The sale of Colt's arms from January 1st, 1856, to December 30th, 1865, was as follows: Pistols, 554,283; rifles, 6,693; muskets, 103,970. On the opposite page will be found an illustration of the Colt system as applied to rifles and carbines. The present attention of the Colt Arms Company is devoted to the special production of the revolver or pistol, of which several varieties are manufactured and of which the sales are very large.

The revolving pistol consists essentially of: 1st, the barrel; 2d, the cylinder; 3d, the lock frame (containing the lock); 4th, the stock.

I. The barrel is made of steel and is rifled. It is in all respects

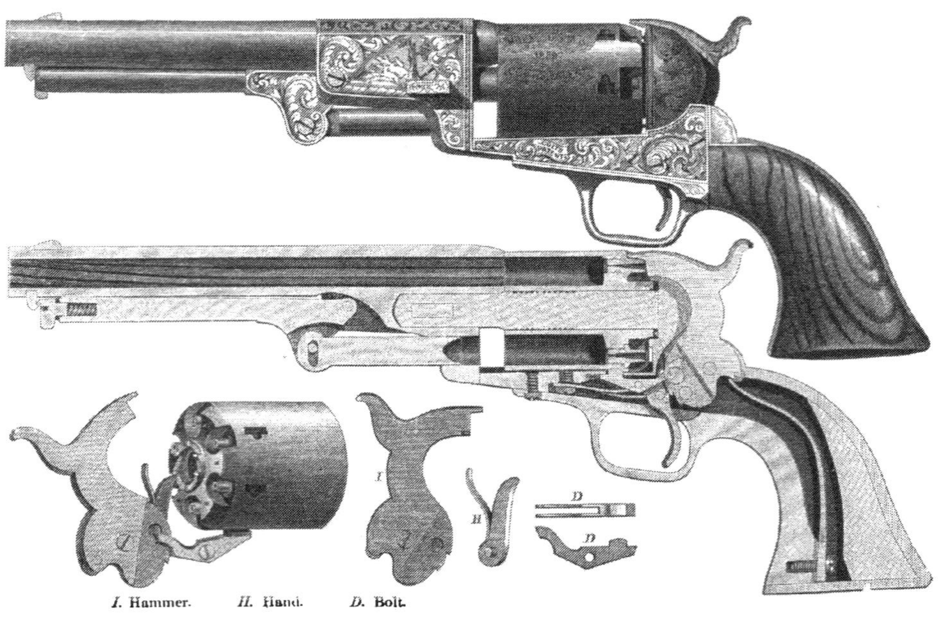

I. Hammer. *H.* Hand. *D.* Bolt.

like the barrel of any muzzle-loading arm, except that it is open at both ends, and on its lowest side are a socket for the rammer and the fixtures for fastening the rammer and its lever to the barrel. These fixtures are all forged in one piece with the barrel. There is also a slot below for holding key of the cylinder-pin, hereafter described.

II. The cylinder is a piece of steel in which five or six chambers parallel to the axis are bored. Their bore and that of the barrel are the same. They are open at the front and stop at a distance from the rear of the cylinder, great enough to leave sufficient metal behind the chamber to give proper security against bursting. Behind each chamber and entering it, an orifice is cut, which the screw on the base of the cap-cone fits, so that the cone is fixed directly in rear of the chamber. Beside the chambers, there is another hole in the cylinder, whose axis is the axis of the cylinder, and which is bored entirely through it. Through this, and fitting it precisely, passes a pin from the lock-frame to the barrel. The pin is paralleled to the bore of the barrel, and so far below it that the revolution of the cylinder brings in succession each chamber directly behind the barrel, so that the chamber and bore of the barrel can be made continuous. This pin secures the cylinder in position between the lock-frame and barrel, allowing it only to revolve about its axis. It is secured to the barrel by a key passing through a slot cut in the pin, and a corresponding one in the barrel. On the rear of the cylinder is cut a ratchet having five or six teeth, as the cylinder has five or six chambers. The centre of the ratchet is on the axis of the cylinder, and the teeth are so arranged that when the piece is at full-cock a chamber is directly in rear of the barrel. On the surface of the cylinder are cut as many small slots as there are chambers. The lowest of these slots is entered by the end of a bolt, which is movable by the action of the lock, and is pressed into the slot by a spring constantly acting. So long as the bolt is in the slot, the cylinder is immovable.

III. The lock-frame is directly in rear of the cylinder, and consists of the recoil-piece, into which the cylinder-pin is fastened; the lock, which contains the machinery for exploding the cap, as well as revolving and locking the cylinder; and a frame which contains and holds in place the mainspring. In the lock the sear and trigger are in one piece, as are also the hammer and tumbler. In these respects

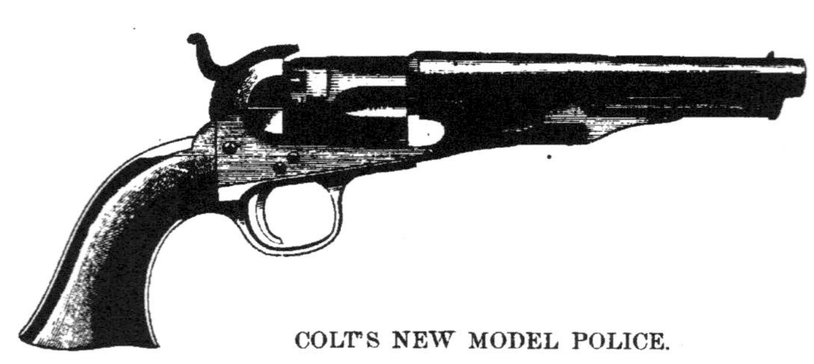

COLT'S NEW MODEL POLICE.

Calibre or size of bore, 37-100 of an inch in diameter, carrying 92-50 elongated, or 86 round bullets to the pound.

the lock differs from that used before the invention of the revolver by Colt. The mainspring acts upon the tumbler and hammer directly. The tumbler has fastened on its face a "hand," which engages the ratchet on the rear of the cylinder, and is held against it by a spring. It also has a projecting pin which is so arranged that at the proper time it engages the bolt which locks the cylinder, lifting it out of its seat in the cylinder slot, and giving it freedom to move under the action of the "hand." When the pin no longer acts upon the bolt, the spring which constantly acts upon it forces it into the first slot which it meets in the revolution of the cylinder, thus locking it. The action of the lock is as follows: The hammer is supposed to be resting upon one of the cap-cones. The hammer being slightly raised, there is at first no motion of any other part, except that of compression ot the main-spring. This device is used to permit any pieces of exploded caps to fall out at the raising of the hammer, before the other parts are in motion. The raising of the hammer being continued, the pin in the face of the tumbler disengages the bolt from the slot in the cylinder; immediately afterwards the "hand" engages a tooth of the ratchet, and as the hammer is raised the cylinder is revolved by the "hand" one-fifth or one-sixth of a revolution, according as there are five or six chambers. When the hammer arrives at full-cock, the tumbler-pin is disengaged from the bolt, which flies back into the cylinder-slot by the action of its spring, and bolts the cylinder. The piece is then ready for discharge, and the cap can be exploded by pulling the trigger.

IV. The stock, composed of wood or ivory, is immediately in rear of the lock, and embraces that part of the lock-frame which contains the main-spring. It forms the handle or grip.

The piece is loaded by inserting the cartridge in the front ends of the chambers. These are successively brought under the rammer, and the loads are pressed home by the action of an ingenious lever arrangement attached to the barrel and worked by the hand. The piece is then capped, when it is ready for discharge. Although in the various forms and models of revolving arms made since the date of Colt's inventions there have been some deviations from the details of this description, the principle of the arm is in all of them the same as that given here. The Colt's Armory Company now manufacture breech-loading revolving pistols for metallic cartridges

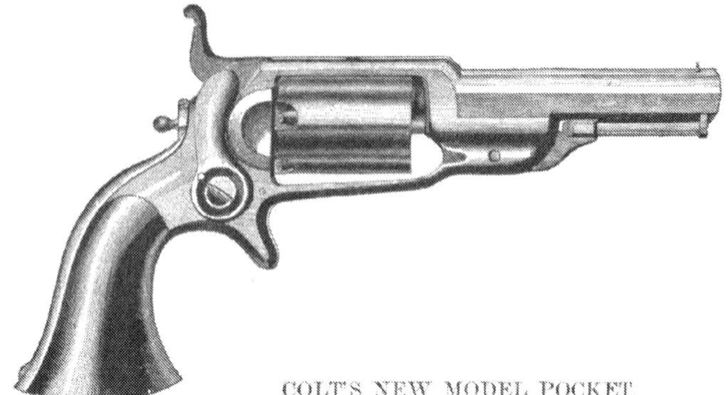

COLT'S NEW MODEL POCKET.

Calibre or size of bore, 31-100 of an inch diameter, carrying 92 elongated or 140 round bullets to the pound.

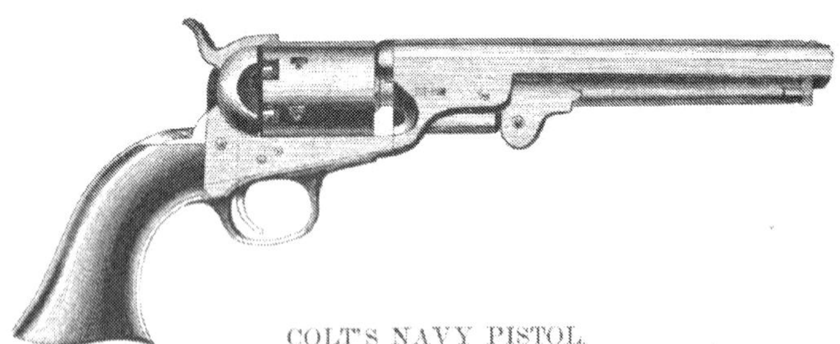

COLT'S NAVY PISTOL.

Pattern now used by the U. S. Navy. Calibre or size of bore 36 100th of an inch diameter, carrying 50 elongated or 86 round bullets to the pound.

of the same calibre as those using powder and ball, and of the same model.

The demand for these pistols is very great; during the past year the sales having reached the large number of 300,000. The capacity of the armory in this direction admits of the turning out of 500 per day. The Navy Pistol has been introduced largely in the United States Navy, and also by foreign governments.

NATIONAL DERINGER PISTOL.—These pistols are made with wood stocks, exact size.

Directions for use.—To Load.—Set the hammer at half-cock; grasp the stock in the right hand, and drawing back the steel button with the forefinger, rotate the barrel toward you with the left hand. Holding the barrel thus turned aside, introduce the cartridge and then rotate it to its original position.

After firing, the empty shell may be ejected by rotating the barrel as directed for loading.

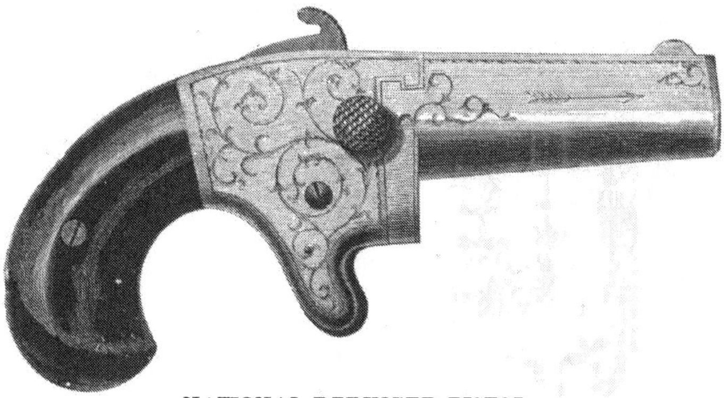

NATIONAL DERINGER PISTOL.

Since the publication of American Breech-Loading Small Arms in 1872, the Colt's Arms Company has perfected a new and superior arm known as the

COLT'S NEW DOUBLE ACTION, SELF-COCKING, CENTRAL FIRE, ARMY SIZE SHOT.

45 in. calibre, Revolving Pistol.

1880.

COLT'S NEW MODEL ARMY METALLIC CARTRIDGE REVOLVING PISTOL.

GENERAL DESCRIPTION OF COLT ARMY REVOLVER, CALIBRE 0".45.

It differs from other revolvers in the following points, viz.: The hand, or finger, or pawl, which revolves the cylinder has two points, one above the other. The upper engages the ratchet of the cylinder when the revolution begins. But before the necessary sixth of a revolution could be made, as the pawl moves in a plane, and the ratchet tooth in the arc of a circle whose plane is perpendicular to the pawl's plane of motion, the pawl would lose its hold on the tooth, and the revolution of the cylinder would stop. To prevent this, the second point is added, and just as the first point will disengage from the ratchet, the second or lower point engages another tooth of the ratchet and completes the revolution. By this arrangement the pawl actuates a larger ratchet than it could otherwise, and therefore exerts more force upon the cylinder, by acting upon a longer lever-arm. This permits a smaller sized cylinder for the same diameter of ratchet.

The cylinder has a bushing, which projects in front of it, and gives three surfaces upon which the cylinder revolves, thus diminishing the chance of sticking from dirt or rust, and also giving a very small axis upon which to revolve, decreasing the moment of friction.

When the ejector is used it springs back to its place and is ready for use again, avoiding the necessity of putting it back.

To Take Apart the Pistol.—Half-cock the pistol, loosen the catch screw which holds the center-pin, draw out the center-pin, open the gate, and the cylinder can then be withdrawn.

To remove the ejector, turn out the ejector tube screw, then push the front end away from the barrel and pull it towards the muzzle. The barrel can then be unscrewed.

The stock can be removed by turning out the two screws just behind the hammer and that at the bottom of the strap. All the parts of the lock are then displayed and can be readily separated.

The cylinder bushing should be pushed out for cleaning.

To remove the gate, turn out a screw in the lower side of the frame, (hidden by the trigger guard,) then the gate spring and catch can be withdrawn, and the gate can be pushed out. The best sperm oil should be used for oiling the parts.

To Load the Pistol—1st motion: holding the pistol in the left hand, muzzle downwards, half cock it with the right hand and open the gate. 2d motion: insert the cartridges in succession, with the right hand, close the gate, cock and fire it, (taking it in the right hand,) or bring the hammer to the safety notch, as may be desired.

To Eject the Cartridge Shells.—1st motion: holding the pistol in the left hand, half cock with the right hand and open the gate. 2d motion; eject the shells in succession with the ejector pushed by the right hand, moving the cylinder with the thumb and forefinger of the left hand. When the shells have been ejected, the pistol is ready for the 2d motion of loading.

N. B. There are three notches in the hammer of this pistol. The first is the safety notch, the second is the half-cock notch, and the third is the cock notch. The pistol cannot be fired when the hammer rests in the safety notch or half-cock notch, and can be fired by pulling the trigger when the hammer rests in the cock notch. The pistol should be carried habitually with the hammer resting in the safety notch.

No. 2.—Vertical section showing arrangement of working parts—Half size.

NOMENCLATURE.

A. Barrel.
B. Frame.
B′. Recoil plate.
C. Cylinder.
D. Base pin.
D′. Base-pin bushing.
E. Guard.
F. Back strap.
G. Hammer.
H. Main-spring.
I. Hammer roll and rivet.
J. Hammer screw.
K. Hammer cam.
L. Hand and spring.
M. Bolt and screw.
N. Trigger and screw.
O. Hammer notches.
P. Firing pin and rivet.
Q Ejector rod and spring.
Q′. Ejector tube.
R. Ejector head.
S. Ejector tube screw.
T. Short-guard screw.
U. Sear and bolt (combined) spring and screw.
V. Back-strap screw.
W. Main spring screw.
X. Front sight.
Y. Base-pin catch screw.

WEIGHTS.

Total weight, ... 2.31 lbs.
Weight of powder charge (service), 28 grs.
Weight of bullet, ... 230 grs.

The powder charge and weight of ball have been lightened to adapt the cartridge to the Schofield-Smith & Wesson revolver.

THE NEW DOUBLE ACTION, SELF-COCKING, CENTRAL-FIRE SIX SHOT REVOLVER, is the last improvement from the Colt factory. These arms are made of two sizes, 41 and 38 calibres with a length of barrel 5 and 6 inches for 41. The pistols of both calibres are furnished with rosewood stock, and case-hardened frame, also finished with hard rubber, ivory or pearl stock and nickel plates. For 38 calibre the lengths of barrels are 3½ and 4½ inches. These pistols have the double hand or pawl, which makes the revolution more free, and adds to the endurance of the arm. They can be cocked by either the trigger or the thumb, and in materials and workmanship cannot be surpassed.

Directions for Using the Reloading Tools, viz.: the bullet-molds, the loading chamber, the cap-punch, the rammer and the safety base.

To Remove the Exploded Cap.—Place the shell, cap downwards, in the recessed end of the loading chamber, placed vertical, insert the cap-punch into it, and strike the head of the punch with the bullet-molds or a mallet.

To Cap the Shell.—Place it in the recessed end of the loading chamber, place the cap in its cavity, and also insert the rammer into the other end of the loading chamber to make a firmer grip. With the hook end of the molds-handle engaged in the notch near the end of the loading chamber, press the cap firmly into its place.

To Charge the Cartridge.—The capped shell being in the recessed end of the loading chamber, invert the chamber and place it in the safety base. Fill the shell with powder, measuring from another empty shell. Place the bullet in the chamber, base downward, insert the rammer, and drive it in until the shoulder on the rammer is flushed with the upper end of the chamber.

Before using the cartridges the bullets should be dipped in melted tallow or some other good lubricant.

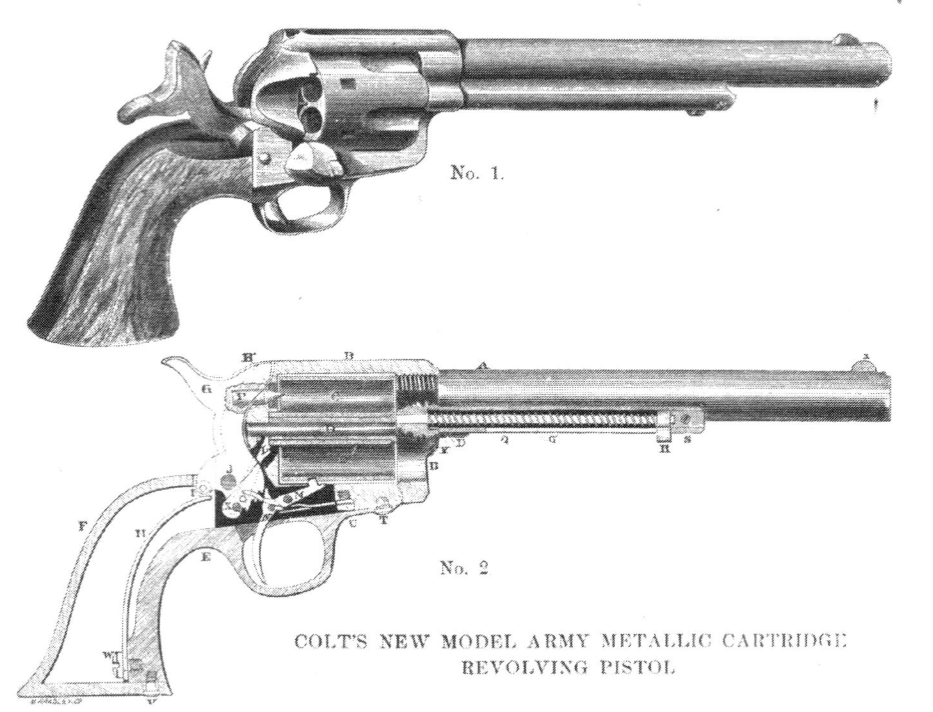

No. 1.

No. 2

COLT'S NEW MODEL ARMY METALLIC CARTRIDGE
REVOLVING PISTOL

The two back-strap screws just behind the hammer, the stock, the long-guard screw, gate, gate-catch screw, gate-spring and gate-catch are not shown in Fig. 2. The gate is shown in Fig. 1.

OPERATION OF THE PARTS.

As the hammer is cocked, the hand, which is pivoted to its lower portion, rises and engages the ratchet on the base of the cylinder, and causes it to revolve. The lower point or finger of the hand engages with one of the teeth of the ratchet just as the revolution of the cylinder has carried away the preceding tooth from the upper finger of the hand. This completes and insures the revolution by increasing the effective leverage of the hand.

The bolt M engages the stop notches in the surface of the cylinder, to prevent the momentum of the cylinder from carrying it past the firing point. It is caused to disengage from them by the action of the hammer cam K, which, rising during the cocking of the hammer, presses up the rear end of the bolt and liberates its front end from the notch. When the revolution is about complete the beveled lower surface of the hammer cam comes opposite the point of contact on the bolt. At this moment the tail of the bolt (being slit so as to have a lateral spring, and the head being pressed upward by the flat spring U,) slides down over the inclined surface of the cam, and the head engages with the stop-notch in the cylinder. The spring U is slit and bent so as to act upon both the bolt and the trigger.

The bushing around the base pin is useful by affording another surface for the revolution of the cylinder, and thereby diminishes the chances of sticking from dirt or rust. Both the cylinder and bushing may revolve on the base pin, which in turn may revolve in its own bearings.

DIMENSIONS.

Total length, ...	12″.5
Length of barrel, ...	7″.5
Diameter of bore, ...	0″.45
Grooves, number of, ...	6
Grooves, twist of, uniform, . . .	1 turn in 16″—left-handed.
Grooves, depth, uniform, ...	0″.005

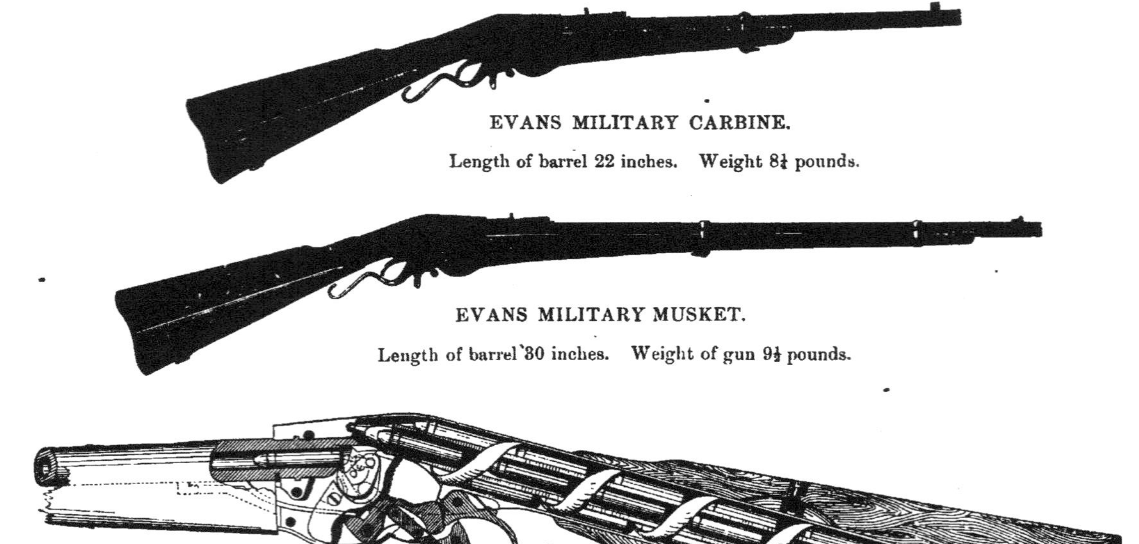

EVANS MILITARY CARBINE.

Length of barrel 22 inches. Weight 8¼ pounds.

EVANS MILITARY MUSKET.

Length of barrel 30 inches. Weight of gun 9½ pounds.

EVANS SHOOTING RIFLE.

Octagon barrel—26, 28 and 30 inches. Sectional view, quarter size. The cartridges in the Evans Magazine Gun are carried in separate chambers, a sure safeguard against accidental discharge.

Exact size of cartridge for model of 1877, 26 rounds in magazine.

EVANS MAGAZINE RIFLE.

It is claimed by the manufacturers that this Rifle is of positive mechanism throughout; that it widely differs from the magazine guns heretofore made, which have uniformly contained in their magazine a spiral spring for the purpose of feeding the cartridges through and from the magazine to the breech mechanism of the arm. This system of spiral spring feed has been and to-day is defective, from the inevitable weakening of this spring from use, rust, &c. In the "Evans" the magazine is located in the stock of the arm, a locality regarded as far preferable to a magazine located under the barrel, where the poise of the arm is constantly changed by the varied number of cartridges contained therein; while in the "Evans" the poise is in no way effected or its accuracy impaired, whether partially or fully charged.

The magazine of the "Evans" consists of a cylinder of forged iron, running from the breech to the butt plate; around the inner circle of this cylinder is affixed, in the form of a spiral, a flat-wire of the proper conformation. Into this cylinder with its fixed spiral is introduced a shaft of fluted, or grooved iron, this shaft being revolved by movement of the lever in the breech mechanism. The cartridges are introduced into the magazine through the butt plate; with the introduction of each cartridge the breech mechanism is moved, thus carrying forward the cartridge until the magazine is filled.

The cartridges as they lie in the magazine are in separate cells, and cannot come in contact with each other, thus precluding any possibility of discharge; while in all spiral spring magazine guns the cartridges bear or rest one upon the other, thus rendering a premature discharge possible. The system of feed in the "Evans Magazine" strongly resembles the Archimedean Screw. The magazine carries twenty-six rounds of cartridges of two inches in length, and may be loaded in one-half of a minute, and the entire magazine of twenty-six rounds discharged at will, in from fifteen to twenty seconds, thus embracing the greatest repeating capacity of any rifle made.

This arm may be fired twenty rounds per minute, while used as single loader, introducing the cartridges into an aperture at the side of the receiver at the breech. It can also be fired twenty rounds per minute, holding the magazine full and in reserve, by introducing cartridges into the magazine at the butt, as each cartridge is discharged.

Plate 2.

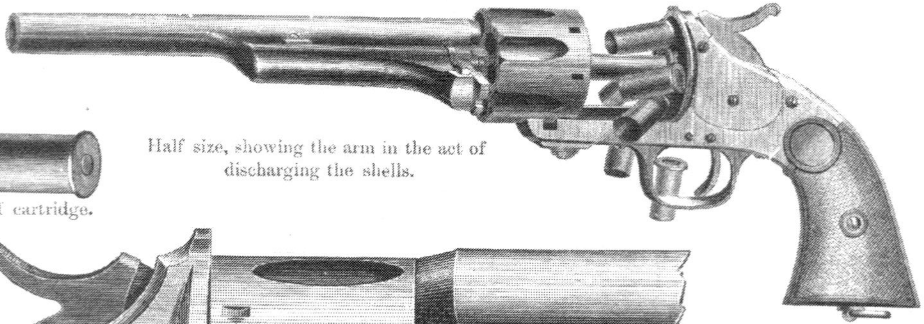

Half size, showing the arm in the act of discharging the shells.

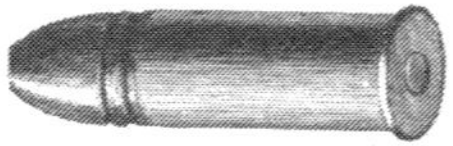

Exact size of cartridge.

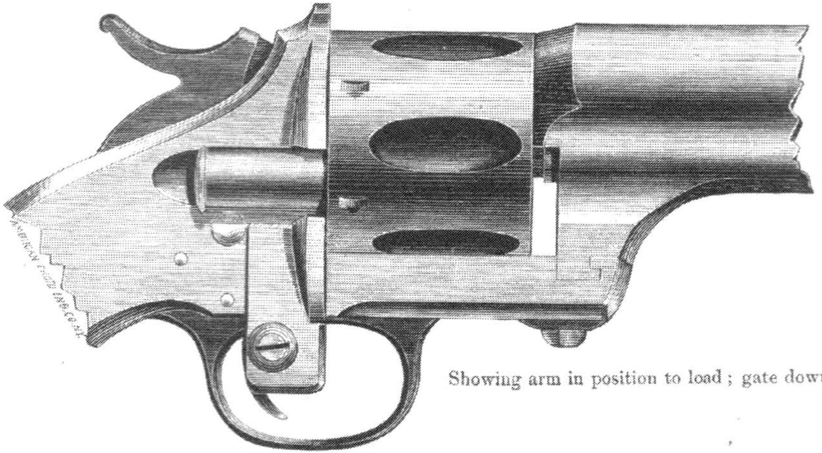

Showing arm in position to load; gate down; hammer half cock.

MERWIN, HULBERT & CO'S NEW ARMY REVOLVER,
With Automatic Ejector.

The lock works are very simple and strong. The following are claims made for this gun:

Novelty of its magazine; magazine of positive mechanism; locality of magazine in butt stock of arm; cartridges situated in separate cells in magazine; impossibility of cartridges coming in contact with each other in magazine; safety of magazine; unfailing transit of cartridges in magazine by positive movement; unfailing transit of cartridges from magazine to chamber of barrel by positive movement; inability to discharge cartridge before cartridge is home in barrel and breech-block closed; extraction and ejection of shells by positive mechanism; exclusion of water and dust from arm when closed; simplicity and durability of magazine and lock works; capacity of magazine, twenty-six rounds of ammunition; simplicity of manipulation, but three movements, viz.: forward and return movement of lever, and pull of trigger; a magazine gun of positive mechanism throughout; general substantial construction of the arm.

MERWIN, HULBERT & COMPANY'S ARMY REVOLVER

(Plate 2) makes the following claims for superiority:

Compactness, symmetrical easy outline, and general neat appearance.

No salient points to prevent its ready and easy insertion into or withdrawal from the holster.

In handling, not liable to injure the hand; all the projecting parts being rounded and smooth; cleaning being thereby facilitated.

The circular form of cylinder front gives a continuous cover to breech of barrel; prevents sand or dirt entering therein.

Accidental unlocking of the parts prevented, as hammer must first be set at half-cock.

The front sight forged solid with the barrel; not liable to be separated therefrom or injured.

The extractor ring prevents the interior of the lock and the ratchet from fouling by escape of gas about the primer when using outside primed ammunition.

The hood and collar at front of cylinder covering base pin and base pin hole prevents fouling.

The flanged recoil plate covers and protects the heads of the cartridges; prevents sand or dirt entering between face of recoil plate and cylinder, which might clog it and prevent rotation.

Plate 3.

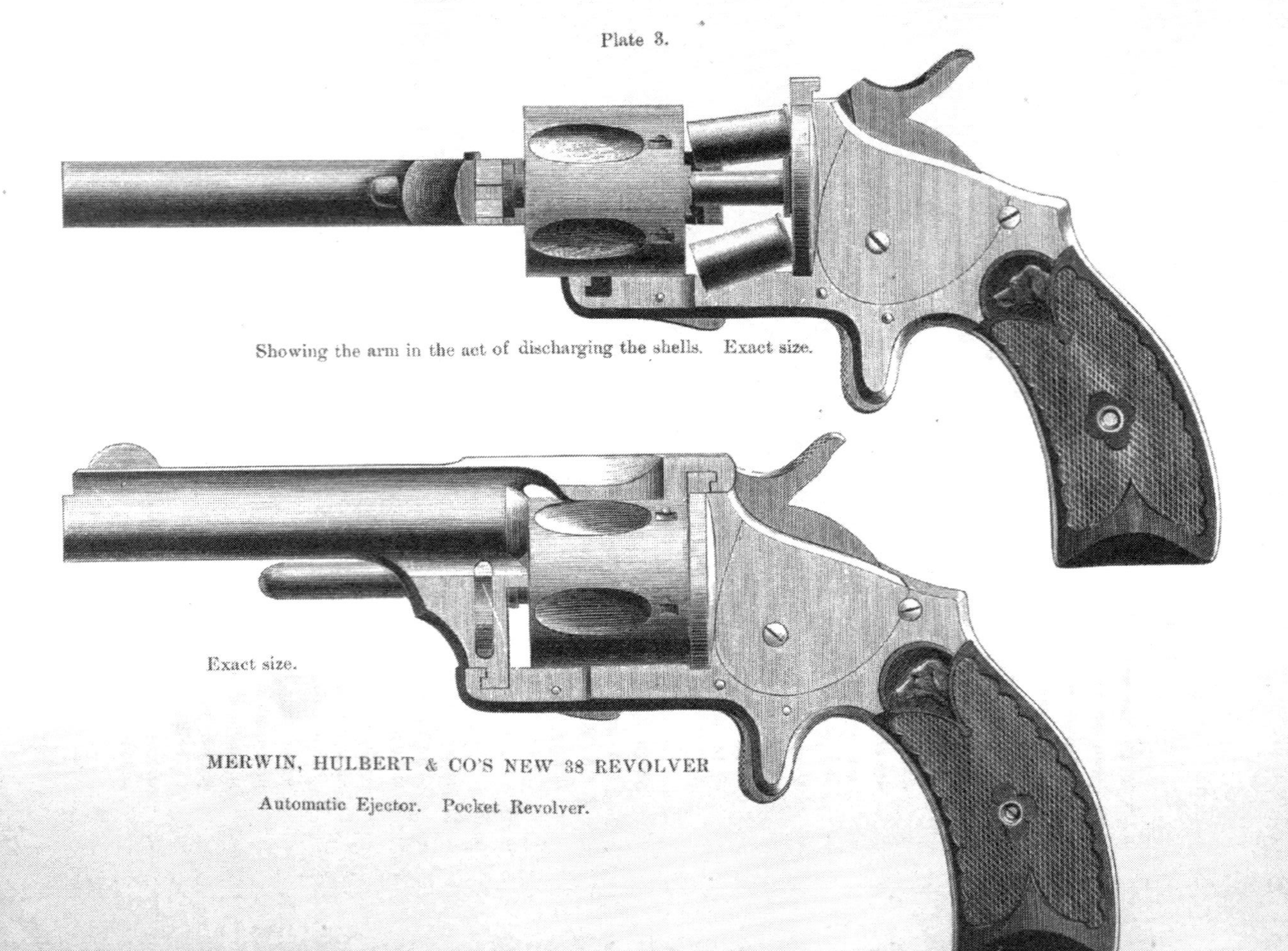

Showing the arm in the act of discharging the shells. Exact size.

Exact size.

MERWIN, HULBERT & CO'S NEW 38 REVOLVER

Automatic Ejector. Pocket Revolver.

The cylinder and barrel can be dismounted from the frame and re-assembled thereto without the use of screw driver or any tool.

The construction is not intricate nor fragile, and the extractor is a solid part of the bore pin.

Strength, durability and endurance.

Simultaneous, positive, and easy extraction of shells; great power obtained for starting the shells before final extraction by the incline screw action on the base pin.

Less lateral escape gas is deflected downward into the works, as no top strap is used.

The face of the collar on cylinder takes against the bracket, prevents forward movement of cylinder when pressed by the ball in rotating; gives a central bearing; prevents abrasion of cylinder face against rear of barrel; gives easy rotation; permits a close joint without friction, reducing the escape of gas; the cylinder is not forced backward on firing, but is held forward by the hood clutch taking into the recess of the cylinder collar.

The lines of recoil and resistance are close together, lessening upward inclination of barrel when fired.

DIRECTIONS FOR MANIPULATING THE ARM.

To Load.—Place the hammer at half-cock, press the gate downward and insert the cartridges.

To Eject the Shells.—Push back the thumb-bolt under the frame, turn the barrel outward, and draw forward, when the shells will fall out.

To Take the Arm Apart.—When the barrel and cylinder are drawn forward, press the small pin in the barrel catch even with the frame, *then* press the catch down and draw forward.

Complimentary letters have been received as regards these arms from all parts of the world; the following are extracted: Col. George T. Denison, author of the Russian Imperial Report on Arms and Cavalry Tactics, for which he received the government reward of five thousand dollars and gold medals, as well as medals from other governments. Colonel Denison says: "Your army revolver is, in my opinion, the most perfect cavalry pistol in the world." He gives his reasons for this conclusion.

Lieut. Weitzenberg, inspector of arms for the Imperial Russian navy, says: "Your army revolver and Evans magazine gun are the best pieces of workmanship and the best working arms for military use that I have ever inspected."

General W. H. Morris, late quartermaster-general, state of New York, says: "It seems to me that your army revolver meets every requisite called for in a military weapon. It is the perfection of workmanship and simplicity of motion. For strength and beauty of outline it has no peer."

The new pocket revolver (Plate 3) is made upon the same system as the Merwin, Hulbert & Co's Army revolver, and the workmanship is as perfect as the Army, which has been accepted by the best judges and experts as having no superior.

This system insures great rapidity of fire, but is strong, of few parts, durable, and will not injure in warm climates. They claim the following advantages as compared with any other revolver:

It can be taken apart for cleaning without use of any tool, the barrel, cylinder and frame being separated by two motions.

The extractor is of one piece, a solid part of the base pin, which is attached to the recoil plate, and cannot get out of order.

It has the screw power to start the exploded shells, which gives easy extraction. It has no small parts exposed to rust. The parts are all interchangeable, and of such strength as to avoid breaking. It is rifled by improved machinery that gives the best results in shooting, is well balanced, and pleasant to handle. It extracts one or more exploded shells without removing the loaded ones, by drawing forward the cylinder far enough to allow the exploded shells to fall, the loaded ones remaining, when the weapon can be again closed. Both ends of the cylinder are covered and so protected as to exclude dirt that might hinder rotation. It can be ascertained whether any or all the chambers are loaded, without opening the pistol, by looking through the loading aperture.

The escape of gas while firing cannot work the cylinder loose upon the base pin as in other revolvers, from the fact that the cylinder has a solid collar that sets into the recess of the barrel, and cannot be forced back by the gases. This clutch or recess also acts as a gas deflector, keeping the base pin always free from fouling. It is believed to be the most perfect and efficient arm for police, house, or personal use.

CHAPTER IX.

SPORTING ARMS.

MAYNARD'S BREECH-LOADING RIFLE AND SHOT GUN — PARKER SYSTEM—BAKER GUN—STEVENS GUN—BUCK SYSTEM.

The Maynard Sporting rifle is manufactured by the Massachusetts Arms Company, at Chicopee Falls, Mass. While special attention has been paid to the manufacture of a superior hunting rifle and sporting gun, the interest in rifle shooting at long range, has led to the invention and introduction of what is known as the "New Creedmoor Rifle," in which the acknowledged and superior merits of the system are introduced, securing convenience, safety, accuracy and efficiency, all made applicable to meet the present demand for long range practice.

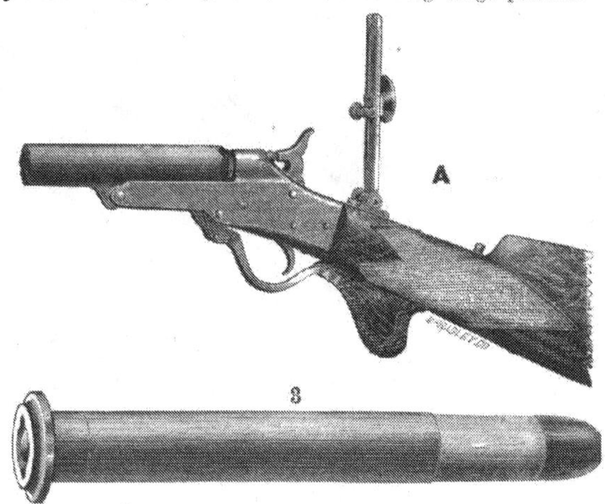

The "New Creedmoor Rifle," see cut A, represents a model 32 inch, 44 calibre rifle, specially adapted to the requirements of the Creedmoor range, and to which has been applied every facility and appendage which has been found by trial and experience best adapted to secure the most satisfactory results,—including ammunition. vernier and wind gauge sights, spirit level, pistol-grip, and all of superior models and workmanship. One valuable and special feature of the Maynard system is, that it admits of an interchange of barrels of any length or calibre, between the Creedmoor Mid-range, or sporting models. The Creedmoor rifle, cut A, weighs just under ten pounds; barrel—round, 32 inches, 44 calibre, oiled stock, checkered with pistol grip, vernier and wind gauge sights, spirit level and cartridge retractor. It is sold with the following appendages:

25 cartridge cases — 100 grs., cartridge capper, charger, loader, loading-block, cap-picker, cartridge cleaner, 3 rods and brush, 2 rag-holders, screw-driver, and 100 patched and swaged bullets—520 grains.

Full Size Target.
5
4
7
7
TEN CONSECUTIVE SHOTS. 220 YARDS,
WITH A
MAYNARD CREEDMOOR RIFLE.
By Geo. W. Hadley, Chicopee Falls, Mass.
January 29th., 1877.
String, 10 inches.

All the advantages comprised in the Creedmoor rifle, have also been applied to a new model "Mid-Range and Hunting Rifle," 32 inch, .4 calibre, and is designed and especially adapted for close target practice up to 600 yards, and for hunting where one is likely to meet large or dangerous game. This rifle is represented in cut B, together with two models of targets selected from the large number in possession of the Massachusetts Arms Company, and representing a fair average result for the distance named. The weight of the Mid-Range Rifle is about 9 lbs. 32 inch, calibre .4, stock checkered and oiled, with elevating

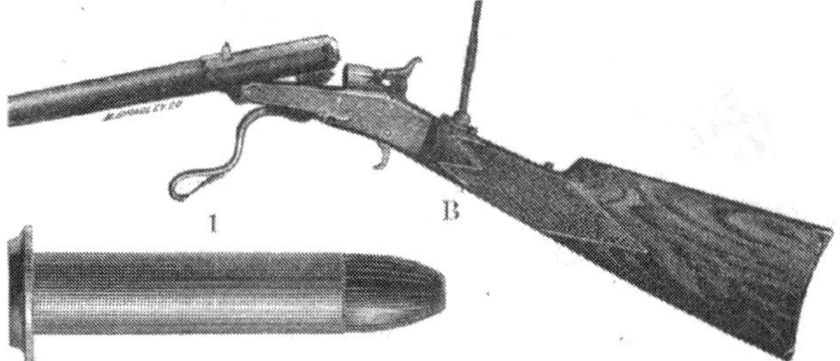

MID-RANGE AND HUNTING RIFLE.

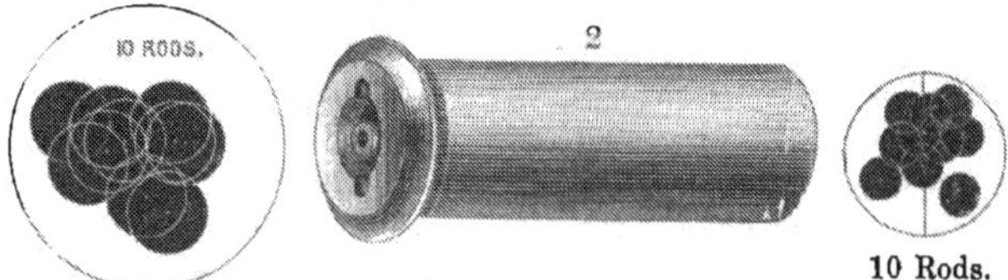

10 Rods.

peep, adjustable rear leaf, and Beach's combination sights, and is supplied with the necessary appendages:

NEW OFF-HAND RIFLE.

The new off-hand rifle, is one of the most recent and improved specimens of the Maynard system, specially adapted for hunters and sportsmen, it has been received with approval by all who have tested it.

The following are some of the scores recently made at Walnut Hill by members of the Massachusetts Rifle Association:—J. N. Frye, President, in all-comers match; 15 shots; 200 yards; off-hand; without cleaning: 5 4 5 4 5 5 5 5 5 5 5 4 4 5 5—71. L. L. Hubbard, Executive Officer, 200 yards; off-hand: 4 5 5 5 5 5 5 5 5 5—49. O. M. Jewell, 300 yards; off-hand: 5 4 5 5 5 5 5—34. O. M. Jewell, 300 yards; off-hand: 5 5 5 5 5 5 5—35.

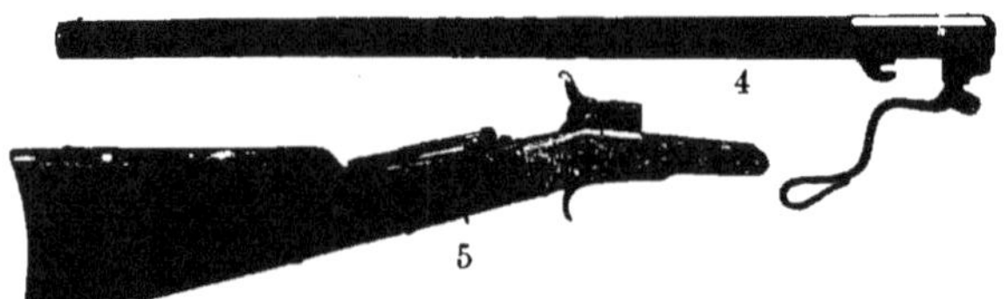

Another special advantage claimed for the Maynard arm is, that it can be taken apart with great ease and packed in a small compass as indicated in cuts 4; and both stock and barrel can be placed in shawl or valise while traveling without attracting observation. The Maynard patent central fire cartridge cases, cuts 1, 2 and 3 are manufactured with great care, and are noted for their uniform accuracy and durability.

The following targets were made by Prof. Chas. E. Dwight of Wheeling, West Va., with a Maynard Creedmoor Rifle, Aug. 12 and 13, 1878, and are the *most remarkable on record*, the grand total of six targets being 437 out of a possible 450. The nearest to it was made by Blydenburg, with a total of 429 out of a possible 450. These scores were made without sighting shots, Fulton position, and in competition for place on the American Team for 1878. It will be seen that the last thirty shots (herewith represented) were all bull's eyes.

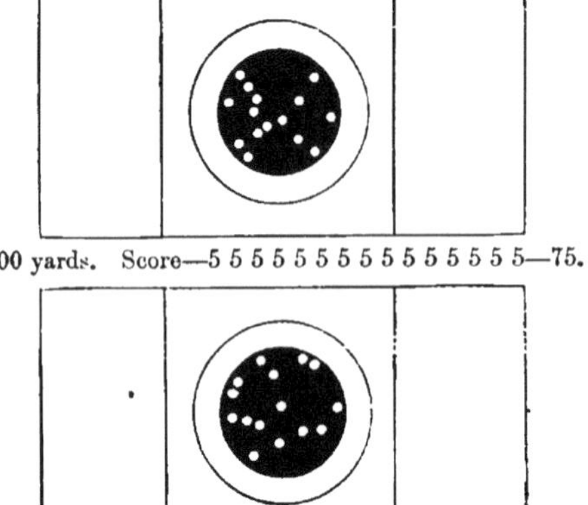

900 yards. Score—5 5 5 5 5 5 5 5 5 5 5 5 5 5 5—75.

1000 yards. Score—5 5 5 5 5 5 5 5 5 5 5 5 5 5 5—75.

THE PARKER SHOT GUN.

The Parker Gun is a distinctively American production, and has all the advantages of the American system of manufacturing. The number of parts is reduced to a minimum, and the construction is so simple that any sportsman with no tool but a screw-driver can take his gun apart for cleaning or repairs.

All the materials used are selected with the greatest care, and no metals but the best cast-steel and wrought iron are used in its construction. These arms are all made with the Parker patent self-acting snap action, which is both convenient and secure. The same principle has been used with eminent success from the beginning, but has since been much improved and simplified, and is undoubtedly one of the most convenient methods in use for securing the barrels to the frame, and opening the gun to load and unload. The locking bolt is held back while the gun is open, doing away with the wear on the hinge joint, which all breech-loaders are subjected to when the barrels are forced down against a strong spring in the rear of the bolt. In connection with the lock attention should be called to the direct blow of the firing-pin exactly in the center of the cap and at right angles with the head of the shell. By this arrangement the chance of a miss-fire is very much lessened, and the efficiency of the arm increased.

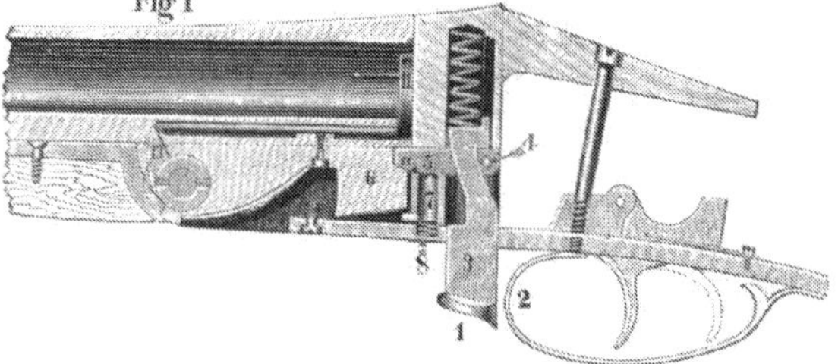

Fig. 1 represents the gun as closed.

The Action.—Pressing up on the finger piece (1) in front of the guard (2) raises the lifter (3), and its beveled side—coming in contact with the screw (4)—acts as a wedge to draw the bolt (5) from the mortise which is cut in the lug (6), and releases the barrels as shown in Fig. 2, ready for the insertion of the cartridges. It will be observed

THE PARKER SHOT GUN.

that when the bolt (5) is back to the position as shown in Fig. 2, the small hole which is drilled in the under side of said bolt comes directly over the trip (7), which by the assistance of the small spiral spring (8) is made to enter this hole in the bolt (5), and thereby holds it in position as shown in Fig. 2.

The finger-piece (1) is solid and a part of lifter (3).

The action of *the lifter* (3) *is positive*, not only to withdraw the bolt from, but to force it forward into the mortise in the lug (6).

For the purpose of cleaning, it can be very easily removed by taking off the locks and removing the small screw (4) from the end of bolt (5), then press down on trip (7), which will allow the lifter to be withdrawn without removing either stock, guard or trigger plate. The improved roll (13) gives great strength to joint.

Fig. 2 represents the gun as opened.

When the barrels are brought to place for firing, the bottom of the lug (6) strikes the trip (7), withdrawing it from the bolt (5), which then enters the mortise in the lug (6), and securely locks the gun as shown in Fig. 1.

The taper bolt (5) locks the barrels positively firm, and the use of a taper bolt for fastening the gun gives it a decided advantage over others, as it does not allow a little dirt (which is very liable to get under barrels when open) to prevent the gun from locking. Many times, when shooting, sportsmen are balked this way, but this gun closes with the same ease, and locks as securely if there is a little dirt in the way.

Parker Brothers are established in the town of Meriden, Connecticut, where they have a large factory employing many workmen, who are kept continually occupied.

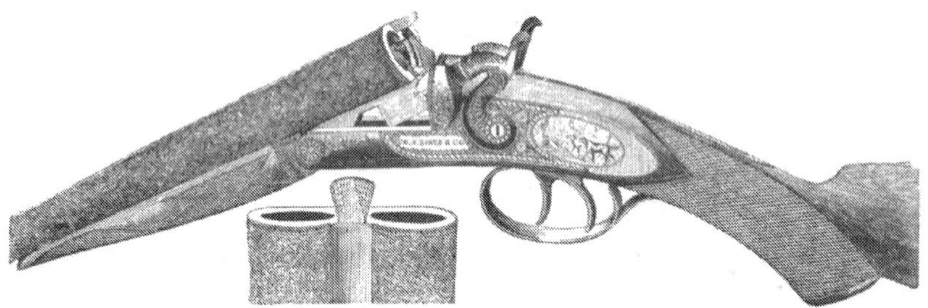

BAKER'S PATENT NEW TOP FASTENER.

BAKER'S PATENT THREE-BARREL GUN.

THE BAKER GUN.

The Three Barrel Breech-loading gun has been introduced to the public to meet every requirement that could be wished for upon any occasion, and for all kinds of game. As happens to every hunter or sportsman, unexpected opportunities offer themselves to shoot at a class of game that a shot-gun will either not reach at all or fail to kill, and this arm will give confidence to those who are in the habit of hunting in localities where there are animals that are dangerous, and which are liable to be encountered at any moment without warning. The weight, not over nine pounds, is sufficient to prevent an unpleasant recoil, and this arm is as light and easy to carry as any double shot gun that has metal enough to do satisfactory work.

It is demonstrated by actual use that there is less spring or recoil in a gun with three barrels than though the same weight of metal was put in one barrel, and this may be accounted for by the fact that the same weight of metal in a hollow tube is much stiffer than though it was in a solid bar; and, also, each barrel forms a brace to help support the other, and especially in regard to the rifle barrel in which use are the heaviest charges that are manufactured for a sporting gun.

It is well known that there is a tendency in all breech-loading shot guns to become loose and open from the effects of heavy and repeated firing, and it has been the great aim of all makers to overcome this objection, and the top fastening or extension of the upper rib *locking* into the top of the breech has been adopted as a necessity, as from the manner in which many guns are constructed the metal of the breech is cut away to such an extent to receive locks that it is so weakened as to be readily displaced by hard shooting, and even with all the precaution that can be brought to bear, many of the best guns require frequent repairs. To avoid this weak point, Mr. Baker invented the lock and construction of the gun now manufactured by this firm, it being peculiarly adapted to the construction of the Three-Barrel guns, as well as perfect for the Double Shot gun, making them much stronger without the top rib extension than others are with it.

The plan adopted is that of extending the solid rib into the breech and making the locking part of the regular dovetail shape, as seen in cut on foregoing page. This gives it the strongest and most bearing surface, and one that will always be sure to fit, as can be seen by inspection. These guns are manufactured by W. H. Baker & Co. of Syracuse, N. Y.

THE STEVENS GUN.

J. Stevens & Co. of Chicopee Falls, Mass., have obtained a special reputation for their sporting arms, of which illustrations are herewith given.

DOUBLE BARREL BREECH-LOADING SHOT GUN.

The evidence received by them from hunters and marksmen, is of the most favorable character as regards the simplicity, strength, and dura-

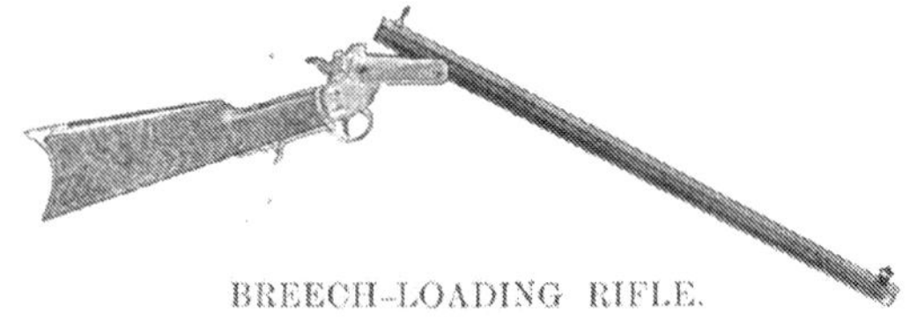

BREECH-LOADING RIFLE.

bility of the arms they manufacture. In target shooting also the result in competition has been very satisfactory for the Stevens Gun. They

HUNTERS' PET.

NEW MODEL POCKET SHOT GUN.

make a special arm for the use of taxidermists, which will, with a very small charge, do most effective work.

THE BUCK SYSTEM.

This arm is presented to the public for the first time in these pages. The inventor, Henry A. Buck, claims for it many special advantages, not only as a sporting arm, but also as a military breech-loading rifle. In his specification for a patent, Mr. Buck states as follows:

"The object of my invention is to produce a breech-loading fire-arm which shall have the fewest parts possible consistent with safety and effectiveness, with all the motions of all the parts, except the hammer and trigger, positive, and not dependent upon springs, and in which a tightly-fitting cartridge can be used with ease, in which the recoil is reduced to a minimum, and in which one motion cocks the gun, opens the breech, and ejects the shell, and a return motion places the arm in readiness for firing after the cartridge is inserted.

"The invention therefore consists in a shell or frame, to which the barrel is rigidly attached, within which frame the breech-block and lock mechanism operate; in the combination of a breech-block having a side cam device, provided with a pin, a hammer, a slotted connecting-arm, and an operating-lever; and, finally, in the general construction and arrangement of the parts by which the gun is cocked, the breech opened, and the shell extracted by one motion of the lever, and the cartridge forced in, and the breech closed, and the block locked in place by another motion of the lever, leaving the gun cocked."

The inventor claims, as also susceptible of proof, that in simplicity of construction and economy in manufacture this arm will enter into competition with any military arm now used, either in this country or Europe. There are only six working pieces, all made of large size, with great strength and solidity, which, together with two springs, comprise all the parts used, and insure a durability to the arm of great value when exposed to the wear and tear of active service. Experiments in rapid firing have proved its great efficiency in this direction, as it has been loaded and fired thirty-four times a minute with perfect ease, and at one hundred feet distance *twenty-eight shots* have been placed in the target also within a minute.

The Buck gun is made on the interchangeable system, so that it can be adopted by any Government as a military arm with the certainty that every available advantage in cost, strength, simplicity and durability has been secured, together with the advantage of a weight not to exceed eight pounds. Plate No. 1 shows the position of the parts of the arm when opened ready to receive the cartridge. The lever being pushed forward, acts upon the connecting arm to raise the hammer until it is brought to full cock, when the cam-slot acts upon the breech-block pin to depress the breech-block, and thus make ready for the cartridge. For the purpose of extraction after the lever has passed

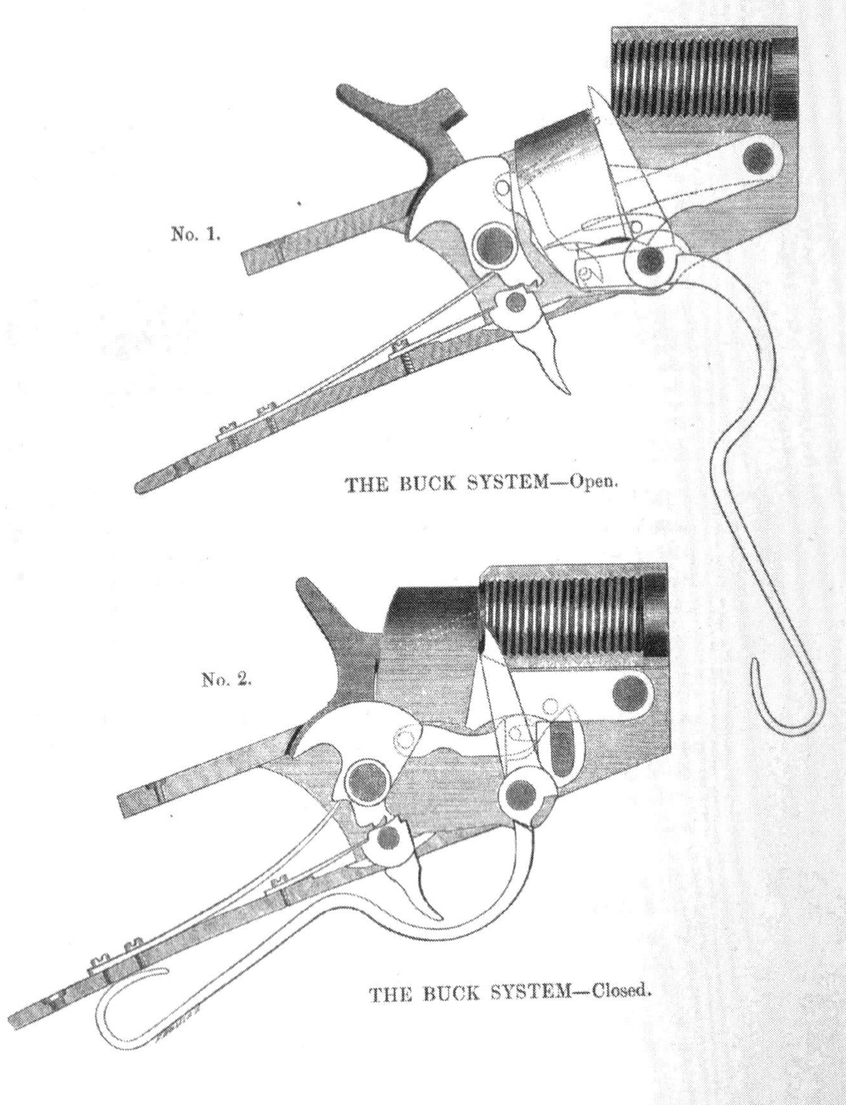

THE BUCK SYSTEM—Open.

THE BUCK SYSTEM—Closed.

through that part of the circle necessary for the previous operations, it strikes the shoulder on the under side of the extractor, giving it a powerful and rapid movement rearward, and thus throwing out the shell with great certainty. Plate No. 2 indicates the breech mechanism at the moment of discharge, the lever cam standing directly underneath the breech-block, and the hammer passing underneath the bottom of the block. The inventor claims that he has secured a perfectly *safe* gun, inasmuch that after the cartridge is inserted it cannot be discharged by closing of the breech-block in any manner, the breech-block being supported by the cam and locked by it as soon as closed, so that in case even that the trigger should be disengaged and allow the hammer to descend, it cannot do so until the breech-block is closed, and then only as slowly as the lever moves, so that there is no possible chance of an *accidental* discharge.

In the case of a cartridge sticking in the chamber, it would be forced in by the action of the lever and the breech-block with perfect safety. It is also considered as an advantage for the Buck gun as a military arm that the hammer is so placed as not to interfere, and being in the usual position it is perfectly feasible for the soldier to carry at "support arms" As a sporting gun, the inventor claims that it can use a stronger cartridge than any other arm, that the recoil is much lessened by the firmness in which the cartridge is held by the breech-block, and that the exploded shell can be removed with facility.

At a test at the National Armory with a gun weighing eight pounds and three-quarters, the recoil was only one hundred and thirty-eight pounds, being much less than the general average for military arms. The Buck shot-gun is also made on the same principle, using any size cartridge, and claimed to have every advantage. These arms are manufactured by H. A. Buck & Co., West Stafford, Conn.

Fig. 1.

GATLING CAMEL GUN.

CHAPTER X.

THE GATLING GUN.

In the year 1861 the idea of a machine gun was first conceived by Dr. R. J. Gatling, of Indianapolis, Ind. Since convincing himself of its entire practicability the inventor has devoted ten years in most thoroughly experimenting upon it, with what success the records of nearly every Government on the globe faithfully indicate.

As early as 1862 he had progressed so far as to have specimens of his gun in working order, and repeatedly exhibited its working by practice before thousands of witnesses at Indianapolis, where his first experiments were made. At this period it had reached a capacity for firing, of more than two hundred shots per minute, and the gun was beginning to attract public attention, from the peculiarity of its construction and its extraordinary results in practice.

In the autumn of 1862, Dr. Gatling went to Cincinnati, and had six of his guns manufactured at the establishment of Miles Greenwood & Co. The manufactory was unfortunately destroyed by fire while these guns were in process of construction, and guns, patterns, and drawings were destroyed with it, subjecting Dr. Gatling to very severe pecuniary loss. Nothing daunted, however, by this misfortune, he soon after had twelve of his batteries manufactured at another establishment, meanwhile constantly experimenting and practicing with it before Army Officers of rank and distinction, all of whom recognized the weapon as destined to achieve unqualified success, and destined to work ultimately a revolution in the practice of warfare.

Dr. Gatling made no attempt at any time to conceal the character or construction of his new invention ; but, on the contrary, published full accounts of it, illustrated by graphic diagrams, which soon found their way to all parts of the world.

At this period the French "Mitrailleuse" had not been heard of; and, as there is good reason to believe, had not been thought of.

The mitrailleuse is said to have been invented by M. Fafschamps, a Belgian Engineer, and having been improved by the addition of a centre fire cartridge and in other ways, by two mechanics—*Christophe* and *Montigny* respectively—it was put forth as the *Christophe-Montigny mitrailleur*. A secret manufactory is said to have been established at Meudon in 1866 or 1867, under the direct supervision of the Emperor Napoleon III., and there the new gun was manufactured, and from thence all sorts of impossible stories emanated in regard to it.

In the late Prussian war, the Gatling gun was used by the French, conjointly with the mitrailleuse. From the *London Journal* we clip a correspondent's description of its efficacious use in action:

Up to this time we had not seen any Prussians, beyond a few skirmishers in the plain, though our battery of Gatlings had kept blazing away at nothing in particular all the while; but now an opportunity of its being of use occurred. A column of troops appeared in the valley below us, coming from the right—a mere dark streak upon the white snow; but no one in the battery could tell whether they were friends or foes, and the commander hesitated about opening fire. But now an aide-de-camp came dashing down the hill, with orders for us to pound at them at once—a French journalist having, it seems, discovered them to be enemies when the general and all his staff were as puzzled as ourselves. Rr-rr-a go our Gatlings, the deadly hail of bullets crashes into the thick of them, and slowly back into the woods the dark mass retires, leaving, however, a track of black dots upon the white snow behind it. This is their famous and historical four o'clock effort and its failure has decided the day. That one discharge was enough.

Returning to the direct history of Dr. Gatling's invention. On October 29th, 1863, Dr. Gatling wrote Major R. Maldon, of the French Artillery, and enclosed him a full description of his gun, requesting him to hand it to the Emperor. The following is a translation of Major Maldon's answer:

"MINISTRY OF WAR, COMMITTEE OF ARTILLERY,
"PARIS, November 20, 1863.

"SIR: I read the letter you addressed to me on the 29th of last October, and communicated it to the private office of the Emperor.

"In consequence of the answer received, I have to tell you that your cannon has excited a profound interest, and I ask of your kindness to answer the following questions that have been proposed to me:—

"1st. What are the results of the tests in regard to precision at the various distances it was tried?

"2d. What proofs have been made in regard to the solidity of your cannon?

"3d. What is the weight of the ball, and of the charge of powder, in the combination which gives the best results?

"4th. Since your cannon has been adopted by the government of the United States, there should be some official report upon the proofs which has caused its adoption. Can you send me a copy of such report?

"5th. If the information which I ask you, and which, when received, will be transmitted to the Emperor, should cause His Majesty to desire that experiments be made in France with your system, under what conditions would you consent to send to France a cannon complete with all the munitions necessary to make conclusive proofs?

"Do me the favor, Sir, to reply to the five questions which I have placed before you, and after I have received your reply, I will put the matter under the eyes of the Emperor, and cause you to know the decision of His Majesty.

"Receive, Sir, the assurance of my very distinguished consideration.

"Your servant,
R. MALDON,
"Major of Artillery to the Committee of Artillery, Paris.

"MR. RICHARD J. GATLING, Indianapolis, U. S."

Dr. Gatling replied to this letter giving definite answers to the questions asked in it, and proposed to sell one hundred or more of the guns to the French Government. His proposition was declined, and shortly afterwards the government of the United States forbade the exportation of arms or munitions of war. It appears, therefore, that the Gatling gun was formally introduced to the French Government in 1863, before the invention of the French or Belgian mitrailleuse, and that Dr. Gatling was the first inventor of a machine gun which could be of practical use in military operations.

During the years 1863 and 1864, Dr. Gatling continued the manufacture of his guns in Cincinnati, and in the autumn of the latter year he made additional improvements in it—in the locks and rear cam—but without changing its main features, and for which he received his second patent, bearing date, May 9th, 1865.

In the years 1865 and 1866 these improved guns were manufactured at Cooper's Fire Arm manufactory in Philadelphia, but since that time they have been constructed in large numbers at Colt's Armory in the city of Hartford, Conn., where machinery has been fitted up at heavy expense to manufacture them in the very best manner possible.

The first official report on the merits of the Gatling gun was made by a committee appointed by Gov. O. P. Morton of Indiana and was in the following terms:

"INDIANAPOLIS July 14th, 1862.

"*To His Excellency Gov. O. P. Morton:*

"SIR: The undersigned, agreeably to your request, have examined with much care the revolving gun of Dr. Gatling.

"They have also witnessed several trials of it, both with blank and ball cartridges.

"We are aware that nothing but actual service in the field, subject to all the casualties of war, can fully establish the utility of any arm, but in this gun, as far as we have been able to judge, everything has been anticipated to render it effective under all circumstances.

"The lock is certainly ingenious and simple in its construction, and fully protected from injury from any cause. The barrels are so arranged as to fire independently of each other, so that an injury to one does not affect the others. There are no complicated parts, and the common soldier can keep it in order as readily as he can his musket. It is so substantial as to endure without injury the same usage as an ordinary field-piece. The discharge can be made with all desirable accuracy as rapidly as 150 times per minute, and may be continued for hours without danger, as we think, from overheating. Two men are sufficient to work the gun, and two horses can carry it over the field with the rapidity of cavalry. The very low price at which the gun can be made, its superiority in every respect, induce us to hope that your Excellency will order enough to be immediately constructed for a fair experiment in the field.

"We are, very respectfully, your obedient servants,
(Signed) "T. A. MORRIS.
"A. BALLWEG.
"D. G. ROSE."

The date of this report, July 14th, 1862, establishes the fact of the manufacture and firing of Dr. Gatling's first gun, in the early part of 1862. And in this connection it may be stated that one of his battery guns, made in 1862, and bearing that date, can be found in the Ordnance Museum, at Washington City.

The result of this trial was so satisfactory as to impress Governor Morton with the desire to have the gun introduced into the service of the United States, as the following letter from His Excellency to the Assistant Secretary of War will show:

"STATE OF INDIANA, EXECUTIVE DEPARTMENT,
"INDIANAPOLIS, Dec. 2d, 1862.

"*P. H. Watson, Esq., Assistant Secretary of War, Washington, D.C.:*

"SIR: Allow me to call your attention to the 'Gatling gun,' invented by Dr. R. J. Gatling, of this city. I have been present at several trials of this gun, and without considering myself competent to judge certainly of its merits, am of the opinion that it is a valuable and useful arm. Dr. Gatling desires to bring it to the notice of your Department, with the view of having it introduced into the service.

"I cheerfully recommend him to you as a gentleman of character and attainments, and worthy in all respects of your kind consideration. Any favor you may be pleased to show him will be duly appreciated.

"Very respectfully, your obedient servant,
"O. P. MORTON,
"Governor of Indiana."

The following letter from Major-General H. G. Wright, then in command of the United States forces at Cincinnati, where he saw the gun repeatedly fired, to General Ripley, the then Acting Chief of the Ordnance Department at Washington, gives the opinion of another experienced Officer who had ample opportunities to judge of the efficiency of the battery:—

"HEAD-QUARTERS, DEPARTMENT OF THE OHIO,
"CINCINNATI, March 11th, 1863.

"*Brigadier-General J. W. Ripley, Chief of Ordnance, U.S.A., Washington, D. C.:*

"GENERAL: I have examined, in company with Lieutenant Edson, Chief Ordnance Officer of this Department, the invention known as the 'Gatling gun,' and it seems to me to possess much merit.

"As a device for obtaining a heavy fire of small arms with very few men, it seems to me admirably adapted to transport steamers plying upon the Western rivers, where infantry squads are needed for security, against guerilla and other predatory bands.

"Mr. Rindge, the agent for the gun, visits Washington, and I would ask for him the opportunity to exhibit the invention to you, or some designated Officer of your Department.

"Very respectfully, your obedient servant,

"H. G. WRIGHT,

"Major-General Commanding."

Several trials of one of the guns took place at the Washington Navy Yard, in the months of May and July, 1863, and the following extracts are taken from the official reports:—

"NAVY ORDNANCE YARD,
"WASHINGTON CITY, May 20th, 1863.

"*Rear-Admiral John A. Dahlgren, Chief of Bureau of Ordnance:*

"SIR: In relation to the 'Gatling gun or battery,' I have to report as follows:—

"The gun consists of six rifle barrels, of $\frac{58}{100}$ inch calibre; each barrel is firmly connected to a breech-piece by a screw of 1 inch in length. The breech-piece is composed of one solid piece, which is made secure to a shaft $1\frac{3}{4}$ inch in diameter. The barrels are inserted in the breech-piece around the shaft, on a parallel line with the axes of said shaft, and held in the proper position by a muzzle-piece, bored by the same gauge as the holes for the breech-piece for the reception of the barrels. The breech-piece is also bored in the rear end, for the reception of the locks, on a parallel line with the barrels, each barrel having its own independent lock, revolving simultaneously, so that in case one lock or barrel becomes disabled, those remaining can be used effectively.

"Between the locks and barrels is a receptacle for the charges on a parallel line with the locks and barrels. As the entire gun revolves, the charges find their way through a hopper, containing any given number, fed from cases, instantaneously. The breech-piece contains the locks, and is entirely protected by a heavy casing of gun-metal, made fast to a wrought-iron frame, resting on trunnions $1\frac{1}{2}$ inches in diameter. It is screwed to the frame by four bolts. Inside this casing is attached an inclined ring, which the hammers of the locks ride as the gun revolves, until coming to the point of line of fire, when the discharge takes place. The locks are composed of three pieces and one spiral spring, and are entirely protected from dust or any injury. The gun is mounted as other field-pieces, with limber attached."

The report concludes as follows:—

"The gun or battery has stood the limited test given it admirably; has proved itself to be a very effective arm at short range; is well constructed, and calculated to stand the usage to which it would necessarily be subjected. It is suggested that an improvement in the manner of rifling the barrels would be advantageous.

"Respectfully submitted,

"J. S. SKERRETT,

"Lieut. Commanding, U. S. A."

At the suggestion of the writer of this last report, Dr. Gatling had a new set of barrels, with a change in the rifling, made and put in the gun, and it was on the 17th of July, 1863, again fired at the Washington Navy Yard, in the presence of a number of officers. The official report of the trial states that "penetration of the Gatling battery was equal to that of the Springfield musket;" that the gun in its "mechanical construction is very simple, the workmanship well executed, and we are of opinion that it is not liable to get out of working order."

The trials were so satisfactory to Admiral Dahlgren that he gave permission to Commanders of Fleets and Squadrons to order what guns they might think proper for service; but few guns were furnished, however, owing to Dr. Gatling's inability to make them in quantities, and want of time to see Naval officers and impress upon them the value and true character of the arm.

Some of them, however, did get into service before the close of the American war, and were used effectively in repelling rebel attacks upon the Union forces, under command of General Butler, near Richmond, Virginia.

In January, 1865, one of the improved guns was sent to Washington, and submitted by Gen. John Love to the Ordnance Bureau. A trial of the gun was at once ordered to be made, and was accordingly completed at the Washington Arsenal in the same month. The following extracts are taken from the official report of the trial:—

Total weight of gun, exclusive of carriage,	224lbs.
" " carriage,	202 "
" " limber,	200 "

The advantages claimed for this gun are:—

1st. There is no escape of gas at the breech.

2d. There is no recoil which can destroy its accuracy.

3d. It performs the operations of loading, firing, and extracting the case by simply revolving the crank.

4th. Accuracy.

5th. Rapidity of fire.

The gun certainly possesses the advantages of rapidity, accuracy, and loads, fires, &c., while the barrels are revolving.

There is no escape of gas at the breech; it has one lock for each barrel, so that in the event of one barrel or lock becoming disabled, the gun is still efficient, as the rest of the barrels can be used without difficulty.

The report concludes in the following words:—

"All parts of the gun work well.

"J. W. MACLAY,
2d Lieutenant, U. S. Artillery."

The gun used in this trial was $\frac{58}{100}$ inch calibre. General Dyer, Chief of Ordnance, being desirous of the further development of the Gatling system, suggested the construction of guns of 1 inch calibre, and ordered full trials of the same to be made at the Frankfort Arsenal, Philadelphia.

In order to conduct these trials successfully, machinery was constructed at the Arsenal expressly for making the large metallic shells for the 1 inch cartridge. In the meantime, eight of the 1 inch calibre guns were made by the Cooper Fire Arms Manufacturing Company, at Philadelphia, under the superintendence of the inventor. As soon as these arms were completed, they were placed under the charge of Colonel S. V. Benét, the able and accomplished Ordnance Officer, in command of the Arsenal, by whom prolonged series of trials were made.

Colonel Benét's report of these trials says:—

"The gun worked smoothly in all its parts, and the cartridges were fed and the cases thrown out after firing, with ease and certainty. The cartridge also worked well, and no more difficulty is to be experienced with it than with any other metallic cartridge of similar construction, if indeed so much."

Subsequently to the foregoing trials, three of the guns were taken to Washington, and fired hundreds of times, in the presence of General Grant, now President of the United States, Generals Hancock, Dyer, Maynadier, Hagner, and a great many other distinguished Army Officers and Government officials.

The Chief of Ordnance then ordered one of the guns to be taken to Fortress Monroe, Virginia, to be fired, in comparison with the "24-pounder flank defence Howitzer." The following extracts are taken from the official report of this trial:—

"FORT MONROE ARSENAL, VIRGINIA, July 14th, 1866.

"*Major-General A. B. Dyer, Chief of Ordnance:*

"SIR: I have the honor to state that in obedience to your letter of May 31st, 1866, I have tested Gatling's rifle gun, in comparison with the 24-pounder flank defence Howitzer, and I have also fired it with ball cartridges at targets.

"The results of the experiments are herewith forwarded.

"I consider it a superior arm to the 24-pounder Howitzer, for flank defence, as from 80 to 100 buck and ball cartridges can easily be fired from it in one minute, being a discharge of from 1,200 to 1,600 projectiles, while from the 24-pounder flank defence Howitzer only four rounds can be fired in the same time, giving for canister 192 projectiles, and for case shot about 700.

"The moral effect of the Gatling gun would be very great in repelling an assault, as there is not a second of time for the assailants to advance between the discharges.

"The machinery of this gun is simple and strong, and I do not think likely to get out of order. I had the oil rubbed off this gun, drenched it with water, and then exposed it for two nights and a day to the rain and weather, but though it was quite rusty, it was fired 97 times in a minute and a-half, one man turning at the crank.

"In my opinion this arm could be used to advantage in the military service, as a flank defence gun, and mounted on a field carriage, to defend a bridge, causeway, or ford.

"The size of the bore might be increased to advantage, which would allow the buck and ball cartridges to contain a greater number of, and larger sized balls.

"Respectfully your obedient servant,

"T. G. BAYLOR,

"Captain of Ordnance, and Brevet-Colonel U. S. A., Commanding.

"A true copy.

"A. B. DYER, Brevet Major-General, Chief of Ordnance."

Fig. 2.

THE GATLING GUN.

After these trials, the United States Government adopted the Gatling battery gun, and on the 24th of August, 1866, gave an order for 100 of them, 50 of 1 inch calibre, and 50 of $\frac{50}{100}$ inch calibre, which were made at the Colt's Armory, and delivered in 1867.

In May, 1868, another trial of large and small-sized Gatling guns took place at the United States Navy Yard, at Washington City, and the following is copied from the report of the distinguished Naval Officers who constituted the Board to test and report upon the merits of the gun:—

"WASHINGTON, D. C., May 30, 1868.

"*Hon. Gideon Welles, Secretary of the Navy, Washington, D. C.:*

"SIR: The undersigned, composing a Board, appointed by your order of the 14th instant, to examine, test, and report upon the merits of the Gatling gun, as to its value for use in the Navy, have the honor to submit the following report:—

"From the examination made of the gun, and the report of the tests hereto appended, the board is of opinion that, as an auxiliary arm for special service, to be used from top-gallant, forecastle, poop-deck, and tops of vessels of war, and in boat operations against an enemy, either in passing open land works or clearing breaches and other proposed places for landing from boats, &c., if opposing infantry and cavalry, it has no known superior.

"Its great merit consists in its accuracy within the limits of its range; the certainty, and, if need be, rapidity of fire, with additional merit of only requiring three persons to load, direct, and fire each piece, when suitably mounted, afloat or ashore.

"The following detailed report of the trial will, it is believed, fully sustain the opinion of the Board." (Here follows a detailed report of the trial, and a full description of the gun and its ammunition, which is too extended to be inserted in this paper.)

The report proceeds thus:—

"The mechanism (of the gun) is simple, and not likely to get out of order; but in such an event it could be repaired on board ship. Spare pieces, as in musket locks, could be a part of the outfit."

The report concludes by saying that at the close of the trial, ten shots were fired at an elevation of 10° 40′, giving by the plane table an average distance of 2,800 yards. None of the cartridges missed fire.

"Very respectfully, your obedient servants,
"M. SMITH, Commodore.
"THORNTON A. JENKINS, Commodore.
"JOHN L. DAVIS, Commander.
"K. R. BREESE, Commander."

DESCRIPTION OF THE GATLING GUN.

The following is a brief description of the construction of the "Gatling battery."

The gun consists of a series of barrels in combination with a grooved carrier and lock-cylinder. All these several parts are rigidly secured upon a main shaft. There are as many grooves in the carrier, and as many holes in the lock-cylinder as there are barrels. Each barrel is furnished with one lock, so that a gun with ten barrels has ten locks. The locks work in the holes formed in the lock-cylinder on a line with the axis of the barrels.

The lock-cylinder, which contains the locks, is surrounded by a casing which is fastened to a frame, to which trunnions are attached. There is a partition in the casing, through which there is an opening, and into which the main shaft, which carries the lock-cylinder, carrier, and barrels, is journaled. The main shaft is also, at its front end, journaled in the front part of the frame.

In front of the partition, in the casing, is placed a cam, provided with screw surfaces. This cam is rigidly fastened to the casing, and is used to impart a reciprocating motion to the locks when the gun is revolved. There is also, in the front part of the casing, a cocking-ring, which surrounds the lock-cylinder, is attached to the casing, and has on its rear surface an inclined plane, with an abrupt shoulder. This ring and its projection are used for cocking and firing the gun. This ring, the spiral cam and the locks, make up the loading and firing mechanism.

On the rear end of the main shaft, in the rear of the partition in the casing, is located a gear-wheel, which works to a pinion on the crank-shaft. The rear of the casing is closed by the cascable plate. There is hinged to the frame in front of the breech-casing a curved plate, covering partially the grooved carrier, in which is formed a hopper or opening, through which the cartridges are fed to the gun, from feed cases. The frame which supports the gun is mounted upon the carriage used for the transportation of the gun.

The operation of the gun is very simple. One man places one end of a feed-case filled with cartridges into the hopper; another man turns the crank, which, by the agency of the gearing, revolves the main shaft, carrying with it the lock-cylinder, carrier, barrels, and locks. As the gun is revolved, the cartridges, one by one, drop into the grooves of the carrier from the feed cases, and instantly the lock, by its impingement on the spiral cam surfaces, moves forward, pushes the cartridge into the chamber, and when the butt end of the lock gets on the highest projection of the cam, the charge is fired, through the agency of the cocking device, which at this point liberates the lock, spring and hammer, and explodes the cartridge. As soon as the charge is fired, the lock, as the gun is revolved, is drawn back by the agency of the screw surface in the cam acting on a lug of the lock, bringing with it the shell of the cartridge after it has been fired, which is dropped on the ground. Thus, it will be seen, when the gun is revolved, the locks in rapid succession move forward to load and fire, and return to extract the cartridge-shells. In other words, the whole operation of loading, closing the breech, discharging, and expelling the empty cartridge-shells is conducted while the barrels are kept in continuous revolving movement. It must be borne in mind that while the locks revolve with the barrels, they have also, in their line of travel, a spiral reciprocating movement; that is, each lock revolves once and moves forward and back, at each revolution of the gun.

The gun is so novel in its construction and operation that, as before remarked, it is almost impossible to describe it minutely without the aid of drawings. Its main features may be summed up thus:—

1st. Each barrel in the gun is provided with its own independent lock, or firing mechanism.

2d. All the locks revolve simultaneously with the barrels, carrier, and inner breech, when the gun is in operation. The locks also have, as stated, a reciprocating motion when the gun is rotated. *The gun cannot be fired when either the barrels, inner breech or locks are at rest.*

This brief description will convince any intelligent person at all acquainted with mechanical principles that the "Gatling Battery" in its distinctive features is unlike all other fire-arms. There is a beautiful mechanical principle developed in the gun, to which special attention should be directed, viz: that while the gun itself is under uniform constant rotary motion, the locks rotate with the barrels and breech, and at the same time have a longitudinal reciprocating motion, performing the consecutive operations of loading, cocking, and firing without any pause whatever in the several and continuous operations.

It may be here appropriately remarked as to other "Machine guns" now existing, that their complex mechanism has always been an objectionable feature in their construction, and has greatly militated against their success. But this is by no means the case with the Gatling gun.

If there is one thing more than another for which it can justly claim superiority it is its simplicity, as has been repeatedly stated by the eminent Army and Naval Officers who have witnessed its operations. Its locks are made interchangeable, and are strong and durable, but should they get out of order, the gun is so constructed that any one or all of the locks can be, in a few moments, taken out, and new ones inserted in their places, and so the gun can be kept in perfect working order at all times on the field of battle. It will not be denied that this is a feature of the greatest value, and is peculiar to the "Gatling" system, for no other machine-gun is made with removable locks and interchangeable in all its parts.

The lock mechanism is the most essential part of a machine-gun, and is the only part which is liable to get out of order from use, for all the other parts are of sufficient strength to withstand all usage incident to the service. In this most important particular the Gatling stands pre-eminent.

There is still another peculiar and valuable feature in the "Gatling" system, which should commend it as a military arm for special service, range and accuracy. It fires not by volleys, but a shot at a time, in rapid succession, thus dividing the time used in rapid firing into equal parts between each discharge, and preventing an accumulation of recoil. Thus, the Gatling system admits of larger discharges and heavier balls, consequently greater range than can be used in any other machine-gun. For instance, the larger sized "Gatling" fires a shot at a time, in rapid succession, weighing a half-pound, without displacing the gun-carriage by the recoil. This firing a shot at a time also allows a lateral motion of the gun to be kept up during the time of firing, which result is attained in the Broadwell carriage upon which the "Gatling guns" are mounted.

Now, suppose a volley of this class of ammunition was fired from a 37-barreled mitrailleuse, would not its carriage, by the accumulative recoil, be sent back to a great distance, necessitating re-sighting the piece after each volley? Most clearly so. It is true the mitrailleuse can be fired a shot at a time, but to do so would greatly lessen its rapidity of fire.

Again, the steel barrels used in the 1 inch calibre "Gatling" gun weigh each 28 lbs. Now, if a mitrailleuse, with its 37 barrels, should be made of 1 inch calibre, the barrels alone would weigh over 1,000 lbs. Of course this would make the weapon, including its massive breech-action, &c., too heavy for field service. To reduce the number of its barrels would again lessen its rapidity of fire and efficiency.

There is another important fact which it may be as well to state in this connection. The largest sized "Gatling gun," with a range of 2,000 to 3,000 yards, can be taken apart, packed on mules, and carried up or across mountains, and re-assembled in a few minutes. With no other heavy machine-gun can this be done, and here again the "Gatling" bears the palm of superiority.

The effectiveness of the large calibre "Gatling battery" does not depend, as some suppose, wholly upon feeding the cartridges to the gun from the feed-cases. The large cartridges used in this arm can be fed to the gun when the hopper is thrown back, by an active man, by hand, at the rate of 90 to 100 per minute; and this rate of discharge is, perhaps, quite fast enough when long and continued firing is to be kept up. The use of the feed-cases and rapid firing need only be resorted to in repelling a charge or in forcing the key of a position.

In feeding the cartridges to the gun by hand, all that is necessary is for one man, when the hopper is turned back, to lay the cartridges one at a time, into the grooves of the carrier. The revolving the gun by the man at the crank will load and fire the cartridges in rapid succession. It will take no more time to feed the cartridges to the gun by hand, in the way stated, than it would to load like cartridges into the feed-plates of a mitrailleur.

It is true the larger sized improved "Gatling gun," of which a representation is here given, and which has an effective range of from 2,000 to 3,000 yards, has, when the feed-cases are used, a rapidity of fire of only 150 to 200 shots per minute, but it is far more effective than the smaller Gatling, which has less range, and more than double the rate of fire. It is the quality of the shooting, that is, the efficient execution at long range, which gives the greatest value to a machine-gun.

There is no doubt that the principle upon which the "Gatling" gun is constructed admits of its range being extended, so as to cover not only the interval between musketry and artillery fire, but that occupied by artillery, thus combining in one arm the effectiveness and execution of both infantry and artillery fire. It must be evident to every thinking mind that the use of such a weapon would be invaluable.

Let us briefly examine this question. First, as to musketry fire.

The execution of the shots fired from a small "Gatling" would be, no doubt, shot for shot, much greater than the fire of infantry. This valuable result grows out of these facts:—

When the gun is once sighted, its carriage does not move but at the will of the operator, and the gun can be moved laterally when firing is going on, so as to sweep the sector of a circle of 12 or more degrees, without moving the trail or changing the wheels of the carriage.

Fig 4.

LIGHT GATLING GUN TRANSPORTED BY SOLDIERS.

It can be trained with far more accuracy and delicacy than small arms from the shoulder. It has no nerves to be disturbed in the din and confusion and carnage of the battle field, nor will the smoke of battle prevent its precision. There is another advantage which it may be proper to state here. The exposure of life is very small with a gun of this character, compared with infantry.

In a competitive trial, made at Carlsruhe, Baden, in August, 1869, between a small sized "Gatling" gun and 100 infantry soldiers, armed with the celebrated "needle-gun," the "Gatling" at 800 paces put 88 per cent. of its shots in a target, while the soldiers, in firing at the same sized target and at the same distance, only placed 27 per cent. of their shots in the target. Who can doubt that this difference would have been greater had the firing taken place during the heat and smoke of battle?

Second, as artillery. There is abundant data to prove that only a small per cent. of the missiles fired from field-guns in the excitement of battle prove effective. During an action, and when the smoke frequently prevents the enemy being seen, the firing is done, in many cases, in the most random manner, and especially is this so when the ground is uneven, and the enemy is frequently changing his position. The gun is also changing its position, particularly when the enemy is pressing forward, and rapid firing is kept up. Often, in such cases, the gun is not moved forward, for want of time, to its original position after each discharge, but is fired in the position in which the recoil has left it. And this is repeated while the battle lasts, when, at its close, it is often found that the gun has receded for a considerable distance from its first position. It must be evident that, under such excitement and conditions, the most of the missiles discharged have failed to do execution.

On this head, the testimony of an experienced artillery Officer may not be out of place. We quote from Major Fosbery:—

With the field-gun in its best condition we produce per round 20 effective fragments or bullets, capable of inflicting serious wounds or death, and we can throw these into a column or other body of troops up to 1,500 yards. We can throw 2½ such rounds per minute under favorable conditions, or 5 rounds in two minutes of time, that is 100 such effective pieces. When these pieces come to be analyzed, we find that some are segments or bullets, some broken pieces of the envelope of iron which fits the gun, and carries them up to their destination. We employ for the purpose at the gun itself a certain amount of apparatus for piercing the fuzes, cutting or otherwise adjusting them; or we employ a fuze already prepared, which depends on some careful adjustment of the gun itself for its efficacy. When all is done, about one-half of the weight of metal put into the gun is finally effective at the object.

But if this is the case, and it would not be difficult to prove that more is so, it must be evident that somewhere a great waste of material occurs. For could a larger portion of metal be made effective, it is clear that it would be useless to carry into the field so large a weight as we now do, in order to produce an equal effect; but if a less weight of metal would suffice, then also would a less amount of powder be required to drive it, a gun of smaller calibre might be used, and the whole of our field equipments would become easier to move, handier in the working, requiring fewer men and fewer horses for its transport and service; and as a matter of course, both in a military and in an economical point of view, fitter for service of the country.

So far is this now from being the case, that we find the 9-pr. guns of the horse artillery unable to produce the effects which we would wish to see, and a proposition entertained for exchanging them for 12-prs., which will doubtless add to the efficiency of their fire, though the additional weight to be dragged must detract to a large extent from their mobility. Supposing for a moment such a change to be carried out, and a horse artillery battery of 12-prs., to be brought into action, not to breach a wall, batter a farm-house, nor oppose an enemy's artillery, but merely to play upon troops either waiting an attack, or forming to make one, what do we find? We find guns weighing 900 lbs., each brought rapidly to the front, with limbers and wagons weighted with at least twice as much powder, lead, and iron as will ever produce, under the best of circumstances, either death or wounds to an enemy; and we find these deaths and wounds dealt out very slowly indeed, at the rate only of about 50 per minute under these exceptionably favorable conditions.

If a "range-finder" is used, a minute and a half is consumed in finding the distance of the enemy; if it be not used at any but the shortest distance, the fire is mere guess work, and may be either good or bad, with a strong presumption in favor of the latter. Superior as our artillery is acknowledged to be, we can scarcely wonder, knowing what we know of its performances, at the failure of either the Austrian or Prussian rifled field services to influence largely the fate of the battles, where both were so freely and ably made use of. Neither succeeded in any instance, as far as I am aware, in stopping the advance of infantry, or even in greatly impeding the operations of cavalry in the field, though doubtless both were efficient and well served."

In another part of his communication, Major Fosbery says:—

"In order to produce these twenty fragments (above alluded to) and render them efficient, many independent operations must be truly performed, and even then sudden gusts of wind, or considerable barometric variations may render all of no avail by their influence on the flight of the projectile, by delaying or accelerating the burning of the fuzes. * * *

"The gun must be laid between each discharge, an operation demanding time and care, necessitating a clear view of the object, and all but impossible to get exactly repeated by the most highly-trained and skilful gunners when on an artillery practice-ground, and neither greatly pressed for time, nor deprived, in however small a degree, of that *sang froid* which few persons possess completely, when exposed to a lively fire, and endeavoring to crush it by the rapidity of their own."

This is the evidence of an Officer who has had the best opportunities of judging, and whose experience entitles him to speak advisedly on the subject.

At the risk of being considered tautological, we will enumerate the advantages of the larger sized "Gatling gun" over such an arm, when used to play upon troops either awaiting an attack or forming to make one.

1st. Its great range, equal to that of the field gun for all practical purposes, and its greater accuracy and precision.

It is the use of the elongated leaden bullet, which has great specific gravity and small air resistance, that gives the "Gatling gun" its superior range and precision.

2d. Its rapidity and continuity of fire, 200 shots per minute, when well served, each ball weighing a half-pound; 1,200 shots a minute from a single battery of six guns; 7,200 shots per minute from six batteries! "It would be difficult to find the troops who could face such a hailstorm as this."

3d. No re-sighting and re-laying are necessary between each discharge. As before stated, "when the gun is once sighted, its carriage does not move, except at the will of the operator, and the gun can be moved laterally when firing is going on, so as to sweep the sector of a circle of 12 degrees or more without moving the trail, or changing the wheels of the carriage." The smoke of battle, therefore, does not interfere with its precision.

4th. It is lighter than a 12-pr., therefore, more easily moved, and requiring fewer horses and men to serve it.

5th. The balls of the "Gatling gun" ricochet for a greater distance than the balls or shells of the field-piece.

6th. The Gatling system is more economical, not only in requiring less horses and men to manage the gun, but also in its ammunition.

The ammunition now used in the "Gatling gun" has been greatly improved. The large 1-inch metallic case ammunition first made for the use of the larger sized "Gatling gun," and which was used in the first European trials, proved defective. Its defects grew out of the fact that the cases or shells were made out of sheet metal, which had not the proper solidity to enable them to withstand even the small charge of powder then used. The result was that in firing the heads of some of the cartridges came off or burst, interrupting, of course, the firing. Moreover, the cartridge shell-extractors first used in the locks were imperfect, failing, at times when the heads of the cartridges were small, to extract the shells after they had been fired.

All these defects have been entirely overcome by subsequent improvements.

Instead of making the cartridge cases or shells of thin material, as in the first instance, they are now manufactured by the aid of powerful machinery, out of sheet metal, which is one-tenth of an inch thick; the heads are made solid, and, in order to increase their solidity, solder is used in their base. The shells are now so constructed as to admit of being reloaded. Indeed, they have been loaded and fired 100 times, without being perceptibly injured.

If one of these shells, or "loading chambers" cost, say, 10 cts., and it can be reloaded and fired on an average of, say 50 times, without injury, it is evident that it must be cheaper than ordinary metallic cartridges, the shells of which can be fired only once.

This class of reloading metallic ammunition will, probably, ere long, be adopted by all civilized nations. These cartridges are waterproof, and strong enough to stand all usage incident to the service. They are not only cheaper, but they are safer in the transport and are of less weight, and occupy less space, requiring, therefore, fewer men and horses for their transportation and service than artillery ammunition.

Besides the trials of the "Gatling gun" in the United States, to which we have already referred, and that at Carlsruhe, Baden, also noticed, numerous competitive trials have taken place at various points in Europe, of which we shall give the results in diagrams hereafter.

One would have reasonably concluded that such results as were attained at Vienna, where, at a distance of 800 paces, the ½ inch "Gatling gun" made 208 sharp hits out of 216 shots, and at a distance of 1,200 paces made 149 sharp hits out of 191 shots—and then at Carlsruhe, where, in a contest between 100 infantry soldiers armed with the celebrated needle gun, the ½ inch Gatling, at a distance of 800 paces, made in the space of one minute, 216 hits out of 246 shots, against 196 hits out of 721 shots made by the infantry, would have sufficiently demonstrated its vast superiority and undoubted merit as a death-dealing instrument. But Governments are slow to believe in new inventions and to act in their adoption, and the *London Times* actually sneered at the Russian Government as making undue haste to adopt "most American inventions, whether good or bad," because, after experiments and trials, that Government ordered a number of the "Gatling guns" for the use of its army and navy. The recent war between France and Prussia, however, in which artillery played so prominent a part, and so largely contributed to the Prussian victories, had the effect of awakening the other Powers of Europe to the urgent necessity of equipping their armies with the best and most effective weapons in this branch of the service. The trial at Shoeburyness, was the result of this necessity. A special committee was organized to conduct these experiments.

The English Government prided itself in the possession of a new nine-pounder Indian bronze gun, from which great deeds were expected, and it is but justice to say that the weapon at the trial at Shoeburyness, maintained its high reputation, but it is equally true that that trial demonstrated beyond a peradventure, that the artillery branch of no army is complete without the "Gatling gun." The experiments were made with the small, medium, and large Gatling, the nine pounder Indian bronze muzzle-loading field gun, the twelve-pounder Armstrong breech-loader field gun, the mitrailleuse, the Martini-Henry breech-loading rifles, and the breech-loading Snider rifle—the three last only at the short distances, up to 1200 yards. It will thus be seen that the "Gatling gun" contended against the best arms, both for short and long ranges, known to modern warfare.

The great importance attached to the trial at Shoeburyness, and the high character and distinguished military knowledge, impartiality, and experience of the able members composing the Committee under whose direction and superintendence these trials were made, will be sufficient excuse for giving their report in full.

REPORT.

President, Colonel E. Wray, C. B., R. A. Members.—Captain the Hon. F. Foley, R. A.; Colonel G. Shaw, R. A., Assistant Adjutant General; Lieut. Colonel Fletcher, Scots Fusilier Guards; Captain Beaumont, M. P., R. E.; Captain W. H. Noble, R. A. Secretary, Lieut. Colonel Heyman, R. A.

28th October, 1870.

SIR:—1. The special committee on Mitrailleuse have the honor to submit their Report upon the results of the trials they were directed to carry out, to ascertain the relative value of two systems of Mitrailleuse, known as the Montigny and Gatling guns, as compared with the fire of field artillery and infantry.

2. Concurrently with the above systems, the committee have had under their consideration several other designs (on paper) of multiple guns, alike in general character, but different in respect to mechanical detail.

The names of the proposers are given in Appendix D., together with a brief description of each of the systems referred to, the majority of which were dismissed on the grounds of their inapplicability to the service, while the remainder were rejected on account of their apparent inferiority to the Montigny and Gatling guns.

3. The mechanical action and constructive features of the two machine guns actually under trial, will be found detailed in Appendixes A. and B. Photographs are likewise transmitted.

4. The results of the comparative experiments carried out by the committee are tabulated in Appendix C., in which also is given the calibre and weight of the respective guns, as well as of the ammunition used.

Previous to proceeding to compare the relative merits of the two systems of Mitrailleuse which have been under trial, the committee think it desirable to submit a few remarks upon the general application of machine guns of this nature for purposes of war.

5. Up to a very recent period the opinions of the majority of the great military Powers were decidedly adverse to the introduction of these weapons for service in the field, and the early experiments carried on in this country appeared also to justify their condemnation.

6. The Prussians, who within the last eighteen months had instituted a searching enquiry into the merits of these machine guns, came to the conclusion that the very narrow sphere within which their effect was restricted, did not at all compensate for the *personnel* and material required in serving them.

7. The French, however, appear to have taken a different view, and have adopted the mitrailleuse in comparatively large numbers.

8. Judging from the accounts received from time to time through the public press of the effects produced by mitrailleuse fire during the present war, the committee are disposed to think that practical experience has led the Prussians to attach more importance to the value of the machine guns.

This question might be readily set at rest by reference to Colonel Walker, Military Attaché at Berlin, but the committee are the more disposed to adopt their view of the case from the circumstance that three great military nations, viz.: Russia, Austria and Turkey have apparently been induced, by the experience of the present war, to recognize the value of these weapons, by giving large orders for immediate supply.

9. Of the two system of machine-guns which have been under consideration of the committee, the Gatling has been proved to be far superior, and the committee can only account for the preference expressed by Major Fosbery for the Montigny, in his report of the 2nd September, 1868, by the supposition that he had not personally a trial of the Gatling in its present perfected condition.

At any rate he could not have seen the gun worked with the "feed drum," which is one of the most recent improvements, the original mode of feed to which Major Fosbery probably refers, was undoubtedly most defective. The particular points for which the committee claim the superiority of the Gatling gun over the Montigny are as follows:—

1st. Greater destructive effect, owing to the rapidity with which it can be fired.

2d. Greater command of range, the Montigny system being necessarily restricted to small calibres, whereas the Gatling is equally adopted to large as to small calibres.

3d. The Gatling gun, so far as the experience of the committee goes, is capable of being worked by fewer men than the Montigny.

4th. Greater strength and simplicity of mechanism.

5th. Greater facility of repair, the locks of the Gatling being removable, and easily replaced in a few minutes if out of order, or otherwise injured; whereas, with the Montigny mechanism a similar accident renders the gun for the time unserviceable.

6th. The greater demoralizing effect produced by the continuity of the fire of the Gatling as compared with that of the Montigny.

7th. The "drum" arrangement affords a better means of carrying the ammunition uninjured than the plan proposed by Major Fosbery for the Montigny.

The results of the recent enquiry have fully satisfied the committee of the expediency of introducing a certain proportion of these machine guns, to act as auxiliaries to the other arms of the service, and of the several designs which have been submitted for their consideration including those that have been under trial, they are persuaded that the Gatling gun is the best adapted to meet all military requirements.

To assist in defending such positions as villages, field entrenchments, &c., the committee feel satisfied that the small Gatling would be invaluable.

For the defence of caponnieres, for covering the approach to bridges or *tetes depont*, for defending a breach, and for employment in advanced trenches or in field-works, where economy of space is of the utmost importance, the same sized Gatling would unquestionably be a most effective weapon.

For Naval purposes the small Gatling would apparently be well adapted for use in the tops of vessels of war to clear the enemy's decks, or open ports; while for gunboats that carry only one heavy gun, and for boat operations, the medium sized Gatling would be most effective in covering the landing of troops, or for service up close rivers.

The committee are also impressed with the effect produced by the medium sized Gatling 0.65 inch calibre, at long ranges as compared with that of a field-gun, but looking to the weight of ammunition required to produce this effect, and to the exceptional conditions under which the larger Gatling could be used with advantage in the field, they are satisfied that a gun is far preferable at long ranges, and consequently they do not recommend the introduction of the larger description of Gatling for land service.

In advocating the introduction of the small Gatling gun, the committee wish it to be distinctly understood that they do not for a moment contemplate their supplanting or displacing a single field-gun, the proportions of which have been laid down by the best military authorities, as indispensable for an army in the field.

The characteristics of the two weapons are essentially different. Except against an enemy in the open, the fire of a mitrailleuse is comparatively worthless, whereas artillery fire will search out an enemy from almost any position, whether covered by trees, brushwood, earthworks or houses, and at distances far beyond the range of a mitrailleuse; but in the open, and at distances up to 1,200 yards, there is reason to believe that the latter will be found the more destructive, owing to the rapidity and continuity of its fire.

The committee have now the honor to submit the following recommendations:—

The immediate introduction of the small Gatling gun for employment in the field.

The guns to be mounted on suitable carriages adapted for two-horse draught.

	cwts.	qrs.	lbs.
Weight of Gun	3	1	0
Six Drums containing each 368 rounds 2,208 .	3	2	0
Carriage and limber	10	0	0
Total,	16	3	0

The whole of the carriages for these guns should be fitted with musket proof shields, and range-finders should be used in connection with them.

The exact number to be attached to each brigade or divison, as well as the mode of horsing and manning the guns, to be left to the decision of the proper authorities. For the defence of caponnieres and field works, &c., to be mounted on carriages suitable for confined spaces.

For the Navy to be mounted on such carriages or swivels as may be found best adapted.

Should these recommendations be approved, the committee would suggest that for a first instalment 50 guns of the small calibre for land service, and as many of the small and medium sized guns as the Lords, Commissioners of the Admiralty may consider requisite for the Navy, be ordered from Dr. Gatling pending the preparation of suitable plant either at Enfield or Woolwich for future production.

The carriages to be designed and manufactured in the Royal Carriage Department.

With regard to ammunition the cartridges used in the recent trials were supplied from America, and were manufactured at Bridgeport, Connecticut.

As compared with the Boxer cartridge, they are expensive, and before proceeding to make provision for supply of ammunition, the committee recommend that the Superintendent Royal Laboratory be asked if he can make a cartridge on the Boxer principle which will be equally suitable for service with the Gatling guns.

The calibre of the small Gatling tried by the committee was 0.42 inch, but looking to the probable introduction of a small bore rifle at a period not far distant, the committee consider it indispensable that the bore and rifling of the Gatling barrels should be made to correspond, viz.: 0.45-inch bore, so as to provide for the possibility in future of having an interchangeable ammunition.

The committee have ascertained from Dr. Gatling that there will be no difficulty or delay by the adoption of a 0.45 calibre, with the rifling and weight of bullet and charge of the Martini-Henry rifle.

We have the honor to be, Sir, your obedient servants,

E. WRAY, Colonel R. A., President.
F. A. FOLEY, Captain, R. A.
G. SHAW, Colonel, R. A.
H. C. FLETCHER, Lieut. Colonel, Scots Fusilier Guards.
FRED. BEAUMONT, Captain, R. E.
W. H. NOBLE, Captain, R. A.
H. HEYMAN, Lieut. Colonel, Secretary.

The Director of Artillery, War Office, Pall Mall.

This is a candid admission from a source that only two months before had "laughed" at the machine-gun system, and conclusively shows that the Gatling achieved no ordinary triumph at the trial at Shoeburyness. The official accounts of those experiments have been published by the committee, and a brief reference to them is essential to establish the relative positions of the several weapons used on the occasion.

In the first experiment at targets, practice against time, (two minutes,) only Shrapnel shell fired from the field guns, the results were:

AT 300 YARDS' RANGE.	Hits.
Small Gatling, with 53 lb. of ammunition	369
Twelve-pounder breech-loader field gun, with 121½ lb.	268
Nine-pounder muzzle-loading field gun, with 107 lb	208
Montigny mitrailleuse, with 25 lb	171
Six Martini-Henry breech-loading rifles, with 15 lb	74
Six breech-loading Snider rifles, with 8 lb	63
AT 400 YARDS' RANGE.	
Small Gatling, with 39 lb	310
Nine-pounder muzzle-loading gun, with 118 lb	236
Montigny mitrailleuse, with 30 lb	178
Twelve-pounder breech-loading gun, with 121½ lb	166
Six Snider rifles, with 9 lb	77
Six Martini-Henry rifles, with 17 lb	68
AT 600 YARDS' RANGE.	
Small Gatling, with 56 lb	522
Nine-pounder muzzle-loading gun, with 75 lb	283
Twelve-pounder breech-loading gun, with 94½ lb	142
Montigny mitrailleuse, with 30 lb	127
Six Snider rifles, with 9 lb	63
Six Martini-Henry rifles, with 11 lb	52

AT 800 YARDS' RANGE.

Small Gatling, with 30½ lb.	229
Montigny mitrailleuse, with 25 lb.	154
Twelve-pounder breech-loading gun, with 82 lb.	152
Nine-pounder muzzle-loading gun, with 53 lb.	118
Six Martini-Henry rifles, with 10 lb.	66
Six Snider rifles, with 10 lb.	48

But the differences come out still more prominently in the grand totals of work of all kinds done in the experimental trials by each weapon. Thus, taking first the totals of all work done within the musketry range, we have:

	Hits.
The small Gatling mitrailleuse, weighing 8 cwt., expended of ammunition, 492 lb., scoring	2,803
The Montigny mitrailleuse, (8 cwt.,) expended 472 lb., scoring	1,708
The twelve-pounder breech-loading gun, (8 cwt.,) expended 1,282 lb., scoring	2,286
The nine-pounder muzzle-loading gun (8 cwt.,) expended 1,018 lb., scoring	2,207

Making the same comparison of the field guns with the medium Gatling, for work done at ranges beyond musketry distances, up to 2,100 yards range, we have:

	Hits.
The medium Gatling (5 cwt.,) expended 241 lb., scoring	309
The twelve-pounder breech-loading gun, (8 cwt.,) expended 312 lb., scoring	258
The nine-pounder muzzle-loading gun, (8 cwt.,) expended 225 lb., scoring	219

This last comparison is not so reliable as the other, for the reason as stated by the committee, that the practice with the weapons on this occasion was unusually bad, and showed them to a manifest disadvantage. The careful observer will not fail in his calculations, to take into consideration the amount of ammunition expended by, and the weight of each gun.

The sights of the larger sized Gatling guns used in these trials had been adjusted only for ranges of one thousand yards and less, and this fact materially affected the practice made with them at longer ranges.

It is confidently believed that, with improved ammunition, and a more perfect system of rifling, the larger calibre Gatling guns, worked by men perfectly familiar with their use, will be as effective at long ranges as the best field guns, and far more effective at short ranges.

The committee also reported the result of a competitive trial, on the same occasion, between the Montigny Mitrailleuse, using the latest pattern of ammunition submitted, and the small Gatling gun, at a row of ten targets, 9 feet by 9 feet, as follows:

	Time.		Hits			
	Min	Sec	Through.	Lodged.	Struck.	Total.
At 600 yards, 720 rounds from each deliberately						
Montigny Mitrailleur	4	0	536	2	0	538
Small Gatling	3	31	608	3	7	618
At 800 yards, 555 rounds from each deliberately						
Montigny Mitrailleur	3	8	284	5	3	292
Small Gatling	3	26	423	6	10	439

In this long range firing we have in the third experiment the following results between the large and medium sized Gatlings and the field guns:

AT 1,400 YARDS' RANGE.

Firing against time (2 minutes) at a column of targets 9 feet by 9 feet, representing 90 infantry divided into 3 troops or companies 20 yards apart.

	No. of Balls Through & Lodged.	Infantry Disabled.	Time.
Large Gatling	99	54	1 Minute and 18 Seconds.
Medium Gatling 0.65 inch	236	103	1 Minute and 9 Seconds.
Small " "	104	55	
Nine-pounder bronze M. L. R. Shrapnel	178	66	
Segment	90	42	
Twelve-pounder B. L. R. Shrapnel	224	104	
Segment	102	53	

AT 2,070 YARDS' RANGE.

Firing against time (2 minutes) at a column of targets 9 feet by 9 feet, representing 36 cavalry or 45 infantry, divided into 3 troops or companies 30 yards apart.

	Total Hits.	Cavalry Disabled.	Infantry. Disabled
Large Gatling	99	38	46
Medium Gatling 0.65 inch	164	34	44
Nine-pounder bronze M. L. R. Shrapnel	35	16	20
Segment	6	22	31
Twelve-pounder B. L. R. Shrapnel	41	22	24
Segment	115	36	37

The committee also reported the experiments, the result of which is shown in the following tables:

FOURTH EXPERIMENT.

Firing at 134 dummies, placed in loose order on uneven ground, representing broken infantry retiring; left of the line thrown back; front, 98 yards; *average depth, 35 yards; firing from three positions at unknown ranges, the distance judged by officers in command, a different subaltern being appointed for each series.*

Date.	Data.	Elevation.	Length of fuze.	Time of firing.	Number of rounds fired.	Total disabling hits.	Infantry disabled.	Remarks.
26. 8. 70.	9-pr. M. L. R., firing shrapnel. Lieut. Day, R. A., in command.		ins.					
"	1st position—judged at 400 yards	0° 20'	.2 / .15	1' 55''	5	74	30	2 rounds burst *beyond* the line of dummies—ineffective.
"	2d position— " 700 "	0° 50'	.3					
	" 750 "	1° 0'	..	3' 10''	5	34	26	Gimlet borer broken, causing considerable delay.
	" 780 "	..	..					
	" 800 "	..	.35					
"	3d position " 1,000 "	1° 50'	.5	2' 15''	5	47	37	Service hook borer broken, causing delay.
	Total of 15 rounds	..	.	..	.	155	93	
"	12 pr. B. L. R., firing shrapnel. Lieut. Halliday, R. A., in command.							
"	1st position—judged at 570 yards	0° 45'	.25	2' 45''	5	29	18	1 round blind and 1 over—ineffective.
	" 520 "	..	.2					
"	2d position— " 650 "	1° 5'	.3	2' 11''	5	62	45	Safety pin broken in the fuze first round, causing delay.
"	3d position— " 900 "	2° 0'	.45 / .5 / .45	2' 45''	5	39	33	The changes in length of fuze considerably reduced the rate of firing.
	Total of 15 rounds	..	..	..	.	150	96	
	The mean time firing 5 rounds from each gun, viz.: 2⅓ minutes, taken as the period for the Infantry and Mitrailleur to fire for comparison.							
"	Mitrailleur—firing for 2⅓ minutes. Lieut. Murray, R. A., in command.							
"	1st position—judged at 330 yards	0° 36'	..	..	Plates. 9	122	69	1 miss fire. 1 case jammed.
	" 300 "	..	..	.	328 / 9	83	59	6 cases jammed.
"	2d position— " 650 "	1° 18'	..	.				
"	3d position— " 950 "	2° 20'	..	..	333 / 11	9	8	9 plates were loaded with an improved pattern cartridge, and 2 with the old cartridge hitherto used. 8 of the new cartridges jammed, and 15 of the old ones. This indifferent result is attributed by Mr. Cristophe to the new cartridge being loaded with a much stronger powder, for which due allowance had not been made.
	Total of 1,073 rounds	..			407	214	136	
15. 9. 70.	300 yards. Further trial with 12-pr. B. L. R., firing case shot.	1°	.	2' 30''	7	83	57	
	Total of 7 rounds	..	..	..	..	83	57	
"	Small Gatling gun. Captain Ellis, R. A., in command.							
15. 9. 70.	1st position—300 yards	..	..	2' 30''	453	212	100	
16. 9. 70.	2d position—450 yards	..	..	2' 10''	736	162	92	
"	3d position—650 yards	..	.	2' 5''	736	177	85	
	Total of 1,925 rounds	.	.	..	1,925	651	277	

And yet, after these experiments, it was not until after the Gatling guns were brought to Woolwich, and, in the words of the London papers, "subjected to a general and exhaustive trial at the Government Butts, Royal Arsenal," that they were finally adopted by the British Government! After all these trials, so thorough, searching and exhaustive, culminating at all, in the most complete triumph, is it necessary to waste words in commendation of the Gatling gun?

These experiments have shown the main features and superiority of this gun to be:

1. Its rapidity and continuity of fire.

2. Its simplicity—there is nothing complex about the gun.

3. Each barrel in the gun is provided with its own independent lock or firing mechanism.

4. These locks are made interchangeable, and are strong and durable, but should they get out of order, the gun is so constructed that any one or all of them can be, in a few moments, taken out and others inserted in their places, and so the gun can be kept in perfect working order at all times, on the field of battle. It will not be denied that this is a feature of the greatest value, as the lock mechanism is the most essential part of a machine gun, and is the only part liable to get out of order from use.

5. All the locks revolve simultaneously with the barrels, carrier, and inner-breech, when the gun is in operation. The locks also have a reciprocating motion when the gun is revolved. The gun cannot be fired when either the barrels or locks are at rest.

6. The gun is made of single barrels, open at muzzle and breech, with space between them for the free circulation of air and radiation of heat, thus preventing to a great extent that heating and fouling of the barrels, which, otherwise, the rapidity and continuity of its fire would cause.

7. The isolation of the barrels makes their expansion and contraction equal and uniform, and thus they suffer no distortion from these causes, as they would if massed together.

8. The barrels are open from end to end, and can easily be kept clean by the use of a swab or wiper.

9. The cartridges are loaded directly into the rear ends of the barrels, thus all leakage of gas at the breech is prevented.

10. The gun fires a shot at a time in rapid succession, and thus

by dividing the time used in rapid firing into equal parts between the discharges and preventing an accumulation of recoil, it admits of larger charges, heavier balls, and consequently, greater range.

11. This peculiarity of no recoil is of special value in the defences of bridges, fords, mountain passes, etc., which are frequently attempted during darkness, fog or storm, as also in the smoke of battle, when the movement of the enemy cannot be accurately observed.

12. Firing a shot at a time also allows a lateral motion of the gun to be kept up during the time of firing, which result is attained in the Broadwell carriage upon which it is mounted, or by the Kinne attachment to the carriage manufactured at Colt's Armory, Hartford, Conn., by which the gun is traversed automatically.

13. No re-sighting and re-laying are necessary between the discharges. When the gun is once sighted, its carriage does not move but at the will of the operator, and the gun can be moved laterally when firing is going on, as heretofore remarked, so as to sweep the sector of a circle of 12 or more degrees, without moving the trail or changing the wheels of the carriage.

14. The continuous firing, a shot at a time, avoids all deflections of the balls.

15. As musketry fire, the small Gatling can be trained with far more accuracy and delicacy than small arms from the shoulders, and has no nerves to be disturbed in the din, confusion, and carnage of the battle-field, nor will the smoke of battle prevent its precision.

16. It requires fewer horses and men to serve it. The weight of the small Gatling is only 3 cwt., of the medium 5 cwt., and of the largest size 6 cwt. Two men serve the first, and from five to seven men the last two.

17. Its great economy, not only in men and horses, but in ammunition.

18. The great safety in the transportation of this ammunition. The cartridge cases or shells for the larger Gatling guns are constructed of sheet metal, which is of an $\frac{15}{100}$ inch thick, the heads are made solid, and solder is used in their bases. These shells can be reloaded and fired from 50 to 100 times. They are also waterproof, strong enough to stand all usage incident to the service, and

Fig. 5.

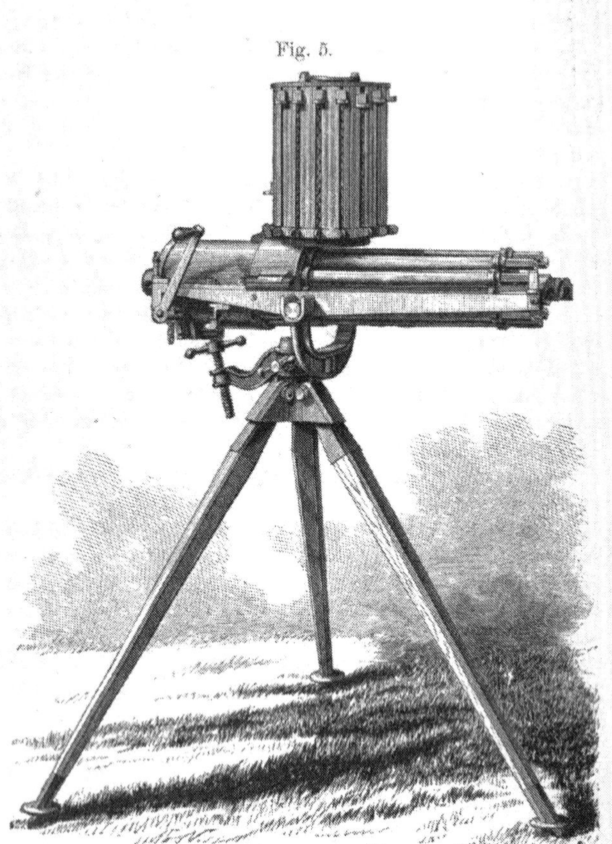

TRIPOD GATLING GUN.

are safer in transportation, are of less weight, and occupy less space, thus requiring fewer men and horses for their transportation and service than artillery ammunition. By carrying loading-machines, with extra balls and powder, and detailing men to reload the shells after they have been fired on the field of battle, a supply of ammunition can always be kept up in time of action.

19. The operation of loading is greatly simplified. There is no need of sponging, capping, priming, adjusting of fuses, cocking, etc. All that is required is to supply the hopper with the cartridges and to turn the crank, when a continuous stream of balls can be discharged.

20. The flanges of the cartridges have square faces in front, which enable the shells to be easily extracted from the chambers of the barrels, after they have been fired, by the improved extractors with which the locks are now made.

21. The great range of the large gun, equal to that of the field gun for all practical purposes, and, in accuracy and precision, greater, given to it from the use of the elongated leaden bullet, which has great specific gravity and small air resistance.

22. The projectiles of the large gun may be either solid shot, shell, or canister, like those of field artillery.

23. The balls of the Gatling gun ricochet for a greater distance than the shells or missiles of the field-piece.

24. The feeding drums and feed cases of the gun can all be used with any gun of the same calibre.

25. The working parts of the gun are encased in the breech covering so as to be entirely protected from dust and bad weather.

26. The largest sized gun, with a range of from 2,000 to 3,000 yards, can be taken apart, packed on mules, (see Fig. 7, p. —,) carried across mountains, and on its arrival at its destination can be reassembled in a few minutes.

In order to supply the demand for these fire-arms, the following various sizes are now manufactured by the Colt's Fire-Arms Manufacturing Company, at Hartford, Conn., U. S. A. Gatling guns are also now being manufactured by Messrs. Paget & Co., in Vienna, Austria, and by Sir W. G. Armstrong & Co., at Newcastle-on-Tyne, England.

1st. The smallest size (Fig. 4, p. 233) has ten steel rifled barrels, and is made of any proper calibre to suit the musket cartridges used by different governments.

2d. The second sized gun (Fig. 2, page 226) has ten steel rifled barrels, is $\frac{65}{100}$ inch calibre, and discharges solid lead balls weighing 3½ ounces.

3d. The third sized gun also has ten steel rifled barrels, is $\frac{75}{100}$ inch calibre, and discharges solid lead balls weighing 4½ ounces. This gun in its exterior dimensions is precisely the same as the $\frac{65}{100}$ inch calibre gun.

4th. The fourth or largest-sized gun, (Fig. 3, p. 231,) is of one-inch calibre, is made with six (sometimes with ten) barrels, and discharges solid lead balls weighing one-half pound. This gun also uses a canister cartridge which contains sixteen balls, (a cut of which is shown in Fig. 6.) It also discharges explosive balls with great effect.

5th. Guns of 6 and 10 barrels are made, adapted to the size of cartridge used by the infantry, so as to use their ammunition. (Fig. 6, p. —) also shows the cartridge used by the infantry and the Gatling gun in the Russian army.

Special attention is called to the new improved Gatling gun (a cut of which is shown in Fig. 2.) In this new model, the mechanism of the locks has been greatly strengthened, as well as otherwise improved, and there are means provided for their insertion and removal without taking off the cascable-plate. These means consist of the perforation of the covering and back diaphragm in the outer casing, and by the closure of the apertures through both these plates by a single removable plug, as shown at *B*. This is a very valuable improvement, inasmuch as the repairing or inspection of the locks is thereby greatly facilitated.

As stated heretofore, the cartridges used with this and one-inch-calibre guns, have been greatly improved ; (a section of one of them is shown in Fig. 6.)

6th. A new model Gatling gun, weighing 125 pounds, using infantry ammunition, and having ten barrels, the calibre being the same as that of the musket, has just been completed.

It is designed to be carried on mules or camels, and will be particularly useful in mountainous countries, where the roads are impassable for vehicles.

1-2 inch GATLING GUN.

Distance 800 paces. * Trial shots, 3. Shots, 216. •Sharp hits, 208. °Hits which did not penetrate, 5. Total, 213.

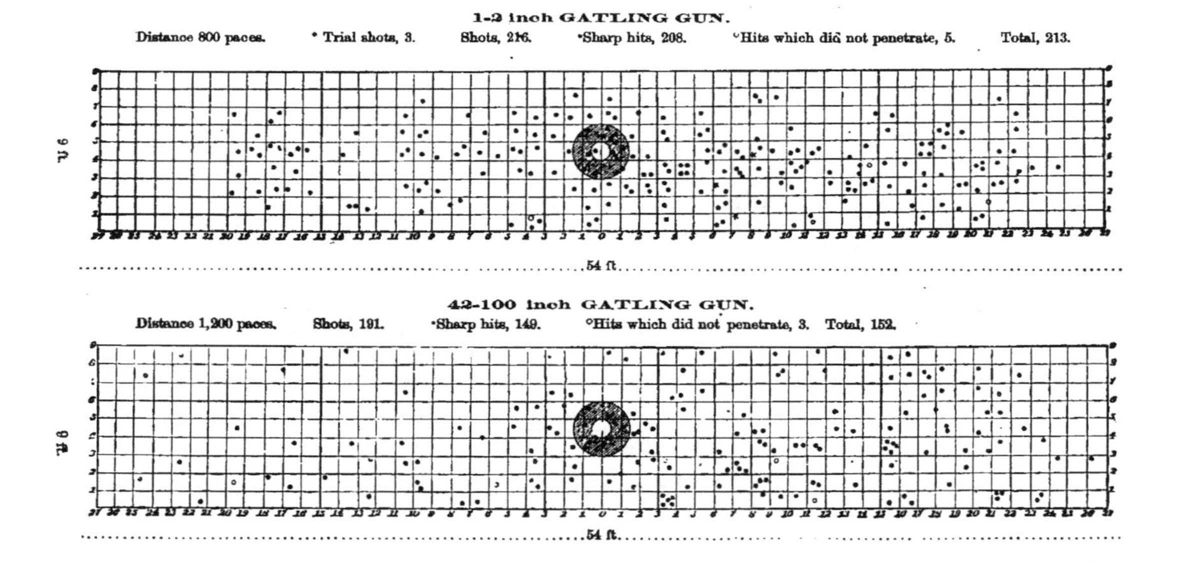

42-100 inch GATLING GUN.

Distance 1,200 paces. Shots, 191. •Sharp hits, 149. °Hits which did not penetrate, 3. Total, 152.

Results of Target Practice made at Carlsruhe, Baden, August, 1869, between 100 Infantry Soldiers, armed with the "Needle Gun," and a single "Gatling Gun.

INFANTRY TARGET.

Distance, 800 paces. Shots, 721. Hits, 196. Time, 1 minute.

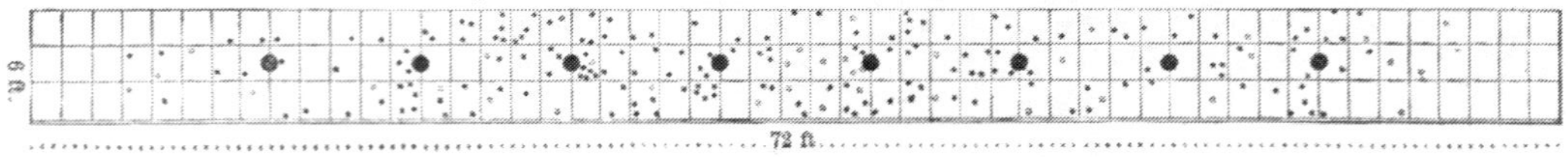

6 ft.

72 ft.

1-2 inch GATLING TARGET.

Distance, 800 paces. Shots, 246. Hits, 216. Time, 1 minute.

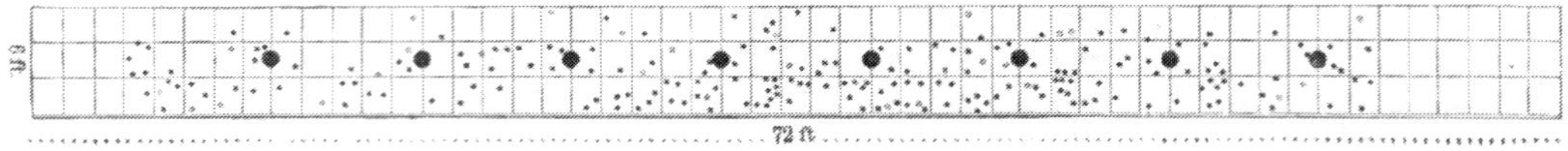

6 ft.

72 ft.

PRACTICE MADE AT VIENNA, July 17th, 1868.—1-2 inch GATLING TARGET.

Distance, 400 paces. Shots, 399. Time, 2 minutes.

9 ft.

54 ft.

Shots which penetrated.

Shots which did not penetrate.

Bulls eyes.

Trial shots.

Results of Target Practice made at Fortress Monroe, U. S. A., between 24-pdr. Howitzer, and a 1-inch Gatling Gun.

24-pdr. HOWITZER.

Distance, 150 yards. Hits, 89. Number of rounds, 4, each charge having 48 Canister Balls. Time, 1 minute, 30 seconds.

6 ft.

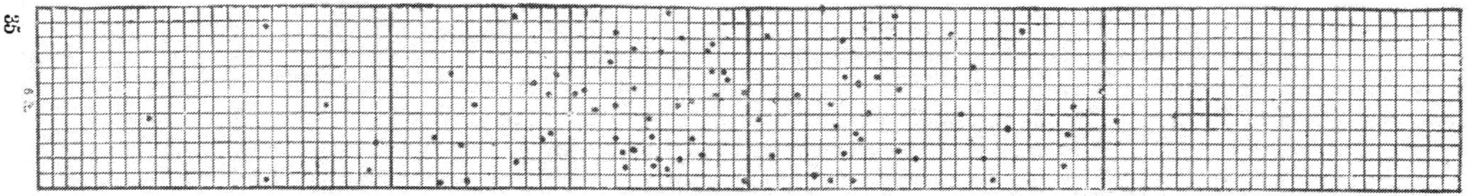

48 ft.

1-inch GATLING TARGET.

Distance, 150 yards. Hits, 691. Number of shots, 101, each cartridge having 16 balls. Time, 1 minute, 30 seconds.

6 ft.

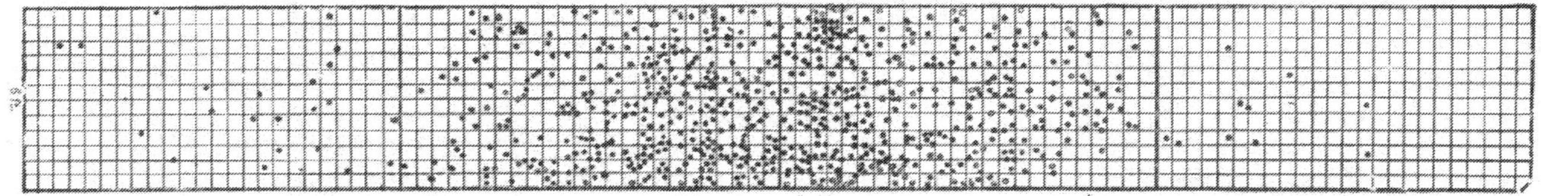

48 ft.

DIRECTIONS FOR USING, LOADING AND FIRING THE GUN.

The gun should be kept clean and oiled to prevent its getting rusty.

In working the gun, the man at the crank should keep cool and turn steadily.

When the gun is at work, the man at the crank should keep his eyes on the hopper to see if the cartridges are feeding properly, and the man that feeds should do the same. In time of action, one man should remain at the hopper to attend to the feed and to remove each feed case as soon as it becomes empty, and a second man should receive the loaded cases from a third man, and set them in the hopper. By this arrangement, the firing can be kept up incessantly.

The feed cases should be filled with cartridges before the firing commences, and as follows: Take an empty case in the left hand, resting its upper end in the elbow-joint or against the upper part of the left arm, holding the mouth of the case *inclining downwards*, with the fingers of the left hand partly over the mouth of the case; then with the right hand feed in the case a cartridge at a time, with the cap ends all one way, until the case is full. If this precaution be not taken in loading the cases, the cartridges are likely to get reversed in the case, and in that event could not be fed to the gun.

The gun should not be unnecessarily snapped.

COMPONENT PARTS OF GATLING'S BATTERY GUN.—1. Main Shaft; 2. Rear Plate, (into which the barrels are screwed); 3. Front Plate, (which supports front ends of barrels); 4. Barrels; 5. Cartridge Carrier; 6. Lock-Cylinder; 7. Rear Guide Nut; 8. Cocking Ring; 9. Cocking Ring Clamps; 10. Screw Cam; 11. Breech Casing; 12. Cascable Plate; 13. Diaphragm; 14. Diaphragm Plug; 15. Gear Wheel; 16. Pinion; 17. Crank Shaft; 18. Crank; 19. Gun-Frame; 20. Trunnions; 21. Hopper; 22. Rear Sight; 23. Front Sight; 24. Lock Butt; 25. Lock Tube, or Plunger; 26. Lock Hammer; 27. Lock Spring; 28. Firing Pin; 29. Extractor; 30. Casing Screws; 31. Rear Cam Screw; 32. Hopper Screws; 33. Rear Sight Screw; 34. Cartridge Shell ejector.

DIRECTIONS FOR TAKING THE GUN APART.

1st. Block up the frame and barrels

2d. Take off the hopper.

3d. Take off the butt plate or cascable. *First raising the rear sight.*

4th. Take the pin out of the pinion and then turn the crank downwards and remove the crank shaft in that position.

5th. Take out the rear sight, and then remove the large gear wheel.

6th. Take out the rear plug in the diaphragm, and then gently revolve the gun until a lock presents itself on a line with a hole in the diaphragm, through which one lock after another may be taken out.

7th. Take out the large screws on the sides of the breech casing and then remove the casing to the rear. (Be careful to have the lock cylinder and gun supported, so as to keep the axis of the main shaft in the plane of the top of the frame, which is necessary to prevent the inner breech, or rear of the gun, from dropping when the casing is removed.)

8th. The large rear nut, on the shaft in the rear of the lock cylinder, and which serves as a guide for the rear ends of the locks, is fastened to its place by a pin and a *left-handed screw.* To remove this nut, the pin must be taken out and the *nut turned to the right.* Then remove the lock cylinder and carrier from the main shaft.

The spiral cam need not be taken out of the casing in order to take the gun apart.

NOTE.—In the *new* models (where the plug is in the cascable plate,) first remove the plug before unscrewing the cascable plate.

DIRECTIONS FOR PUTTING THE GUN TOGETHER.

1st. Put the main shaft to its place, through the plates which hold the barrels, and then put to their proper places, the carrier, lock-cylinder, and rear large nut. The latter should be screwed up tight and have the tapered pin put through the nut and shaft.

2d. Place the gun within the frame, and let the front end of the main shaft rest in the hole designed for it, in the front of the frame. Care should be taken to keep the axis of the main shaft in the plane of the top of the frame. When the gun is in the above position, the cocking ring should be shoved over the lock-cylinder and left to remain for the time, loosely around the carrier.

3d. Let the breech of the gun be slightly raised, when the breech casing can be shoved over the lock-cylinder, &c., to its place. Then

Fig. 6.

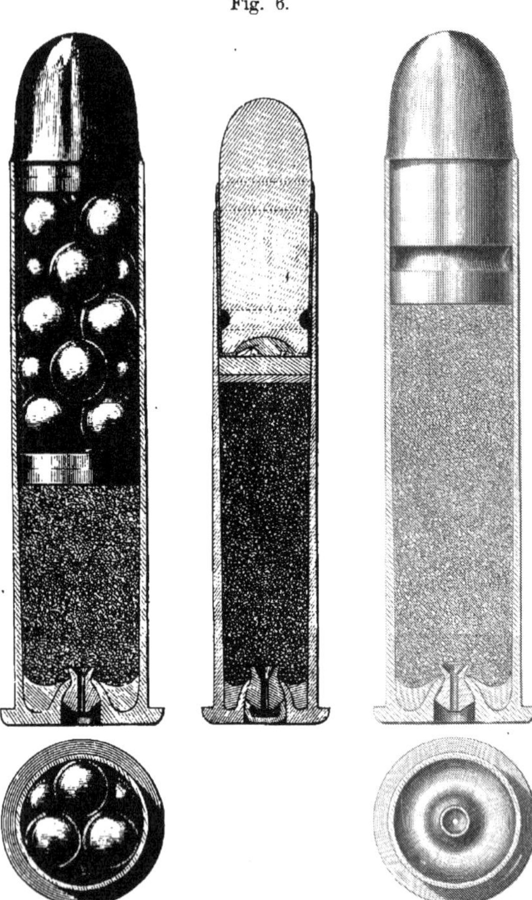

CARTRIDGES USED IN THE GATLING GUN.

screw the casing to the frame—putting the cocking ring, in the meantime, to its proper place. Then revolve the gun, to the right or to the left, so that the places for the locks will come on a line with the hole in the diaphragm, through which one lock at a time can be inserted to its proper position ; afterwards the screw plug should be inserted to close the hole through the diaphragm.

4th. Put on the cog-wheel, replace the crank shaft, pinion, and taper pin. Then put on the rear sight and screw on the butt plate and hopper, when the gun is ready to be mounted.

EXPERIMENTS WITH THE CAMEL GUN.

The *Broad Arrow* gives the following account of some experiments made in England with Dr. Gatling's last modification of his weapon:

At first sight, this smallest species of the Gatling system resembles a model-gun. Even when examined closely and critically, so minute and perfect are the component parts, one might remain under the impression, were it not for the strength and solidity of what may be termed the frictional portions of the gun. The barrels, for instance, at once dispel the delusion that the weapon is only for ornament, showing as they do more weight of metal than is usually seen in small-bore rifles. This is, of course, exceptionally requisite in the Gatling, from the continuous strain caused by a flow of bullets fired at the rate of 300 or 400 rounds a minute. Just at the base or chamber thickness is indispensable to resist the first pitch of the discharged cartridge, but there seems no good reason why the barrels should not taper to the muzzle a little more than they do, and thus lessen the weight without impairing the effectiveness of this gun, which even as it is, weighs only 125 pounds.

Perhaps the best idea of the Gatling can be formed by perusing a description of the operation of taking a camel gun to pieces, as, although simple in action, it is rather difficult of comprehension by a mere reader, however scientifically informed.

Assuming, then, the presence before us of a small Gatling, we will proceed to disconnect its several parts, commenting on the nature of each as it is dismounted :—

1. Remove the drum—this is is a cylinder, fourteen inches high, separated into sixteen divisions, each capable of containing twenty-five cartridges.* Each division is provided with a small brass running weight designed to sit on the column of cartridges when resting dove-tail fashion one on the top of the other, point inclining downwards, so as to facilitate their descent and to indicate the gradual deduction of their number as they disappear into the hopper. The base of the drum is provided with a keying plate which has to be manipulated previous to the "commence fire" so as to let the cartridge drop through into the grooved carrier, and on the periphery are arranged a series of thumb lugs, by which the drum is resolved to bring the loaded divisions successively over the opening in the hopper.

2. Raise the hopper—this is a brass curved plate hinged to the framework of the gun, and provided with an aperture through which the cartridges descend to their places in the grooves of the carrier at the chambers of the barrels, whereupon the cartridges are taken instant possession of by the locks, forced into the barrels and fired. The hopper encases the chambers of the barrels, and although there is no absolute necessity for raising it as a first operation, it must at some time be done, so as to remove the barrels. The drum is pivoted on a brass pin in the gun-metal disc attached to the hopper.

* The height of the present drum is out of all proportion to the length of the gun ; it will therefore be reduced one-third, and the replacement of an empty by a charged drum occupies an inappreciable space of time, the new drum will only contain 200 instead of 400 rounds.

Fig. 7.

3. Take out the rear-plug and unscrew the cascable plate. The rear-plug in the larger guns is fitted with an apparatus for withdrawing the locks, but in the Camel gun it is simply a plug. The cascable when unscrewed lays bare the worm-gear and pinion.

4. Reverse the crank handle and bring a lock coincident with the aperture in the diaphragm or division plate, withdraw the ten locks separately through the boss or guide which is fitted into the division plate.

5. Take off the screw on the left end of transverse shaft and remove the automatic traversing screw; then unscrew the small pin securing the worm-gear on the shaft, and withdraw the latter—the worm-gear will thus fall into the hand.

6. Take out the pin securing the pinion on the rear end of the main shaft and remove the gear-wheel.

7. Unscrew and remove caseside screws (three on each side); at the same time block up the barrels, so as to prevent them falling to the ground, and draw off the case; this lays bare the interior mechanism—*i. e.*, the cam and cocking device.

8. Take out the screw of the division plate and the two other small screws on either side, and remove cam; this lays bare the cocking arrangement, which, when unscrewed, completes the disconnecting process.

In considering the mechanism of any new piece of ordnance, we naturally note suspiciously the multiplicity and strength or otherwise of the component parts, for it is evident that no rapidity and continuity of fire under exceptional circumstances could ever compensate for the slightest deterioration or derangement of a Gatling in a practice. But again we must not be too exacting in our desire for simplicity; economy of detail will often be dearly purchased when the presence of an extra screw would make security doubly sure, and, at all events, the lock mechanism of a ten-barrelled Gatling is less complex in the long run than the multiplied component parts of the several rifle-locks which represent an analogous "fire action," by which we mean to imply the generally admitted axiom that a Gatling gun, properly manipulated, is equal to the *accurately* sustained fire of twenty or thirty rifles—*ex. gr.*, the camel gun fires at the rate of 400 rounds per minute. Thirty riflemen fire at the rate of twelve rounds per minute—or 360 rounds per minute *en masse.*

The idea has even been suggested that the mechanism of the Gatling might be advantageously increased; indeed, we believe, a device has been invented and experimentally put in practice with this object, so that by the addition of a second worm-gear and pinion in connection with the transverse shaft, the feeding drum is made to revolve automatically, and thus enables the firer to devote all his energies to the object aimed at, and to the rapidity and continuity of firing. But we venture to think that such a step, if permanently taken, will overshoot the mark and cause unnecessary, if not careful, complication.

Rapidity of fire is all very well in itself, and there are circumstances under which it would be inestimable; but to increase the means of hasty firing for such exceptional cases would, we fear, be opening the door to sheer waste of ammunition. Indeed, it has been well remarked that more money has been lavished upon extreme length of range and rapidity of fire than can ever be justified by the event. To send an elongated shot six or seven miles at all close to a vessel at sea, or to "get off," anyhow, twenty-five or thirty rounds a minute from a breech-loading rifle, is by some considered the acme of perfection in a military weapon. Undoubtedly to have the *power* residing in the gun, by the addition of an automatic revolving apparatus, of a slightly increased rapidity than can be obtained manually, arising from the accuracy of a machine in bringing each division of the drum over the hopper (whereas a gunner, through flurry or carelessness, is liable to error) may be very captivating in theory, but, nevertheless, we contend that the substitute would be bad in practice. When thirty rounds a minute can be multiplied by ten times that number, *combined with a due degree of accuracy in aim*, then, and not till then, is great rapidity of fire justifiable, and in the Gatling camel-gun we have all the conditions for each of these cardinal virtues without having recourse to and apparently needless and deceptive innovation. There is, moreover, no actual necessity for the firer to attend to the drum at all. A second man should manipulate it when full and remove it when empty, thus permitting the firer to remain seated on the trail, calmly and judiciously revolving the crank and traversing or elevating the gun, according to circumstances.

On the other hand, a few small Gatlings on board ship might, we grant, be advantageously provided with this automatic apparatus, but to be used only *as an adjunct*, in situations where a second man cannot conveniently work the drum, as when the gun is lashed in the tops of ships for sweeping decks, etc.

With these rather lengthy preliminary observations, we will proceed to give the result of the experiments on the 22d ult., at the Woolwich proof-range, in presence of the Ordnance Select Committee. It was evident that the chief object in view was to note the working of the gun when fired from the tripod; so after one or two divisions of the drum had been fired at 500 yards from the gun-carriage the gun was moved up closer to the target, and when mounted on a tripod the experimental firing took place. Distance 300 yards.

1st Practice. One division of the drum, *i. e.*, twenty-five cartridges, fired in two and a half seconds.

The hits were fairly grouped on the target, but not nearly so well as in a preliminary practice from the gun-carriage at the same range on the day previous, when every shot "told" within half a yard of the bull's eye. However, it should always be borne in mind that it is possible to be too accurate with guns of this description, and that, in fact, the more the shots would scatter at close quarters, as on board ship, the better the effect. Even in the field a spreading fire would produce good results, for it would be so much the worse for the enemy, who would not know which way to fly.

2d Practice. Two divisions of the drum, *i. e.*, fifty cartridges, fired in five seconds.

The wind was very strong about this time, and the legs of the tripod seemed to "give" in the wet and marshy soil, consequently a few of the shots missed the target. But this wild firing was also owing to the inferiority of the ammunition, which had lain in store for two years after use on a former occasion. For, be it remembered, the cases of the cartridges are manufactured out of solid metal so as to allow of their being recharged several times. The cartridges used were of the Russian rifle or bottle-nose pattern; but the cartridge of such guns should be the best procurable, for economy in this point is simply fatal to the success of the piece as a multiple gun.

3rd Practice. Two divisions, fifty rounds, fired in five and a half seconds.

The tripod was on this occasion placed upon a platform, and the recoil of the gun, slight as it was, caused it to slip about, producing still wilder results than the previous discharge. Some modification of the tripod, as regards its legs and feet, will therefore be needful.

But we venture to suggest that the tripod should be regarded as a secondary consideration, an adjunct to be made use of or not in the field, according to circumstances, as when a small detachment in the open is surrounded by numbers, and for this purpose the tripod should be lashed to the trail of the gun-carriage.

But the gun-carriage is itself capable of infinite improvement. It ought to be light in weight and narrow in beam, something similar in dimensions to the seven-pounder gun carriage used in the Abyssinian campaign, so as to run into gateways, breaches in walls, etc., and to be carried by manual labor when requisite.

The tripod, *per se*, would, however, be still applicable for use on board ships and in boat operations, as well as also in the defence of buildings, causeways, bridges, and the like, and in mountain warfare to be mounted on the back of an animal. In fact, it was for these objects, and particularly the last named, that the gun was invented by Dr. Gatling at the suggestion of Colonel Maxwell, R. A.

Since the publication of our first edition, wonderful improvements have been made in the construction of Gatlings, and marvelous results achieved in their performances. The guns now fire over one thousand shots a minute. The weight has been so reduced, that now the lightest gun weighs but little over ninety pounds. Everything has been simplified, and we have as near perfection in the result as it seems possible to come.

We present some new illustrations of the guns, but cannot show all—six different models of the musket calibre gun alone being made, and three new models of the larger calibres.

The guns are still manufactured by the Gatling Gun Company, at Colt's Armory, Hartford, Connecticut.

The Gatling gun received the only award for machine guns at the Centennial Exhibition.

INTERNATIONAL EXHIBITION, [No. 235.]
PHILADELPHIA, 1876.

The United States Centennial Commission has examined the report of the judges, and accepted the following reasons, and decreed an award in conformity therewith.

PHILADELPHIA, January 8, 1877.

Report on Awards.

Product, The Gatling Gun. Name and address of exhibitor, Richard J. Gatling, Hartford, Conn.

The undersigned, having examined the product herein described, respectfully recommends the same to the United States Centennial Commission for award, for the following reasons, viz.:

Eminently entitled to recognition, not only as one of the best machine-guns in existence, but also as the first really serviceable weapon of its class A new five-barrel gun is exhibited, showing improvements over the usual pattern in respect to simplicity; the automatic spreading of the shot; the feeding arrangement; an adjustment for adapting the gun to receive metallic cartridges having rims of varying thickness; diminished weight; increased facility in extracting the locks, and generally, in separating the gun for cleaning, etc.

HENRY L. ABBOTT, *Brevet Brig.-Gen. U S. A.*
Signature of the Judge.

Approval of Group Judges.
W. H. NOBLE, ALPHONSE LESNE,
S. C LYFORD, L. F. DESALDANHA.

A true copy of the record.

FRANCIS A. WALKER, *Chief of the Bureau of Awards.*

Given by authority of the United States Centennial Commision.

J. R. HAWLEY, *President.*

A T. GOSHORN, *Director-General.*
J. L. CAMPBELL, *Secretary.*

NAVY CARRIAGE FOR GATLING GUN.

In the first volume of the "British Reports on the Philadelphia International Exhibition of 1876" containing reports made by the English judges of what they deemed especially worthy of notice,

Major W. H. Noble, Royal Artillery, speaking at length of the Gatling gun, says: "This celebrated weapon is so well known that it does not need a description, but several important improvements have recently been made in its construction. The latest model is a five-barreled gun in which the improvements are as follows: The crank handle is attached to the rear instead of the side, thereby increasing the speed of revolution of the gun and the rapidity of its fire; the drum is abolished, and a new pattern feed-case substituted for it; it stands vertically, and thus insures a direct fall into the receivers; all the working parts, as well as the barrels, are encased in bronze to afford protection from rust and dirt; the arrangement of the locks has been much simplified, and the size of the whole breech arrangement reduced by about one-half; the rapidity of fire has been more than doubled; the traversing arrangement has been improved. This gun has been fired at the rate of one thousand rounds a minute, but the ordinary rate of rapid firing is about seven hundred rounds per minute. Fired deliberately at a target 19 feet long by 11 feet high, range 1,000 yards, it scored 665 hits out of 1,000 shots."

Gatling guns are also made with ten barrels, having the improvements mentioned by Major Noble. Particular attention is called to these new model guns, which have *center feed*, cuts of which are shown in this book.

These improved guns are easily operated and have more than double the effectiveness of the older style of Gatlings.

The following extracts are taken from the various official reports of trials of both old and new model guns.

TRIAL AT FORT MADISON, MARYLAND.

A very interesting trial of the 0.50-inch-calibre Gatling gun (old model) was made at Fort Madison, Annapolis, in October, 1878, under the supervision of Commodore Jeffers, chief of the Ordnance Bureau, United States Navy, during which 100,000 cartridges were fired, (64,000 without stopping) to test the quality of the cartridges and the durability of the gun. The official report says:

MUSKET CALIBRE, FIVE BARREL GATLING GUN.

"The working of the gun throughout this severe trial was eminently satisfactory, no derangements of any importance whatever occurring."

A TRIAL TOOK PLACE AT FORT MONROE, VA., IN 1873.

before a mixed Board of Officers (the Engineers, Artillery and Ordnance being represented) General Q. A. Gillmore being President of the Board.

After a discussion and comparison of results of the firing by the Gatling gun and its competitors, and particularly as to its use as applied to Forts, the report of Gen. Gillmore's Board says:

If, in addition, this hypothetical gun shall have proved itself capable not only of *delivering* but of *maintaining* uninterruptedly for hours a most destructive fire at all distances, indifferently, from fifty yards up to and beyond a mile, a power conspicuously absent in our present service ordnance, its introduction into the armament of our fortifications, as an auxiliary, would seem to be an obvious necessity. *The Gatling gun is such an arm, and is, beyond question, well adapted to the purposes of flank-defense at both long and short ranges.*

Views and Recommendations of the Board.

Among the advantages possessed by the Gatling gun may be enumerated the lightness of its parts, the simplicity and strength of its mechanism, the rapidity and continuity of its fire without sensible recoil, its effectiveness against troops at all ranges for which a flanking gun is required, its general accuracy at all ranges attainable by rifles, its comparative independence of the excitement of battle, the interchangeableness of its ammunition with the same calibre of small arms, and its great endurance.

For the defense of detached field fortifications placed in defensive relations to each other, and intrenched positions with long lines of defense, the Gatling gun would be superior to any other species of artillery against troops exposed to view, and therefore a most valuable auxiliary to shell-guns.

One advantage possessed by the Gatling gun is its lightness, and hence the ease with which it can be withdrawn from position, when exposed to breaching-batteries or any overpowering or disabling fire, and replaced in battery to meet the critical moment of an assault.

The Board recommend the adoption of the Gatling gun as an auxiliary arm for flanking purposes.

The board have necessarily limited the scope of their recommendations to the restricted field of inquiry contemplated in the order, and have therefore not touched upon the most prominent advantages claimed and generally conceded for the Gatling gun. Among these may be enumerated its peculiar power for the defense of intrenched positions and villages; for protecting roads, defiles, and bridges; for covering the embarkation or debarkation of troops, or the crossing of streams; for silencing field-batteries or batteries of position; for increasing the infantry fire at the critical moment of a battle; for supporting field-batteries and protecting them against cavalry or infantry charges; for covering the retreat of a repulsed column; and generally the accuracy, continuity, and intensity of its fire, and its economy in men for serving and animals for transporting it.

ORDNANCE OFFICE, January 21, 1874.

The foregoing report is respectfully submitted to the Secretary of War with the following recommendations:

1. The adoption of the Gatling gun, calibre 0 45, using the service-cartridge, as an auxiliary arm for flank defense of fortifications.

2. The adoption of a special canister for 8-inch flank-defense howitzer, to contain lead balls.

3. The designing and manufacturing of two casemate-carriages for the Gatling gun, as suggested by the Board.

4. The adoption of the Gatling gun, calibre 0.45, as an auxiliary arm for all branches of the service.

5. The appointment of a Board of Engineers and Ordnance Officers to determine on the proportionate number of such guns in fortifications for flank defense, and the whole number required on July 1, 1874.

6. The relations it shall occupy to the different arms of service, and the number to be held in reserve for that purpose, should be settled by competent authority.

By order of the Chief of Ordnance,

S. V. BENET, *Major of Ordnance.*

This most careful and exhaustive investigation and trial of the Gatling gun resulted in its adoption as an auxiliary arm by the United States War Department, not only for the flank defense of fortifications, but for all branches of the service. The United States Navy also adopted it for shore service, and for use on ships and small boats.

TRIALS AT SANDY HOOK, N. J., IN 1876.

Extract from Report of the Board.

Two guns were submitted by the company for tests, one being a short five-barreled gun, designed for cavalry service, the other a long ten-barreled gun for flank defense.

The improvements in the gun intended for service with cavalry, consist in a change of the position and attachment of the crank from the side to the rear, greatly facilitating and increasing the speed of revolution of the gun and rapidity of its fire; the feed-cases are entered more readily to the receiver, and stand vertically, thus insuring a direct fall and feed of the metallic cases; the exterior form of the receivers admits of reversing the motion of the crank without danger of jamming the cases. All the working parts as well as the barrels are encased in bronze, affording better protection from dust and dirt to the gun. It is lighter and of less expensive construction, and more compact in appearance. An automatic device attached to the breech of this gun gives a traversing motion through a small angle, which can be set to suit range and circumstances of fire, and is worked by the crank operating the gun. The increased rapidity of fire is seen, from the examination of the record, to be more than double that of the old model ten-barreled gun, and its accuracy is by no means impaired.

The board is of opinion that the application of the crank to the rear, vertical feed, automatic transversing motion, lightness, cheapness, etc., are all important improvements.

All the changes and improvements in the Gatling gun for cavalry service are equally applicable to the long-barreled gun for flank defense.

TRIAL AT SANDY HOOK, N. J., IN 1879.

Extract from Report of the Board.

"The Board find the changes in the elevating and traversing fixtures of the Gatling gun since its last report in April, 1879, are such as simplify and economize the construction and add facility to its manœuvres, and are therefore to be preferred to the fixtures then applied. The various firings made with the gun, as will be seen from the records of firing, show that the gun is handled with great ease and facility, and the fact that one man can work the gun alone, firing 500 rounds in 1 1-6 minute, and making an excellent target, undoubtedly indicates that the improvements have very much simplified and perfected all the operations with this gun to a degree not heretofore attained." Total number of rounds fired 5,000. Mechanism of gun worked well during entire firing.

Record of Firing.—Number of rounds fired, 500. Time of firing, 28¼ seconds.

Great Britain, after an exhaustive examination of the Gatling gun, has adopted it for land and naval service.

Russia, Turkey, Egypt, China, and many other of the leading governments of the world, have also adopted it.

On account of the lightness and the convenience of having the same ammunition for the Gatling gun and the musket, the greater number of guns sold hitherto have been of the musket calibre. The United States, England, China, Egypt, and other nations have, however, also adopted guns of the larger calibres, and the results of the trials demonstrate that these guns may and ought to take the place to some extent of Field Artillery.

MUSKET CALIBRE GATLING GUN,
With New Pointing Fixture.

In a lecture delivered by Lieut.-Col. H. C. Fletcher, Scots Fusileer Guards, a member of the committee of which Col. Wray was president, before the United Service Institution, he says: "From a comparison of a series of eleven trials of the small-sized Gatling, of the 9-pounder muzzle-loading field-gun, firing shrapnel, and of the Martini-Henry rifle, fired by six guardsmen, at ranges from 300 to 1,200 yards, and under various conditions in regard to time and known and unknown distances, I find that the Gatling made 2,699 hits, the 9-pounder muzzle-loader

MUSKET CALIBRE, TEN BARREL GATLING GUN.

MUSKET CALIBRE, TEN BARREL GATLING GUN.
With Carriage and Limber complete.

1,620 hits, and the Martini-Henry 718 hits; that is, the Gatling was about 3⅔ times and the 9-pounder 2¼ times more effective than the Martini-Henry in the hands of six soldiers, a result I would venture to term satisfactory as regards infantry fire. Not that I mean to affirm that this comparison is a true measure of the efficiency of the 9-pounder and Gatling as compared with infantry. To say that the fire from a field-gun was only equal to that of fourteen infantry, and that that of a Gatling was not more deadly than the fire of twenty-two infantry, and to measure their efficiency in the field by this standard, would lead to very erroneous conclusions. Each arm, I contend, has its own duty to perform, and there are moments in battle when no field-gun or Gatling would counterbalance the absence of even a section of infantry, as there are times when a single shell from a 9-pounder, or a volley from a Gatling, would be worth more than the presence of a battalion."

The following extracts from reports on the performance of the Gatling gun in the field are given to show what has been done with the gun in actual warfare.

ASHANTEE WAR.

(*London Times, October* 6, 1873.)

The Gatling guns which accompany the expedition are those known as the 0.45 inch. They will be mounted on carriages somewhat similar to the guns, and, we presume, are mainly intended for the defense of stockaded positions. If by any lucky chance Sir Garnet Wolseley manages to catch a good mob of savages in the open, and at a moderate distance, he cannot do better than treat them to a little Gatling music. The gun is fitted with an arrangement by which a traversing motion may be given to the barrels while the firing continues. It is obvious that it would be absurd constantly to fire a Gatling gun in one direction. A few men immediately in front would be perforated, while those on the flanks would escape. But the traversing arrangement enables us to "waterpot" the enemy with a leaden rain. Altogether, we cannot wish the Ashantees worse luck than to get in the way of a Gatling well served.

(*Army and Navy Journal, March* 7, 1874.)

We are not surprised that the Ashantees were awe-struck before the power of the Gatling gun. It is easy to understand that it is a weapon which is specially adapted to terrify a barbarous or semi-civilized foe. The Ashantee correspondent of the *New York Herald* says that the reputation of the Gatling is now spread throughout Ashantee. "It is a terrible gun which shoots all day. Nothing could stand before it; the water of the Prah ran back affrighted." "The effect of this," remarks the writer, "combined with many other things, has been to induce the King and his Council to deliberate and reflect on the possibility of peace."

THE GATLING GUN IN KHIVA.

Extract from an article by Capt. A. Litvinoff, entitled, "Action of Battery Guns in Khivean Expedition," in the Russian Artillery Journal, January, 1874. The guns were of Gatling model.

Particular attention is called to the fact that Capt. Litvinoff reports that his expenditure of cartridges with two Gatling guns was 408 on the first day, and the reader will find that the effect produced was enormous. It is probable from Capt. L.'s description that a battalion of infantry could not have effected more than did his two field Gatling guns.

* * * "We left Zmukshir on the 13-25th of June, and after a march of twelve verstes, stopped near the village of Chandir, close to the gardens which stretch without interruption from Chandir to Illialee. About 3 P. M. parties of horsemen commenced to make their appearance from different sides; they approached us nearer and nearer, and behind them we could descry larger masses. They commenced to engage our picket line with great determination and daring. One of these pickets, composed of one officer (Ensign Kamentzky) and five Cossacks, swords in hand, threw themselves forward against an approaching mass of Toorkomans, and were completely cut to pieces. Two companies of the third battalion of sharpshooters, two of the eighth battalion of the line, and two battery guns (Gatlings), were ordered forward to drive away these bands of Toorkomans. The road we had to follow was very difficult, even for infantry and cavalry, as at every step we had to cross wide ditches dug for irrigation, which had abrupt sides; for artillery the road would have been impassable. Our light battery guns went on this road with perfect ease, the ammunition pack-horses alone giving us some trouble. When we stopped, a line of sharpshooters and battery guns was formed along one of these ditches.

"First I had to find out the range; for this purpose I fired three cartridges, changing each time the height of the sight. The distance found was between the limits of 1,050 and 1,170 yards. Then I laid down both guns, aiming one at a large band of Toorkomans, and the other at another band formed not far from the first. Opening at the first band, I fired rapidly twenty-five rounds; the band immediately dispersed, part of the men joining the second band. Opening from the second gun I fired fifty rounds without interruption; the second band dispersed at once, the men betook themselves to the broken ground, and disappeared behind some hills and in the irrigation ditches. Several times the enemy, collecting in masses of some strength, moved against us, but was each time driven back by our fire; thus I had several opportunities of firing a succession of twenty-five or fifty rounds, the directions of guns and their elevations varying somewhat, according to the circumstances. In the whole, the battery guns fired that day 408 cartridges. The guns were permitted a very slight side motion. The ground was of clay, covered with scant vegetation, and the fall of the bullets on such ground and their ricochets were easily seen from the battery, even at a distance of 1,170 yards.

* * * "June 15-27th a general order was given to move forward early next morning, leaving all trains and baggage behind. As to this train and baggage, they received the order to remain on the same spot (Illialee), and at the break of the next day to form a wagenburg (a large square made of wagons), under the guard of two companies of the fourth battalion of sharpshooters, two battery guns, and a few men of each command sent back to take care of their respective baggage wagons.

"At nightfall it was ascertained that in the vicinity of our camp the enemy had congregated in large numbers. Soon after midnight there was an alarm, when all the troops took up arms, but it proved to be without consequence. Apprehending a night attack, and considering that the wagons were much scattered about, it was ordered to collect all the wagons at once, without waiting for the breaking of day. These being collected, the formation of the wagenburg began.

The left side and part of the front side of the square were well lined with wagons put close to one another. A company of sharpshooters of the fourth battalion occupied that line, the men either getting on top of the wagons or sitting under them on the ground. The enemy being expected chiefly from the right, I put my two guns in the corner formed by the front and right sides of the square. The right side and rear having as yet no wagons in line, and being somewhat protected by shallow ditches, were guarded, first by miscellaneous men of different commands taking charge of their wagons, officers' servants, sutlers, etc., all armed with pistols, revolvers, sporting-guns, etc., second by a platoon of sharp-shooters lying on the ground. At 3 o'clock the attack of Toorkomans commenced.

[Here follows the description of the fight of the other troops.]

"At the first howls of the attacking enemy I hastened to form a cover for my guns. I put on the right wing ten privates of Soonja and Daguestan, who were with the train guarding their wagons; on the left, fifteen sharp-shooters and twelve men of my battery guns command, with whom I could dispense for the present; these men were also armed with rifles. Leaving thus with the battery guns only the most indispensable men to assist in firing, I took myself the crank-handle of the first gun, invited Capt. Cachourin (Cossack) to take the handle of the other gun, and enjoined on all my group not to commence the fire before the word of command was given.

"The guns formed an obtuse angle one with another, as it was necessary to direct them to the precise spot where the shoutings of the enemy were heard, and whence they were approaching us. We had not long to wait. The cries of the Toorkomans who had succeeded in breaking through the lines of our detachment and turning their flanks, suddenly rose from all sides and became deafening. Though it was dark, we perceived in front of us the galloping masses of the enemy with uplifted glittering swords. When they approached us to within about twenty paces, I shouted the command 'Fire.' This was followed by a salvo of all the men forming the cover, and a continuous simultaneous rattle of the two battery guns. In this roar, the cries of the enemy at once became weak, and then ceased altogether, vanishing as rapidly as they rose. The firing at once stopped, and as no enemy was visible before us, I ventured to get a look at the surrounding grounds, availing myself of the first lights of dawn. About 200 paces to the right of our square stood the eighth battalion of the line. Between it and us no enemy was to be seen, but at every step lay prostrated the dead bodies of the Yonoods, their hats being pushed up to their eyes. I saw no wounded—they were probably all carried away according to the usual Toorkoman warfare."

In the naval engagement that took place in Peruvian waters on May 28, 1877, between the Peruvian rebel iron-clad ram *Huascar*, and the British men-of-war the *Shah* and *Amethyst*, a small Gatling gun, stationed in the foretop of the *Shah*, rendered excellent service.

The correspondent of the *Illustrated London News*, in a semi-official report of the conflict, says:

"About five o'clock, the *Huascar* being clear of the shoals, we seized the opportunity to close. The enemy likewise closed, with evident signs of ramming, firing shell from her 40-pounder. Our Gatling gun then commenced firing from the foretop, causing the men on her upper deck quarters to desert their guns."

Captain Aurelio Garcia y Garcia, one of the most distinguished officers of the Peruvian Navy, in his account of the above engagement, says:

"The firing became even more severe from the English frigates, and as the distance between the antagonists had been reduced to two cable-lengths, more or less, the admiral brought to bear all his attacking forces, which on board the *Shah* were very formidable in character. From the tops a Gatling gun threw a hail of bullets at the decks of the *Huascar*, together with steady volleys of musketry and rifles."

Another account from Peruvian sources says:

"A small Gatling gun stationed in her tops very seriously incommoded the combatants on the ram, and her smoke-stack is riddled with bullets."

It is evident that Gatling guns, when used on shipboard or in tops of war-vessels, would be of inestimable service in firing into the port-holes, or in clearing the decks of the ships of the enemy. Moreover, large Gatling guns can be used on shipboard to great advantage for repelling torpedo-boats; solid shot or shell fired with rapidity from the inch-calibre Gatling would be able to penetrate and sink Thorneycroft torpedo-launches—thus saving the ship attacked from destruction.

The Russians used Gatling guns in the siege of Plevna. A special correspondent of the *London Times*, writing under date of November 26, 1877, from the head-quarters of the army of Bulgaria, at Bogot, says:

"The mitrailleurs [Gatling guns] were in constant action until midnight, splitting the air with their harsh, rattling reports." Another account (Nov. 26th) says: "The Russians are using their mitrailleurs [Gatlings] a great deal now at night, probably with the intention of keeping the Turks occupied, so as to relax the tension on the infantry in the trenches."

No arms in the world are equal to Gatling guns for night service. They can be placed in a position in the daytime so as to cover any point desired, and as they have no recoil to destroy the accuracy of their aim, an incessant fire can be kept up during the night with the same precision as in daylight.

INDIAN WAR IN IDAHO.

(*New York Times, July* 17, 1877.)

The stubborn fight which Chief JOSEPH made last week, near the mouth of the Cottonwood, against a superior force of our troops, has roused the country to an appreciation of the fact that we have a war within our domains quite worthy of public attention. This affair derives additional interest from the successful employment of Gatling guns and howitzers, to which, in fact, the dislodgement of JOSEPH was largely due.

THE ZULU WAR.

(*London Army and Navy Gazette, February* 22, 1879.)

The Gatling guns landed with the naval contingent from the Active and Tenedos have astonished the Zulus, who have been trying an engagement with our blue jackets. They found the fire much too hot, and the naval force has had the satisfaction of carrying more than one contested position. It is a pity that Gatlings are not more plentiful with Lord Chelmsford's army. The naval brigade have got some, but the artillery have none. If there had been a couple of Gatlings with the force annihilated the other day, the result of the fight might have been different, for Gatlings are the best of all engines of war to deal with the rush of a dense crowd.

THE NAVAL FIGHT OFF IQUIQUE, PERU.

(*New York Times, July* 20, 1879.)

The Huascar attacked us again, directing her bow to the middle of our ship. I steered to prevent the shock, but our want of speed made it impossible and the iron-clad struck our vessel midships. In that moment Lieut. Serrano, followed by a dozen sailors, jumped on the deck of the Huascar and they were all killed by the shots of musketry and Gatling guns fired from the turret and behind the parapets of the stern.

THE CHILENO-PERUVIAN WAR.

(*New York Herald, December* 17, 1879.)

A letter from Lima, describing the defeat of the Peruvian army at San Francisco heights, says: "The earthworks were defended by a strong Chilian force, plentifully supplied with Krupp field pieces and Gatling guns. Here Buendia committed the error which has cost the allies the best division in their army. Instead of making a detour, which he could easily have done, and thus compelling the enemy to descend to attack him in the pampa at the rear of the hill, or submit to having his communications with Pisagua cut off, Buendia gave the order to charge up the rugged hill and carry the works by storm. The attempt was gallantly made. Three times the shattered regiments, which had undertaken a feat which it was impossible to perform, were compelled to fall back and re-form, leaving the hillside thickly covered with their dead and dying, who had fallen in masses before the Krupps and Gatlings long ere they could make their rifles tell.

The Royal Artillery Institution Gold Medal Prize Essay for 1879, by Lieutenant F. M. Goold-Adams, R. A., advocates at length the place of Gatlings in an army; and urges incorporating them with artillery in such proportions as may be determined.

This essay has been published in the United States, as Ordnance Note No. 119, and its cogent reasons for the use of Gatlings will well repay perusal.

By the above extracts—official and otherwise—the *actual work* of the Gatling gun in action is shown. The success of the gun is brilliant, and it is inevitable in future warfare that its power must be greatly felt. Within the last two years it has been perfected and the work it has already done proves it to be a necessary part of a nation's armament.

Truly the world moves! for a hundred men armed with Gatlings could easily prove more than a match for the mighty host of Xerxes.

Unquestionably the most interesting problem in the next great war will be the changes rendered necessary by the use of Gatlings.

CHAPTER XI.

CARTRIDGES—CARTRIDGE METAL—GUNPOWDER—SWORDS.

The success of breech-loading small arms is due in a great measure to the cartridge, in the improvement of which there has been the same advance as in the arms themselves. No matter how inferior may be a breech arrangement, a perfect cartridge can be used with safety and efficiency. A cartridge containing the means of its own ignition is, by no means, a recent discovery, for such a one was patented as early as 1827, and in 1836 a Parisian gun-maker introduced the metallic cartridge, which with modifications is in general use at present for smooth-bore sporting arms.

The needle gun cartridge to which reference is made more particularly hereafter, has been in use in the Prussian service many years, and though not metallic, it contains its own ignition. But the metallic cartridge for weapons of war was first largely adopted in our own armies during the rebellion, and was, as already hinted, the parent of many beautiful inventions in breech-loading small arms, both in our own and other countries. Prior to the introduction of the metallic cartridge it was estimated that there was a loss of forty per cent. from wet or breakage, the preventive of the escape of flame through the joint of the breech was almost impossible, and the most elaborate arrangements of the breech mechanism were of but little avail. By the use of the metallic cartridge this difficulty is entirely overcome, the cartridge being itself a perfect gas-check renewed at every firing and preventing fouling and wear of the mechanism, exercises the most vital functions in the life of the arm.

The advantages of the metallic cartridge are many, its completeness and simplicity, being either self-primed or capped with great facility, and used as a whole in loading; its strength and safety, withstanding the roughest usage and thoroughly protecting the powder and fulminate; its accuracy, because of the coincidence of the axes of the bore and bullet, and, added to these, the impossibility of using more than one cartridge at a time. The American cartridge consists of four parts, namely, the shell, the fulminate, the charge of gunpowder and the bullet. The shell is formed from one piece of copper, brass or iron, is without joining or welding of any kind, being drawn out from the sheet metal by machinery, and is gradually taken from the thickness of sheet at the head to the requisite thinness at the bullet end, thus arriving at a complete prevention of escape of gas by sudden expansion of this end. In the rim-fire cartridge the means of ignition is in the shell, round the rim at the base, and when loaded with the charge of gunpowder, this shell is made to grip the projectile so as to unite it with the gunpowder and fulminate in one compact body. The projectile is solid and composed altogether of lead. In addition to the small number of its component parts this cartridge has much to recommend it. It is impervious to moisture, and may even be used after immersion in water. It is gas-tight, for the shell expanding with the combustion of the charge, combined with the resistance offered by the initial movement of the bullet, completely seals the breech, and thus effectually prevents the escape of the gas breechwards. It has, however, the disadvantage that the copper shell can not be reformed and reloaded after the contents have been discharged. So much for the rim-fire.

CENTRE-FIRE CARTRIDGE.

This cartridge is rapidly taking the place of the former, and its superiority over the rim-fire is so marked as will undoubtedly lead to its adoption universally. By concentrating the percussion composition in the centre of the head the quantity used is reduced to a minimum, to less than one-fourth of what is required to prime the entire circumference in the rim-fire, and this smaller quantity is so much better protected as not to be at all liable to accidental explosions. The central portion of the head is better able to resist the strain upon it from the sudden action of the fulminate, besides having the additional advantage of permitting the reinforcing of the rim, thus strengthening the weakest portion of the cartridge case. The case is the copper tube which forms the receptacle for the powder charge, the percussion composition and the leaden bullet. Its exterior conformation is designed to facilitate its ready extraction from the chamber of the gun after firing. Besides the rim at the end, which is intended primarily to assist extraction, the case is tapered from the rear to a point where it seizes the bullet, whence it merges into a right cylinder. The centre fire cartridge was adopted only after the most thorough and exhaustive experiments, and the non-explosive character of the same was tested at the U. S. Frankford Arsenal, under direction of the Ordnance Bureau, as follows:—

On the 21st April, 1868, the following experiment was made to determine whether the explosion of one or more metallic cartridges in a box of ammunition will communicate fire to the remainder:—

A wooden box, packed ready for issue, containing six hundred and eighty metallic cartridges, calibre .50, in paper packages, with the latter in two horizontal layers, was fired into from the 1-inch Gatling gun, carrying a ball weighing seven and a half ounces. Three shots perforated the box and upper layer of paper packages, destroying the upper half of the wooden box, breaking up ten paper packages containing two hundred cartridges, exploding some, bruising and crushing others, and scattering many to a considerable distance. The damage done was as follows:—

Twenty-nine cartridges exploded.

Ninety-seven badly bruised and crushed out of shape; some with bullets knocked out and the powder exposed, but none exploded.

Thirty-eight loose, uninjured

Four hundred and eighty, in paper packages, were uninjured; these included the entire bottom layer.

Thirty-six missing.

The cartridges that exploded were undoubtedly of the number actually struck by the passing ball, but it is a curious fact that so large a proportion should have been subjected to such rough usage with impunity. Although the flame from each of the three explosions was distinctly seen at the distance of two hundred yards, even the paper of the packages was not ignited.

This trial seemed to prove that the explosion of a caisson or an ammunition wagon, if not an impossibility, is at least robbed of its greatest terrors, by being confined to only a small number of the few cartridges that may be struck by the enemy's shot.

The Ordnance Bureau of the U. S. War Department has devoted much attention to the question of cartridges, and the experiments made at the Frankford Arsenal have been carried through with the greatest care and precision. In addition to the large number of metallic cartridges manufactured by the War Department, private enterprise has also entered the field, and at the present time there are several cartridge factories all fully employed, and admitted to produce better ammunition than those of any other nation. The one which stands the most prominent, however, is the Union Metallic Cartridge Company of Bridgeport, Conn. This establishment comprises several large buildings fitted up with the latest and most expensive machinery, and is in a position to turn out 400,000 cartridges per day. Its price list comprises over thirty distinct and

38

separate patterns applicable to breech-loaders of all descriptions, revolvers, repeaters, pistols, carbines, and the Gatling gun. During the past two years special attention has been paid to the production of the Berdan Central Fire Cartridge, the ammunition adopted for the Russian army, and of which a description is here given extracted from the patent.

Fig. 1.

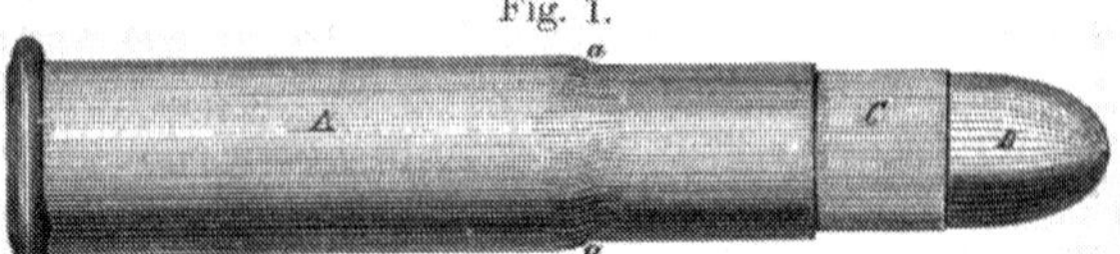

"Figure 1 is a side view on an enlarged scale of my improved cartridge, and Fig. 2 a longitudinal section of the same.

The object of my invention is to produce a superior cartridge for military arms, one which shall fulfill all the required conditions to a greater degree than any heretofore produced. In cartridges of this kind the following conditions are to be complied with: First, the ball must have great range, with a flat trajectory, and to obtain this it must have a large propelling charge. To withstand the explosive effect of this heavy charge the head of the shell must be made unusually strong. Second, in order to reduce the resistance of the atmosphere to the passage through it of the bullet it is necessary to reduce the diameter of the latter; and in order to retain its momentum it is necessary that the weight of the bullet shall not be lessened. To do this I make the bullet of less diameter, but of greater length, it being preferably two and a half or three diameters long. Third, as this elongated bullet will have a long bearing on the walls of the barrel it is necessary that it shall be patched in such a manner as to prevent leading, and at the same time pass through the barrel with the minimum of friction consistent with the insuring of its rotation; and, fourth, the body of the shell must be made of some material that will admit of the insertion of the patched bullet without bulging or misshaping the shell, and which shall, at the same time, hold the bullet firmly and accurately in place.

Fig. 2.

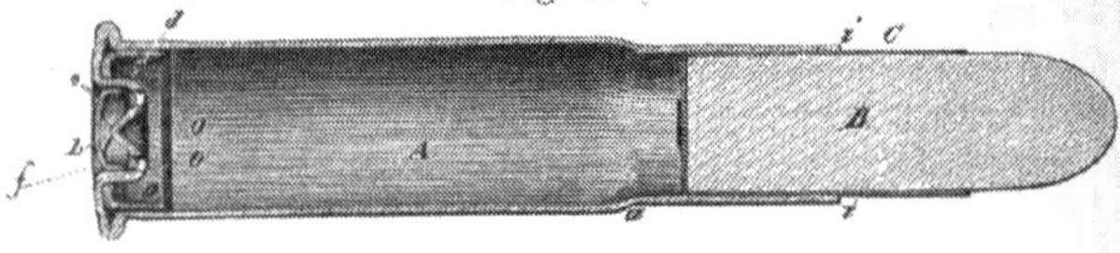

To make a cartridge which shall comply with these requirements I proceed as follows: In the first place I select a good quality of sheet-brass, from which I draw the shell by means of dies and punches in the usual manner. This material forms a shell that is more springy or elastic than the copper heretofore and generally used, and, being stronger and not so easily set, it permits the patched bullet to be shoved in with sufficient force to retain it securely in place, and, at the same time, not bulge or swell out the front portion of the cartridge. I then form the head of the shell as represented in Fig. 2, by which a recess is produced on its exterior, with a point therein to act as an anvil for exploding a cap applied exteriorly. I then form a cup, *b*, which has a hole at its center of such a size as to fit over or around the inwardly-projecting part of the head of the shell, this cup being inserted at the mouth or open end of the shell and pressed firmly down upon the base, as shown in Fig. 2. I then compress the front end of the shell A to a diameter corresponding with that of the bullet B, the compression extending back as far as the bullet is to be inserted, and as indicated between the letters *a i*, Fig. 2. I then make a bullet, which is of the form represented in Fig. 2, the same being from two and a half to three diameters in length. I next prepare a patch by cutting sheets of tough thin paper —bank-note paper being preferred—into strips. These strips I apply to the bullet by first moistening the paper and then rolling it smoothly and snugly around the bullet, so as to cover the latter for nearly its entire length, and fold or twist its rear portion down over the rear end of the bullet, the end being secured by a little paste, if desired. This patch C should be of such a length as to make one or more complete turns around the bullet so as to envelop the latter on all sides with a uniform thickness, and thus insure its being perfectly centered in the bore of the gun when inserted therein. After the patch has dried, by which means the paper is contracted and made to fit the bullet smoothly and snugly, I then insert this patched bullet securely into the front end of the shell A, taking care to insert it far enough to hold it true and firmly in place, the shell, of course, having been previously filled with powder. A cap, *b*, is then applied to rear end of the shell, as shown in Fig. 2, and the cartridge is complete.

It is obvious that in case it be desired to make this style of cartridge of a smaller size for use in pistols or other smaller arms, then the cup B may be omitted; and it is also obvious that the brass shell and patched bullet may be used with the fulminate arranged within the shell; but in such case the shell cannot be refired, which I consider a great object, because in case of necessity, where, for instance, a new supply cannot be readily obtained, these shells can be reloaded and used many times over. By this method of constructing a cartridge I am enabled to produce an article much superior to anything of its kind heretofore known. The paper patch is the only thing that can be relied upon to adhere to the bullet and pass with it through the bore of the gun, and thus prevent leading. A cartridge made on this plan has sufficient strength to withstand the effect of a large charge, thus insuring great range, a flat trajectory and consequent accuracy of flight of bullet. By reduction of the diameter and lengthening the bullet its momentum is preserved, while its resistance in passing through the air is lessened, and by means of the paper patch the leading of the barrel is prevented and the friction thereby kept at its minimum, thus fulfilling all the required conditions for success.

Having thus described my invention, what I claim is—

1. The combination of the drawn brass shell with the patched bullet, substantially as described.

2. The combination of the metallic shell with a paper-patched bullet and a re-enforce cup, all constructed and arranged to operate as set forth.

3. The combination of the metallic shell A with the paper-patched bullet, and a cap or primer applied exteriorly, substantially as described, whereby the same shell may be repeatedly used, as set forth."

This cartridge is so perfect in all its parts that, while it admits of being reloaded and fired a full average of fifty times, it is perfectly water-tight, as will be seen from the following taken from the Russian Inspector's Report from February 22d to April 19th, 1871:

"There have been fired in our regular work 20,720 cartridges without one miss fire, and 1,200 re-loaded ten times, making 32,720 without a miss fire in the inspection of 2,000,000."

"The Barque *Freya*, from New York for Cronstadt, with 3,645,120 cartridges aboard for the Russian Government, made by this Company, was dismasted in a gale, had the deck stove in, and was abandoned at sea. She was found by the steamer *Iowa*, from Liverpool, partly full of water, pumped out and towed to the port of New York, arriving April, 1871. A large part of this ammunition had been under water five weeks. The whole was taken out and returned to this factory, the wet paper boxes removed, and 10,450 of the cartridges fired, proving that they were uninjured."

So far as regards heat the severe test undergone by the Berdan cartridge while in use by our navy in the tropics subject to the moist heat of the tried thermometer 135, is the best proof of their perfection in quality.

The same results have been arrived at by the Spanish navy, the Berdan cartridge withstanding all the heat of a two years station in the waters of the West Indies. That they are equal to all varieties of climate may be considered settled, as this cartridge has been adopted by the Russian Government, which has had many millions manufactured by the Union Cartridge Company under the supervision of its own officers.

The great value of the American cartridge may be in part owing to the quality of the native copper used in the manufacture, which is specially adapted to this purpose. The heating of the barrel by firing does not expand the brass, the nature of the metal being such that, although the shell expands on firing, its immediate contraction thereafter leaves it in a condition to be easily extracted. This quality is not obtained by those made in other countries, and the natural result is that the governments of Russia, France, Spain, Sweden, Denmark, Switzerland, Roumania, Egypt, and other European nations, have ordered in the aggregate over 100,000,000 of American cartridges made of native copper. In Russia, a simple reloading apparatus has been adopted, which enables the armorer of each company to reload shells. A strict accountability is kept with each soldier, to whom is given 40 cartridges, for which he is personally responsible, unless in actual engagement with an enemy. Each night he must hand his empty shells to the armorer, who returns them to him in the morning reloaded, when they are inspected by his officer. As a special evidence of the safety of these cartridges, it may be mentioned that a box filled with them was dropped in the hold of a vessel without explosion; and that on another occasion a nail was driven through one cartridge in a box filled with the same, only that single cartridge exploding.

The following models are selected from the large number manufactured by the Union Metallic Cartridge Company, as an evidence of the variety and type.

Fig. 3.

This is the smallest size Pistol Cartridge made. The consumption is very large, the daily product being 100,000, or 30,000,000 a year.

Smith & Wesson.

Fig. 4.

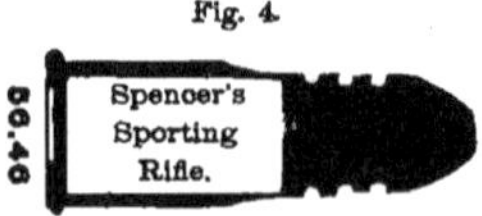

This is used in the Spencer Repeating Rifle specially for large game.

Fig. 5.

Berdan Patent, adapted to Smith & Wesson's new Army Pistol as the latest and best pistol cartridge. The Russian Government have ordered several millions.

Fig. 6.

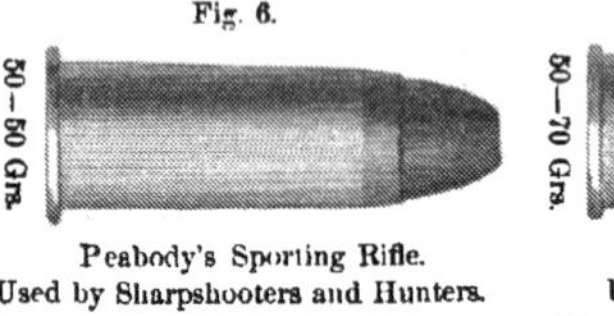

Peabody's Sporting Rifle.
Used by Sharpshooters and Hunters.

Fig. 7.

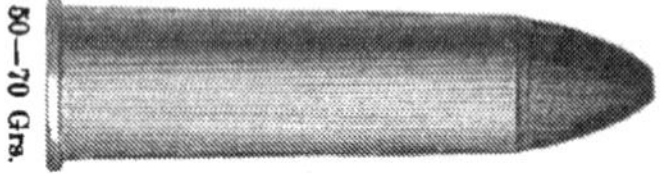

Remington's Muskets.
Used in all 50-calibre central fire arms.

Fig. 8.

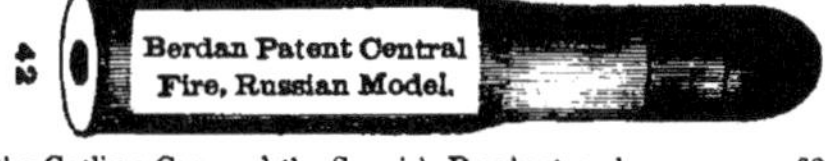

Used in the Gatling Gun and the Spanish Remington, has a range of 2500 yards.

Fig. 9.

Adapted to use a variety of ammunition for sporting purposes.

The great desideratum of ordnance officers of all nations has been to obtain a solid head cartridge that will retain its shape and force under repeated firing, the difficulty lying in the inability to use sheets of metal $\frac{1}{16}$ in thickness, leaving that thickness at the head and tapering the mouth of the cartridge to $\frac{1}{100}$. The Union Metallic Cartridge Company have control of several patents (which cover this objection) for the manufacture of solid cartridges, and are prepared to manufacture the same whenever required.

Among the machinery used by the Union Metallic Cartridge Company special attention should be directed to the

HEADING MACHINE.

The head or rim of the cartridge case is formed by this machine, which consists of a horizontal die countersunk at one end for shaping the head ; a feed punch to insert the tubes into the die ; and a heading punch to flatten the closed end of the tubes into the countersink.

The tubes, which are a little longer than the headed case, are fed into the inclined trough of the Heading Machine, whence they are taken up on the feed punch. A shoulder on this punch, at a distance from its extremity equal to the inner depth of the headed case, prevents it from extending to the full depth of the tube, and a surplus of metal is thereby left at the closed end of the tube for the formation of the head.

The feed punch inserts the tube into the die, and holds it there, while the heading punch moves forward by a powerful cam and presses and folds the unsupported, projecting portion of the tube into the countersink of the die, forming and accurately shaping the head or rim.

The headed case being left in the die as the feed-punch recedes, is pushed out by the succeeding tube, and thrown by a flipper into the receptacle below.

No oil is used in this operation, the moisture of the tubes from the recent washing sufficing as a lubricant.

The machine is fed at the rate of sixty-five per minute.

LOADING MACHINE.

The cases are now loaded with powder and bullet by means of the Loading Machine, which consists of a revolving circular plate with holes or receivers, and a hopper and powder measure. The cases and bullets are fed on revolving plates, thirty-five a minute ; the former are lifted into the receivers, passed under the hopper and measure for a charge of powder, and then under the bullet feeder for a lubricated bullet. In order to insure a full charge in each cartridge the machine is provided with a bell which gives notice to the operative of any failure in this particular. The edge of the case is then crimped on the bullet in a very simple manner. The receivers are smaller at the top where the bullet enters than at the bottom where the case is received, the diameter of the former being only equal to that of the interior of the open end of the latter. After the bullet has been pressed into the case, the cartridge is lifted, so that the edge of the case is forced into the conical surface of the receiver, between its larger and smaller diameters.

The powder is placed in a brass hopper, about two feet above the machine, and is fed to the cases through a paper tube one inch in diameter; the hopper and tube stand inside of a large conical shield of boiler iron.

During the process of manufacture accidents are only possible with the Loading Machine, and consequently every precaution has been taken to provide against their occurrence. As the machine is now made and arranged, the explosion of one cartridge may communicate fire to the few charged cases near it without danger. The entire charge of powder in the hopper may be thus exploded without the possibility of injury, either to the operative or to the machine, as the hopper and tube offer but slight resistance to the action of the gases that expend their forces in every direction without affecting the stability of the protecting shield. This has been proved by experimentally exploding full charges of two and a half pounds in the hopper itself. But the explosion of a cartridge in the operation of loading is of very rare occurrence. Out of the many millions loaded in the past four years, a trifling number only have exploded prematurely, resulting in no damage whatever.

After loading, the cartridges are wiped clean, and put up in paper packages, and packed in wooden boxes for storage or sale.

The following reports are added as evidences of the value of the Berdan Cartridge manufactured by the Union Metallic Cartridge Company:—

Office of Colt's Patent Fire Arms Manf'g Co.,
Hartford, Conn., Aug. 6, 1868.

Colonel:

In a series of experiments made by this Company, to test the strength of certain steel gun barrels, eleven barrels were tested, the maximum loads of gunpowder, varying from 175 to 600 grains, and the maximum loads of lead varying from 1,800 to 11,700 grains.

All of the barrels were tested to destruction; and in all cases Berdan Cartridge Shells were used. In no case was the head of the Cartridge affected by the enormous pressure, although in some cases the heat developed was great enough to melt the front ends of the Cartridge Shells.

Very respectfully yours,
(Signed), W. B. Franklin,
Vice-Pres't, Gen. Agent Colt's Arms Co.

Col. H. Berdan,
Hartford, Conn.

[CERTIFICATE.]

Don Enrique Barbaza y L'Arden, Col. of Infantry, and Lieut.-Col. of Artillery, Secretary to the Inspector General of the Island of Cuba, in the Regular Army of Spain:

By order of His Excellency, Senor Marshal of the Army, General Don Antonio Venene y Andrada de Wanderwhorilde, Knight of the Grand Cross of the Royal and Military Orders, etc., etc.,

HEREBY CERTIFIES, That the manufactory of cartridges called the "Union Metallic Cartridge Company," of Bridgeport, Conn., in the United States of America, have made six millions of cartridges, of different calibre and systems, for the use of the army of this island, which have proved to have a perfect construction in all their parts, and to be of the very best materials of the kind best adapted for their manufacture.

Of the different systems that have been used on this island, the cartridges of the Berdan system, central fire, have always proved, without one single exception, to be the best, and are uninjured in the shell by firing—and water-proof, not admitting dampness, when exposed to it. The metal has an elasticity, perfect and equal to all required tests.

Wherefore this Certificate is granted at Havana, on the 20th April, 1870.

Approved, VENENC, Inspector General.

ENRIQUE BARBAZA, Col. of Artillery.

Extract from the report on Breech-loading systems, made by a Board of Naval Officers, to the Bureau of Ordnance, in the year 1869, from Navy Department, 16th February, 1870 :—

"Five hundred rounds were then fired, as rapidly as practicable, in series of one hundred rounds, with a short interval between each one hundred rounds to cool, BUT NOT TO CLEAN, the gun. Average time per one hundred rounds, four minutes fifty-five seconds.

"At the conclusion of the five hundred rounds, the gun was carefully examined, cooled and cleaned. NOT A TRACE OF LEADING WAS TO BE SEEN IN THE BARREL, and very little fouling, which was removed by washing. Barrel and stock greatly heated. No injury to the breech parts. Gun worked well.

"DURING THIS TEST BRASS CASE CARTRIDGES, CALIBRE 42, BERDAN PRIMER, LUBRICATED BETWEEN POWDER AND BULLET, AND PAPER PATCH ON BULLET WERE USED."

1880.

UNION METALLIC CARTRIDGE COMPANY.

Since the publication of the preceding remarks the capacity of this company has been increased threefold, so that it is now enabled to turn out one million of cartridges daily. Every effort has been made to add the latest improvements and suitable machinery to meet all the requirements for military and sporting arms, including paper shells for shot-guns, gun-waddings, etc., etc., the present price list of the company comprising over one hundred varieties of metallic cartridges, all distinct and separate patterns, including the new inventions for magazine arms and battery guns. The special water-proof character of these cartridges has been shown most conclusively, the writer having witnessed the firing of some specimens taken at random from a case sunk on board the steamer Guatemala and destined for one of the South American Governments. These cartridges after being under water some months, were brought to the factory in the original cases, which when opened were found full of water; upon firing, every cartridge exploded promptly, as has been the case whenever these cartridges have been fired. The best evidence of the high value placed upon the cartridges manufactured by the Union Metallic Cartridge Company, is the fact that the Governments of Russia, Germany, France, and Spain have established manufactories for making this system of cartridges which has been adopted by them as the ammunition of their respective armies.

In addition, it is a well known fact, that the Turkish Government ordered some hundreds of millions for their use during the Turco-Russian campaign, and have since then purchased a large plant of machinery for the establishment of a manufactory of this special cartridge in Turkey. These statements are very conclusive evidence as to the approval of this system by the leading military authorities of the world. For the past eight years they have been largely in use by the various South American Governments. The perfect freedom from accidents as the result of the transportation of such an immense quantity of cartridges has satisfactorily proven that they are perfectly safe to handle, and can be transported without difficulty. With the view to secure the most perfect cartridge possible, both the United States Ordnance Department and private manufacturers have expended much time and labor in exhaustive experiments upon the subject. The question as to the relative merits of the solid and the re-enforced folded head has attracted much attention, as also the system upon which the anvil is made for exploding the primer.

THE FOLDED RE-ENFORCED HEAD CARTRIDGE

is claimed to have the following properties, viz., that it being constructed of metal so treated that it will expand equally upon being fired, so as to completely fill the chamber of the gun, and thereby be equally supported in all its parts by the walls of the chamber, at the same time being elastic, it immediately contracts after the firing so as to admit of easy extraction. The head of this shell, which is the part most liable to give out, is strengthened by the re-enforced cup, which is so placed in the shell that if a fracture should occur in or near the head of the shell there would be no leakage or escape of gas at the breech of the gun. Should any such defect occur the shell could be easily extracted, and it would at once be discovered in the event of reloading the arm. The service cartridge of the United States army fabricated by the Ordnance Department is of this character, and known as the folded head cartridge, and is regularly issued at the present time for use in the army. Admiral Selwyn of the Royal Navy of Great Britain has recently at a meeting of military and scientific men alluded to the American cartridge as follows: "I was in Turkey during the whole of last year, and I noticed particularly that the supply of cartridges given to the Turks was both highly efficient in itself, and provided for much larger expenditure than had ever been thought probable in any other army before." The cartridges thus referred to were those supplied to the Turkish army and manufactured by the Union Metallic Cartridge Company, and were made on what is known as the Berdan principle with folded heads.

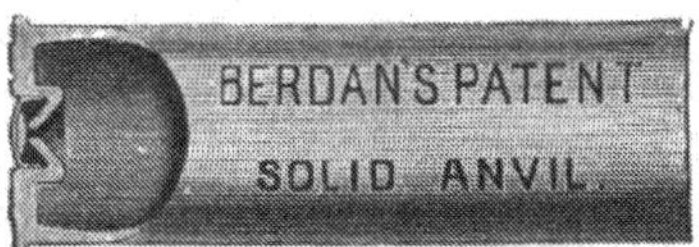

THE SOLID HEAD CARTRIDGE

on the other hand rests its claims upon the following points: First, that the metal being much thicker, consequently the shell itself must be stronger, and, especially, the metal is left much thicker in and near the head of the shell, and tapers rapidly to near the center of the body. In consequence of the great difference in the thickness of metal in different parts of the shell the thinner portion expands when fired, and is supported by the walls of the chamber of the gun, that portion of the shell nearer the head being much thicker, and in consequence expanding in a less degree, does not bear against the chamber of the gun sufficiently hard to hold it in position. By that means a longitudinal strain is brought on the cartridge to that extent that when a break in the cartridge does occur the shell parts longitudinally a short distance from the head, and upon an attempt to extract the same, the head portion with a small piece is drawn out, while the remaining portion is broken off by the discharge, and is usually carried forward into the barrel and completely disables the arm.

THE PRIMER.

The system of priming used in the Berdan cartridge, as made by the Union Metallic Cartridge Company, is formed as follows: The anvil upon which the primer is exploded is formed in a cavity in the head of the shell by raising a portion of the metal from which the shell is made, the primer is a shallow cup which holds the fulminate, before the fulminate is placed in this cup the cup is covered with a coating of varnish and carefully dried, which is a sure prevention of its coming into contact with the metal. The priming is then covered with a piece of tin foil, also varnished, which prevents any amalgamation of the mercury with the metal of which the primer is made. This primer is very largely used by Foreign Governments in their cartridge manufactories as it can be applied to either the solid or folded head cartridge. The other system of priming is best known as the French system, and also consists of a small cup with a flat anvil of different forms pressed in the cup on the priming and held in by the rim of the cup. It is claimed that the Berdan primer is less liable to allow gas to escape, and in consequence the primer is left entirely free to expand by the explosion of the fulminate, while in the French cartridge the pressure of the anvil in the cap sufficiently tight to hold it there, strains the periphery of the cap out of place and allows the gas to escape around the primer.

CARTRIDGE METAL—THE COE BRASS COMPANY.

Since the adoption of fixed ammunition for use in small arms there has been a steadily large and increasing demand for copper and brass. The great success of the cartridges made in the United States is due in a large measure to the admirable condition of the metal from which they are made, and which has led to the shipment of millions of cartridge shells to many of the foreign governments. Official experiments for the past ten years indicate beyond a peradventure that the strength and tenuity of American copper has never yet been equaled, and specially that which is mined in the Lake Superior region, and which is used particularly in the manufacture of cartridges. The great importance of this interest is well indicated by the success of the Coe Brass Manufacturing Company, located at Wolcottville, Connecticut, where it was started in 1834, under the name of The Wolcottville Brass Company. The business of this company is confined entirely to the manufacture of brass and copper in sheet, roll and wire, with special arrangements to facilitate the turning out of blanks and cups for metallic cartridges, in which condition the metal is delivered to the various manufacturers of cartridges. General Gorloff, of the Russian army, who is well known for his thorough knowledge of the subject of fixed ammunition, paid special attention, while in this country, to the manufacture of the Berdan cartridge, and freely admitted that the success and adoption of that cartridge by the Russian government was due in the largest degree to the admirable character of the metal supplied by the Coe Brass Company. The copper used by this company is entirely the product of the Lake Superior region, so well known as the best in the world. The zinc used in combination with the copper for the manufacture of brass comes from the state of New Jersey and the Lehigh region in Pennsylvania, and it is unexampled for its purity. The reputation of the Coe Brass Company for purity of metal has secured not only a majority of the business in cartridge metal in this country, but also in sales, in *sheets and cups*, to Russia, Spain, Italy, Peru and the Argentine Republic, while, in the form of manufactured cartridges, their product has been sent in enormous quantities for use, on *both sides*, in the Russian-Turkish war; and the average daily capacity of their works, often tested to the utmost, is equivalent to the production of ten tons of cartridge metal per day in addition to the general supply of sheet metal for miscellaneous purposes, and requiring the services of three hundred workmen. For the manufacture of pins, shoe-nails, eyelets for shoes, and other purposes of an industrial character, an immense daily amount of sheet brass is turned out, as well as of brass wire. The Coe Brass Company are also largely engaged in the manufacture of copper wire for electric machines, electro-dynamic machines, and for telegraph purposes; experimental tests showing a purity of metal equal to 99 degrees.

The view of the works, as indicated in the steel plate, covers some three or four acres—comprising, however, in all the land occupied, over twenty acres. These buildings comprise casting-shops, rolling-mills, annealing-furnaces, wire-mills, press-room, boiler and engine rooms, store-houses for wood, coal, etc., etc.

The water power used is from the Naugatuck river, with twenty-seven feet fall, using two water-wheels, one overshot wheel and one turbine, in addition to steam power to the amount of 400 horse power.

The fuel used for annealing purposes is entirely wood, of which at least three thousand cords per annum are consumed. In the casting furnaces, fifteen thousand bushels of charcoal and three thousand tons of Lehigh coal are used.

Every facility for transportation to tide-water by the Naugatuck Railroad, connecting directly with New York.

THE COPPER-BRASS CARTRIDGE.

The circumstances which led to the invention of the copper-brass cartridge which is illustrated, were, principally, the reports received in this country, in 1876, relative to great losses by corrosion of cartridges whose shells or cases were made of brass alone, and whose construction permitted the powder to come directly in contact with the inner brass surface of the shell.

It was reported that, under certain climatic or atmospheric conditions, brass shelled cartridges, which had been stored for a certain time in arsenals, were found to have been so badly corroded on the interior as to render them unserviceable, and that the quantity so spoiled, in European countries alone, amounted to many millions; and samples of very badly corroded shells were shown to the inventors and patentees

Copper – Brass

Brass.

Section of Cup.

Section of Cup.

Section of Shell.

Section of Shell.

Brass and Copper Cartridge Metal

Manufactured by the

COE BRASS MF'G. CO. WOLCOTVILLE, CONN.

of the copper-brass shells, Messrs. Leet & Chapin, of Springfield, Massachusetts, in 1876, and there was an apparent necessity that shells possessing all the elastic qualities of brass, and also non-corrosive, should be provided as a substitute for brass shells.

The inventors of the copper-brass shell caused considerable quantities of their shells to be made and tested in the winter of 1876-7. These tests were made by the ordnance officers of this and foreign countries, for the purpose of determining, first, the elastic properties of the compound shell; second, the adhesiveness of the two metals one to the other, under excessive expansive and retractive strains; third, strength under excessive and numerous successive charges of powder; and, fourth, the rigidity of the metal relative to the requisite qualities of anvil-resistance against the blow of the hammer, at the point where the primer is inserted in the head; and the results of said tests were eminently satisfactory.

The qualities of cartridge-shells made of either copper or brass alone were perfectly well known when the copper-brass shell was invented; but when such a new construction as this shell is produced, embodying, as it does, several new conditions, which no previous experience could indicate the practical results of, it became necessary that certain experiments should be made, which would require several years to determine the results of, and consequently, at the request of Messrs. Leet & Chapin, the United States Ordnance Department kindly consented, in April, 1877, to make a certain number of copper-brass shells, and to test them in comparison with the regular-service shells made of copper.

The results of the above test disclosed that in the matter of "extracting pressure" the difference, in pounds, in favor of the copper-brass shells was as 1.65 to 11.5; 4.25 to 20.2; 4.8 to 19; and the report says:

"The results of the firing were very satisfactory. The pocket cases were uninjured, and with the excessive charges the swelling of body or head was scarcely perceptible. The same is true with the service form of case. In one instance, however (with eighty grains of English rifle powder), a head was torn slightly at the fold. The pressure necessary for extraction (as shown by the table) was light. It therefore in this respect possesses the same advantages as brass cartridges. Whether the inner coating of copper will protect the metal from the corrosion which is said to take place in brass cartridges, is a question which will require time to fully answer. There is every reason to believe that in this respect all the advantages of copper may be derived from this metal.

"One hundred cartridges have been set aside that this, as well as other qualities, which time may develop, may be investigated. Specimens showing the metal at different stages of manufacture are forwarded with this report."

In January, 1880, the United States Ordnance Department, in response to the request of Messrs. Leet & Chapin, reported upon the condition and quality of the cartridges, which were set aside at the time, and for the purpose mentioned in the above-named report, and the results as to preservation in good firing condition, no corrosion, etc, are reported as follows:

"I have the honor to report that the cartridges referred to in the accompanying letter were, upon its receipt, taken out of the fulminate cave (under ground), where they had remained since April, 1877.

"The pasteboard boxes had rotted away from them, leaving black streaks upon the exterior surface of the bodies of the shells. These streaks were found, upon examination, to be simply discolorations which did not injure the shells. Some were cut open and carefully examined, to see whether any corrosion had taken place upon the interiorly-lined copper surface. *None was discovered.* One half of a shell was flattened out, to see whether the metal had preserved its toughness. The sample flattened out indicated that it had. The two halves of the shell are inclosed herewith.

"Ten velocities were taken, to ascertain the effective condition of the powder and fulminate in comparison with ten others taken from the storehouse. Mean initial velocity of those taken from cave, 1,318 feet; mean initial velocity of those taken from store, 1,308 feet. Showing an actual gain in velocity of 10 feet by those deposited in the cave. To be sure of this, I weighed the charges from two cartridges, and found that the one from storehouse had 69 grains powder in it, and the one from the cave 68 grains. This proved that the cartridges from storehouse were rather overloaded than underloaded, in comparison with those from the cave, although not giving as much average velocity by 10 feet. Both were made and loaded about the same time, with same kind of powder.

"The conclusions arrived at from an examination of these cartridges are both interesting and important:

"1st. Re-loading cartridges can be stored in a damp place underground for two-and-a-half years without impairing their efficiency as to strength of shells, certainty of fire of primer, and effective force of powder charges.

"2d. That a re-loading shell, made with any care, protects the powder charge from injury under *ordinary* and extraordinary exposure—as the greater includes the less.

"3d. That Japan wax, as a lubricant, has little or no tendency to injure the metal from which the shell is made, even when that metal is a combination of two metals—brass and copper. The brightness and cleanliness of the bullet-seat in the shell proves that.

"4th. That a brass cap can be used with safety on a copper anvil in the pocket of a brass shell whose interior surface is lined with copper."

The manufacture of the double metal for the production of the above-described copper-brass cartridge-shells requires that the metals be firmly united previous to rolling; that nothing shall enter into their composition which can in any way render the quality of the scrap metal unfit for re-melting and working; that the metal shall possess such ductility and homogeneousness as will permit it to be rolled, drawn, annealed and headed, and in every way treated, in the manufacture of cartridges, identically like a single metal sheet. These results are all successfully obtained from this metal, which is manufactured and furnished by the Coe Brass Manufacturing Company.

GUNPOWDER.

The earliest notice of the manufacture of gunpowder in this country is found in an order of the General Court of Massachusetts of June 6, 1639, when Edward Bowen was granted 500 acres of land at Pecoit, "So as he goes on with the powder if the saltpeter comes." A powder-mill was built at Dorchester, Mass., previous to 1680. In 1774 a powder factory was started in Pennsylvania, and in the same year a premium was offered by Cumberland county, Va., to establish a powder factory there, and in 1776 William Pitkin started the manufacture of powder in Hartford, Conn. In 1775 the Rhinebeck Powder Mill sold powder at twenty pounds per cwt.; in 1793 the powder-magazine in Philadelphia contained nearly 50,000 mortar casks that had been manufactured in Pennsylvania. A mill was also established at Southwick, Mass., in 1805.

DU PONT'S GUNPOWDER WORKS.

Eleuthere Irenée du Pont was the founder of the immense works distinguished as the "Brandywine Powder Works," near Wilmington, Del. He was a native of France, and emigrated to the United States in the fall of 1799, landing at Newport, R. I., January 1, 1800. Having noticed the poor quality of the gunpowder then made in America, he resolved to engage in its manufacture, of which he had a knowledge, having been a pupil of the celebrated French chemist, Lavoisier, who had charge of the "Bureau de Poudres et Salpetres" under the French Government. After some time spent in selecting a location, Mr. Du Pont established himself on the Brandywine creek, about four miles above the town of Wilmington, in the State of Delaware, where he prosecuted the business with such success that, at the time of his decease, at the United States Hotel in Philadelphia, in 1834, his establishment was the most extensive of its kind in this country, as it now is in the world.

Since the decease of its founder, the business has been managed by his sons and grandsons, who maintain the old firm style of E. I. Du Pont de Nemours & Co. The works of the firm comprise fourteen complete manufactories,—four on the Brandywine, two in Luzerne county, Penn., seven in Schuylkill county, Penn., and one in Northumberland county, Penn. The original works on the Brandywine commenced operations in 1802, and have a capacity for producing five thousand pounds of sporting powder per day. The middle, or Hagley works, commenced in 1812, comprise two complete sets of works in one inclosure, under a fall of twenty-two feet—so arranged that both can work on the same description of powder; or, if required, one set can manufacture one kind of powder, and the other set another kind; the two combined having a capacity of twenty-five thousand pounds of blasting powder per day.

In 1816 Du Pont de Nemours & Co. agreed with the Ordnance Bureau to re-manufacture damaged powder, the manufacturers to furnish saltpeter and allow a reasonable price for barrels. The lower works, commenced in 1836, are under a fall of twelve feet, and have a capacity of five thousand pounds of sporting powder per day. The Saltpeter Refinery, with laboratory attached, is two hundred and fifty-eight feet by ninety-six feet, with ample appliances for supplying all the niter required for the fabrication of powder, and also considerable quantities for the market, for such purposes as require an article chemically pure. In proximity to the refinery are large warehouses for the storage of saltpeter. The Charring Houses for the preparation of charcoal—three in number—are capable of furnishing all the coal required for the mills, the wood being stored and seasoned in extensive buildings adjacent.

The firm have two shipping points—one on the river Delaware, with magazines, and a wharf at which large vessels can lie; the other on the Christiana creek, with ample wharfage for coasters, and for landing coal, wood, etc. They have, also, a station and siding for the works on the Wilmington & Reading railroad, which passes through the property, intersecting the Pennsylvania railroad at Coatesville, and uniting with the Philadelphia & Reading railroad at Birdsboro. A passenger railway has been established between the city of Wilmington and the property of the Messrs. Du Pont. Attached to the powder works are extensive machine and millwright shops, where all repairs are made and most of the machinery is built; also a saw-mill, planing-mill, carpenter and blacksmith shops, and capacious buildings for the manufacture of wooden and metallic kegs and barrels, and of powder canisters. Railroad tracks are laid through the powder works, and the bulk of the transportation of powder, in its various stages of manufacture, is done in cars drawn by horses, and the transportation to and from tide-water and the railroad station is done in wagons by horses and mules, of which the firm have over one hundred at their Delaware and Pennsylvania mills.

Besides the powder-mills, the firm owns over two thousand five hundred acres of land, that stretch for a distance of three miles on both sides of the stream; and on the property there are three woolen-mills, a cotton-mill, a merchants' and grist-mill, and a population of nearly four thousand persons. The aggregate fall of the various water-powers of the firm on the Brandywine, including two which are as yet unimproved, is ninety-one feet. The farms attached to the works are in a high state of cultivation, and the roads are all macadamized for ease of transportation. The buildings on the estate are mostly of stone, and very substantial, and the machinery is of the best and most costly character.

The Luzerne County mills have about seven hundred acres of land on the Big Wapwallopen creek, with an aggregate fall of over one hundred feet, and a capacity for twenty-five thousand pounds of blasting powder per day. The Pennsylvania canal and the Lackawanna & Bloomsburg railroad pass through a part of the property.

The Schuylkill and Northumberland County mills, situate near the railroad connections of the Philadelphia & Reading railroad, have about nineteen hundred acres of land, and an aggregate water-power of one hundred and seventy-five feet fall; mining powder for the collieries being largely made.

The high reputation so long maintained for the Brandywine powder is due to the care bestowed on its manufacture, and to the constant personal supervision of the owners. The consumption of saltpeter and nitrate of soda, (including the Pennsylvania mills,) the principal ingredients in the manufacture, in the year 1871, was over eight million five hundred thousand pounds. The machinery in operation for the manufacture of gunpowder is driven by fifteen steam-engines and ninety-three water-wheels, of which the greater part are turbines.

The manufacture embraces all descriptions of powder, viz.: hexagonal, square, mammoth, cannon, mortar, musket and rifle, for army and navy ordnance service; diamond-grain, eagle, and the various grades of canister and sporting powders; shipping, blasting, mining, and fuse powders. The production of the mills is principally consumed in the United

States, the firm having agencies and magazines at all the important points, with a principal depot for the Pacific States at San Francisco, and agencies in South America, and in the East and West Indies.

To illustrate the progress which has been made in the manufacture of powder in the United States, it is only necessary to recall the fact that during the Crimean war the allies, to enable them to prosecute the siege of Sebastopol, were obliged to procure large supplies of gunpowder in the United States (one-half of which was furnished by the Brandywine powder-mills), and that the American powder compared favorably with the best they could procure in Europe.

At the present time there are five varieties of gunpowder used in the United States for the army and navy. The sizes being known as follows:

Hexagonal, adapted to fifteen inch guns.

Cannon, adapted to smaller sea-coast guns and mortars.

Mortar, adapted to field and siege cannon.

Musket, adapted for rifled muskets.

Rifle, adapted for pistols.

Diameters of large and small holes:

Hexagonal, ...	0.9 inch and	0.64 inch.
Cannon, ...	0.31 " "	0.27 "
Mortar, ...	0.1 " "	0.07 "
Musket, ...	0.06 " "	0.035 "

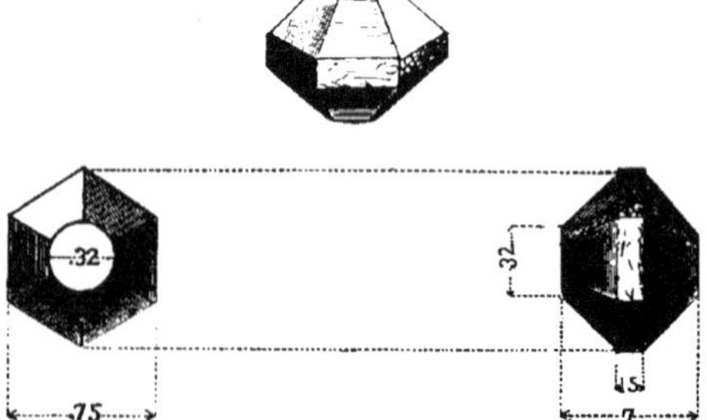

Initial velocity required for Hexagonal powder in a fifteen-inch gun, with a charge of 100 lbs., weight of projectile 450 lbs., 1,500 feet, with a pressure of not over 30,000 lbs. to the square inch; and in the eight-inch rifled gun, with charge of powder 35 lbs., weight of projectile 180 lbs., the initial velocity should be 1,400 feet for a pressure not to exceed 36,000 lbs. For cannon powder the initial velocity should be 1,450 feet, and for musket powder 1,350 feet. These are the government requirements for contract powder.

The opposite cuts illustrate the hexagonal-grained powder made by Messrs. E. J. Du Pont de Nemours & Co. The granulation is very uniform. The grains are polyhedral, the dies in which they are pressed being almost perfect dodecahedrons. It is called "Hexagonal" by the manufacturers, probably because it is nearly so in cross sections. These cuts indicate not only the shape of the grains but also the exact dimensions.

THE HAZARD POWDER COMBANY, HAZARDVILLE, CONN.

The name of Col. A. G. Hazard has been connected with the manufacture of gunpowder since 1833, when he commenced the business in the town of Enfield, Conn., where the works of the Hazard Powder Company are now located. These works cover an area of about six hundred and forty acres. The principal factories are established at Hazardville (a part of Enfield). These factories comprise twenty-two pairs of rolling mills with iron wheels six to seven feet in diameter and in weight averaging about fifteen tons for each pair. There are five granulating presses each separated from the other, six hydraulic presses of from four to five hundred tons working power, and also screw presses, refineries and tent houses. Special buildings have been erected for pulverizing, mixing, dusting, drying, glazing, sorting and packing, and in every instance attention has been paid to a systematic plan of arrangement so that in no contingency of accident could any serious result occur. Store-houses for charcoal, sulphur, brimstone and nitrate of soda, furnaces for burning charcoal, foundries and other buildings, making in all over two hundred separate buildings which are required by the Hazard Powder Company in their manufacture of gunpowder. Although these buildings are thoroughly isolated, not only from the village in which the workmen and their families reside, but also from each other, the means of transportation to market are quite feasible either by the Connecticut river or by railroad. Additional works are located at Burnside and Scitico, both in the same state. A very large capital is invested in these works, which have a capacity of from ten to fifteen tons per day. About one hundred and fifty men are now employed, a small town has grown up with a population of nearly one thousand dependent upon the mills and amply supplied with good schools, churches, a library, etc., etc. A system of mutual insurance has been adopted by this company for the benefit of the workmen which has proved of great service to all interested. The powders manufactured by this company comprise government, sporting and blasting powders. Those used by the government are known as:

CUBICAL.—A powder used in very heavy guns, average size $\frac{5}{8}$ inch, its special advantages being that while the propelling qualities are the same, the shape of the blocks secures a longer burning and more effectual consumption of the powder together with the utilization of the gases and greater power in the initial velocity, thereby saving the chances of bursting of the breech.

HEXAGONAL.—Which shape is claimed to be of special value, inasmuch as the air has more facility in passing between the grains and thus securing complete consumption.

MAMMOTH.—This is a large grain powder of irregular shape, being the first step from the manufacture of small powder to the regular grain as now used.

ARMY CANNON NO. 5.—About half the size of the mammoth, and in general use by the U. S. army for which it is specially adapted.

ARMY CANNON NO. 7.—This is a still smaller grain for army use in cannon of small calibre.

NAVY CANNON.—A size still smaller, and used exclusively by the United States navy.

MORTAR POWDER.—The finest of all the ordnance powders, and only one size coarser than

MUSKET POWDER.—Used in the manufacture of fixed ammunition by the government at its various arsenals.

The Hazard sporting powder is world-wide in its reputation and is manufactured of all sizes and adapted for every species of large and small game, and is well known under the general term of "Kentucky Rifle." The brand F. G. is used particularly at Creedmoor, where it has invariably been well received.

Duck Shooting.—There has been a very decided change in the adoption of a larger grain powder for duck shooting, and it has proved very successful in practice; the sizes having been increased from one to six during the past year. The Hazard Powder, made for this purpose, has been generally adopted.

Electric Gunpowder.—This brand is especially known for its rapidity of discharge and certainty of action; it is designed for bird shooting, and is manufactured in the most careful manner and from selected ingredients of the best quality. The Hazard Powder Company have taken advantage of all the improvements introduced into the manufacture, and the best of skilled labor and experience is made use of in superintending the various processes through which the ingredients have to pass,—the saltpeter alone requiring three separate refinings before it reaches the point required by the ordnance department, that the impurities shall only exist as one in three thousand.

AMES MANUFACTURING COMPANY, CHICOPEE, MASS.

The earliest notice of the manufacture of swords in this country indicates that they were first made by Ezekiel Hopkins, in Scituate, Rhode Island, in 1760, and from all accounts they were of excellent quality. In 1826 Nathan Star commenced the manufacture of swords at Middletown, Conn., producing an article which, in temper and finish, was pronounced equal to the famous Damascus blades. Swords made by Mr. Star were presented to Generals Jackson, Gaines, Johnson, and Commodore Hull. To the Ames Manufacturing Company is due in a great measure the present high character of the swords made in the United States. N. P. Ames commenced the manufacture of tools in Chelmsford, Mass. (now Lowell), and was considered one of the most skilled mechanics in his trade, at a time when labor of that class was very scarce. Up to 1812 nearly all swords were imported; in 1831 Ames & Co., commenced the manufacture of swords for the Government, their improvement in finely finished tools having led to this undertaking. At this date, there being no steel, manufacturers were dependent upon hoop-iron and blister steel, all imported from England. Agricultural implements were largely made from German steel, and German shear steel. All the swords used by the United States army were made by the Ames Manufacturing Company up to the commencement of the war, and in 1840 six presentation swords were made for the State of Virginia at a cost of one thousand dollars each. The most successful experiments were made with cast-steel, which was subjected to very severe tests, and the first swords manufactured were so perfect that they would cut the blades of all foreign swords. Since the production of American swords from cast-steel, all foreign makers have commenced using the same metal. Ames & Co. made the first sabre bayonets used by the United States army.

At the commencement of the war of the rebellion the demand for swords was so great that the entire force of the Ames Company —some eight hundred men—was employed, turning out one thousand swords a day, making a total production of nearly three hundred thousand, all standing the government test. Special attention was paid to the manufacture of swords for officers, and it is believed that in every respect they were equal to any made elsewhere.

In 1836 the Ames Manufacturing Company commenced the manufacture of bronze 6-pound and 12-pound Howitzers, by contract for the army, also Coehorns, Napoleon guns, and mountain Howitzers. The manufacture of James projectiles was also carried on here, some two thousand tons being turned out, varying from small calibres six and twelve pounders up to forty-two pounders. In addition, the services of the company were used in the manufacture of round shot, canister and shell largely for foreign Governments, especially for the various South American States, Mexico, and the Republic of Texas. The Ames Manufacturing Company have devoted much time and experience to the subject of gun machinery, having supplied the famous Enfield Armory in England, not only with gun machinery but also with engineers and workmen, by the special action of a commission sent from Great Britain. This class of machinery is all based on the interchangeable system, gauges being made to each set of machines, and they were supplied to the London Armory Company, the Birmingham Small Arms Company, the Russian and Spanish Governments, and the South American Republics. The introduction of this interchangeable gun machinery led to an entire change in the manufacture of small arms in all the countries of the world. In 1858 Mr. J. T. Ames was selected by the Secretary of War to visit Europe, to secure the best machinery for rolling gun barrels, a process which had taken the place of the welding process. On his arrival Mr. Ames was supplied with government permits to all the foundries, arsenals, and armories in Great Britain. Mr. Ames as agent for the United States Government secured all the machinery required for the armories at Springfield, Mass., and Harper's Ferry, Va., all of which was delivered in season to be of great and immediate service and to the advantage of the government. At the present time the Ames Manufacturing Company are not only largely engaged in the manufacture of swords for the United States army, but also for the various purposes required for secret societies, etc., etc. The new improvements in gilding which have originated with the Ames Manufacturing Company have led to a great change in this branch of sword manufacture.

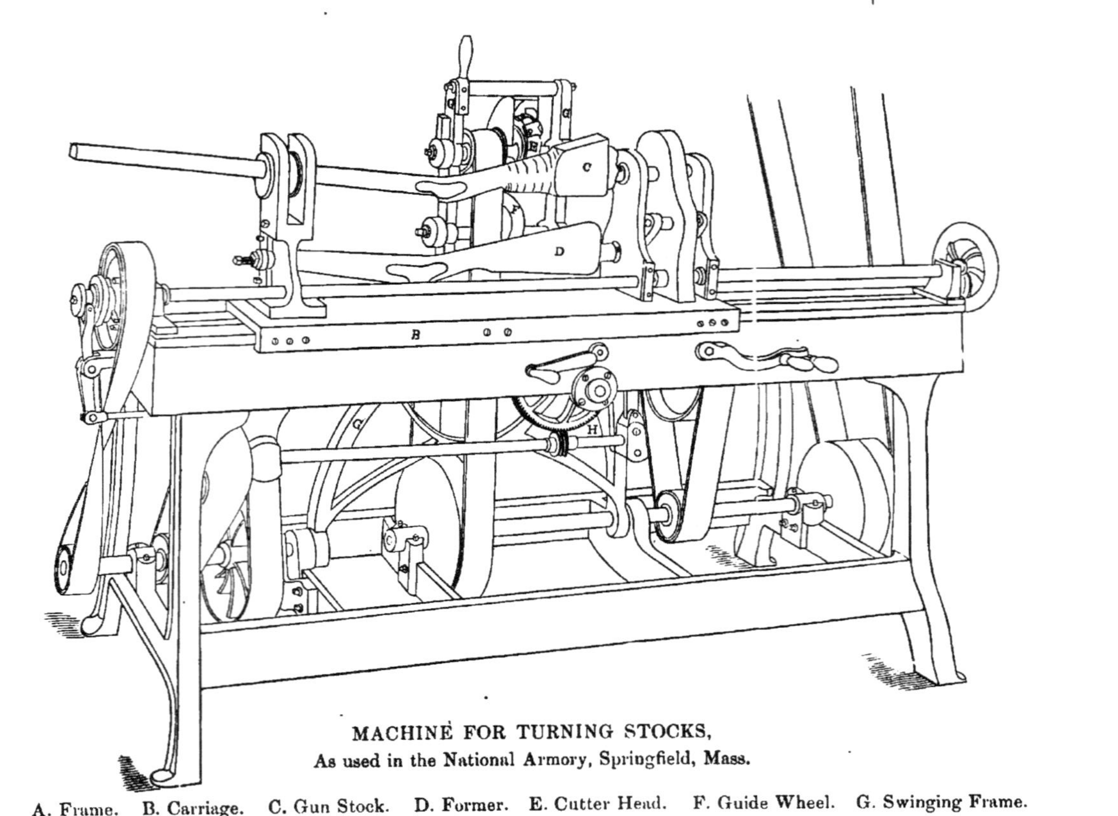

MACHINE FOR TURNING STOCKS,

As used in the National Armory, Springfield, Mass.

A. Frame. B. Carriage. C. Gun Stock. D. Former. E. Cutter Head. F. Guide Wheel. G. Swinging Frame. H. Feed Motion. I. Revolving Shaft.

CHAPTER XII.

PRATT & WHITNEY COMPANY—GUN MACHINERY.

The present system of manufacturing small arms as generally adopted by all nations is due to American invention. All of the large gun factories in Great Britain are now using the numerous machines originally designed in this country, and which have never been equaled by foreign manufacturers. At first these machines were imported from here, but now having the models before them foreign manufacturers are making them largely themselves. In the early introduction it was found necessary to import American skilled labor, and there may be found American mechanics now in charge of some of the most important factories. The Pratt & Whitney Company, of Hartford, Conn., have devoted special attention to the manufacture of gun machinery in all its various forms, with most satisfactory results. Their orders come from all countries, and their work has received the most favorable commendation. A complete set of this machinery is now in use in Germany, having been ordered by that government in 1873, at a cost of a million and a half of dollars. This machinery was put in place by American mechanics, sent over for that purpose, and is now busily employed turning out two hundred thousand rifles per annum. Illustrations and descriptions are given herewith of the most important machines supplied by this Company.

CARTRIDGE VARNISHING MACHINE.

The design of this machine is to coat the interior of metallic rifle shells with an impermeable elastic varnish, that will prevent chemical action between the salts of the gunpowder and the material of the shells. The result is to insure the preservation of the shells, and of the quality of the cartridges, for a definite period. The operation is also adapted to the preparation of once-discharged shells, making them

available for re-charging. The shells are placed in a hopper, several hundred at a time, and fed singly, forty passing through the different stages of the process at once, at the rate of 2,000 or more per hour. Beside revolving around the central spindle, the shells are rotated in the chucks which hold them, to prevent the accumulation of the varnish in any one spot, and to insure its being spread evenly. This rotary motion "sets" the varnish, which should afterwards be hardened and thoroughly dried, by means of a cheap sheet-iron furnace, that may be readily heated by steam pipes, or in any other convenient manner. One operator may attend two or three machines, as all the motions of the machine are entirely automatic, including an effective stop-motion, that acts promptly at any obstruction. To insure uniform results, the temperature of the room in which the machine is used should be maintained, as nearly as possible, at 70° Fahr., and the air should be dry and free from dust. The machine may be adapted to shells of any calibre. Weight, 1,800 pounds.

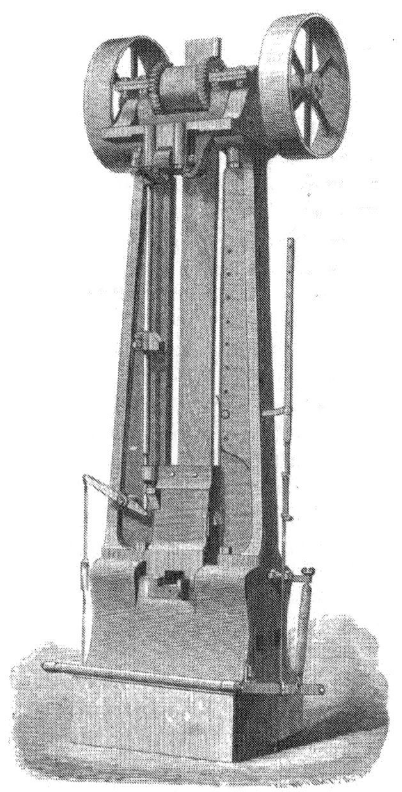

PATENT IMPROVED DROP-HAMMER.

This Drop-Hammer is made under the Goulding & Cheney patent, with F. A. Pratt's improvements. It has borne the test of a large practice successfully, is a convenient substitute for the trip or steam-hammer, and is also an efficient drop-hammer. The drop is raised by means of a flat-surfaced strip of tough wood, which engages with the faces of finished cast-iron rolls, driven by gears at the ends. One of these rolls runs in fixed bearings, and the other has its bearings in a yoke suspended on journals which allow it to be moved toward its fellow, to engage with the surface of the lifting-board. This yoke has a central portion projecting downward and engaging by a connecting bar with a cam operated by a vertical starting-bar through the medium of a crank-lever. By this combination, a much greater force is exerted, instantaneously, in placing and retaining the roll in contact with the lifting board, than is possible when the starting-bar is connected directly with the roll bearings. The two rolls, with their gears, and the cam movement, are all parts of the head-piece, which may be removed as a whole, or the rolls may be removed separately. The gears are made very strong, and have a peculiar form of tooth specially adapted to the work they perform. There are two to each roll. An automatic and adjustable stop holds the drop suspended at any hight desired. An automatic trip may be attached, which will secure a series of blows of uniform force, at the will of the operator, who can, however, instantly change it from the full impact of the drop falling from the extreme hight of the lift to the simple pressure of the weight of the mass without motion. This absolute control and instant adjustment of the force of the blow will be appreciated by all practical forgers. The workman has the free use of his hands in operating the machine, as its action is governed entirely by his foot. The addition of the automatic trip will increase the price of the hammer to a certain extent; but experts in the use of the hammer do not attach much value to it as having any advantage over the foot motion, while the latter has many over the former. With each machine are furnished wrenches, and also a wrought-iron die-bed secured by a key. This die-bed saves the trouble and expense of dressing the main bed by chisel and file, or by planer, in case of damage, and also adds to the strength of the machine by increasing its resistance to the shock of the blow. These machines are offered as superior to others heretofore used, in the following respects: Weight and quality of metal, size of shafts, bearings, and bolts; simplicity of construction, and of the adjustment, which is made at one point only. Dies of any required form furnished as ordered.

No. 1 HAND-MILLING MACHINE.

This machine is used on the lock-parts of small arms, where small cuts are taken, not necessitating an automatic feed.

The spindle is of steel, running in boxes lined with best Babbitt-metal, and carrying a cone of 3 grades, for 1¾ inch belt. The horizontal adjustment of the slide is 6 inches, and the vertical and horizontal movement by the levers is 2 inches. The greatest distance from the top of the table to the center of the spindle is 4 inches, and from the top of the vise 2¼ inches. Weight, with vise and countershaft, 450 pounds.

COLD-PRESSING AND STAMPING MACHINE.

For stamping medals, coin, etc., and for finishing by pressing in dies, instead of milling, wrought-iron forgings, such as gun hammers, etc. The gearing, nicely cut, is inclosed in the hollow base. The crank and knuckle-joint with which the machine is constructed give a stroke of 1½ inch, which exerts its maximum power at the extreme end, when the crank passes the center and the joint is nearly straight. The machine will sustain a maximum pressure of 800 tons, may be started and stopped instantly without a shock by means of the Pratt patent friction clutch. Weight, with countershaft, 12,000 pounds.

DRILLING OR CHUCKING MACHINE, WITH HORIZONTAL REVOLVING-HEAD.

This machine is used on lock-parts and in chambering the barrels.

Is designed for a variety of work, such as drilling, facing, and tapping holes before removing the piece to be finished from the chuck or face-plate. The revolving-head carries several spindles for the reception of tools. Each one is brought to the work successively, by a single movement of a lever or handle, and is fed forward by a rack and pinion, operated by a convenient hand-wheel. The machine is rapid in its operation, and very accurate in its results. The number of spindles in the head may be varied to suit the work to be done, and the length of the bed may be increased or diminished, as ordered. They are made in three sizes, 13, 18, and 24 inches swing.

HORIZONTAL TAPPING MACHINE.

Specially used for lock-parts in small arms.

This machine taps holes from $\frac{1}{16}$ inch to $\frac{3}{8}$ inch diameter. The head-spindle carries 2 pulleys, 8 inches diameter, 2 inches face, and is provided with a chuck for holding the taps, which, being made of round steel, may be secured to project any desired distance. Between the pulleys is a covered clutch for reversing, which is operated by merely drawing back the piece that has been tapped. The foot-stock spindle carries a rest, upon which the nut, or other work to be tapped, is held by the hand, or by suitable clamps. The rear portion of the spindle is threaded to receive a check-nut, which governs the depth to be tapped where the tap is not to pass through, obviating all liability of breaking even the smallest tap. The foot-stock is secured to the bed at any point by a binding-screw. Weight, with one countershaft, 320 pounds.

NO. 3 POWER MILLING MACHINE.

For milling the barrels and heavier portions of the lock-parts.

The Nos. 3 and 4 Power Milling Machines are built on the same general plan as No. 2, though upon larger scales. They have four speed and four feed changes. Weight, with vise, foot-stock, and countershaft, 2,150 and 3,100 pounds, respectively.

INDEPENDENT FOUR-SPINDLE DRILL.

Used for drilling the receiver or "culas." Intended especially for work on which two or four tools are necessary to finish a hole, as for example, for use with four tools, a starting drill, through drill, enlarging drill, and a straightening reamer. In such cases the piece is secured in a holder, is carried around and indexed under the drills perfectly, and finished before it is removed from its fastening. All of the spindles run and do their work simultaneously, an operator being able to attend to several machines. But as each spindle has an independent feed, the machine may be used with one, two, or three spindles, as well as with the entire set. Drills holes from ¼ to 1½ inch diameter and 9 inches depth. Changes in speeds and holders can be made to suit the work. Weight, with countershaft, 2,850 pounds.

BROACHING PRESS.

For broaching out the interior of barrels, receiver, &c.

This machine is designed for broaching holes of such diametrical form in the interior of barrels, receivers, &c., that they cannot be finished by rotary motion, as drilling or reaming. It will work cavities up to 2½ inches diameter. It is adapted also for drawing, or for finishing the outside of work. The head is operated by worm and gear, the teeth of the latter running in a pan of oil. The connection and operation is made and produced by a pitman and crank action. All the gearing is inclosed in the hollow base. The driving-wheel is 26 inches diameter, and carries a 4½-inch belt. It may be started and stopped instantly, without jar, by Pratt's Patent Friction Clutch. Machines of strokes varying from 1 to 9 inches are made, as ordered. Weight, 3,400 pounds.

MARKING MACHINE.

This is a handy tool for impressing textual or emblematic designs on the barrel of the gun into finished work, as the titles of firms, monograms, or trade-marks. The design is formed on the face of a circular die, which revolves with an arbor that is held in a carriage sliding in uprights, and is brought to its work by a foot-lever (not shown in the engraving), the device being impressed on the piece to be marked, as it is moved, with the table to which it is secured, by hand-lever under the die. Pieces of varying diameters may be marked in the same machine. Rests, or holders, for articles, will be furnished, as adjuncts to the longitudinal carriage, to suit the demands of the purchaser. The machine is mounted on legs of convenient hight. Weight, 300 pounds.

SCREW SHAVING MACHINE.

For finishing the heads of the gun screws and pins.

Is furnished with ten spring collets, a cross-rest with two shaving tools, oil tank, dripper, and countershaft. The collets are opened and closed in the spindle by a hand-lever, and hold screws $\frac{1}{4}$ inch to $\frac{5}{8}$ inch diameter, increasing by sixteenths; $\frac{5}{8}$ inch to one inch diameter by eighths. The shaving tools are circular, and may be sharpened by grinding without changing their form.

Weight, 750 pounds.

No. 1 SCREW-SLOTTING MACHINE.

The head carries a cone-pulley of three grades for $1\frac{3}{8}$ inches belt. The spindle has longitudinal adjustment of 1 inch. In the plain machine the screw, held in a chuck mounted on a slide, is raised, by means of a hand-lever, pinion, and rack, to the cutter revolving in the spindle for simply sinking a nick in the head. This vertical slide has a movement of 4 inches, which may be limited by a screw and check-nuts. A rod, arranged to pass up through the chuck as it descends with the slide to starting point, pushes the screw out of the chuck, to be caught by the table. For slotting across screw heads, and for light milling cuts, a cross-slide with traverse of 3 inches, operated by hand-lever, is added to vertical slide. Weight of machine, with countershaft, 225 pounds.

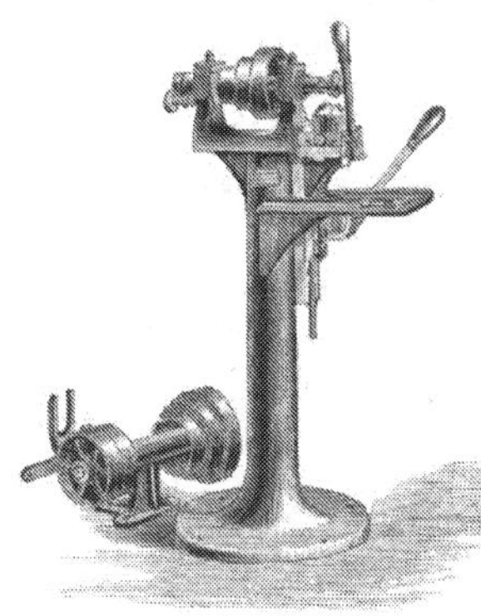

NO. 1 SCREW MACHINE, WITH WIRE-FEED.

The engraving shows No. 1 Screw Machine, with the Parkhurst Patent Wire-Feed Attachment. The device is simple in construction and efficient in operation. It is not liable to derangement, and is operated by the movement of a hand-lever. It feeds the wire forward to a length regulated by an adjustable gauge-stop held in the turret, and the same movement that brings the wire forward, closes the jaws of the chuck, holding the wire firmly. The reverse movement opens the jaws to receive another length. These movements are performed instantaneously, without stopping the machine, so that the use of the device results in a great saving of time. There are several sizes of these machines for making the gun screws and pins, etc.

All of these machines require special "Fixtures" for holding the pieces when being machined. These are made especially for each particular piece. The Pratt & Whitney Company are prepared to furnish these, with cutting tools and gauges, complete; also, forging dies for the hammers—completing everything; so that it is ready for use, without further expense, before it leaves the works, and making in all a perfect plant for gun machinery.

RIFLING MACHINE.

For rifling gun-barrels with a uniform twist, from one turn in twenty inches to one in thirty-six inches. The cutter-rod carries from one to three cutters, as the rifling is four, five, or six to the circumference. An adjustable feed-stop gauges the depth of the rifling, and the racks, which are of steel, are double, to take up all back-lash, so that the cutters cannot ride on the lands. An oil-pump feeds automatically at each end of the stroke. The carriage is gibbed on the outside of the long slide, allowing free access to its working parts. Weight 1,600 pounds.

This machine rifles by the filing process which is more correct than the planing process, and will turn out about one gun-barrel an hour.

THE IMPROVED GARDNER BATTERY GUN.

Notwithstanding the general competition and the varieties of inventions in all classes of small arms there have been but few changes in Battery Guns, and only one or two systems have received much public attention. In presenting the Improved Gardner, the manufacturers and owners of the patent (the Pratt & Whitney Co. of Hartford, Conn.) feel assured that upon a careful examination its advantages will be apparent and must necessarily lead to its adoption by all nations. The various exhaustive trials to which it has been exposed since its presentation to the Army and Navy Departments of the United States and the triumphant results are significant evidence of the value of the *improved* Gardner in the eyes of experts, and the manufacturers look with confidence to a similar or better result wherever tested. It is claimed for this gun, as now improved, that in simplicity, durability and lightness it is unequaled by any other gun of a similar character; also, that it can be turned with much more ease.

The original gun was invented by William Gardner, of Toledo, Ohio, in 1874. In the following year arrangements for the construction of the Gun were made with the Pratt & Whitney Co., and the first gun was carefully tested by the Ordnance Board U. S. Navy at the U. S. Navy Yard, Washington city, in November, 1875. There were present on this occasion Commodore Jeffers, Chief of Ordnance U. S. Navy, and General Benét, Chief of Ordnance U. S. Army.

In this trial the system was greatly commended. Since then the feeding apparatus has been greatly improved by adopting the one now in use, the invention of Mr. E. G. Parkhurst, of the Pratt & Whitney Co., which is very simple and efficient. The system of swinging levers (known as the *Gardner* System), that transfer the cartridge from the feed guide to the perforated plate, with the help of gravity, have been superseded by a system that positively carries the cartridge to its place, and retains the shell in position until it is ejected. With these improvements, the gun was again presented to the Naval board at Washington, for trial June 17, 1879, the official report of which is appended. This report gives no miss-fires, six failures of one lock to extract cartridge shells; perfect working of the other lock during the trial. The recent introduction of an extractor, that has a positive movement, and will in

TO ACCOMPANY ORDNANCE NOTES No. 124.

PLATE VI.

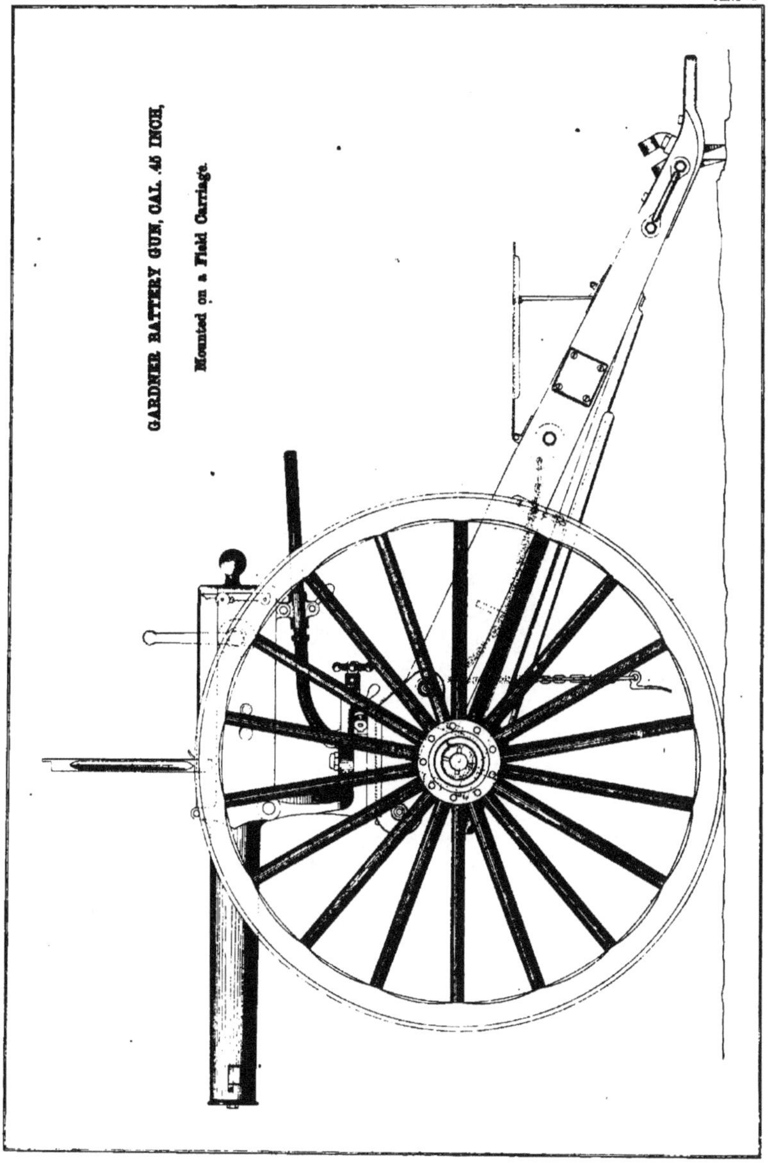

GARDNER BATTERY GUN, CAL. .45 INCH,

Mounted on a Field Carriage.

all cases remove the *shell*, has strengthened the only weak point that was developed by the trial above referred to, and has made the gun reliable and worthy of confidence in all respects. This gun possesses every quality desirable in a machine gun, namely: lightness, strength, simplicity and durability, ready accessibility to all the working parts, an independent feed for each barrel and adaptation to firing one or more barrels at will. The gun can be arranged for any calibre of small arm, or any length of barrel. As improved, it works perfectly, and commends itself to the critical examination and consideration of all governments.

In the present system of springs for locks, the tension is *entirely* taken from the springs at each discharge of the gun, the firing pins and springs are relieved from unnecessary *strain*, the crank can be *revolved* without compressing the mainsprings, and ammunition can be run through the gun without being fired.

DESCRIPTION.

The Improved Gardner Gun, as shown on tripod and carriages, consists of two simple breech loading rifled barrels, placed parallel to each other, about 1.4″ apart, in a *case* or *compartment*. These two barrels are loaded, fired and relieved of shells by one revolution of the hand-crank. The working of the gun is simple. One man inserts the heads of cartridges projecting from a feed block into the feed-guide, drawing the block from the cartridges; another man turns the crank, by which the gun is fired, and as the cartridges disappear down the feed-guide, their places are supplied from another block; in this manner the firing may be made continuous. The barrels are open from end to end, and chambered at the rear to admit a flanged center-fire metallic cartridge. The barrels are firmly screwed into a *rear barrel ring*, which is pinned fast to the rear case, and the muzzles pass through another similar ring called *front barrel ring*, which is fitted into the front case and made fast with a taper pin. The rear case extends from rear barrel ring far enough to contain all lock parts, together with the *driving crank* and *safety stop*. A swinging cover, hinged at forward end of case, is firmly locked in position by a cascabel having a screw thread cut on its stem that enters the rear case. When the cover is raised, which can be quickly done after turning back the cascabel, all the working parts of the gun are fully exposed; and should an accident occur, like the bursting of cartridge heads, or derangement of locks, the trouble can be instantly discovered, and as quickly remedied. The hand-crank that operates the gun is pinned fast to the *main crank*, which is supported by journal boxes. The boxes are locked into the rear case, and serve as a protection to the swinging cover from side thrusts. The body of *main crank* is circular, having journals, or crank pins, for operating the locks, diametrically opposite each other (the firing being alternate) and eccentric enough to give the required motion to the locks as they are moved forward and back, driving in cartridges and withdrawing shells. The outer portion of crank pins or journals are flattened to the circle of the periphery of main crank for the purpose of holding the lock stationary while firing, about one-fifth part of the revolution of hand-crank, and allowing ample time for *hang fires*. The lock in form resembles the letter U, having an extension from its side, which contains the *firing pin*, main (spiral) spring, sector or spring compressor, sector-sleeve, extractor, and lock head. The U part of the lock, that works under and around the crank pin, is curved at the inner front to correspond with the outer circle of the crank; the office of the curved front being to hold the lock in position for firing. The circular firing pin is flattened a portion of its length near the front end, to allow it to pass under the extractor by which it is held in position. It extends from the head of the lock, through the mainspring and sector-sleeve, terminating in a flange or head, for locking into the sear. The sear, having the form of a bell crank, pivoted in the center to the lock, holds the firing pin securely, and prevents it from touching the cartridge until it is released from its hold by the action of the crank journal when the lock is in its extreme forward position.

The sector or spring compressor, hinged in a recess of the lock, and engaging by means of gear teeth with the sector-sleeve, has its arm forced against the safety stop as the main crank advances, thus compressing, through the medium of the sector-sleeve, the main spring, and holding it tense until released by action of the sear.

The lock heads serve as breech plugs, and receive the recoil when the cartridges are fired. Each lock carries a *hook extractor*, which rides over and catches the flange of the cartridge, when the lock is forced forward, and when the lock retreats, withdraws the empty shell until it comes within reach of the ejector, by which it is positively thrown out. The shell starters have a positive movement in connection with the lock head. Should the cartridge be driven by the extractor, into the barrel, to its head, (as is the case when the gun is worked rapidly,) before the lock is in firing position, it is forced from the chamber by the shell starter as the lock advances, and is held long enough for the extractor to engage with the head, when the lock, extractor, and cartridge are driven home together.

The ejectors, hinged to the case, are driven by projections on the sides of the locks which give them positive movements to eject the empty shells. They also serve as stops to prevent the cartridges from falling through the perforated plate as they are forced down through the feed-valve.

The perforated plate extending across the rear case, to which it is fastened by a pin, has two parallel semi-circular grooves, which are enlarged *extensions* of the chambers in barrels. From the back part of the groove, slots large enough to pass freely the cartridges, (being wider at the rear, behind the ejector, than at the front,) are cut downward through the plate. When the retractor has drawn the shell back nearly to the extent of the throw of the crank, the ejector forces the shell through the slot, and is then in position to receive another cartridge from the feed plate or valve. The feed valve, attached to the swinging cover, has a reciprocating motion across the perforated plate. It has two angular openings, of the size and shape of the outline of the cartridge, with centers equidistant with centers of barrels. After a cartridge has dropped one-half its diameter into the valve, it is forced by the action of the latter into its true position, and held positively against the *cartridge support.* When the valve is again moved back, the cartridge is forced downward into the perforated plate, and the column of cartridges is cut off in the swinging cover feed-ways, which are extensions of the *feed guide*, that is located above and in line with the perforated plate.

The feed valve is driven by the *feed plate* lever; this also is attached to the swinging cover and is operated by the locks, using about one-eighth the stroke of the crank in its forward motion, thereby giving the valve ample time to hold both cartridge and shell down in position as they move in and out from the barrel. The *feed guide* is a simple plate having two parallel T-grooves, extending from end to end, their centers equidistant with the centers of the barrels. The upper end of the guide has a trumpet-shaped mouth, to facilitate the entrance of the cartridge heads. The lower end is provided with a cartridge stop, which lifts all cartridges contained in the guide when it is taken out from the swinging cover by which it is supported. The guide is held fast in firing position by a spring catch. It can be quickly released, by drawing back the spring catch by pressure on its exposed arm. In placing the guide in position, the spring catch becomes self-acting. These operations require but one hand, leaving the other free to place the safety-stop arm in position. The safety-stop is an oblong block having an angular face, against which the arm of the sector in the lock may engage when the locks are moved forward by the crank. It is held in position by two links which are moved by an arm that is pinned fast to a shaft passing through the rear case, to the outer end of which is pinned the stop arm. This arm is constructed in the form of a hand crank, having a stop spindle placed in its handle, behind the shoulder of which is placed a spiral spring that forces the spindle out from the arm into the stop holes, two in number, in the rear case. When the stop spindle is in the upper hole, the *arm* is in *line* with barrels, the safety stop is thrown within reach of the sector-arm by which the mainsprings are compressed, and the gun is in firing position. When the spindle is in the lower hole the stop is carried forward out of the way of the sector-arm, and in no case can the springs be compressed while the safety-stop arm is down.

LOADING AND FIRING.

The commands of the officer in charge of the gun are—I., Load; II., Fire; III., Cease firing.

At the command load, No. 1 steps to the gun, sees that it is properly pointed, then takes hold of the cascabel knob with his left, and the crank handle with his right hand. No. 2 steps forward, places feed guide, sees that safety-stop arm is in firing position. No. 3 steps forward, hands a block of cartridges to No. 2, who takes them in his left hand, inserts the cartridge head into the trumpet mouth of feed guide, steadying the block cover with his right hand as he forces the cartridges down the guide, until the cover is removed, when he pulls the block from the cartridges with a quick motion, throwing aside both block and cover. *At* the command fire, No. 1 turns the crank with a *steady motion*, No. 2 inserts the cartridges into the feed-guide, No. 3 hands the cartridges to No. 2. The cartridges may be taken from haversacks or from limber, using the fourth man to pass cartridges to No. 3. In this manner an unbroken fire is maintained for almost any length of time. *At* the command, cease firing, No. 2 takes out feed guide, puts safety stop arm down; No. 1 continues to turn crank until all the cartridges are out (in no case can there be more than 4), No. 1 and No. 2 and No. 3 return to their original positions, which will be dependent upon the field tactics of the nation using the gun.

TO DISMOUNT THE GUN.

1st. Unscrew cascabel far enough to relieve breech cover, swing over the same until it rests on barrel case. This will expose *all* working parts of the gun.

2nd. Drive out the pins that hold front and rear barrel rings: Force forward by the locks moved by the crank (using a shell or other article to lengthen the locks) the rear barrel ring into the enlarged part of the case. This will carry the barrels and front ring into such a position that they can be easily removed by hand, and the barrels be unscrewed from rear ring with a socket wrench.

(In replacing the barrels in the ring, see that it is done according to the number on each, for the extractor recesses in the barrels are unlike.)

3d. Take out ejectors by the knobs on their pins.

4th. Drop safety arm out of firing position. *Caution*.—This safety arm should in *all* cases be "down," except in *actual* firing. It is a sure preventive of accidents in careless handling of ammunition, also a relief for firing pins, and mainsprings.

5th. Take crank handle with right hand, turn main crank nearly to the top of U part of lock, grasp the lock at the small part, with the left hand, raise the front end enough to clear perforated plate, make a slight backward movement of lock with the hand crank, at the same time raise forward end until it swings clear of safety stop; this will allow the U part of lock to clear the crank. In returning locks to place, have crank uppermost, keep steady with right hand, place U part of lock over crank, and drop the lock into place.

6th. Grasp the crank and journal box with the right hand, the opposite journal box with the left hand, and raise them with the main crank, out of the recesses in the case. To remove the journal boxes from the crank, drive out the pins that hold hand crank and left hand box to the crank gudgeons, and remove by hand.

7th. Drive out the pin that holds the perforated plate to the case, move back and raise the plate.

8th. Turn out from the bottom of the case the screw that holds the cocking cam, and lift out the latter. Drive out the taper pin that holds the safety stop arm on the shaft, take out the shaft from the case, draw back and remove the safety stop.

TO ACCOMPANY ORDNANCE NOTES No. 124.

PLATE V.

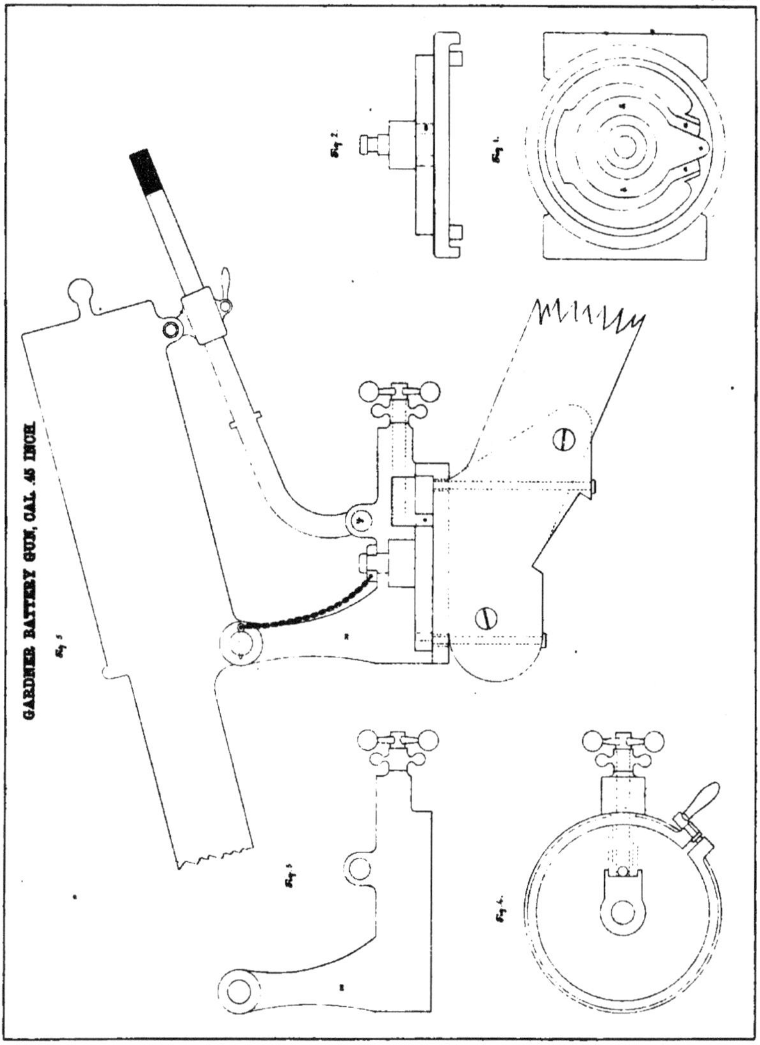

GARDNER BATTERY GUN, CAL. .45 INCH.

REPORT OF TRIAL AT WASHINGTON NAVY YARD.

ORDNANCE OFFICE, NAVY YARD,
WASHINGTON, D. C., June 24, 1879.

SIR: In obedience to your order of the 16th instant, convening a Board to conduct the experiments with the Gardner Machine Gun and Cartridges, presented by F. A. Pratt, Esq., we have the honor to report as follows:

The gun arrived at the Yard on the 16th June, and on the same day a careful examination of it was made by the Board, the gun being taken entirely to pieces, and its mechanism and working fully explained by Mr. Pratt.

The following description, with the accompanying drawings, will explain the changes and improvements, principally in the feeding device, that have been made in the gun since its trial in March, 1877.

After the cartridge has fallen through the feed guide (a) to the top of the feed valve (b), into which, as the valve passes out from under it, it is received and held in position by the abutment (c) and cartridge support (d), as the valve passes back again, the cartridge is forced downward by the angular sides of the feed valve (e) into the perforated plate (n), then held in a position beyond or lower than the point of the extractor (f), and when the lock (g) comes forward the cartridge is forced still farther down in line with the barrel (h) by the angle at the front of the feed valve.

The feed-plate lever (I) and ejector and abutment combined (i), also stop (K) on the bottom of the feed guide, are new. It will be observed that in the feed-plate lever and ejector there are no springs and the motion is positive. The cartridge support (d) is new, and holds the cartridge in position, so that the bullet cannot drop. The edges of the perforated plate (n) are of necessity parallel, which would allow the point of the cartridge to depress; hence the use of the said piece whose edge conforms to the shape or taper of the cartridge.

The advantages claimed for these improvements are—

1st. Keeping the cartridge in line of the barrels. 2d. In assisting gravity to bring the cartridge to a position where it cannot fail to enter the barrel. 3d. The certainty with which the empty shell is thrown out of the gun, after having been taken from the barrel by the extractor.

Hardened steel pieces have been introduced into the cams, and also in the locks when they take against the cams.

The trial of the gun took place on the 17th inst., ten thousand rounds being fired: The cartridges used (brass shell with reinforced folded head; outside primed; weight of ball four hundred and fifty grains; weight of powder charge seventy grains) were those of caliber 50, manufactured at Bridgeport, Conn., by the "Union Metallic Cartridge Co." The accompanying record shows in detail the working of the gun, and gives a full account of the experiments made; the maximum number of shots fired in one minute; all stoppages, their causes; and the condition of the gun at different times during, and at the conclusion of the firing.

The gun was not provided with spare locks or any other spare parts for use in case of failure or accident. The only circumstance, however, which interfered to prevent the completely successful working of the gun, occurred after four thousand six hundred and fifty charges had been fired, when the extractor of the right lock failed to extract an empty shell from the right hand barrel. Several similar failures occurring in quick succession, and there being no spare lock to replace this one, it was found necessary to take it out and stiffen the extractor, and also file its hook slightly. After this had been done, the experiments were continued, and the remainder of the ammunition was fired without any further trouble, the gun working perfectly in every respect.

The ease with which this gun is worked deserves special notice. The crank is turned with little effort, and the speed of firing is only dependent upon the rapidity with which the person turning it can make his hand revolve.

The jacket covering the barrels, while it would act as a good protector in case of rough usage, has some disadvantages; the principal of which is in its confinement of the heat when the gun is being worked. It should be perforated to allow the free access of air to the barrels, and should also be fitted so that it could be readily removed if required.

As the gun is at present, it is necessary to take out all of its working parts before the barrels can be removed. The barrels should be fitted so that they could be removed from the gun without interfering with any other parts of its machinery.

The gun is exceedingly simple in device and light in construction, weighing, with its tripod, two hundred and one pounds, and without the tripod, one hundred and forty-seven pounds.

The cartridges come from the Cartridge Company in wooden boxes, each containing one thousand rounds put up in paper boxes, twenty cartridges in a box. They were here transferred to the wooden feeding blocks, with tin covers, peculiar to the Gardner system. The space occupied by a thousand cartridges thus put was to the space occupied by the same number in the paper boxes, nearly in the ratio of nine to seven, increasing the weight of one thousand cartridges, exclusive of weight of wooden packing boxes, by fourteen pounds. All of the faults noted in the gun were those of construction; and the general results of the experiments were highly satisfactory in every respect.

We are, sir, your obedient servants,

H. L. HOWISON, Commander, U. S. N.
R. D. HITCHCOCK, Lieutenant, U .S. N.
T. C. McLEAN, Lieutenant, U. S. N.

To Commodore WILLIAM N. JEFFERS,
Chief of Bureau of Ordnance, Navy Department.

NOTE.—All alterations suggested in this report have been made, with such additional improvements in the extracting mechanism as will overcome all difficulties.

TO ACCOMPANY ORDNANCE NOTES No. 124.

PLATE I.

TARGET RECORD. 2 BARREL GARDNER BATTERY GUN, CAL. .45 INCH.

At Sandy Hook, N. J., January 7 th, 1880.

Target 200 Yards from Gun.

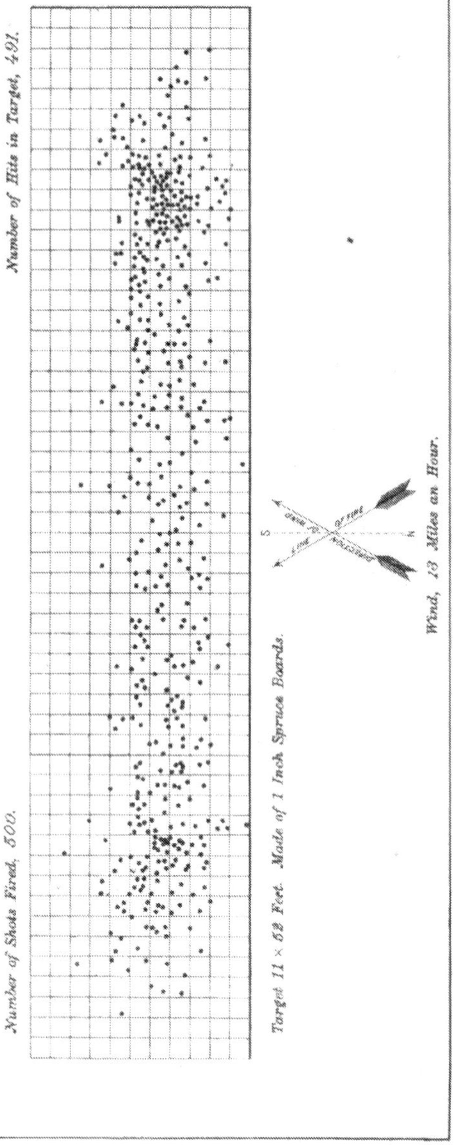

Number of Shots Fired, 500.

Number of Hits in Target, 491.

Target 11 × 52 Feet. Made of 1 Inch Spruce Boards.

Wind, 13 Miles an Hour.

RECORD OF FIRING OF THE GARDNER BATTERY GUN, WASHINGTON NAVY YARD, JUNE 17, 1879.

REMARKS.

The gun was mounted on its tripod, thirty feet from the butt, and laid level.

Mr. F. A. Pratt, assisted by Messrs. Saunders and Whitney, represented the proprietors of the gun.

The mechanism of the gun was explained, and the locks were taken out and lightly lubricated with tallow.

Two hundred cartridges were fired at the rate of 429 per minute. Mr. Whitney at the crank, and Mr. Saunders feeding.

The gun was then examined and found to be in good condition.

The ammunition in two boxes was placed on the ground, at the left of the gun.

One thousand cartridges were fired in three minutes, forty-one seconds, which is at the rate of 271 per minute.

One ordnance man was at the crank, and two ordnance men were feeding. All parts worked smoothly.

The gun had a slight motion in a vertical plane, owing principally to the working of the feet of the tripod.

There was no perceptible motion in a horizontal plane.

The barrel cover was quite hot. The small amount of fouling on the locks and extractors was kept soft by the tallow.

An ammunition box was placed on the ground to the left of the gun.

Two ordnance men were feeding, and Mr. Saunders was at the crank; 431 cartridges were fired in one minute. The barrel cover was very hot, and a cartridge taken from the right barrel was too hot to be held in the hand.

The fouling of the locks and extractors was light and soft. The barrels were moderately foul. Owing to the limited number of feeding blocks, there was some delay in preparing ammunition for continuance of trial. Commenced firing, with the intention of firing 5,000 cartridges without stopping.

The ordnance men relieving at the crank, and two feeding from ammunition boxes on the ground to the left of the gun.

Fired 3,019 cartridges in eight minutes, thirty seconds, which is at the rate of 355 per minute.

A cartridge failed to extract from the right barrel when the men were changing at the crank. Backed out the cartridge with a cleaning rod. Examinations made of extractor. Delay of one minute, twenty-five seconds. Cartridge failed to extract from the right barrel, and was backed out as before.

One hundred and three cartridges were fired in fifteen seconds. Delay, one minute, sixteen seconds. Cartridges failed to extract from right barrel after firing 259 in forty-two seconds, which is at the rate of 370 per minute.

The locks were taken out and the extractors carefully examined. The extractor hooks were in good condition, but the shank of the right extractor seemed less stiff than that of the left one. The extractor recess in the barrel, and the grooves in the locks for the extractor shanks were only moderately foul.

The barrels were very foul. As each failure had occurred with the right extractor, it was evident that the ammunition was not at fault, and it was decided to go on with the trial.

Fired 694 cartridges in one minute, forty-two seconds, which is at the rate of 408 per minute.

Cartridge failed to extract from right barrel. Thoroughly cleaned the extractor recess in right barrel. Delay, one minute, three seconds.

In one minute and five seconds, fired 420 cartridges at the rate of 388 per minute.

Cartridge failed to extract from right barrel.

Cleared out the chamber of right barrel. Delay, fifty-three seconds.

In one minute, twenty seconds, fired 430 cartridges at the rate of 323 per minute.

Cartridge failed to extract from right barrel. Delay, forty-five seconds.

In eight seconds, fired seventy-five cartridges at the rate of 563 per minute.

Total time of firing 5,000 cartridges, twenty-five minutes, fifty-three seconds.

Time including delay for examination of locks and extractors at eleven hours, forty-six seconds, nineteen minutes, one second.

TO ACCOMPANY ORDNANCE NOTES No. 124.

PLATE II.

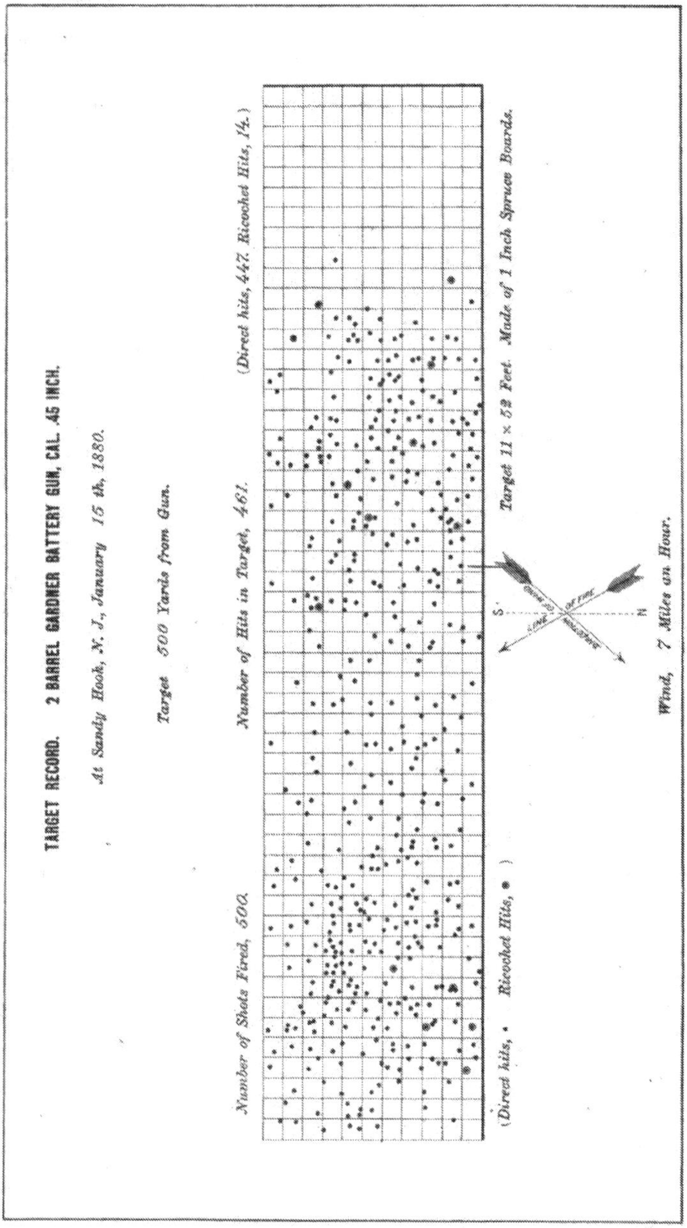

TARGET RECORD. 2 BARREL GARDNER BATTERY GUN, CAL. .45 INCH.

At Sandy Hook, N. J., January 15 th, 1880.

Target 500 Yards from Gun.

Number of Shots Fired, 500. *Number of Hits in Target, 461.* *(Direct hits, 447. Ricochet Hits, 14.)*

(Direct hits, • Ricochet Hits, ●)

Target 11 × 52 Feet. Made of 1 Inch Spruce Boards.

Wind, 7 Miles an Hour.

Longest delay (except that at eleven hours, forty-six minutes, sixteen seconds,) one minute, twenty-five seconds.

The gun was carefully examined. The barrels were very foul and very hot. The cover or jacket for the barrels was also very hot, charring paper and pine splinters.

The working parts were moderately foul, but in excellent working order, with the exception of the right extractor, which appeared to have not enough stiffness in the shank. Permission was given to the exhibitors to take out the locks and put the right extractor in working order. The hook of the right extractor was filed slightly, and the shank was bent in a little more toward the lock.

Gave the ordnance men their noon hour.

Two thousand cartridges were fired in one series for rapidity. Before commencing the firing the jacket for the barrels was still too warm to be borne by the hand.

Three ordnance men at the crank and two feeding. At one hour, twenty-four minutes, twenty seconds, there was a delay of eight seconds owing to awkwardness of the men feeding.

In five minutes, sixteen seconds (excluding the eight seconds delay), 2,000 cartridges were fired at the rate of 380 per minute.

One hundred cartridges were fired for rapidity in eleven seconds, which is at the rate of 545 per minute.

Mr. Whitney was at the crank, and two ordnance men were feeding. About two quarts of water were poured through the barrels, which were then swabbed out, and the gun moved to the sea wall, where it was mounted on its tripod, and depressed to an angle of twenty-nine degrees. With two ordnance men feeding and one at the crank, 430 cartridges were fired in one minute; gun in good condition and working smoothly.

With three ordnance men at the crank and two feeding, using the full traverse motion, in two minutes, fourteen seconds, 839 cartridges were fired at the rate of 376 per minute. The gun was carefully examined, and found in good working condition.

The barrels were very foul and very hot, but the working parts were only moderately foul and worked as smoothly as at the beginning of the trial.

During the whole of the trial a light breeze blowing across the line of fire (from right to left) carried the smoke clear of the men serving the gun. Ten thousand cartridges were fired during this trial.

ORDNANCE NOTES.—NO. 124.

WASHINGTON, MARCH 17, 1880.

GARDNER MACHINE GUN.

[6 Plates.]

TRIAL OF THE GARDNER MACHINE GUN BY THE ORDNANCE BOARD, U. S. A., COMPOSED OF LIEUTENANT-COLONELS S. CRISPIN AND T. G. BAYLOR AND MAJOR CLIFTON COMLY, ORDNANCE DEPARTMENT.

PLATE IV.

The Gardner gun, as submitted to the Board and as shown with its carriage on the drawings herewith transmitted, consists of two breech-loading rifled barrels, calibre .45, chambered for the service cartridge, placed horizontally and parallel, 1.4 inches apart, which with the working mechanism are inclosed in a brass casing. By one complete turn of the hand crank both barrels are loaded, fired, and the shells ejected. The barrels are held in position by rear and front barrel rings pinned to the case. The casing extends sufficiently from the rear barrel ring to contain the lock mechanism, together with the *driving crank* and *safety stop*. A swinging cover, hinged immediately over the rear barrel ring, gives easy access to all working parts of the gun in case of defective cartridges, derangements of locks, or other accident. The cover when closed is secured in position by a few turns of the cascabel, which for that purpose has a screw-thread cut on its neck or stem entering the rear of the case. The hand-crank that operates the gun is pinned fast to the *main crank*, which is supported by journal boxes. The boxes are locked into the rear case, and serve as a protection to the swinging cover from side thrusts. The body of the *main crank* is circular, having journals or crank-pins for operating the locks diametrically opposite each other—the firing being alternate—and eccentric enough to give the required motion to the locks as they are moved forward and back, driving in cartridges and withdrawing shells. The outer portion of the crank-pins or journals are flattened to the circle of the periphery of the main crank for the purpose of holding the lock stationary while firing, about one-fifth part of the revolution of hand-crank allowing times for *hang-fires*. The lock in form resembles the letter U, having an extension from its side, which contains the *firing-pin*, *main* (spiral) *spring*, *sector* or *spring-compressor*, *sector-sleeve*, *extractor*, and *lock-head*. The U part of the lock that works under and around the crank-pin is curved at the inner front to correspond with the outer circle of the crank, the office of the curved front being to hold the lock in position for firing. The circular firing-pin is flattened a portion of its length near the front end, to allow it to pass under the extractor, by which it is held in position. It extends from the head of the lock through the mainspring and sector-sleeve, terminating in a flange or head for locking into the sear. The *sear*, having the form of a bell-crank, pivoted in the center to the lock, holds the firing-pin securely and prevents its forward motion until it is released from its hold by the action of the crank-journal when the lock is in its extreme forward position.

The sector or spring-compressor, hinged in a recess of the lock and engaging by means of gear-teeth with the sector-sleeve, has its arm forced against the safety-stop as the main crank advances, thus compressing, through the medium of the sector-sleeve, the mainspring and holding it tense until released by action of the sear.

The lock-heads serve as breech-plugs, and receive the recoil when the cartridges are fired. Each lock carries a *hook extractor*, which rides over and catches the flange of the cartridge when the lock is forced forward, and when the lock retreats withdraws the empty shell until it comes within reach of the ejector, by which it is positively thrown out. The shell-starters have a positive movement in connection with the lock-head. Should the cartridge be driven by the extractor into the barrel to its head (as is the case when the gun is worked rapidly) before the lock is in firing position, it is forced from the chamber by the shell-starter as the lock advances and is held long enough for the extractor to engage with the head, when the lock, extractor, and cartridge are driven home together.

The *ejectors*, hinged to the case, are driven by projections on the sides of the locks, which give them lateral movements to eject the empty shells, or full cartridges in case of miss-fires. They

TARGET RECORD. 2 BARREL GARDNER BATTERY GUN, CAL. .45 INCH.

At Sandy Hook, N. J., January 16 th, 1880.

Target 1,000 Yards from Gun.

Number of Shots Fired, 500. *Number of Hits in Target, 260.* *(Direct hits, 235. Ricochet Hits, 25.)*

(Direct hits, • Ricochet Hits, ●) *Target 11 × 52 Feet. Made of 1 Inch Spruce Boards.*

Wind, 3 Miles an Hour.

also serve as stops to prevent the cartridges from falling through the perforated plate as they are forced down through the feed valve.

The perforated plate extending across the rear case, to which it is fastened by a pin, has two parallel semi-circular grooves, which are enlarged *extensions* of the chambers in the barrels. From the back part of the groove slots large enough to pass freely the cartridge (being wider at the rear behind the ejector than at the front) are cut downward through the plate. When the retractor has drawn the shell back nearly to the extent of the throw of the crank the ejector forces the shell through the slot, and is then in position to receive another cartridge from the feed plate or valve. The feed valve, attached to the swinging cover, has a reciprocating motion across the perforated plate. It has two angular openings of the size and shape of the outline of the cartridge, with centers equidistant with centers of the barrels. After a cartridge has dropped one-half its diameter into the valve it is forced by the action of the latter into its true position and held positively against the *cartridge support.* When the valve is again moved back the cartridge is forced downward into the perforated plate and the column of cartridges is cut off in the swinging cover-feed ways, which are extensions of the *feed guide* that is located above and in line with the perforated plate.

The feed valve is driven by the *feed plate* lever. This also is attached to the swinging cover and is operated by the locks, using about one-eighth the stroke of the crank in its forward motion, thereby giving the valve time to hold both cartridge and shell down in position as they move in and out from the barrel. The *feed guide* is a simple plate, having two parallel T grooves extending from end to end, their centers equidistant with the centers of the barrels The upper end of the guide has a trumpet-shaped mouth, to facilitate the entrance of the cartridge heads. The lower end is provided with a cartridge stop, which lifts all cartridges contained in the guide when it is taken out from the swinging cover by which it is supported. The guide is held fast in firing position by a spring catch. It can be quickly released by drawing back the spring catch by pressure on its exposed arm. In placing the guide in position the spring catch becomes self-acting. These operations require but one hand, leaving the other free to place the safety-stop arm in position. The safety-stop is an oblong block having an angular face, against which the arm of the sector in the lock may engage when the locks are moved forward by the crank. It is held in position by two links, which are moved by an arm that is pinned fast to a shaft passing through the rear case, to the outer end of which is pinned the stop-arm. This arm is constructed in the form of a hand crank, having a stop spindle placed in its handle, behind the shoulder of which is placed a spiral spring that forces the spindle out from the arm into the stop-holes, two in number, in the rear case. When the top spindle is in the upper hole the *arm is in line* with barrels, the safety-stop is thrown within reach of the sector arm, by which the main-springs are compressed, and the gun is in firing position. When the spindle is in the lower hole the stop is carried forward out of the way of the sector arm, and in no case can the springs be compressed while the safety arm is down

The cartridges are contained in perforated wooden blocks (holding twenty each), channeled on the sides for receiving the fitted tin covers in the manner adapted to the Gardner gun. The cartridges thus arranged are simply and readily conveyed through the feed guider to the gun, and as the block is emptied before the cartridges previously inserted are expended a continuous fire can be sustained.

In the service of the gun three men are required; one at the lever and turning the crank, one inserting and withdrawing the cartridge blocks, the other in passing cartridges properly fitted in their blocks.

Carriage.

Plate V.

The distinctive feature of the carriage lies in the bed-plate, with its arrangement for oscillation, and in the manner of attaching or mounting the gun For the latter purpose the frame fitted to the bed-plate has at its forward portion a projecting arm (x) bored at the upper end for attachment by an ordinary pinned hinge to the casing of the gun at a point just below the rear barrel rings The second attachment is at the rear of the casing by means of a sliding clamp to the elevating (and oscillating) lever, which in its turn is attached to the plate at the point (y).

Oscillation and Field of Fire.

PLATE V.

The bed-plate holds a spring (a, Fig. 1) by means of which the oscillation of the gun can be increased or diminished, as follows: The lug c, Fig. 5, which governs the lateral motion of the gun, has a screw attached to the upper end, this screw passing through to the rear of the bed-plate and arranged with an adjustable handle and stay-nut. When the lug is drawn by the screw to its rearmost point the lug enters the semi-circular notch c, Fig. 1, and side motion of the gun is checked; as the lug is pushed forward by running in the screw, the lever being worked from side to side, it strikes the sides of the springs, (a, a,) the amplitude of the oscillation increasing as the lug is pushed forward, until passing the spring it reaches the circular channel k, where it is checked by a stop-pin when the gun has the full range of the horizon. When in this position the lateral motion can be checked at any point by using the clamp R, Fig. 4, encircling the rim s, Fig. 1, which, being a part of the bed-plate and attached to the carriage, is immovable.

Results of Firing.

Twenty cartridges, fired for the purpose, gave an average initial velocity of 1,280 feet. A test for rapidity of fire gave an average of 357 per minute.

The target firing at targets of spruce boards, 11x52 feet, resulted as follows:

At 200 yards, 98.20 per cent. of hits.
At 500 yards, 92.20 per cent. of hits.
At 1,000 yards, 52 per cent. of hits.

There were no miss-fires, and the gun worked evenly and well.

TO ACCOMPANY ORDNANCE NOTES No. 124.

PLATE IV.

GARDNER BATTERY GUN, CAL .45 INCH,

Top view, with breech cover open showing all working parts of gun.

Vertical Section.

Recommendation.

The trials of this gun at Sandy Hook having shown it to be one of simple construction, easily manipulated, and of sure action, (though of less rapidity of fire than other machine guns heretofore tested by the Board,) and in view of the fact that its cost, for a machine gun, will be comparatively light, the Board would recommend the purchase by the Department of a limited number for actual trial in service, as compared to other machine guns now in the hands of troops.

Nomenclature of the Gardner Gun.

PLATE I.

1. Main case.
2. Breech cover.
3. Breech cover pin.
4. Breech cover pin washer.
5. Cascabel.
6. Cascabel screw.
7. Barrels.
8. Front barrel ring.
9. Rear barrel ring
10. Rear barrel ring pin.
11. Front barrel ring taper pin.
12. Main crank.
13. Main crank steel pieces.
14. Main crank steel pieces screws.
15. Main crank journal boxes.
17. Hand crank
18. Hand crank handle.
19. Hand crank handle spindle.
20. Hand crank handle spindle nut.
21. Hand crank taper pin.
22. Feed valve.
23. Feed valve guide
24. Feed valve guide screws.
25. Feed valve lever.
26. Feed valve lever slide.
27. Feed valve pivot screw.
28. Perforated plate.
29. Perforated plate taper pin.
30. Perforated plate cartridge support.
31. Perforated plate cartridge support screws.
32. Shell starters.
33. Shell starter pin.
34. Ejectors.
35. Ejector pin.
36. Lock frame.
37. Lock frame head.
38. Lock frame truck.
39. Lock frame truck pin.
40. Lock frame sectors.
41. Lock frame sector pin.
42. Lock frame sector sleeve.
43. Sear.
44. Sear pin.
45. Sear spring.
46. Sear spring pin.
47. Sector stop pin.
48. Firing pin.
49. Mainspring.
50. Extractors.
51. Extractor pin.
52. Safety stop.
53. Safety stop link.
54. Safety stop link pin.
55. Safety stop lever.
56. Safety stop shaft.
57. Safety stop shaft taper pin.
58. Safety stop arm.
59. Safety stop arm stop.
60. Safety stop arm stop head.
61. Safety stop arm stop spring.
62. Safety stop arm stop head pin.
63. Cocking cam.
64. Front sight.
65. Rear sight bar.
66. Rear sight guide.
67. Rear sight pinion.
68. Rear sight pinion head.
69. Rear sight pinion head pin.
70. Rear sight guide screws.
71. Rear sight tension spring.
72. Feed guide.
73. Feed guide catch.
74. Feed guide catch pin.
75. Feed guide catch spring.
76. Feed guide cartridge stop.
77. Feed guide cartridge stop pin.
78. Feed guide cartridge stop slide.
79. Feed guide cartridge stop slide spring.
80. Feed guide cartridge stop slide pin.

Weight of gun, 142 pounds.
Weight of gun and carriage, 502 pounds.

No. 1.
Total number of hits on target, 491.

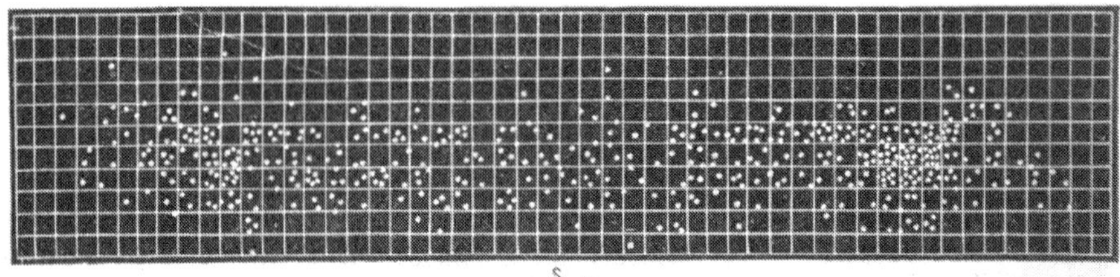

Distance, 200 yards.

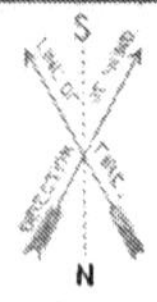

Wind, thirteen miles an hour.

No. 2.
Total number of hits on target, 461.

Distance, 500 yards.

Wind, seven miles an hour.

No. 3.
Total number of hits on target, 260.

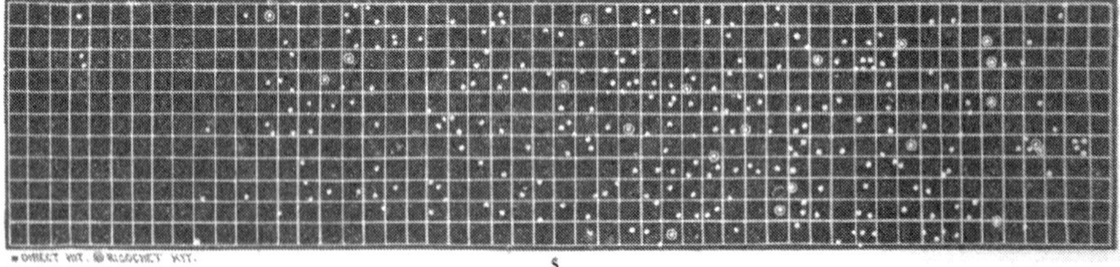

Distance, 1,000 yards.

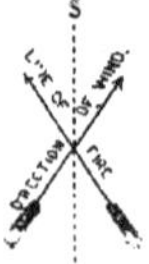

Wind, three miles an hour.

TARGET RECORD OF THE IMPROVED GARDNER BATTERY GUN—Cal. 45,
As tested by the U. S. Ordnance Bureau at Sandy Hook, N. J., Jan. 15, 1880.

TARGET RECORD OF FIRING WITH CAL. .45 GARDNER MACHINE GUN, AT SANDY HOOK, N. Y. HARBOR, FROM OCTOBER 31, 1879, TO JANUARY 29, 1880.

	No. of cartridges fired.	Date.	Ammunition.	Time of firing.	Initial velocity feet.	Wind, strength and direction.	By whom fired.	Remarks.	Special remarks.
	500	Oct. 31, 1879 ...	Bridgeport brass shells,	1′ 22½″.	....	S; LINE OF FIRE; DIRECTION OF WIND	Saunders, an expert..	Fired deliberately into sand butt to test mechanism of gun.	Before firing, the gun was taken apart by an expert; barrels being taken off and inside mechanism taken out and then put together again, ready for firing. Time taking apart, 1′ 2″. Time putting together, 1′ 21″. After firing the 4th series of 500 rounds, the gun was again taken apart while hot, and after cooling the disk at, and the rear end of barrels, was put together again. Time taking apart, 1′ 14″. Putting together, 1′ 43″. During the firing considerable more effort was required to work the gun when using the Frankford ammunition than when using the Bridgport. Three men required to work gun, one to turn crank and oscillate, one to pass ammunition, and the other to feed it. The gun was not cleaned during the firing, and there were no halts or delays owing to defects of mechanism, and no failures to extract. The firing of 500 rounds for rapidity, with either cartridge, required about all the effort one man could make.
	500	Oct. 31, 1879. ...	Frankford copper shells,	.. . .	....				
	500	Oct. 31, 1879.....	Bridgeport brass shells,	1′ 39″.	....		New hand.		
	500	Oct. 31, 1879.....	Frankford copper shells,	1′ 28″.	....		New hand		
	500	Oct. 31, 1879.....	Bridgeport brass shells,	1′ 17″	....		Saunders, an expert...	Fired into sand butt for rapidity.	
	100	Oct. 31, 1879	Bridgeport brass shells,	13″	....		New hand		
	100	Oct. 31, 1879. ..	Bridgeport brass shells,	12½″	....				
	100	Oct. 31, 1879	Frankford copper shells,	12⅝″	....		Saunders, an expert..		
Barometer, 30.347; thermometer, 44, rel. humidity, 76 per cent.; wind, 13 miles an hour.	500	Jan. 7, 1880......	Bridgeport brass shells.	1′ 41″	....		....	Fired at 200-yard target. Target 11 by 52 feet, made of 1 inch spruce boards. Total number of hits in target, 451.	
Barometer, 30.256; thermometer, 42; rel. humidity, 82 per cent.; wind, 7 miles an hour.	11	Jan. 15, 1880. ...	Bridgeport brass shells,	....	....		....	Fired at 500-yard target; sighting shots.	
	500	Jan. 15, 1880.....	Bridgeport brass shells,	1′ 24″.......	....		....	Fired at 500-yard target. Target 11 by 52 feet, made of 1-inch spruce boards. Total number of hits in target, 461 Direct hits, 447. Ricochet hits, 14.	
Barometer, 30.225; thermometer, 38; rel. humidity, 72 per cent.; wind, 3 miles an hour.	32	Jan. 16, 1880. ...	Bridgeport brass shells,	....	....		....	Fired at 1,000 yard target, sighting shots.	
	500	Jan. 16, 1880. ...	Bridgeport brass shells,	2′ 03″	....		....	Fired at 1,000-yard target. Target 11 by 52 feet, made of 1 inch spruce boards. Total number of hits in target, 260. Direct hits, 235. Ricochet hits, 25.	
	1	Jan. 29, 1880. ...	Bridgeport brass shells,	....	1249		....		
	1	Jan. 29, 1880.....	Bridgeport brass shells,	....	1267		....		
	1	Jan. 29, 1880. ...	Bridgeport brass shells,	....	1320		....		
	1	Jan. 29, 1880. ...	Bridgeport brass shells,	....	1290		....		
	1	Jan. 29, 1880.....	Bridgeport brass shells,	....	1306		....		
	1	Jan. 29, 1880.....	Bridgeport brass shells,	....	1296		....		
	1	Jan. 29, 1880.....	Bridgeport brass shells,	....	1303		....		
	1	Jan. 29, 1880. ...	Bridgeport brass shells,	....	1293		....		
	1	Jan. 29, 1880.....	Bridgeport brass shells,	.. . .	1288		....		
	1	Jan. 29, 1880.....	Bridgeport brass shells,	....	1311		....		
					Average, 12[illegible].3.				
	1	Jan. 29, 1880. ...	Frankford copper shells,	....	1264		....	Fired into sand butt for velocities.	
	1	Jan. 29, 1880.....	Frankford copper shells,	....	1267		....		
	1	Jan. 29, 1880.....	Frankford copper shells,	....	1257		....		
	1	Jan. 29, 1880. ...	Frankford copper shells,	....	1266		....		
	1	Jan. 29, 1880. ...	Frankford copper shells,	....	1258		....		
	1	Jan. 29, 1880.....	Frankford copper shells,	....	1261		....		
	1	Jan. 29, 1880.....	Frankford copper shells,	....	1275		....		
	1	Jan. 29, 1880.....	Frankford copper shells,	....	1261		....		
	1	Jan. 29, 1880.....	Frankford copper shells,	....	1266		....		
	1	Jan. 29, 1880.....	Frankford copper shells,	....	1270	N	....		
					Average, 1261.5.				

ORDNANCE OFFICE,
WASHINGTON, March 17, 1880.

Publication authorized by the SECRETARY OF WAR.

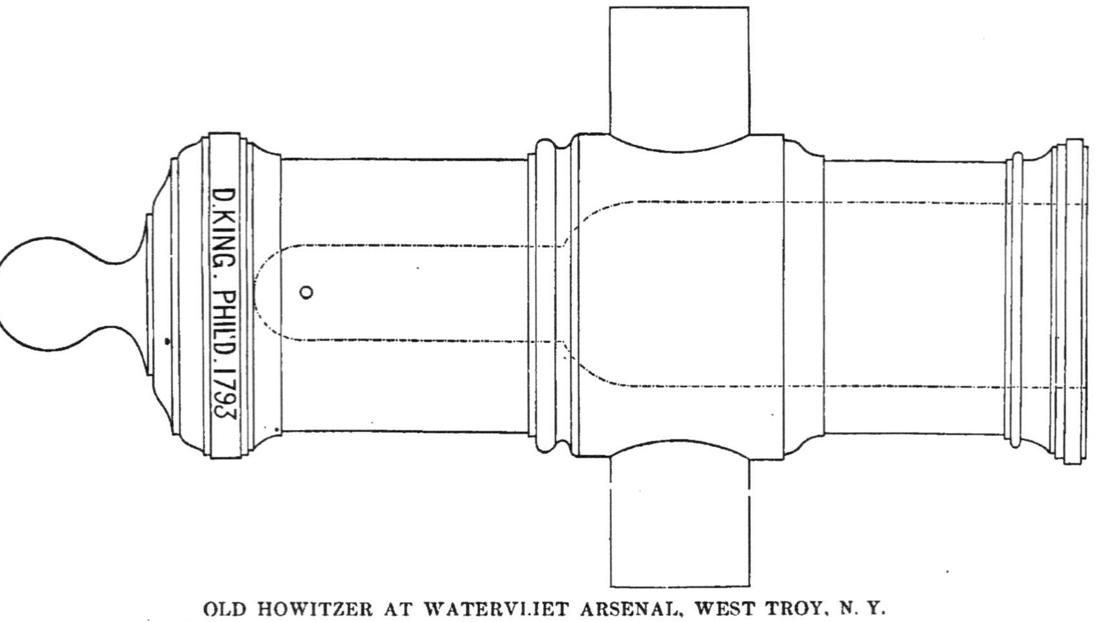

OLD HOWITZER AT WATERVLIET ARSENAL, WEST TROY, N. Y.

CHAPTER XIII.

HEAVY ORDNANCE—WEST POINT FOUNDRY—SOUTH BOSTON IRON COMPANY.

The manufacture of ordnance to any extent in the United States dates back to about the period of the Revolution; previous to that time such small cannon as were in use on the forts were brought over from England, Holland and France. The first positive evidence of the casting of cannon for the Provinces was the manufacture by Henry Leonard at his foundry in Lynn, Mass., as early as 1647; in 1648 there is also a record of the casting of iron and brass cannon at Orr's Foundry, at Bridgewater. The Hope Furnace was established in 1735 in Rhode Island. In 1739 the following pieces of ordnance were ordered from England for the fortification of New York: Fifteen 32-pounders, twenty-four 18 pounders, nine 12-pounders, ten 9-pounders, eighteen 6-pounders.

In 1775 sixty heavy cannon were ordered by the State of Rhode Island and were cast at the Hope Foundry. In 1776 the Board ordered cast either of bronze or iron, six 6-pounders, six 12-pounders, four eight-inch howitzers, four six-inch howitzers, six Coehorn mortars.

The heaviest guns used at this period were 18-pounders. Foundries were established for casting cannon in Massachusetts and Pennsylvania; Daniel Joy of Reading, Pa., turning out one 9-pounder daily. In Salisbury, Conn., the Committee of Safety expended £1,450, in fitting up a furnace to cast cannon and shot, employing fifty nine men where guns were made from 4 to 32-pounders, and mostly supplied to the navy. In 1776 Silas Deane as agent for the Provincial Government purchased in France two hundred brass cannon, and twenty-four mortars; at about the same period the Massachusetts Committee of Safety resolved "that £43 1s. 10d. be paid in full to Preserved Clap; and whereas said Clap says that he has invented a machine for boring cannon, therefore, resolved that if said Clap will exhibit a plan or model to Hugh Orr, Esq., and a committee, if satisfactory will grant adequate pay."

In 1794 an estimate was submitted by General Knox, Secretary of War, for the casting of two hundred cannon for the fortifications of the United States at a cost of $96,745, 32-pounders to be nine feet six inches in length from the hind part of the bore ring to the extremity of the muzzle, with a total weight of 5,500 pounds; 24-pounders, length nine feet, and weight 5,000 pounds. The same for the navy, eight feet, with a weight of 4,500 pounds. A contract was also made with the Hope Furnace "for 34-inch cannon to carry a 32-pound ball at the cost of $106.66 for every ton weight of said cannon as the same shall weigh when bored. The cannon to be cast solidly with a spruce head of metal of at least 500 pounds weight, and to be bored out with machinery, each cannon to be proved by two successive discharges."

In 1790 one William Denning made wrought iron cannon of iron staves, hooped like a barrel, with wrought iron bands firmly bound together and then boxed and breeched; one of these guns captured by the English may be seen in the Tower of London. The only authentic piece of ordnance of these early dates, now in existence in this country, is a small Howitzer made by Daniel King, 68 South Front street, Philadelphia, 1793, and of this through the courtesy of Capt. J. G. Butler, Ordnance Department, an illustration is herewith given. Several of these guns may be seen at the Watervliet Arsenal, West Troy, N. Y. They are supposed to have been ordered by Gen. Anthony Wayne for special purposes.

In 1795 Secretary of War Pickering authorized the securing of the services of experienced iron founders from abroad, and the following estimate was made as to the cost of 1,300 cannon:

One hundred	32-pounders,	$420 each,	$42,000
Two hundred	24-pounders,	350 each,	72,000
Two hundred	18-pounders,	318 each,	63,600
Three hundred	12-pounders,	211 each,	63,000
Three hundred	9-pounders,	140 each,	42,000
Two hundred	6-pounders,	130 each,	26,000
			$308,900

By this time foundries were established in nearly all the States and actively at work turning out small calibre guns. In 1798 a bill was offered in Congress for the establishment of a national foundry for cannon, and the President was authorized to take or lease one or more suitable places for the purpose. In 1811 The Committee of Congress on arms, ammunition, etc., reported "the foundries in Rhode Island, Pennsylvania, Maryland, District of Columbia, etc., as having arrived at perfection, the art of boring cannon being so well understood that our inspector of artillery has declared to the world 'he never was compelled to reject a gun on account of a defect in the bore, although he examined upwards of two thousand cannon of different calibres.'"

An estimate was made that it would cost $30,000 to establish a national foundry at Washington, but the successful working of the various private foundries established at heavy cost prevented any action being taken. In this same year the Congressional Committee reported that the government had on hand, 462 brass pieces; 1,876 iron pieces, of which 201 were 24-pounders, and 277 were 32-pounders; 46,677 grape strapped and canister shot of all sizes; 217,652 cannon balls of various sizes; 378,719 pounds of grape shot; 486,064 pounds of powder.

In 1812 the Board of Ordnance was established, and in 1816 the Navy Department made contracts with the foundries to secure supplies for eight guns with the assurance that said foundries should have permanent work. In 1816 a contract was made with John Mason to supply thirty-two 42-pounders at $125 per ton; thirty-six 32-pounders at $135 per ton; twenty-four 32-carronades at $135 each; 130 tons round shot, five cents per pound; 60 tons grape shot eight cents per pound; this contract to include turning and chiseling at $8 per ton.

In 1818 Col. Bomford, Chief of Ordnance made a contract with R. L. Stevens of Hoboken, N. J, for 2,000 elongated shells, the manufacture of the shells to be a secret between said Stevens and the Secretary of Navy. At about this time brass cannon were made at the Government Arsenal, Watervliet.

In 1819 foundries were established in Ariel Co., Maryland, near Washington, and at Richmond, Va, with a capacity of three hundred pieces of artillery a year. In 1825 experiments were made in London with steam artillery, invented by Jacob Perkins, an American, with a result showing the discharge of balls at the rate of 1,000 per minute, iron targets shattered to atoms, and eleven planks each one inch thick placed at a distance from each other were pierced by balls fired in this manner, but no practical result has ever been arrived at. At the com-

BREECH-LOADING RIFLED CANNON FOR NAVAL USE.

Manufactured at the West Point Foundry, Cold Spring, on the Hudson.
Paulding, Kemble & Co., Proprietors.

commencement of the late war there were in the possession of the War Department 1,052 pieces of siege and coast artillery of all calibres, 231 pieces of field artillery. The Navy Department had on hand 2,966 guns of all calibres, of which 1,872 were 32-pounders of different patterns, 107 12-pounders, 29 24-pounders, 575 8-inch guns, 27 10-inch guns, and 30 9-inch Dahlgrens.

The interest shown by the Ordnance Bureau in the subject at the present time is clearly indicated by the following extracts from the reports of the Chief of Ordnance:

Report of Chief of Ordnance, 1873.

"In my last report attention was specially invited to the absolute necessity of provision being made for the armament of our sea coast defenses. The importance of the subject increases with the earnest and continued efforts on the part of all nations not only to improve the quality of their guns, but in providing in quantities those that have given best results in experimental trials.

Large grain powder for heavy guns was first adopted by this Department in 1861, at a time when other nations continued the use of small grain. This great improvement in the mode of manufacture was the result of careful study and experiment by the late Gen. Rodman, who successfully used it in his first 15-inch gun. This and his invention of "perforated cake" powder, which has been adopted by and is now in use in both Russia and Germany, and the "pebble" powder similar to our "mammoth" adopted by England, created that revolution in the manufacture of gunpowder, based upon purely scientific principles of combustion and evolution of gases, that has enabled all nations to increase the size of their ordnance."

Report of Chief of Ordnance, 1874.

"I desire to call attention to the fact that the first grand strike toward the introduction of great guns in any service was made in this country by the late General Rodman of the Ordnance Dapartment, whose reputation as an ordnance officer is world-wide, and that the 15-inch gun he first made in 1861 was the most powerful weapon then known, soon to be surpassed by his 20-inch smooth bore made in 1864, weighing 116,000 pounds and throwing a shot weighing 1,080 pounds. * * * In this country the success of the Ordnance Department in improving the quality of our cast iron for cannon has been marked and satisfactory, and we may lay claim with good reason, to the best cast-iron guns in the world."

Report of Chief of Ordnance, 1875.

"Since the report on the 8-inch rifle was made, the Board has continued its trials with that gun; and up to the present time it has been successfully fired 700 rounds with battering charges and still remains "sound and serviceable," giving an endurance that fully justifies the recommendations of the Board, and my approval, that our large number of smooth-bore guns ought to be converted into rifles, as it is entirely practicable to give the requisite strength and consequent endurance by the invention of a wrought-iron tube. Additional proof of the correctness of this decision is found in the results obtained by the firing of the 9-inch rifle (10-inch Rodman lined with wrought-iron tube) which has thus far sustained 250 rounds with battering charges of 40 to 45 pounds of hexagonal powder, and shot of 200 to 247 pounds weight, the gun remaining sound and in good condition. * * * We have the best cast-iron metal known, and this plan of conversion enables us to utilize our own products. * * * We cannot stand with folded hands and permit other nations to get far in the van in a line of improvement in which the United States not many years ago knew no superior. * * * Rifle guns of size, endurance and power, to enable us to meet on fair and equal terms a foreign foe, must be provided while we have the time, and it is certainly not the part of wisdom to delay making such provision until the enemy invades our shores."

Report of Chief of Ordnance, 1876.

"It must now be conceded that the strength and value of conversions by using coiled wrought iron lining tubes for 8-inch rifles have been proved and established. The success which has attended these experiments at Sandy Hook in the effort to utilize our smooth bore cast iron guns by converting them into rifles of great power and efficiency is a source of great satisfaction, and this uniform success justifies us in the conclusion that equally satisfactory results will follow our trials with the higher nature of 10-inch and 12-inch rifles which are now in course of preparation. If our anticipations are realized in the success of these larger calibres, the Department will have developed a system of heavy ordnance at small expense which will compose an armament for our forts fully able to cope with foreign guns of equal calibre. Such a system will bring the manufacture entirely within the capacity of our private foundries, using our own raw material and with no dependence on foreign establishments."

Report of Chief of Ordnance, 1877.

"A consideration of the urgent wants of our sea coast defenses, the length of time required to supply these wants, the absolute impossibility of providing for them in time of danger when the even's of years are crowded into days, the wisdom and policy of fostering our mechanical industries for the manufacture of warlike stores in the absence of a government providing the economy of products which are the results of passing orders and steady labor satisfies me that a permanent annual appropriation for the amount of fortifications would be most judicious and satisfactory in the interest of the public purse and the public service."

Report of Chief of Ordnance, 1878.

"The 12¼-inch rifle was completed and mounted at Sandy Hook the past year. It has been fired only twenty-four rounds with charges varying from 60 to 120 pounds power, and shot weighing 600 to 700 pounds. The report shows that with 115 pounds powder and shot weighing 700 pounds, it gave a velocity of 1,485 feet with pressure of 33,500 pounds to the square inch; a very satisfactory result, and comparing favorably with results obtained in other countries with guns of the same calibre. To the length of bore and the excellent character of our powder and projectiles may be attributed its superiority, if any, over others. While unable to make an exact comparison between this gun and those used abroad as to capacity for work because of differences in charges of powder and weights of projectiles, the following favorable indications may be noted: The English 28 ton gun with 85 pounds powder and 600 pounds shot has given 450 foot-tons *less* energy than ours; Krupp's with 88 pounds powder and 664 pounds shot has given 1,254 foot-tons *less* than ours. The Italian with 110 pounds powder and 770 pounds shot has only given about 400 foot-tons *more* than ours. Our gun uses only eighty pounds powder and 600 pounds shot. With 110 pounds powder and 700 pounds projectile our American rifle yields 9,551 foot-tons, an energy about as great as given by any gun known using this charge, and decidedly superior to the Krupp and Italian using *heavier* charges."

THE WEST POINT FOUNDRY.

This foundry was established under the special patronage of the government in 1817. In 1819 an agreement was made with the Ordnance Bureau to receive all the old unserviceable cannon, carronades, shot, stools, etc., at the Navy Yard, Brooklyn, N. Y., and to return kentledge therefor; to pay $25 per ton for old iron, and deliver the kentledge at $55 per ton. On July 11, 1820, the first contract was made and signed by Gouverneur Kemble, President of the West Point Foundry Association, for 32 42-pounders, long guns at $125 per ton, to be delivered in New York in twelve months; December 1st the same year the following guns were ordered by the Ordnance Board: 24 42-pound carronades at $185 each; 32 42-pound cannon at $125 per ton; 36 32-pound cannon at $125 per ton; 4,500 42-pound round shot at five cents per pound; 3,500 32-pound round shot at five cents per pound; 1,200 42-pound stools at five and one-half cents per pound; 640 32-pound stools at five and one-half cents per pound; 14,400 42-pound grape shot at eight cents per pound; 7,680 32-pound grape shot at eight cents per pound; 300 32-pound double head at six cents per pound.

From the establishment of the West Point foundry until the commencement of the Rebellion this establishment was engaged in the manufacture of cast iron smooth-bore Dahlgren and Rodman guns, which were at that date as efficient as any ordnance then manufactured in the world. At the commencement of the civil war immediate demands were made by the government upon the West Point foundry, and its whole force was devoted to the production of rifled cannon on the Parrott system, a peculiarity of which consists in the band or reinforce of wrought iron made by coiling a bar of iron upon a mandrel and the welding of this coil into the breech of a cylinder which is afterwards bored and turned and shrunk upon the breech of the gun; the manner of attaching the band to the gun is another peculiarity, as is also the mode of rifling and the expanding projectiles used in this system. In 1860 were first manufactured the 10-pound Parrott guns, and in the following year 20 and 30-pounders, the Parrott projectile, and also the 100-pounders; still later were made the 200 and 300-pounders; of this special system of ordnance were manufactured of the various sizes about three thousand, and one million six hundred thousand projectiles. Since the close of the war the West Point foundry has received orders for supplying ordnance from Spain, Peru, Chili, and Venezuela and have also *converted* for the U. S. Government a considerable number of ten-inch Rodman guns into eight-inch rifles, and eleven-inch Dahlgren guns into eight-inch rifles, for use in the army and navy. The original Rodman and Dahlgren guns are of cast iron, and the conversion consists in the inserting of a coiled wrought iron tube inside of the old gun. The system adopted by the United States after careful experiments is a combination of the cast iron shell with the wrought iron tube, a gun being thereby produced which, it is believed, will stand as heavy charges and repeated firing as the built up

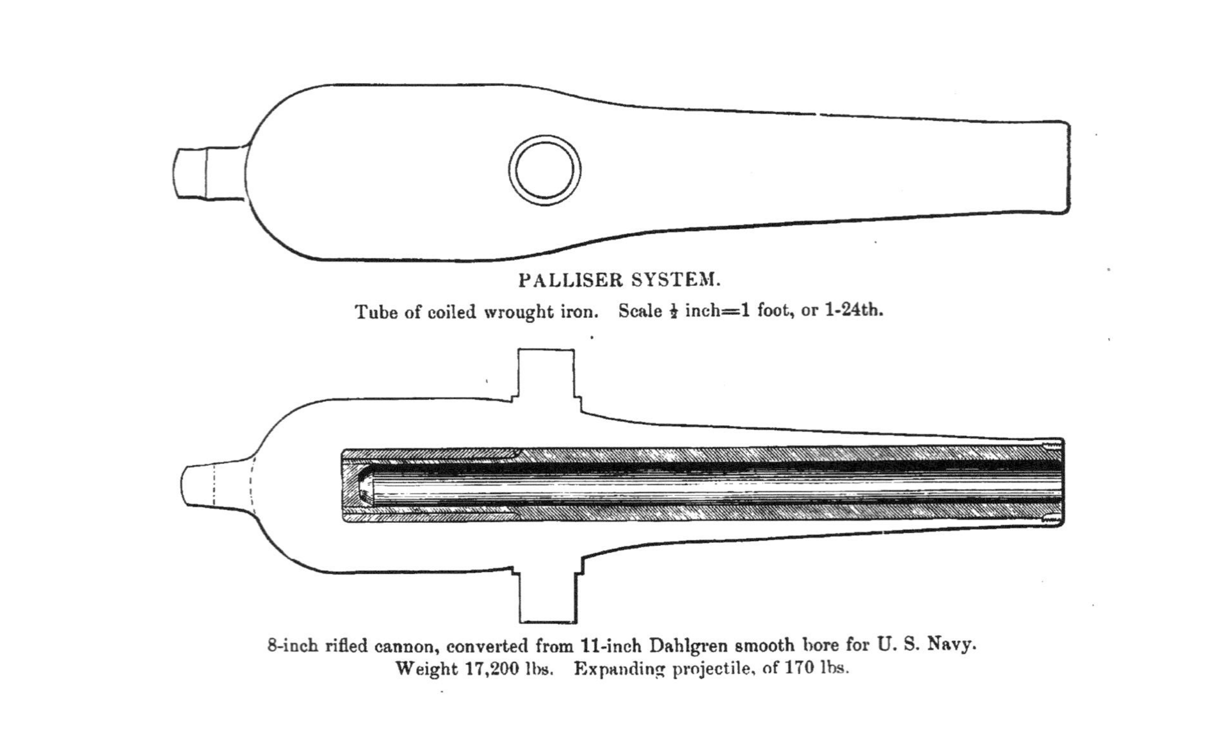

PALLISER SYSTEM.

Tube of coiled wrought iron. Scale ½ inch=1 foot, or 1-24th.

8-inch rifled cannon, converted from 11-inch Dahlgren smooth bore for U. S. Navy.
Weight 17,200 lbs. Expanding projectile, of 170 lbs.

wrought iron guns lined with steel, manufactured at Woolwich by the British Government, and at Elswick by Sir William Armstrong, or even as the forged steel ordnance made by Fred Krupp in Germany. These guns can be produced at much less cost than the European ordnance, more particularly for the reason that the largest portion is composed of cast iron, a much cheaper material than either steel or wrought iron. The plates given herewith represent converted ordnance constructed from guns now belonging to the United States, and in length of bore and other details are not what experience indicates as producing the very best results as regards initial velocity and penetration. The performance of these guns however is sufficiently satisfactory to demonstrate that they would be very effective against the powerful iron-clads of Europe, and their success has led to the adoption of the system by the Government of the United States, and it is quite evident that with new guns built upon this system and adopting the latest European improvements, there can be no question but that equally good results could be obtained. The experiments made in Europe during the past ten years have been at a vast expense, and we can take advantage of all the results arrived at, and, adopting such improvements as seem advisable, omit the errors that have been committed, with no outlay for experiments beyond the cost of the firing of trial guns as required by the U. S. Government when a new model or calibre is introduced.

The West Point Iron Foundry is supplied fully with all the necessary appurtenances for manufacturing heavy ordnance of all classes, including wrought iron tubes up to eighteen-inch bore, also muzzle-loading and breech-loading rifled cannon of all calibres, and which are in every respect fully up to the standard of quality required by the Ordnance Department of the Army and Navy. They also have facilities for the manufacture of expanding projectiles of all the new patterns together with shells and battery shot with chilled ends. There seems no question but that the use of muzzle-loading rifled guns will be discontinued, and that they will be superseded by breech-loaders, of which the advantages are now admitted and the difficulties of construction have been overcome, thus securing through the new system adopted by the United States greater initial velocity, heavier projectiles and guns of much greater strength, sufficiently powerful to destroy any iron-clad which can cross the Atlantic.

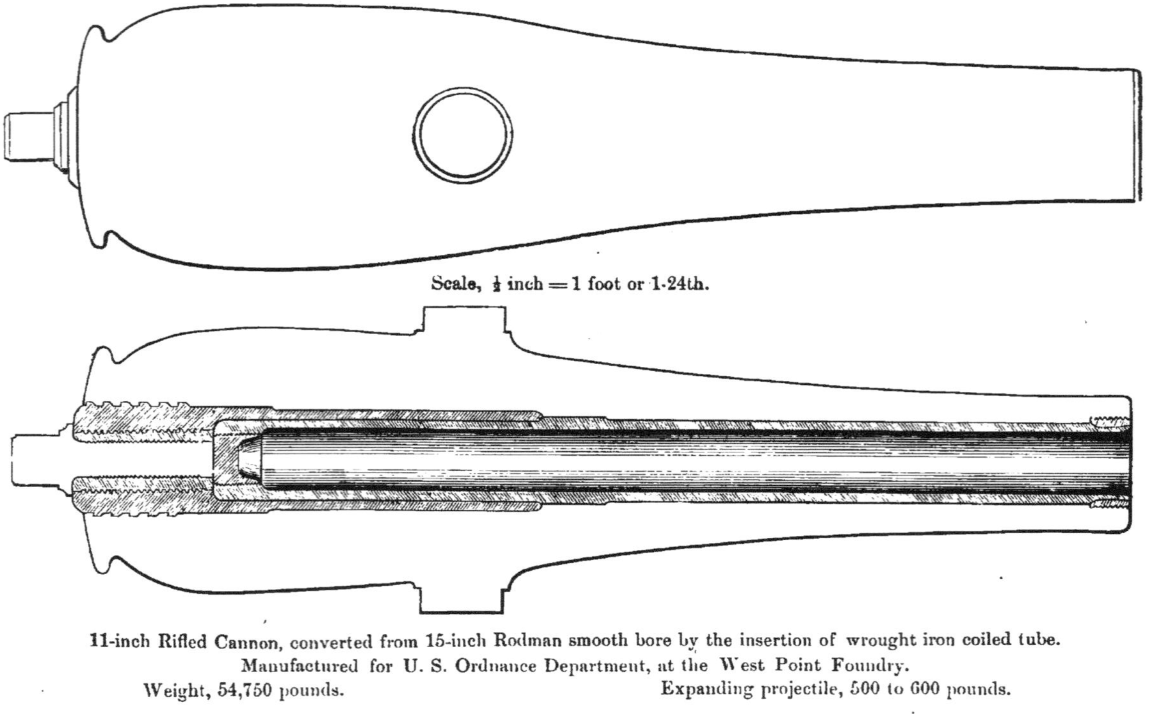

Scale, $\frac{1}{2}$ inch = 1 foot or 1-24th.

11-inch Rifled Cannon, converted from 15-inch Rodman smooth bore by the insertion of wrought iron coiled tube.
Manufactured for U. S. Ordnance Department, at the West Point Foundry.

Weight, 54,750 pounds. Expanding projectile, 500 to 600 pounds.

ALBERTYPE FORBES CO.

SOUTH BOSTON IRON CO. WORKS,
BOSTON.

THE SOUTH BOSTON IRON FOUNDRY.

The South Boston Foundry possesses the only works for heavy ordnance existing in the country, and can cast guns weighing ninety tons in the rough. The West Point Foundry makes the production of coiled wrought iron tubes a specialty and produces medium and light ordnance. Both make all varieties of guns and projectiles, but the South Boston Foundry has, also, with the Ames Company of Chicopee, Mass., been since 1826 recognized contractors for bronze guns.

The survival of the existing ordnance works has been due not to chance but to their excellent work and, failing proper support on the part of Congress, to their engaging in other lines of manufacture. The South Boston Iron Company, for instance, was the first maker of chill rolls in this country, Mr. Alger having patented the method in 1811, also improvements in plows and cylinder stoves for anthracite before 1840, later, fine statuary castings in iron; and heavy machinery was made from the first or since 1828. At all times many foundry specialties such as gearing, pulleys, kettles, &c., have been made. About forty years ago almost all the machine shops of Boston and vicinity drew their castings from "Alger's foundry." Capt. Thomas A. P. Catesby Jones writes in 1835 concerning the different foundries: "The Boston Foundry, owned by Mr. Alger, has not, I believe, cast *any* guns for the navy, nor am I certain that he has for the army; but for shot he had a considerable contract with the Ordnance Department in 1833, and his specimens were the best I have ever seen. And from the extensive plan, perfect machinery, and experienced workmen connected with that work, I should place great confidence in the productions of that foundry."

All the cannon and shot required for the gradual increase of the navy were cast at the Columbian, Bellona and the West Point Foundries. The quality of the castings of these three works does not materially differ, but the shot turned out by the West Point Foundry are decidedly superior in every respect to those cast at the Bellona and Columbian Foundries.

Lieutenant Wahlback states, in his Annual Report in 1847, that "the cannon furnished by the South Boston Iron Foundry have all been

Plate 1.

cast since the revised regulations of 1840, and are not, therefore, included in the foregoing. The few trials I have made of guns from this foundry have afforded the most favorable results, and the quality of the metal is unsurpassed."

About 1840 the character of "gun-iron" used for ordnance became definitely fixed, largely due to the efforts of Major Wade. Previous to that time, each foundry used its own iron in its own way, taking either hot or cold blast, and of the grade the founder thought best. But it was found about that time that only cold blast charcoal iron carefully made, properly mixed, and refined in air furnaces, gave uniformly good and reliable results.

A knowledge of the mechanical properties of metals was first exactly obtained by Major Wade's testing machine, which has gone all over the world as the American testing machine. Originally called the "Metallo-Dynamometer," it was built by Mr. Alger about 1840 under the directions of Major Wade, and the original machine is still in daily use at the foundry, giving accurate results.

The knowledge thus gained enabled the value of new guns to be fixed, from the character of their metal, without subjecting them to the damaging proof previously applied to each gun. Their reliability was shown by a few rounds of service charges, and American guns cast under the United States regulations since 1840 have had the highest reputation for strength and endurance.

The South Boston Iron Company began to cast heavy guns about 1839, and erected in 1842 what was then the heaviest shop in the country for ordnance. Previous to that time many light guns of bronze and cast iron up to twenty-four pounders had been made. Beginning at that period it had the advantage of all previous failures and avoided the hap-hazard methods of the earlier foundries.

About 1836 Cyrus Alger patented and made the first guns of malleable iron, cast and converted in an oven, supplying fifteen of them in 1837 and 1838.

The first gun rifled in America was rifled at the foundry in 1834.

About 1840 Mr. Alger invented the following improvements in fuses and in casting shell, which have been adopted and are still in use in the United States service and abroad, but for which he received no compensation whatever from the government.

First.—The use of a fuse composition rammed in a paper case fitting into a wooden or metal plug inserted in the shell.

Second.—A safety plug of lead fitting like a cup in the bottom of the paper case. The top edges of the cup are thin enough to expand tightly against the paper, but be easily detached and the cup thrown into the shell cavity by the shock of discharge. The cup thus ordinarily shuts off the fuse from the powder, but opens the passage as soon as the fuse begins to burn.

Third.—A safety cap to ensure the ignition of the fuse under all circumstances combined with a leaden disc, removed on loading, to prevent ignition out of the gun.

Fourth.—Placing the holes for the escape of gas from the burning fuse in a metal plug and obliquely, and in such a position that the fuse is not extinguished by mud nor by ricochetting on water.

Fifth.—The use of a metal bushing in connection with a hollow core arbor to receive the fuse, "that is, a bushing, with a small hole to receive fuse, which is placed directly upon the core arbor, and is retained in place as a part of the shell by the metal cast around it."

These fuses were immediately adopted, as leaving nothing to improve for a time fuse for smooth bores of the heavier classes. They were used in the Mexican war, and ever since in the United States for all smooth bore ammunition. The metal bushing has been extensively copied everywhere, and a chilled cored shot could not be made without it.

The earliest piece of what would now be called heavy ordnance, cast at the South Boston Foundry, was the ten-inch Columbiad. This gun marked, at the same time, a departure from old ideas and the introduction by Col. Bomford of horizontal shell fire of great power. It was cast 6th September, 1839, under Col. Bomford's superintendence, and was copied soon after by Gen Paixhan, in France. Its dimensions were in extreme length, 111 inches; length of bore, ninety inches; weight of gun, 14,500 pounds; weight of shot, 130 pounds; of shell, ninety pounds; and of powder charge, eighteen pounds.

In 1839 a Board of Ordnance Officers was sent to Europe to inspect European ordnance and ordnance works. It purchased 6 and 12-pounder cast iron guns, and 12 and 24-pounder iron howitzers from Swedish, French and English foundries.

These guns were subjected to extreme proof at Fort Monroe, 1841-42, with the result that the Finspong guns proved themselves the best of all tried, including West Point guns of similar sizes. The proof of the Finspong 6-pounder was as follows, the gun bursting at the last fire. The charges had two wads in each:

Series.	Pounds powder in each round.	No. of balls in each round.	Rounds.
First.	2	1	20
Second.	3	2	20
Third.	3	3	10
Fourth.	6	7	2
Totals.	142	104	52

The Ståfsjo gun stood forty-nine rounds in similar series, the Aker forty-seven rounds, the West Point thirty-nine rounds, and the Gospel Oak gun thirty-eight rounds, respectively. There were twenty rounds each in the first and second, and ten in the third series; the Finspong gun only reached the fourth series.

In March, 1844, the South Boston Foundry submitted a 6-pounder cast iron gun, No. 7 of their make, for extreme proof, which took place at City Point, South Boston. In strength and endurance it was found superior to the Finspong above mentioned.

Rounds.	Powder charge, pounds.	Number of balls each round.	Number of balls.
16	2	1 to 16	136
4	2½	13 to 16	58
2	3	14 and 15	29
14	3	16 each.	224
2	6	7	14
38	102		461

The result of this and other proofs was so much to the credit of the South Boston Foundry, that it again cast for the army, ordnance on 8th July, 1846, the first twelve-inch Columbiad of Col. Bomford's design. This gun weighed, finished, 25,510 pounds; for the period it was truly a colossal gun and was the largest that could be made in the country at that date. The weight of its shell was 172 pounds, with twenty pounds of powder, and ten degrees elevation; the shell ranged 2,770 yards, and its extreme range with maximum elevation was 5,761 yards, or three and one-half miles. The weight of the gun precluded it from sea service at that period. This twelve-inch sea coast gun remained the limit of size of our army guns till 1860.

About 1844 Mr. Alger, taking advantage of Col. Bomford's experiments on the pressure exerted by fired gunpowder at different points of the bore, brought out a 32-pounder which was the first gun wholly plain in outline, and was the original of what is now known as the Dahlgren gun. This 32-pounder gun was known as Alger's 32-pounder, and after its proof and trials was preserved and still exists at the foundry. It is shown on Plate 2. On comparing its outline with the Dahlgren it will be found to differ no more than is due to the powder pressure curves of the respective charges, and to the absence of the tulip muzzle. The trunnions were cast hollow so as to diminish the "shrink" due to their mass of metal.

In connection with this gun Mr. Alger submitted a "Port Carriage" to the Navy Department, involving a friction compressor binding the wooden chassis and the now universally adopted *eccentric axle* for the wheels of the carriage itself. By this arrangement the gun carriage slides back on firing the whole weight of the gun, creating friction, and when raised off the chassis and on its wheels by turning the eccentric axles, rolls back easily into the firing position. Major Wade witnessed about 1843, "in Boston, the trial of several devices for checking the recoil of cannon by friction—by means of clamps, compressors, and eccentric axles—designed by Captain Van Brunt of the Navy, and by Mr. Cyrus Alger. The eccentric axle designed by Mr. Alger, caused the gun carriage to *slide* in its recoil and to move on *rolling wheels* when returning to battery. This appeared to be the best of the methods then tried."

During the course of the improvements of our navy guns by the late Admiral Dahlgren, the South Boston Foundry made many guns remarkable for strength and endurance. Admiral Dahlgren said that Cyrus Alger "possessed that rare quality, sagacity, which constitutes in truth the highest attribute of the intellectual man, and enabled him to arrive at results which others sought by disciplined study and often in vain."

The shell guns of Dahlgren design were introduced largely into our navy not long before the civil war, and the safe limit of charge for the eleven-inch gun was not known till investigation was compelled by the failure of the "Monitor's eleven-inch guns, which were made at the South Boston Foundry to penetrate the armor of the Merrimac." It was perhaps not expected they would be brought against armor, or if the idea was broached it was answered by the statement that "the occasions on which shot could be advantageously used are so rare as hardly to warrant their being considered as part of the regular allowance."

The South Boston nine and eleven-inch shell guns exhibited endurances, which bore comparison with the best forged Armstrong guns of 1862.

A cast-iron eleven-inch gun if fired with thirty-one pounds of powder and ninety-three pounds shot, would be doing more proportional work than the Armstrong wrought iron gun which in April, 1862, pierced the warrior target with a round 156 pound shot and fifty pounds of powder, afterwards bursting under that charge. It is proper to say here, we do not know but that between the two dates it had fired greater charges. But an eleven-inch of South Boston make (No. 1262 S. B. F. 1862) was fired 155 times as follows: 22 rounds, twenty pounds powder; 101 rounds, twenty-five pounds powder; 32 rounds, thirty pounds powder; shot from 165 to 169 pounds each. After this proof the gun exhibited no marks of strain or defects of any kind.

Another eleven-inch gun was fired 170 rounds in two successive days without injury, although the gun became so heated that it was found warm eighteen hours after the last round.

The trial gun, for extreme proof, of a contract in 1857 (No. 1098 S. B. F. 1857) a nine-inch Dahlgren shell gun, 9,090 pounds in weight, endured the following proof before destruction, a series of 1,532 rounds:

Rounds.	Powder charge	Number of shot each round.	Total weight shot each round.
1	15 pounds.	1 shot	91 pounds.
9	10 "	1 shell	72 "
1,500	10 "	1 "	72 "
5	15 "	1 shot	90½ "
5	15 "	2 "	181 "
2	15 "	3 "	271½ "
3	15 "	4 shell	288 "
1	20 "	3 shot and 1 shell	343½ "
1	20 "	2 " " 4 "	469 "
1	20 "	2 " " 6 "	613 "
1	20 "	7 shot	636½ "
1	20 "	8 "	724 "
1	20 "	9 "	812 "
1	20 "	10 "	903 " and burst.

Plate 2.

15–INCH RODMAN GUN, SKIDDED FOR FIRING.

With twenty pounds powder and 343½ pounds weight shot, the gun recoiled nineteen feet; with twenty pounds powder and 469 pounds shot, the recoil was thirty-three feet; and with twenty pounds powder and 636½ pounds shot, the recoil was twenty feet up a steep slope, although the breech of the gun had been completely buried before firing. With ten shot the bore was nearly filled, the fronts of the last being seven and three-fourths inches from the muzzle. At bursting the gun was torn in two from cascabel to middle of chase, the part blown off, about two-fifths the circumference, being broken into five large fragments.

The proof firing was extremely rapid, 500 rounds being accomplished in four successive days. The enlargements due to firing were inconsiderable, the bore remaining in serviceable condition, and the endurance was reported on the 1,527th round as "really astonishing."

Nothing could exceed the confidence these guns inspired in the war, and their efficiency on the new Ironsides is matter of history.

The Monitor was armed with eleven-inch guns fired with 169 pound shot and fifteen pounds powder. It was not known then that the charge could be increased to thirty pounds, as was afterward proved safe in case of necessity. This increase would give a shot of 169 pounds, an initial velocity of 1,400 feet, and a similar increase of the charge of the nine-inch gun from ten to thirteen and one-half pounds of powder, would give an initial velocity of 1,290 feet to its shot. The low velocity of her shot was consequently the reason why in all probability the Monitor failed to sink the Merrimack.

In 1860 the fifteen-inch gun of 49,000 pounds was cast, and proved in 1861. Being demanded for both naval and sea coast armament in great numbers, the South Boston Iron Company erected a new ordnance foundry and machine shop, and began in 1863 to apply the Rodman method to the production of fifteen-inch guns. This shop was designed to cast and finish the largest guns then thought practicable.

During the war the demands of service prevented any extended experiments on the strength of the gun. But after the war, and armored ships had to be met, it was found safe to fire 100 pounds of powder with the 450 shot instead of fifty pounds, the heaviest service charge during the war. The initial velocity was thus increased to 1,600 feet per second. It is a fact that a fifteen-inch Rodman gun made at South Boston Foundry has endured twenty-six rounds with 140 pounds of mammoth powder and 450 pounds shot without bursting.

Perhaps the best instance of the reliability of both guns and shot, made by American methods, will be found in the history of the fifteen-inch Rodman gun of South Boston, model made by Cyrus Alger & Co. in 1867 for the British Government (S. B. F. No. 186).

The report of the Ordnance Select Committee during its trial at Shoeburyness was understood to have stated "that it was doubtful if the Rodman gun can be burst with *any charge* of American powder, as it will not burn more than 100 pounds, which it has fired without injury."

The wood cut shows the gun skidded for firing, at an elevation of thirty-two degrees, with 100 pounds of American (prismatic or mammoth) powder on 6th September, 1867. The shot weighed 452 pounds; time of flight was thirty-three seconds, and range was 7,680 yards or about four and four-tenths miles.

The trial of the gun lasted a year from June 1867, during which it was tried against all the armor shields in use. It was fired thirty-six times; fifteen rounds of these were with charges of 100 pounds mammoth powder or its equivalent (83¼ pounds R. L. G.). The velocities of the shot at impact were 1,174 to 1,500 feet per second, and it was shown that at 200 yards the gun could not penetrate eight-inch armor nor materially injure the nine-inch Hughes elastic shield. This conclusion caused the gun to be regarded as a formidable weapon, but not especially dangerous to British men-of-war as the admiralty had previously adopted heavier armor.

If, however, the force of the shot failed to meet the expectations of American officers, yet their material—gun-iron—also that of the gun itself, exhibited its wonderful tenacity in the best light.

The illustration shows a shot which struck the Gibraltar target with a velocity of 1,174 feet per second and making an indent four inches deep, rebounded twelve feet to the front nearly entire. The striking face was flattened and a few largish fragments splintered off. Many others exhibited similar behavior, the shot rebounding to the front, set up and disfigured. Their toughness induced the belief that they must in some way be made partially of wrought iron.

They were of course wholly of cast iron, but cast iron in its most perfect state, combining all the hardness and toughness possible for cast iron. The essential characteristic of gun-iron is its elasticity, which it

CYRUS ALGER'S 32 PDR. GUN, 1844; 1-16 FULL SIZE.

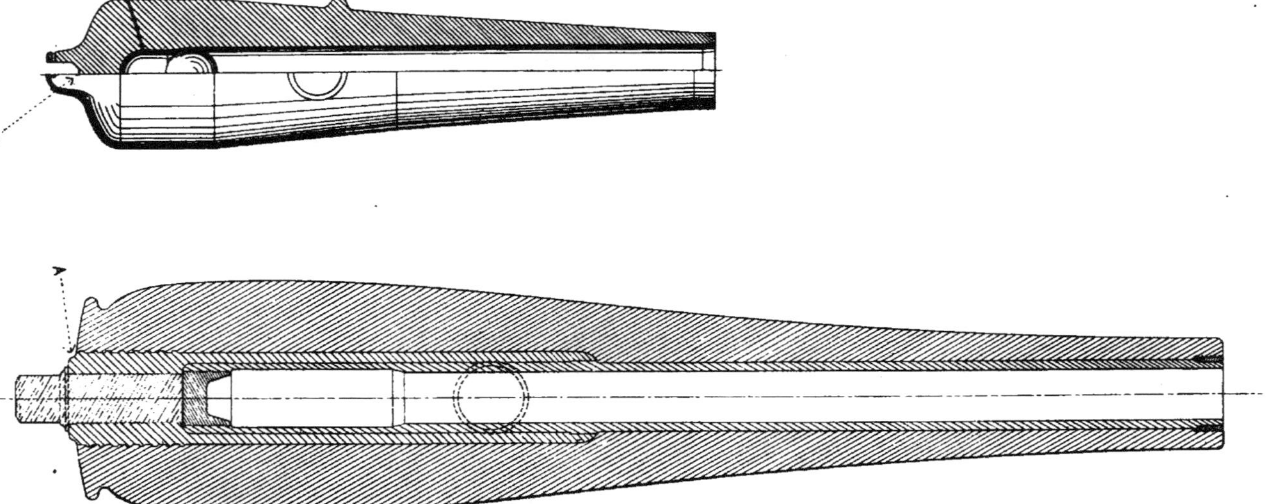

U. S. 12-INCH RIFLE, LINED WITH COILED IRON TUBE, 1-30 FULL SIZE. WEIGHT, 89,350 LBS.

exhibits to a limit of 9,000 to 12,000 pounds per square inch, an amount somewhat less than that of ordinary bronze and nearly half that of average wrought iron.

The South Boston Foundry has made since 1836 a specialty of producing bronze guns, and turned out for the United States and for Massachusetts, probably the first sound ones made in this country. Bronze cast in sand is liable to many defects—porosity, and separation—often the gravest, and the Company is entitled to the credit of at least the

application of cast-iron molds for guns, and it believes it made the first discovery of that improvement before 1855. In sand molds it made bronze gun, the average tenacity of which was 41,270, and density 8.64, which is considered now a first-class bronze. But after the adoption of chill casting very high results were obtained. The average density of 24-pounder navy howitzers, between S. B. F. Nos. 1,417 and 1,693 of 1863-64, was 8.72, and average tenacity 50,041 pounds per square inch. Nine guns included in the above series exhibited an average density of 8.80 and an average tenacity of 60,610 pounds to the square inch. These are believed to be the highest recorded qualities of bronze gun metal.

In 1869 Mr. S. B. Dean, while engineer of the South Boston Iron Company, discovered that bronze guns could be greatly improved and rendered highly useful as rifles by rough-boring the gun, and then forcibly expanding the bore to its finished size by means of mandrels successively enlarging in diameter. This process he patented here, in

France, and unwisely perhaps in Austria, where it has been pirated by the Austrian artillery under the name of the Uchatius system. All the field guns and many siege guns of the Austrian army are now made of so-called "steel bronze," a very good name considering the fact they should be "Dean bronze" guns.

The effect of the Dean method is to bring the exterior of the gun under tension while the interior is hardened and rendered capable of resisting the wear of the rifled projectile. The first condition renders the gun stronger, all portions helping each other against the explosion, and is the counterpart of the Rodman process where the exterior is put under tension by shrinking it, as it were, on the more quickly cooling interior of the gun. The hardening effect is great and highly valuable.

The following table of properties of similar cylinders, one of them cut from the chase of a three and one-half inch Dean rifle after "condensing," exhibits the improvement effected.

	Uncondensed.	Condensed.
Hardness, ...	1.40	5.12
Density, ...	8.35	8.70
Tenacity, ...	35,810 pounds.	51,571 pounds.

In 1863 Mr. Francis Alger, a son of Cyrus, patented the use of a bag or pouch to hold the bursting charge of a shrapnel or a shell. He made the bag waterproof and attached it to the fuse. This method has been widely adopted, and in large shells is an essential safeguard against the explosion of the bursting charge by the shock of the explosion, and consequent friction of the powder against the shell

Various improvements in fuses for rifled shell were experimented with and Mr. F. Alger patented in 1862 a combined time and percussion fuse of merit.

During the civil war the South Boston Iron Company furnished the Government with over 1,700 guns, including 700 bronze guns and howitzers, about 700 solid cast guns of eleven-inch calibre and less, 332 Rodman guns ten-inch calibre and over, and only nineteen rifled guns of all sizes. This record will show how largely the war was fought with smooth-bore guns.

The Rodman guns were barely fifteen-inch guns for the army, and to meet the demand a new ordnance foundry and machine shop put into operation in 1863, which is now the only works for Heavy Ordnance in the United States, and is capable of turning out guns of fifty tons weight. During the war it made nothing heavier than the fifteen-inch gun of 49,000 pounds. It might be expected that the foundry would have many interesting records of so busy a period, but its energies, as well as those of the Ordnance Bureaus of the Army and Navy, were almost wholly devoted to producing guns of serviceable design. Even the usual proofs were dispensed with, so great was the need for ordnance, and after the trial gun of a class had fired 1,000 rounds in proof the rest of the class were accepted according to the tests of their material.

In respect to projectiles, however, the Company did good work. The need of good rifle projectiles became decided when rifles began to be appreciated, as our artillerists became more experienced. Many experimental projectiles claimed attention and the Company decided on the Schenkl plan as affording the best solution of the difficulty. The projectile was cast with a conical base over which a papier mache sabot fitted almost half the length of the shot. The explosion drove the sabot up, the cone thus compressing it between the shot and the gun and causing it to take the grooves. In service eighty-two per cent. took the grooves perfectly in the Parrott gun, for which they were not intended. Being light it fell off almost immediately in flight without danger to troops over whom it was fired. The shot was thoroughly rotated and was considered most reliable until it was found that the sabot, under influence of moisture, often swelled so much as to refuse to enter the gun.

The South Boston Foundry furnished some 500,000 rounds of ammunition of all sizes to the Government, of which some 400,000 were Schenkl projectiles.

Although the question of a perfect projectile remained unsolved, yet the Schenkl percussion fuse furnished with the shot was one of the unqualified successes of the war. It was found absolutely certain in action and combined extreme simplicity with perfect safety. It remains the standard fuse of our Navy and requires very slight modification to render it equal to all requirements. During actual service in the civil war eighty-two per cent. proved perfect.

THE BUTLER PROJECTILE—MUZZLE-LOADING.

The projectile manufactured by the South Boston Iron Company, for use in their guns, is the invention of Captain J. G. Butler, Ordnance Corps U. S. A., and is considered without an equal, either for muzzle-loading or breech-loading guns, with appropriate rifling. It was early adopted by the government, and the very perfect results with it, together with the wonderful conservation of the bores of the lined guns during the experiments of the Ordnance Board in 1873 and 1874, led to quick imitations abroad in both the muzzle and breech-loading field of ordnance.

In 1872, Congress having made an appropriation for the construction of certain heavy guns, the question of rifling and shotting them became one of paramount importance. The defects of existing plans were very grave, and Captain Butler, after much consideration of the subject, aided by a successful but limited range of private experiment, was convinced that the germ, so to speak, of the perfect system, lay in the expanding principle which other countries had thrown aside as unworthy, and which with ourselves had proved hitherto unreliable and especially unequal to the demands of the heavier calibres. But very few were of this opinion. The costly, and presumed exhaustive, experiments in England, and our own want of success with it, had shaken the faith of many in the expansive system, and it was therefore in deprecation of a tendency to abandon the expansive and take up the stud (English) system that this officer laid before the Chief of Ordnance detailed reports upon the subject. He says:

"I maintain that no less important than the question of gun construction are the questions of rifling and projectiles—nay, more important to-day; for whatever be the respective merits of various gun constructions, most of them would be found abundantly strong, if their strength were only properly economized."

An examination of many firing records showed frequent enormous and destructive powder pressures clearly traceable to the bad conduct of projectiles, and it would be difficult to say which of the prevailing systems furnished most of such disastrous failures. The South Boston Iron Company, in a statement compiled from official records concerning the action of their Double-lipped Expanding Sabot Projectile, makes a powerful showing of its value. We quote:

Plate 1.

THE BUTLER MUZZLE-LOADING PROJECTILES.

FIG. 1.

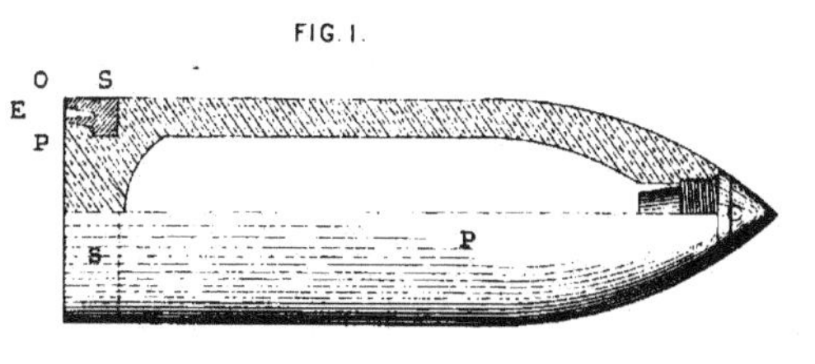

3-INCH FIELD SHELL,— Scale ⅓.

FIG. 2.

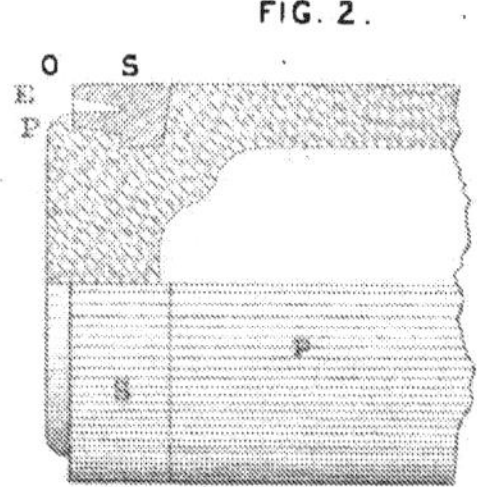

4½-INCH SIEGE SHELL,— Scale ⅓

FIG. 3.

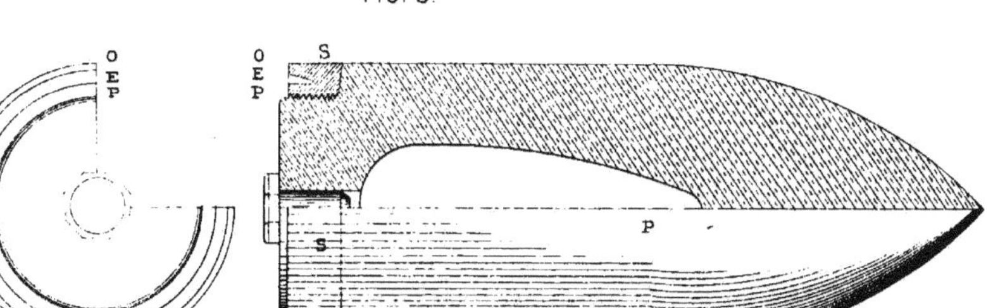

12-INCH 700-POUNDER,— Before Firing.

FIG. 4.

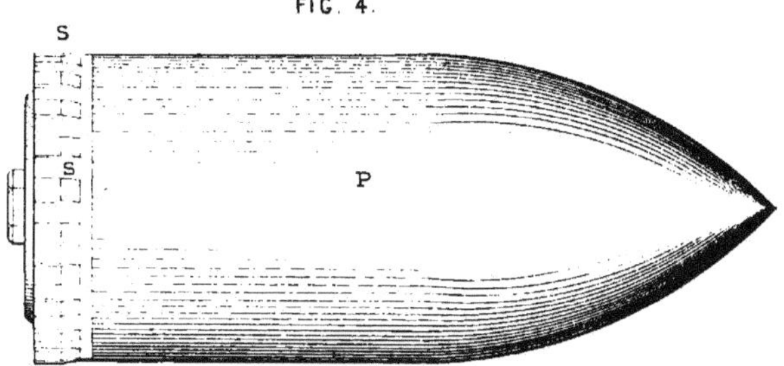

12-INCH 700-POUNDER,— After Firing.
Scale, 1-7

In loading, always measure the distance from the charge to the muzzle with the ramrod or wiper and apply it to the shot. In this manner the gunner can always tell whether the projectile is fully down or is obstructed by dirt or sand.

If the piece be fired when the projectile is not "home," it strains the gun unnecessarily.

II. DIRECTIONS FOR FIRING.

Having the gun and apparatus on the ground, to prepare for firing:

1. Select a place where the gun and carriage may recoil without striking rocks or other obstructions.

2. Note the position of the vessel to be relieved; her distance from the shore, the direction and approximate force of the wind.

3. Place the gun in position, making allowance for the force of the wind and for the drift of the line.

3. Place the faking-box and line on the windward side of the gun, and two or three feet from it—not more. The box should be on a line with the muzzle of the gun. Loosen the hasps, invert the box, and incline it to the front at an angle of about forty-five degrees.

5. See that the vent is clear by inserting the priming-wire.

6. Wipe off the shot with care, freeing it from dirt and sand.

7. Remove the frame and faking-pins, pressing at the same time gently upon the "false" bottom to keep the fakes in place. Then remove the "false" bottom by lifting it slowly until clear of the box.

8. Seize the end of the line, drawing out just enough to reach to the gun without disturbing the fakes in the box, pass the end through the eye-hole in the shank and tie two or three half-hitches in it, drawing the knot down close to the eye; then wet about three or four feet of the line.

[The wetting is a precaution that was not taken in the experimental firing, it not being found necessary. It is better, however, to err on the safe side.]

9. Remove the tompion or muzzle cover from the piece.

10. Insert the cartridge.

11. Insert the projectile slowly until it rests upon the cartridge.

12. Prick the cartridge with the priming-wire to avoid disturbing the elevation after being given.

13. Set the "combination level" to the desired angle.

14. Place the lower arm of the level lengthwise upon the chase.

15. Elevate the muzzle until the bubble of the level stands at the middle of the tube.

16. Adjust the quoin.

17. Unroll the lanyard and insert the hook in the wire loop of the friction primer.

18. Insert the primer gently in the vent.

19. Stand clear of the line.

In the use of this, as of all other apparatus, a certain degree of care and common sense must be constantly exercised by those who have it in charge. The best and most perfect apparatus in the world will prove a miserable failure in the hands of ignorance and carelessness. The necessity for thorough instruction and frequent practice is nowhere so urgently called for as in the fitting of men to handle efficiently the appliances for saving human life.

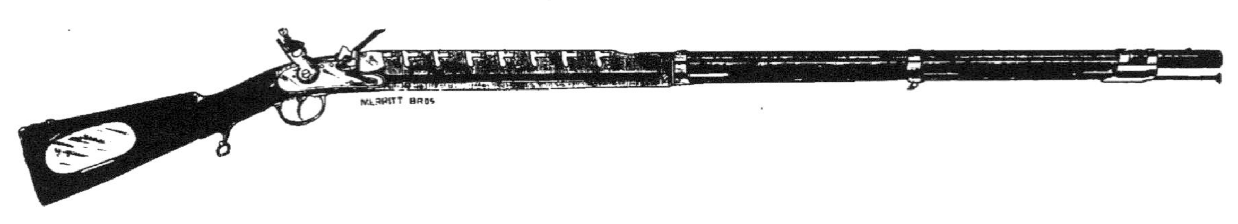

REPEATING ARM MADE BY S. NORTH, MIDDLETOWN, CONN., 1825.

In the possession of the Winchester Arms Co., New Haven, Conn.

APPENDIX.

FERGUSON'S BREECH-LOADING RIFLE.—1778.

Letter from General J. Watts De Peyster.

Gen. C. B. Norton:

DEAR SIR—Life-long study leads me to take great interest in your labors, and I feel much pleased to hear of the approaching completion of your work on "American Breech Loading Small Arms." This, particularly, as I am sure that it will be the means of doing justice to our inventors. The fact that so many of our systems of breech-loading have been adopted by other nations is highly creditable to our people, but the additional fact that these systems have been adopted without credit to their inventors does not speak well for the ingeniousness of those nations who have profited by American intelligence. The special reason I have for addressing you, however, is in connection with a curious fact which long since came to my knowledge relative to the early use of a breech-loader in the Revolutionary war.

At the outbreak of the Revolutionary war, almost without exception every relative or connection of mine of suitable age held commissions or positions of trust under the Government of the Mother Country—in the army from Brigadier-General down to Cornet. The writer's grandfather, Frederic de Peyster, of this city, and two great-uncles, Abraham and James, were all three officers almost before attaining man's estate, the two first Captains, the third Captain-Lieutenant in Fannings, the 4th, or the King's American Regiment, and the two first were wounded and the third killed in the Royal service. A third great-uncle, Major Stephen Watts, lost his leg at Oriskang.

Circumstances transferred their sphere of duty to the Southern Colonies, and there they became intimately connected with one of the most distinguished officers of the British army, Patrick Ferguson, Junior Major of the 71st Regiment, Highlanders, 2d Battalion, who was not only most distinguished for his military abilities and his skill as a marksman, but for his prescience as an inventor. He was particularly charged with the duty of organizing the Loyalists, and Lord Cornwallis seems to have placed the most exalted and implicit confidence in his special as well as general capacity. Indeed Cornwallis—a very superior man himself, although circumstances beyond his control compelled his surrender at Yorktown - expected that the audacious and able Ferguson would infuse his spirit into the preponderating loyal element and extinguish the fires of opposition in the interior districts of the Carolinas; and this he would have done had he not been overcome so shortly afterward by "the inevitable" which rules the affairs of peoples and progress.

As to his rank in the regular army there is no question, but he seems to have been invested with a higher local rank, as likewise the officers acting under him. In one narrative he is styled Brigadier-General; and his tombstone and the American reports qualify him as Colonel. In fact there is the same difficulty in determining his correct title that is experienced in the case of Barry St. Leger, in 1777, who is mentioned as Brigadier-General, as Colonel, and as Lieutenant-Colonel. Whatever may have been his real rank, his command and influence was far more extensive, comprehensive and independent than is consistent with that of a Junior Major.

At all events Ferguson was authorized to arm and drill his troops according to his own ideas; and if tradition and circumstantial evidence are to be relied on, it was his purpose to place in their hands a *breech-loading rifle* with a variety of improvements, considered of recent date. Some of these rifles were used in the battle of King's Mountain, 7th October, 1770, the turning point of the war at the South- as Oriskang, another riflemen's fight, 6th August, 1777, had been at the north—a battle in which he was defeated and slain, and that blew all his hopeful plans into air. In this great battle the writer's great-uncle was second in command and severely injured. He was a particular friend and confidant of

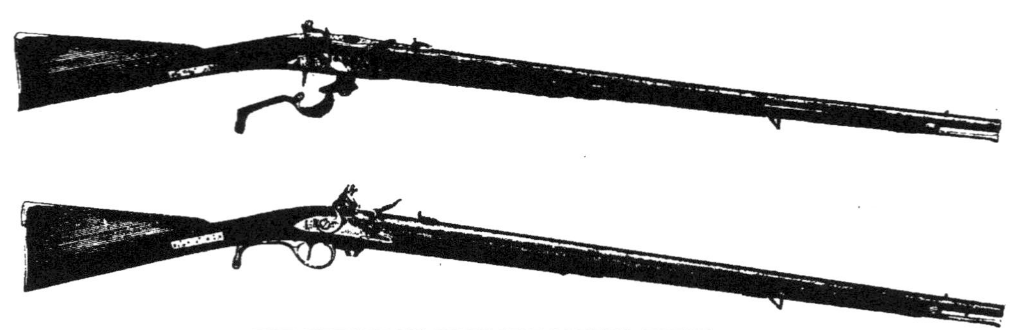

THE FERGUSON BREECH-LOADING RIFLE—1776.

Ferguson, as was his younger brother, the writer's grandfather. The latter, however, who had been detached for special service and likewise severely wounded, commanded a company before attaining his majority, at a time when such commissions were the reward of service and influence, especially those granted by the Crown in the Colonies. To the latter, as a token of affection, Ferguson presented his own rifle—a breech-loader, invented by himself—which, transmitted from son to grandson, has been photographed and engraved for this work.

Although a breech-loader not of American invention, it has become American from the fact that it made its first appearance as a weapon of war on the battle fields of America, and is the first instance of a breech-loading rifle ever having been used on this continent or any other.

The first allusion to this fire-arm is in the *Annual Register* of 1776, June 1st, page 148. In the second part of the same volume, pages 131, 132, &c., its distinguishing feature (132 (2) ¶ 3) is referred to in an article entitled the "Effects of rifling gun barrels," which also contains the first recommendation of oblong bullets as superior to round ones, not carried into effect until within a very few years. For further ameliorations the curious reader is referred to Emerson's "Miscellaneous Treatises," published in the same year, 1776.

The drawings of Ferguson's invention as applied to a breech-loading rifle, likewise of his other inventions for breech-loading cannon, styled (1) "Turn-cock," (2) "Cross-slider," are to be found in volume No. 1,139 of English Patents for 1776, the Text of which is on the lower shelf of Alcove 132 in the Astor Library.

Patrick Ferguson's military sobriquet or title of "Bull Dog," was acquired in consequence of his determination, fearlessness, and contempt of danger. He was the son of the eminent Scotch Jurist, James Ferguson, and the nephew of the noted political economist and writer on the currency and public credit, Patrick Murray, fifth Lord Elibank, who lived 1707-'78. Conspicuous as a partisan leader, he was as renowned in the use of fire-arms, that is, as a marksman, as he had proved himself remarkable as a practical improver of such weapons, and of the discipline best adapted to light infantry. He was as generous as he was brave, as conciliating as decided, a loyal subject, a just commander, a faithful friend, a charming associate, and so good a soldier that, although he had only participated in the American war since 1777, he had acquired the confidence of every commander under whom he had served by his activity, and had so distinguished himself at the siege of Charleston that his services had been deemed worthy of particular mention by the British Commander-in-chief. Those who knew him personally whose opinions were worthy of implicit confidence, declared that his military abilities, great as they were, were less notable than his chivalric courage, stern resolution, devoted loyalty, and generous sentiments.

The writer is well aware that in many histories a far different character has been assigned to this faithful and accomplished soldier. At such times, however, rancor sharpened and prejudice filled the pen which described or misrepresented him. Irving was too much of a gentleman to repeat the harsh remarks in his life of Washington.

"Major Ferguson possessed very distinguished talents as a partisan, and, in the conduct of irregular warfare, was without a superior in the British army."

"He was perhaps the best marksman living, and probably brought the art of rifle shooting to its highest point of perfection." "He even invented a gun (1776) of that kind upon a new construction, which was said to have far excelled in facility and execution anything of the sort ever before known; and he is said to have greatly outdone even the American Indians in their adroitness and quickness of firing and loading, and in the certainty of hitting the mark lying upon the back or belly, and in every other possible position of the body. It is not certain that these improvements produced all the effect in real service which had been expected from those astonishing specimens of them that were displayed in England. Humanity, however, cannot but wish that this barbarous mode of hostility was by universal consent banished from the warfare of all nations. It has been reported that Gen. Washington owed his life at the battle of Germantown to this gentlemen's total ignorance of his person, as he had him sufficiently within reach and view during that action for the purpose. The truth of this report was afterwards fully established by the discovery of a letter from Col. Ferguson to Dr. James Ferguson of and in Scotland. "'We had not lain long (Ferguson is speaking of a detachment of his riflemen who occupied a skirt of wood in front of General Knyphausen's divisions) when a rebel officer, remarkable by a hussar dress, passed towards our army within a hundred yards of my right flank, not perceiving us. He was followed by another dressed in dark green and blue, mounted on a good bay horse, with a remarkably high cocked hat. I ordered three good shots to steal near to them and fire at them; but the idea disgusted me. I recalled the order. The hussar in returning made a circuit, but the other passed within one hundred yards of us; upon which I advanced from the woods towards him. Upon my calling he stopped, but after looking at me proceeded. I again drew his attention and made signs to him to stop, levelling my piece at him; but he slowly continued his way, as I was in that distance at which in the quickest firing I could have lodged half a dozen balls in or about him before he was out of my reach. I had only to determine, but it was not pleasant to fire at the back of an unoffending individual who was acquitting himself very coolly of his duty, so I let him alone. The day after I had been telling this story to some wounded officers who lay in the same room with me, when one of our surgeons, who had been dressing the wounded rebel officers, came in and told us that they had been informing him that General Washington was all the morning with the Light troops and only attended by a French officer in a hussar dress, he himself dressed and mounted in every point as above described. I am not sorry that I did not know at the time who it was.'" Forbearance so generous and unusual in an officer commanding a corps of sharpshooters was in keeping with every act of Ferguson's life."

Again, in another account of the battle of King's Mountain, the following language is used in regard to this officer: "He possessed superior abilities as a soldier, and his spirit of enterprise was uncommon. To a distinguished capacity of planning great designs, he also added the practical abilities necessary to carry them into execution. The advantage which the Americans gained over him and his party in a great degree frustrated a well concerted scheme for strengthening our army by the co-operation of the well affected inhabitants whom he had undertaken to discipline and prepare for actual service."

"The military science possessed by Major Ferguson was profound, and his adaptation of it to the use of small arms more correct than any other officer who preceded him. His execution in firing was such that it almost exceeded the bounds of credibility. He very nearly brought his aim at any given object to a mathemetical certainty."

On the first of June, 1776, he made some experiments at Woolwich before Lord Viscount Townshend, Lord Amherst, General Harvey, Deragliers and several other officers with the rifle gun on a new construction which astonished all beholders. The like had never before been done with any other small arms. Notwithstanding a heavy rain and the high wind, he fired during the space of four or five minutes at the rate of four shots per minute, at a target two hundred yards distance. He next fired six shots in one minute, and also fired (while advancing at the rate of four miles an hour) four times in a minute. He then poured a bottle of water into the pan and barrel of the piece when loaded so as to wet every grain of the powder, and in less than half a minute he fired with it as well as ever without extracting the ball. Lastly, he hit the bull's eye lying on his back on the ground, incredible as it may seem to many, considering the variations of the wind and the wetness of the weather. He only missed the target three times during the whole course of the experiments. A patent was afterwards granted him for all his improvements. It passed the great seal on the fourth of December following (1776).

The following is the reference to or description of this Patent, A. D. 1776, No. 1139. "Ferguson's Improvements in Breech-Loading Fire Arms. Line 9, page 2 to line 15, page 3. No. 1 (figure) of "Ferguson's Specification," is a section along the barrel of a gun, cannon, or pistol, which loads at the breech by means of a screw-plug that descends by one turn as low as the bottom of the bore to admit the ball and then the powder after, which by turning the plug the contrary way the breech is closed and the piece loaded. Something similar to this has been attempted, but has always failed for want of the following improvements, and has never been studied as an object of public utility, or rendered in any degree fit for public service.

The improvements are: First. A projection of the barrel towards the guard (X) to receive the screw plug long enough to allow the plug to descend sufficiently low, occasionally to be cleared after much firing without coming entirely out of the grooves, by which means the difficulty, loss of time, and embarrassment of hitting the proper groove (in occasions of hurry and danger) to re-enter the plug is avoided.

Secondly. That part of the screw plug which forms part of the breech of the barrel is made smooth and hollow by which means it neither retains so much of the smoke or foulness, nor in going round does it lodge it into the female screw so as to clog it and impede the motion of the plug.

Thirdly. There are various channels cut across the outside of the screws of the plug in such directions as not to communicate and occasion any part of the charge to blow out, at the same time that they are contrived to go along the whole surface almost of the female screw in mounting and descending, thereby loosening and receiving any foulness that may have lodged.

Fourthly. There is a hollow or reservoir behind the screw plug at the breech of the barrel into which the smoke which has forced its way through the grooves is thrown, when the plug turns round so as to clear the grooves or female screw from being clogged by the foulness that might otherwise lodge in them.

Fifthly. There is a rising formed on the breech of the barrel, which answers as an elevating sight, which is never in the way, nor to be moved out of its place (like the sights commonly used which are let into the barrel), and into this elevated sight a sliding sight is let in, which, by being gradually pulled out in proportion to the distance of the object, may be adjusted to all manner of distances; whereas these sights usually in use only answer for two or three given distances.

By means of these improvements the piece is to be loaded and fired with much more safety, facility, and certainty, and can be discharged as often as ever can be necessary without any occasion for the cleaning, so that the public is furnished with an arm which unites expedition, safety, and facility in using with the greatest certainty in execution, the two great desiderata in gunnery never before united."

Ferguson's own rifle, to which, as it is now perfectly established (28–5–72) that the preceding refers, is still in existence and hangs amid other family trophies and mementoes, in a librarial sanctuary devoted to the preservation of such interesting objects and the histories of the times when they were employed, situated on the bank of that very Hudson river upon or along which one of the soldiers referred to in this narrative first saw service.

The following—published a few years since in the *United Service Journal*, a periodical edited by Col. W. W. Tompkins, which preceded the *Military Gazette*—in regard to Ferguson's capability as a marksman and his weapon, is very interesting, and will close the remarks in relation to both the inventor and his inventions:—

"So astonishing a marksman had he become, that although earlier in life his right arm or hand had been disabled or amputated, he could take his pistol out of his holster with his left hand, throw it up in the air, catch it, as it fell, by the stock and instantly shoot off the head of a small bird sitting within point blank range.

"Years before he was assigned to partisan service in the Revolutionary war he determined to invent a rifle which, while it admitted of the greatest rapidity of fire and accuracy of aim, should be furnished with a bayonet, which would enable riflemen to cope with cavalry in the open field or meet infantry in a bayonet charge. A variety of experiments resulted in the weapon which, handed down from that generation, finally reached the writer's hands, and is admitted by all who have examined it to be one of the most beautiful and interesting specimens of fire arms ever seen. It is even now as serviceable as when first finished. Experienced workmen who have examined it admit that it is a perfect specimen of their art; that the lock made by the celebrated Egg, of London, is equal to the best of the present day; and that the whole weapon combines three essentials for an active service rifle —which improvements were subsequently claimed by different persons as their own inven-

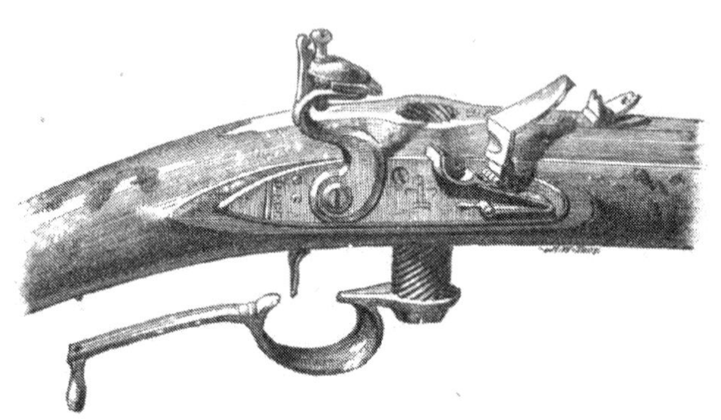

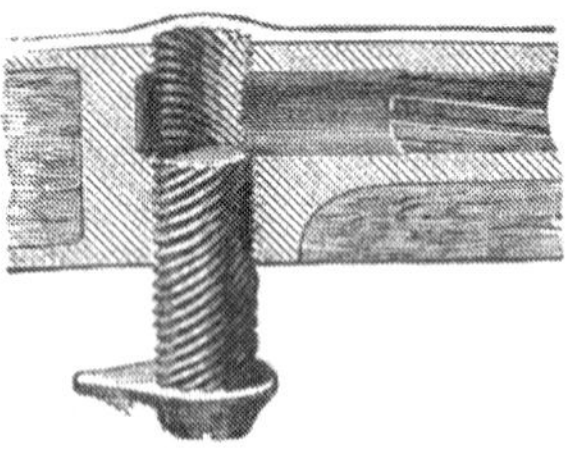

tions. Had Major Ferguson lived, the real utility of his rifle would have been sufficiently tested, for he intended to arm a flying-corps with it.

"In order to explain its peculiarities a few details are necessary. The length of the piece itself is 50 inches, (of a U. S. rifle, 48¾ inches); weight, 7½ lbs. (of a U. S. rifle (1850), 9¾ lbs.) The bayonet is 25 inches in length (a U. S. musket bayonet blade being 16 inches) and 1½ inches wide, and is what is commonly called a sword blade bayonet; flat, lithe yet strong—of fine temper and capable of receiving a razor edge, and, when unfixed, as serviceable as the best balanced cut and thrust sword. The sight at the breech is so arranged that by elevating it is equally adapted to ranges ranging from one hundred to five hundred yards.

"We now come to its greatest curiosity, namely, the arrangement for the loading at the breech. The guard plate which protects the trigger is held in its position by a spring at the end nearest the butt. Released from this spring, and thrown around by the front, so as to make a complete revolution, a plug descends from the barrel, leaving a cavity in the upper side of the barrel sufficient for the insertion of a ball and cartridge or loose charge. This plug is an accelerating screw, and is furnished with twelve threads to the inch, thereby enabling it, by the one revolution, to open or close the orifice; so that the rifle is thereby rendered capable of being discharged, it has been claimed, as rapidly as Hall's United States (flintlock) carbine. This accelerating screw constitutes the breech of the piece, only instead of being horizontal, as is usually the case, it is vertical. Were there not twelve independent threads to this screw, it would require two or three revolutions to close the orifice; whereas one suffices.

"Many of the muskets fabricated in the French arsenals during the last years of Napoleon, had bayonets of the shape mentioned herein adapted to them, specimens of which were deposited among the French trophies in the tower of London.

"In case of any injury to the fire arm, the sword blade bayonet would have been as effective a weapon as the artillery or even the infantry sword carried by foreign troops."

J. Watts de Peyster,

Brig.-Gen. Brev.-Major General, (by special action), S. N. Y.

Since the communication quoted in this book was presented to the public, some additional facts have been ascertained which are of interest. One or two errors have likewise been discovered and require correction. Frederic de Peyster was second Captain in the (Loyal) New York Volunteers. This regiment greatly distinguished itself, leading the way in the famous assault on Fort Montgomery, in the Highlands, 6th October, 1777. It was afterwards transferred to the South with the magnanimous Colonel Archibald Campbell, the captor of Savannah, 29th December, 1778. It made another mark in the battle which resulted in the taking of this place, and was again noted, in the defense of the city, 23d September to the 18th October, 1779, against the combined attacks of the Americans and French; and among a series of other brilliant exhibitions of soldiership, converted victory almost within the grasp of Greene, at Eutaw Springs, into a triumph for the crown. The 4th, or King's American Regiment, was another noted organization. It was second to none in the British service. Colonel

Garden, in his "Anecdotes of the Revolutionary War in America," bears unequivocal testimony to the exemplary good conduct of Colonel (or General) Small; and "this gallant soldier" was not sparing in his praise of Fanning's King's American Regiment. In this regiment Abraham de Peyster, of New York, was the Senior Captain, and his younger brother, James, Captain-Lieutenant. The latter, a particular favorite of Small,—who styled himself the "military father" of the young New Yorker—was afterwards killed under extraordinary circumstances, on the 18th August, 1793, at Menin in Flanders, after having been buried alive in the assault upon Valenciennes, discovered by accident, and resuscitated. The contemporary accounts attribute to him a second similar escape. These two and his death all occurred within a few weeks.

Patrick Ferguson was Junior-Major of the 71st Regiment, British Army,—"Highlanders," so styled. There is a very curious circumstance connected with its uniform:

The Reverend Mr. Gleig, Chaplain-General to the British army, in his Military History, [London, 1845] p. 194, remarks:—

"In addition to the 42nd, the British army can now boast of four *Kilted* regiments in the line; namely, the 78th, 79th, 92d and 93d, all of them distinguished for their bravery in the field, and their quiet and orderly conduct in quarters *The 71st Light Infantry, and 72d, likewise take rank as Highland Regiments; and both are admirable corps. But the adoption of the trowser in room of the philabeg has drawn a line between them and their kilted comrades; which, without producing a shade of bad feeling, hinders the perfect recognition by the one of the claim to be treated as thoroughly Highland by the other.* It is worthy of remark that the whole of these regiments, the 71st, 72nd, 78th, 79th, 92nd and 93d, are the produce of later times. Some of them were raised to meet the demand for men which the war of American independence occasioned; others came into being so late as the war of the French Revolution; but all are covered with honorable badges, and have done good service in various ways, most of them in every quarter of the world."

At first, the Loyal Provincial organizations were all clothed in green: witness the "Johnson Greens," or "Queen's Royal," or "Loyal New Yorkers." Afterwards, as a rule, they wore red like the Regular troops. The portrait of a captain in the 4th King's American, a Loyal New York regiment, represents him in a red coat faced with dark blue, yellow or buff vest, etc. The Loyal New York Volunteers also wore red.

Major Patrick Ferguson was a notable man in many regards. Family tradition says that he was a one-armed man, having lost his right arm through an amputation following compound fracture. Roderick Mackenzie, "late Lieutenant in the 71st [Ferguson's] regiment," in his "Strictures on Lieutenant-Colonel Tarleton's History," (published in London, 1787, and of which there is now a copy in possession of the New York Historical Society) says (page 23) that Ferguson's right arm had been so much shattered at the battle of the Brandywine, that it was rendered ever after useless. Nevertheless he made himself such a master of the sword with his left arm that on one occasion he defended himself for some time against three soldiers armed with bayonets. He was also such an expert with rifle and pistol, that almost incredible accounts were given and handed down to posterity of the certainty of his aim with both.

He was soon brevetted Lieutenant-Colonel, or full Colonel, by Cornwallis, and appointed "local" or "territorial" Brigadier-general of Militia. Previous to coming to America in 1777, he had seen considerable service in Germany. On arriving in the colonies, his fame having preceded him, he was allowed to pick out a number of crack shots to arm with his novel weapon, and the first engagement of the body was at the Brandywine, 11th September, 1777. The following is Bisset's (History of the Reign of George III. [London, 1803,] vol II., pps. 423–4) mention of these sharpshooters in this battle :—

"At the same time General Knyphausen, with another division, marched to Chad's Ford [on the Brandywine] against the provincials who were placed there ; in this service the Germans experienced very important assistance from a corps of rifle-men, commanded by Major Patrick Ferguson. The dexterity of the provincials as marksmen had been frequently quoted and held out as an object of terror to the British troops. Ferguson, a man of genius, which was exercised in professional attainments, invented a new species of rifle, that combined unprecedented quickness of repetition with certainty of effect, and security to the soldiers The invention being not only approved, but highly admired, its author was appointed to form and train a corps for the purpose of practice ; but an opportunity did not offer of calling their skill into action, until the period at which we are now arrived. Ferguson, with his corps, supported by Wemyss's American Rangers, was appointed to cover the front of Knyphausen's troops, and scoured the ground so effectually that there was not a shot fired by the Americans to annoy the column in its march."

As the subject matter of this communication is not the career of the *inventor*, but the employment of the *invention*, it is simply sufficient to say that Ferguson made his mark wherever he was employed at the North in 1777, 1778 and 1779. In December, 1779, Clinton selected him to accompany the troops destined for the siege of Charleston in 1780, and allowed him to form a corps of selected marksmen armed with his rifle. Sometimes mounted and sometimes on foot, these rendered such services under Ferguson, in connection with the siege of the capital of South Carolina and in subsequent operations, that their commander was invested with extensive powers, in the discharge of which he aroused a new antagonism—an element which had not entered into the calculations of the British commander-in-chief, Cornwallis,—to which he fell a victim at King's Mountain.

For a long time curiosity was excited but not gratified, as to the method of loading the Ferguson rifle.

In a rare old book, entitled Osbaldiston's "Universal Sportsman; or Nobleman, Gentleman, and Farmer's Dictionary," [Dublin, 1792] the method of charging this breech-loader is thus described in an article on "Shooting,"—page 562:—

"By far the most expeditious way of charging rifled pieces, however, is by means of an ingenious contrivance, which now generally goes under the name of *Ferguson's rifle-barrel*, from its having been employed by Major Ferguson's corps of rifle-men during the last American war. In these pieces, there is an opening on the upper part of the barrel, and close to the breech, which is large enough to admit the ball. This opening is filled by a rising screw which passes up from the lower side of the barrel, and has its thread cut with a little obliquity, that when screwed up close, a half turn sinks the top of it down to a level with the lower side of the calibre. The ball, being put into the opening above, runs forward a little way; the powder is then poured in so as to fill up the remainder of the cavity, and a half round turn brings the screw up again, cuts off any superfluous powder, and closes up the opening through which the ball and powder were put. The chamber where the charge is lodged is without rifles, and somewhat wider than the rest of the bore, so as to admit a ball that will not pass out of the barrel without taking on the figure of the rifles, and acquiring the rotary motion when discharged."

It is very strange that, although the sword of the second in command at King's Mountain—Captain ("local" Major or Colonel) Abraham de Peyster—is preserved among the trophies of this battle by the Tennessee Historical Society, and although very many—perhaps two hundred—of the Ferguson rifles must have been captured there, not a single specimen is known to be in existence except the one belonging to the writer. Recent replies to interrogations on this subject attest the fact. Questions relating thereto dispatched to England, have elicited nothing farther. Family tradition (all manuscript testimony having been accidentally destroyed by fire) attributes the fact that the specimen in the writer's possession was alone preserved, to the circumstance that its inventor gave it to his favorite, Captain Frederic de Peyster, who was in command of a temporary detachment, looking after a separate American force, and thus escaped the catastrophe which befell the main body to which he belonged, at King's Mountain. As an "inventor of arms," Ferguson must have possessed extraordinary mechanical insight and foresight. He appears to have foreseen every difficulty which could attend the use of his invention, and likewise to have provided against them. The peculiar spring which secures the extremity of the guard plate that serves as a lever to the breech-screw, whose descent admits the charge, is one which is generally considered a recent discovery, and has been applied in the most diverse manners. To prevent the fouling of the screw-plug there is a perpendicular slot by which anything that could clog it is expelled upwards; and behind it there is a cavity to receive any superfluous powder which would also be carried out by the reverse action downwards. Finally the rifle is a muzzle-loader as well as a breech-loader It is very likely that the specimen in existence was finished with more than usual care, for it is truly an elegant piece of work, and the butt is turned or modeled with a grace and lightness which would scarcely have admitted of very severe usage. It seems to have been intended for an officer rather than for a private soldier; but of this nothing is known except that these rifles were used in battle and service for a little over three years; that they were introduced suddenly and only in America; and that they disappeared from history simultaneously with the death of their inventor. It is still more curious that his other inventions, in artillery, etc., equally remarkable, were likewise allowed to fall into disuse after his decease. And yet, after all, it is not so strange. There are hundreds of inventions conceived centuries ago which have shared a like fate, and have been rediscovered and patented as novelties within the present century.

J. Watts de Peyster,

Brig.-Gen., Brev.-Major General (by special action), S. N Y.

CPSIA information can be obtained
at www.ICGtesting.com
Printed in the USA
BVHW041049210819
556415BV00017B/1098/P